Constitutional Law in Cyprus

Constitutional Law in Cyprus

Fourth Edition

Achilles C. Emilianides

This book was originally published as a monograph in the International Encyclopaedia of Laws/Constitutional Law.

Founding Editor: Roger Blanpain†
General Editor: Frank Hendrickx
Volume Editors: André Alen & David Haljan

Wolters Kluwer

Published by:
Kluwer Law International B.V.
PO Box 316
2400 AH Alphen aan den Rijn
The Netherlands
E-mail: lrs-sales@wolterskluwer.com
Website: www.wolterskluwer.com/en/solutions/kluwerlawinternational

Sold and distributed by:
Wolters Kluwer Legal & Regulatory U.S.
920 Links Avenue
Landisville, PA 17538
United States of America
Email: customer.service@wolterskluwer.com

ISBN 978-94-035-5790-8

e-Book: ISBN 978-94-035-5800-4
web-PDF: ISBN 978-94-035-5810-3

Printed in The Netherlands.

The Author

Achilles C. Emilianides is Professor and Dean of the School of Law of the University of Nicosia and a practising advocate and senior partner of the firm A&E C. Emilianides, C. Katsaros and Associates LLP. He has been elected as a Founding Member and President of the Cyprus Academy of Sciences, Letters, and Arts, as an ordinary member of the European Academy of Sciences and Arts, and as a member of the UNESCO Conciliation and Good Offices Commission. He further represents the Cyprus Academy to ALLEA (All European Academies). He holds a PhD and an LLM from the Aristotle University of Thessaloniki and an LLM from Leicester University. He is the Consulting Editor of the *Cyprus Review* and the Chair of the Royal Commonwealth Society Cyprus Branch. His publications in the IEL series, published by Kluwer, are: *Religion and Law in Cyprus* (4th, 2024), *Constitutional Law in Cyprus* (3rd, 2024), *Family and Succession Law in Cyprus* (3rd, 2024), *Media Law in Cyprus* (3rd, 2024), *Labour Law in Cyprus* (3rd, 2024), *Competition Law in Cyprus* (2021), *Tort Law in Cyprus* (2021), *Civil Procedure in Cyprus* (2020), and *Private International Law in Cyprus* (2015).

The Author

Table of Contents

List of Abbreviations

AKEL	Progressive Party of Working People
CJEU	Court of Justice of the European Union
CLR	Cyprus Law Reports
CYBC	Cyprus Broadcasting Corporation
CYTA	Cyprus Telecommunications Authority
DIKO	Democratic Party
DIPA	Democratic Alignment
DISY	Democratic Rally
EAC	Electricity Authority Cyprus
EAW	European Arrest Warrant
ECHR	European Convention on Human Rights
ECJ	European Court of Justice
ECtHR	European Court of Human Rights
EDEK	Socialist Movement for Social Democracy
EDON	United Democratic Organization of Youth
ELAM	National People's Front
EOKA	National Organization of Cypriot Fighters
ETEK	Cyprus Scientific and Technical Chamber
ETYK	Cyprus Union of Bank Employees
FCPNM	Framework Convention for the Protection of National Minorities
ICCPR	International Covenant on Civil and Political Rights
IDT	Industrial Disputes Tribunal
MEP	Member of the European Parliament
NATO	North Atlantic Treaty Organization
NEDISY	Youth of DISY
PAKOP	Pancyprian Party of Refugees and Suffered Persons
PASYDY	Pancyprian Trade Union of Public Servants
PEO	Pancyprian Labour Federation
RSCC	Reports of the Supreme Constitutional Court

List of Abbreviations

SBA	Sovereign Base Areas
SEK	Confederation of Cypriot Workers
TFEU	Treaty for the Functioning of the European Union
TMT	Turkish Cypriot Turkish Defence Organisation
TRNC	Turkish Republic of Northern Cyprus
UK	United Kingdom
USA	United States of America

Preface

This study consists of an extensive analysis of Cypriot constitutional law. This is the fourth edition of this work; the first edition having been published in 2013, the second in 2019, and the third in 2024. Cypriot constitutional law is unique, a fact which is due to the turbulent history of the island. The characteristics of the system can therefore be properly understood only through knowledge of the country's history.

A significant number of people have influenced my views on Cypriot constitutional law, and it would be impossible to mention all of them here. I would like, however, to thank my colleagues at both the University of Nicosia and my law firm for their perspectives and comments. The International Encyclopaedia of Laws and Kluwer Law International have been kind enough to include this monograph in their publications. I would like to thank my family and friends for their support during all these years, without which nothing else would be of significance. Unfortunately, this new edition was published following the passing of my beloved parents, Constantinos and Zeta, and therefore, I did not have the opportunity to benefit from their comments on my work and their overall presence in my life.

This book is dedicated to my daughter Chloe. Hopefully, one day, she will appreciate the importance of a Constitution and why so many people, including her ancestors, have dedicated their lives to safeguarding constitutional principles.

General Introduction

Chapter 1. Concise Description of Constitutional History

§1. Historical Background

1. Cyprus is the third largest Mediterranean island, after the Italian islands of Sicily and Sardinia. Situated in the Eastern Mediterranean, at a distance of 300 km north of Egypt, 90 km west of Syria, 60 km south of Turkey and 360 km to the northwest of Greece, it covers an area of 9,251 sq. km and has 648 km of coastline. Cyprus is divided into six districts, namely Nicosia, Limassol, Famagusta, Larnaca, Paphos and Kyrenia. The capital of the island is the town of Nicosia. The history of Cyprus begins with the early Neolithic period, dating back to the eighth or even tenth millennium BC.[1] The Achaean-Mycenaean Greeks arrived at the island at around 1600 BC and Achaean civilization was introduced into Cyprus. Greek extensive colonization continued in subsequent years and by 1000 BC, the island had adopted the Greek city-state system of government, as well as the Greek civilization, culture and way of living. The Mycenaean influence is particularly evident from a rich collection of archaeological findings. The island's predominantly Greek character therefore dates from that period.

2. Cyprus was conquered successively by Assyria in the eighth century BC, then briefly by Egypt and eventually by Persia in 545 BC. During that period, the Greek element remained dominant on the island. The island was once again brought under Greek rule by Alexander the Great. After Alexander's death, Cyprus came under the rule of the Ptolemies for about two and a half centuries, until the island was annexed by Rome in 58 BC. Cyprus thus became a province of the Roman Empire. During the early period of the Roman rule, Christianity was introduced in Cyprus. The conversion of Cypriots to Christianity had been completed by the beginning of the fifth century. With the exception of sporadic Arab invasions, Cyprus remained for more than eight and a half centuries, between 325 and 1191, a province of the Byzantine Empire.

3. The period of the Byzantine rule in Cyprus ended in 1191, when Cyprus came briefly under the rule of the crusader then King of England, Richard the Lionheart,

---

1. For an extensive history of Cyprus *see, inter alia*, C. Kyrris, *History of Cyprus* (1985); G. Hill, *A History of Cyprus* vol. 1–4 (Cambridge U. Press 1940–1952).

or Coeur de Lion, who immediately sold Cyprus to the Order of the Knight Templars for 40,000 gold besants; the transaction was, however, short-lived, and it was cancelled in view of the Cypriot resistance. The island was once again sold, for the second time in the same year, to the King of Jerusalem, Guy de Lusignan, who was a French knight; this time, Richard received 100,000 gold besants as consideration. The island remained under the rule of the Lusignans for nearly three hundred years, from 1191 until 1489, which is considered to be the period of the Frankish rule of Cyprus.

4. During the period of Frankish rule, Roman Catholic (Latin) Christianity became the official religion of the island. However, the great majority of the population still adhered to the Orthodox Christian religion and were Greeks. The legislation during the Lusignan period was the one contained in the Assizes of Cyprus, which were modelled after the Assizes of Jerusalem.[2] However, the ecclesiastical courts of the Greek Orthodox Church applied, with respect to the family affairs of members of the Orthodox Church, the so-called Hellenic laws of Cyprus, which essentially consisted of a codification of Byzantine law.[3] During the Venetian rule from 1489 to 1571, the Roman Catholic Church remained the dominant church of the island and Assizes continued to be the governing legislation.[4]

5. The conquest of the island by the Ottomans in 1571 resulted in radical changes in Cypriot legislation. The period of Ottoman rule lasted for more than 300 years, until 1878, and marked the first appearance of adherents of the Islamic faith in Cyprus. The Sheri (Sharia) law, namely the interpretation of the Qurani law, was not only the personal law of the Muslims of Cyprus but also the state law, thus replacing the law of the Assizes, which had been the state law during the period of Frankish and Venetian rule. The Sheri law was applied by the Sheri (Sharia) courts, which were the competent courts for the legal affairs of all people living on the island, irrespective of their religion.[5] The only exception to such exclusive competence of the Sheri courts was the law of personal status and family relations of members of the Orthodox Church. The ecclesiastical courts of the Orthodox Church

---

2. *See* N. Coureas, *The Assizes of the Lusignan Kingdom of Cyprus* (Cyprus Research Ctr. 2002); P. Zepos, *The Law of Cyprus During Frankish Rule*, 23 Y.B. Ctr. Research History Greek L. 123–141 (1976) (in Greek); A. Emilianides, *Polyarchy in the Frankish Rule of Cyprus*, in *Mélanges à la Memoire de Michel Dendias* 7–13 (1978); T. Papadopoulos, *Cypriot Legal*, in *Ibid.*, *Studies*, vol. I, 1–142 (Foundation of Archbishop Makarios III 1984, in Greek).
3. A. Emilianides, *The Hellenic Laws of Cyprus During Frankish Rule*, 25 Y.B. Cyprus Research Ctr. 51–74 (2004) (in Greek); A. Emilianides, *The Hellenic Laws of Cyprus and the Hexabiblos of Armenopoulos*, Y.B. Faculty L. Aristotle U. Thessaloniki 33–38 (1951); D. Simon, *Zyprische Prozessprogramme* (Beck, 1973); J. Maruhn, 'Eine Zyprische Fassung Eherechtlicher Titel der Epitome', in *Forschungen zur Byzantinischen Rechtsgeschichte* 218–255 (Fontes Minores, vol. IV, 1981).
4. A. Aristeidou, *Assizes in Cyprus During the Venetian Rule*, 22 Y.B. Cyprus Research Ctr. 95–101 (2001) (in Greek).
5. M. Zekia, *A Short Historical Survey of the Laws Administered by the Ottoman Civil and Criminal Courts and of the Constitution of such Courts During the Ottoman Era in Cyprus During 1571–1878*, in *Proceedings of the First International Cyprological Conference* vol. III, 457–464 (T. Papadopoulos & M. Christodoulou eds, Socy. Cypriot Stud. 1973); V. Bedevi, *A Survey of the Cyprus Sheri Courts Registers*, in *Proceedings of the First International Cyprological Conference* vol. III, 29–36 (T. Papadopoulos & M. Christodoulou eds, Socy. Cypriot Stud. 1973); H. Inalcik,

continued to be the only competent courts with regard to the family relations of their members and continued to apply Byzantine law.

6. The Ottoman Empire assigned to Great Britain the rights of possession and administration of Cyprus by signing the Convention of Defence Alliance on 4 June 1878 in Constantinople.[6] With the signing of the Treaty of 1878, the period of British rule in Cyprus officially began. Great Britain was granted the power to enact laws and conventions for the island of Cyprus and to regulate its commercial and consular relations and affairs. An Annex to the Treaty of 1878 provided that such Treaty would be terminated and Cyprus would be restored to the Ottoman Empire, so long as Russia restored Kars, Ardahan and Vatoum to the former. Thus, while in law, Cyprus still theoretically belonged to the Ottoman Empire and could eventually return on the fulfilment of certain conditions, in effect, the real and only sovereign of Cyprus was Great Britain, which exercised the administration of the island.[7]

7. The Anglo-Turkish Mixed Arbitral Tribunal held that the position of Cyprus during that period was analogous to that of a protectorate in the sense that it fell within the designation of a country under the protection of Great Britain, which in fact governed the island.[8] This peculiar situation ceased in 1914, when immediately after the outbreak of the First World War, Great Britain annexed Cyprus by Order in Council of 5 November 1914.[9] While it could be argued that such unilateral annexation was invalid, it was eventually recognized by Turkey in 1923 by Article 20 of the Treaty of Lausanne. By Article 16 of the Treaty of Lausanne, Turkey renounced all rights and titles whatsoever over Cyprus. The island was proclaimed as a Crown Colony on 10 March 1925.[10]

8. The administration of Cyprus by Great Britain was a colonial one, without genuine involvement by the native population. The objective of the colonial administration was to equalize the influence of the votes of the Greek Cypriots in the Legislative Council, who were the majority of the population, with the combined votes of the British and the Turkish Cypriots. The colonial Government further had the

---

Ottoman *Policy and Administration in Cyprus after the Conquest*, in *Proceedings of the First International Cyprological Conference* vol. III, 119–136 (T. Papadopoulos & M. Christodoulou eds, Socy. Cypriot Stud. 1973).

6. *See* G. Georgallides, *A Political and Administrative History of Cyprus 1918–1926 with a Survey of the Foundations of the British Rule* 3ff (Cyprus Research Ctr. 1979); L. Dwight, *Great Britain and the Cyprus Convention Policy of 1878* (Harv. Historical Stud. 1934).
7. G. Tenekides, 'La Condition Internationale de la République de Chypre' 6 *Annuaire Francais de Droit International* 133ff (1960); M. Dendias, 'L' le de Chypre dans le Droit International', *Revue de Droit International* 130ff [1933].
8. *Parounak & Bedros Parounakian v. The Turkish Government*, Annual Digest 1929–1930, Case N. 11.
9. Cyprus Annexation Order in Council of 5 Nov. 1914 in J. Howarth & C. Gerahty, *Statute Laws of Cyprus* vol. II, 184 (1923); C. Orr, *Cyprus under British Rule* 175 (Robert Scott 1918).
10. Cyprus Gazette 1 May 1925, Notification No. 266.

right to decline to enforce any decision.[11] Eventually, the Legislative Council was itself abolished as a response to the disturbances of 1931, which culminated with the burning down of the Government House in Nicosia; the demonstrations were the outcome of the disappointment of Greek Cypriots towards the colonial Government for what they considered to be a series of arbitrary decisions, as well as the rejection of their plea for Union of the island with Greece.[12] Britain reacted with a degree of military force and administrative repression that combined to sow the seeds of the 1955 liberation struggle.

9. In a referendum held on 15 January 1950 and organized by the Church, more than 95% of the indigenous Greek population voted in favour of the Union (Enosis) of the island with Greece; however, the British colonial Government rejected the Greek position, with the then Minister of State for Colonial Affairs Henry Hopkinson eventually declaring that Cyprus should never be allowed full independence.[13] On 1 April 1955, the National Organization of Cypriot Fighters (EOKA), led by George Grivas (alias Dhigenis), a Greek Cypriot who was a colonel in the Greek army, declared an armed insurrection against the British, demanding the Union (Enosis) of the island with Greece.[14] The political leader of the Greek Cypriots was Makarios III, who was also the Archbishop of the Greek Orthodox Church. This was due to the fact that during the British rule of Cyprus, the Orthodox Church constituted the nation-leading political organization of the Greeks of Cyprus under foreign sovereignty, also known as the Ethnarchy.[15]

10. Emergency measures were introduced by the British colonial Government, including detention without trial, arrest without warrant, curfews, hanging of suspected EOKA fighters, as well as collective punishments. Makarios and three other leading figures of the Greek Cypriots were exiled to the island of Seychelles by the colonial Government in an effort to force the Greek Cypriots to accept its constitutional proposals.[16] During this period, the Turkish Cypriot Turkish Defence

---

11. *See* A. Emilianides, *Justice and Human Rights During British Rule in Cyprus*, 3 Cyprus L. Tribune 66–96 [2006] (in Greek); S. Symeonides, *Introduction to Cypriot Law*, in F. Frantzeskakis, D. Evrigenis & S. Symeonides, *Comparative Law* 375ff (Sakkoulas 1978, in Greek). *See also* C. Kyriakides, *The Cypriot Legislative Council (1878–1937). Establishment, Function and Parliamentary Debates. Constitutional Liberties under Restriction and Doubt* (House of Representatives 2016, in Greek).
12. *See* P. Stylianou, *The Movement of October of 1931 in Cyprus* (1984, in Greek); V. Livadas, G. Spanos & P. Papapolyviou, *The Insurrection of October 1931* (2004, in Greek); G. Georgallides, *Church and State in Cyprus October 1931 to November 1932: A Systematic Humiliation of the Autocephalous Church of Cyprus*, 19 Y.B. Cyprus Research Ctr. 361–448 (1992).
13. *See* in detail A. Emilianides, *The Cyprus Question Before the House of Commons: 1954–1955* in *Great Power Politics: Foreign Interventions and Domestic Perceptions* 11–31 (M. Kontos et al. eds, Cambridge Scholars Publishing 2014).
14. SIMAE, *Fifty Years on from the EOKA Struggle* (Ministry of Educ. 2006, in Greek); R. Holland, *Britain and the Revolt in Cyprus: 1954–1959* (Clarendon Press 1998).
15. *See* A. Gavrielides, *The Ethnarchic Rights and the Referendum for Union with Greece* (2d ed., 1972, in Greek).
16. *See The Reports of the European Commission of Human Rights with Respect to Cyprus. App. 176/1956 & 299/1957* (A. Emilianides ed., Ministry Educ. & Culture 2008, in Greek); Ethnarchy of Cyprus, *Violations of Human Rights in Cyprus: A Factual Documentation* (1957); E. Lauterpacht,

Organisation (TMT) was established, its aim being the partition of the island (*taxim*). Turkey, with the encouragement of the United Kingdom (UK), became involved in Cyprus and negotiations ensued between the UK, Greece and Turkey. Several proposals for a constitutional settlement were rejected[17] since the Greek Cypriots insisted that they should be allowed to exercise their right of self-determination.[18] However, on 11 February 1959, the Zurich Agreement for the final settlement of the Cyprus dispute was concluded between Greece and Turkey. The Agreement, which was in fact imposed on the people of Cyprus, was then signed in London by the leaders of the two communities of Cyprus, Archbishop Makarios and Fazil Kucuk.

§2. Constitutional History Since Independence

11. The constitutional history of the Republic of Cyprus is characterized by continuous attempts to overthrow, modify or replace the constitutional structure.[19] The Republic of Cyprus was established as an independent and sovereign republic on 16 August 1960, when its Constitution came into force and the British sovereignty over Cyprus, as a crown colony, ceased.[20] The Constitution of Cyprus was signed by Sir Hugh Foot, then British Governor of the Colony of Cyprus, representatives of Greece and Turkey, as well as Archbishop Makarios and the Turkish Cypriot Fazil Kucuk. The latter two had already been elected as the first President and Vice-President of the Republic, respectively. The establishment of the Republic was the outcome of the Zurich and London Agreements of February 1959, on which the fundamental provisions of the Constitution were based.[21] Consequently, the people of Cyprus considered that the constitution had been imposed on them.

12. The structure provided by the Zurich Agreement was considered a compromise between the Greek demand for union with Greece and the Turkish demand for

---

European Commission of Human Rights: Complaints Made by the Greek Government in Connection with Events in Cyprus, 8 Intl. & Comp. L. Q. 366–369 (1958).

17. *See* E. Hatzivassiliou, *The Cyprus Question 1878–1960: The Constitutional Aspect* (U. Minn. 2002).
18. *See* S. Loizides, *The Right to Self-Determination and the Cyprus Question* (1957); *Ibid.*, *The Cyprus Question and the Law of the United Nations* (2d ed., Ethnarchy of Cyprus 1954); C. Tornaritis, *The Right of Self-Determination with Special Reference to the Republic of Cyprus* (1973); S. Calogeropoulos-Stratis, 'Le Droit des Peuples à Disposer d' eux – mēmes et la Question de Chypre', in *Das Selbstbestimmungsrecht der Völker* 53–61 (1967).
19. *See* in general A. Emilianides, *Beyond the Constitution of Cyprus* (Sakkoulas 2006, in Greek); K. Chrysostomides, *The Republic of Cyprus: A Study in International Law* (Martinus Nijhoff 2000).
20. Cyprus Act, 1960, s. 1, Republic of Cyprus Order in Council 1960 S.I. 1960 No. 1368, *Cyprus: Presented to Parliament by the Secretary of State for the Colonies, the Secretary of State for Foreign Affairs and the Minister of Defence*, Cmnd. 1093, July 1960.
21. A. Emilianides, *The Secret Negotiations. The Establishment of the Republic of Cyprus* (Papazisis/CECL 2022, in Greek); P. Tzermias, 'Der Neue Status Cyperns', 84 Archiv des Öffentlichen Rechts 459–489 (1959); G. Vlachos, 'L' Organisation Constitutionelle de la Republique de Chypre', 3 Revue International de Droit Comparé 526–559 (1961); P. Liakouras, *Looking Back to See Forward: The 1959 Zurich and London Accords and the Constitutional Order of Cyprus*, 10 Etudes Helléniques 47–61 (2002).

partition of the island. Further, the UK retained – and continues to retain – sovereignty over two Base Areas, one in Akrotiri and the other in Dhekelia, which cover 250 sq. km of the land area of the island of Cyprus.[22] The Constitution is unique in its perplexity and in the multiplicity of safeguards that it provides for the principal numerical minority of the island, namely the Turkish community.[23] The principle of bi-communality permeates the whole constitutional structure, according, in many respects, an equal status to the Greek community, representing 82% of the population, with the Turkish community representing 18%. It has therefore been argued that the constitutional rules embodied in the Constitution might as well have been conceived by a constitutionalist and a mathematician in a nightmarish dialogue.[24]

13. Not surprisingly, the Zurich Agreement failed to establish cooperation between the Greek and Turkish communities of the island[25] and proved to be unworkable in practice.[26] In 1963, the then-President of the Republic of Cyprus, Archbishop Makarios, transmitted to the then-Turkish Cypriot Vice-President, Fazil Kucuk, a thirteen-point memorandum, whereby he suggested the revision of certain articles of the Constitution, which had impeded the smooth functioning of the Republic of Cyprus. Makarios had suggested, *inter alia*, the abolition of separate majorities in the House of Representatives and of veto rights of the President and Vice-President of the Republic, as well as the unification of the system for the administration of justice and the abolition of the Greek Communal Chamber.[27] The Government of Turkey rejected such proposals even before the Turkish Community had submitted any comments on them. There was an outbreak of violence on the island, which led to a constitutional breakdown.[28] In 1964, a United Nations (UN) Peacekeeping operation came to the island and has remained there since.[29] The Security Council of the UN with Resolution 186/1964, and the General Assembly of the UN on 18 December 1965, called upon all States to respect the sovereignty, unity, independence and territorial integrity of the Republic of Cyprus and to refrain

22. A. Emilianides, *A Long-Drawn out Game of Chess. The Confidential Negotiations on the British Bases* (Hippasus, 2021, in Greek).
23. *See* P. Polyviou, *The Problem of Cyprus: Constitutional and Political Aspects* (1974).
24. A.S. De Smith, *The New Commonwealth and its Constitutions* 282 (Stevens & Sons 1964).
25. *See* A. Emilianides, *The Parliamentary Co-Existence of Greeks and Turks in Cyprus* (Epifaniou 2003, in Greek).
26. C. Tornaritis, *Peculiarities of the Constitution of Cyprus and Effect on the Normal Function of the State* (1980, in Greek); T.W. Adams, *The First Republic of Cyprus: Review of an Unworkable Constitution*, 19 W. Political Q. 475–490 (1966); C. Papastathopoulos, *Constitutionalism and Communalism: The Case of Cyprus*, 16 U. Toronto L. J. 118–144 (1965).
27. *See* C. Tornaritis, *Cyprus and Its Constitutional and Other Legal Problems* 67 ff (2d ed., 1980); D. Bitsios, *Cyprus: The Vulnerable Republic* 121ff (Inst. Balkan Stud. 1975); A. Emilianides, *Beyond the Constitution of Cyprus* 87ff (Sakkoulas 2006, in Greek).
28. *See* S. Kyriakides, *Cyprus: Constitutionalism and Crisis Government* (U. Pennsylvania Press 1968); T. Ehrlich, *Cyprus 1958–1967: International Crises and the Role of Law* (Oxford U. Press 1974).
29. A. Emilianides, *The United Nations Forces Function, its International Conflicts and Civil Strifes*, in *Melanges Bridel* 147–168 (Imprimeries Réunies 1968); A. Papadopoulos, *Peace-Making and Peace-Keeping by the United Nations: Cyprus a Case Study* (1969); G. Kaloudis & P. Lang, *Role of the UN in Cyprus from 1964 to 1979* (Peter Lang 1991).

from any intervention with it.[30] The Government of the Republic of Cyprus continued to be recognized by the international community as the only legitimate representative of the Republic.[31]

14. Inter-communal talks began with the aim of achieving a satisfactory solution to the Cyprus Problem.[32] However, in July 1974, the Republic of Turkey, one of the guarantor powers of the independence, sovereignty and territorial integrity of Cyprus, invaded the country with its armed forces and occupied the northern part of the island. Turkey alleged that its invasion had the purpose of restoring constitutional order on the basis of the provisions of the Treaty of Guarantee, following a coup against President Makarios[33] by the Greek military government (junta), which was then in power in Greece;[34] an allegation, which, however, was correctly not accepted by the international community.[35] Resolution 360/74 expressed the official contempt on behalf of the Security Council of the unilateral military force undertaken against the Republic of Cyprus, while Resolution 3212/74 of the General Assembly of the UN demanded that all foreign armed forces leave at once from the Republic of Cyprus and that any foreign intervention with the Republic of Cyprus' affairs should cease immediately. The latter Resolution was endorsed by Resolution 365/74 of the Security Council.[36]

15. As a result of the Turkish invasion, the Greeks and other Christians of the region were displaced to the southern part of the island. The Turks of the southern part of the island were forced to move to the north. The area occupied by Turkey amounts to 36.4% of the territory of the Republic of Cyprus and is the richest part of the island in natural and productive resources. The Turkish invasion resulted in grave human suffering and material economic loss, and its effects are still evident today with more than one-quarter of the population of the island being displaced persons and more than 1,000 people being classified as *missing persons.* 43,000 Turkish military troops armed with the latest military weapons continue to be based

30. Security Council (SC) Resolution 186/64. There followed twenty-eight SC Resolutions up to 1974, affirming SC Resolution 186/64.
31. *See* further C. Tornaritis, *The Legal Position of the Present Government of the Republic*, in *Ibid., Constitutional and Legal Problems in the Republic of Cyprus* 43–55 (1972).
32. *See* P. Polyviou, *Cyprus in Search of a Constitution: Constitutional Negotiations and Proposals* (1976).
33. *See* L. Loucaides, *The Legal Effect of the Coup of 15 July 1974* (2d ed., 1976, in Greek); A. Loizou, *The Coup, the Usurpers and the Rule of Law*, in *Cyprus: History, Problems and Struggle of Its People* 503–533 (G. Tenekides & N. Kranidiotis eds, Hestia 1981, in Greek).
34. For the Turkish position *see* Z. Necatigil, *The Cyprus Question and the Turkish Position in International Law* (2d ed., Oxford U. Press 1993).
35. *See* I. Brownlie, *The Prohibition of the Use of Armed Force for the Solution of International Differences with Particular Reference to the Affairs of the Republic of Cyprus*, in *International Law Conference on Cyprus* 198–213 (Cyprus Bar Council 1979); R. McDonald, *International Law and the Conflict in Cyprus*, Canadian 19 Y.B. Intl. L. 3ff (1981); D. Constantopoulos, *The Turkish Invasion of Cyprus from the Aspect of International Law* (1978).
36. Similar Resolutions of the Security Council from 1974 until 2004 amount to 87.

illegally on the island, while settlers are being brought to Cyprus in an effort to change the demographic character of the island.[37]

16. The Turkish occupation of Cyprus continues to the present day and therefore the Republic of Cyprus is prevented from exercising its powers over the occupied territory. Several attempts to achieve a solution to the Cyprus Problem have so far failed. On 24 April 2004, the fifth and final version of the plan of the Secretary General of the UN, Kofi Annan, for the comprehensive solution of the Cyprus problem was submitted for approval in separate simultaneous referenda. If the plan had been accepted, a new state of affairs would have come into being by the 'United Cyprus Republic' replacing the Republic of Cyprus.[38] The Plan was rejected by the people of Cyprus, since 75.83% of the members of the Greek Cypriot community voted against it, while 65% of the Turkish Cypriot Community voted in favour of it. Therefore, the so-called Annan Plan is, according to its own provisions, null and void and shall have no legal effect.

17. Cyprus became a full member of the European Union (EU) on 1 May 2004.[39] However, the application of the *acquis communautaire* in the occupied areas has been suspended, until a solution to the Cyprus Problem is found. Moreover, the *acquis* does not apply in the British Sovereign Base Areas (SBA). Prior to accession, the Republic of Cyprus was, from 1961 until 2004, a member of the non-aligned movement. It should be pointed out that Cyprus is the only EU Member State which is neither a North Atlantic Treaty Organization (NATO) member nor a member of the Partnership for Peace programme. A decision by the House of Representatives that the Republic should apply for membership in the Partnership for Peace programme was vetoed by the then-President of the Republic, Demetris Christofias, on 2 March 2011. Following his election, Christofias pledged to restart negotiations with the representative of the Turkish Cypriot Community, Mehmet Ali

37. *See* C. Tornaritis, *The Turkish Invasion of Cyprus and Legal Problems Arising therefrom* (1975); L. Clerides, *Violations of Human Rights by Turkey During the Invasion in 1974 and Continuing Violations Today*, 17 Cyprus L. Rev. 2669–2680 (1987) (in Greek); Cyprus Bar Assn., *Turkey's Violations of Human Rights in Cyprus. Findings of the European Commission of Human Rights and Continuing Violations by Turkey* (1995). *See also* K. Chrysostomides, *The Republic of Cyprus: A Study in International Law* (Martinus Nijhoff 2000).
38. For the Annan Plan, *see* A. Emilianides, *Constitutional Study of Annan V*, in *Reunifying Cyprus: The Annan Plan and Beyond* 95–106 (A. Varnava & H. Faustmann eds, Tauris 2009); A. Emilianides et al., *The Annan Plan: Five Critical Essays* (Ypsilon/Aigaion 2003, in Greek); C. Palley, *An International Relations Debacle* (Hart 2005); A. Syrigos, *The Annan Plan: The Legacies of the Past and the Prospects of the Future* (Patakis 2005, in Greek); A. Auer et al., *A Principled Basis for a Just and Lasting Cyprus Settlement in the Light of International and European Law*, Cyprus Y.B. Intl. Rel. 206ff (2006); S. Papasavvas, *The Annan Plan: A Constructively Vague Constitutional Future for Cyprus* (Sakkoulas 2003, in Greek).
39. *See* S. Laulhé-Shaelou, *The EU and Cyprus: Principles and Strategies of Full Integration* (Brill 2010); A. Markides, *The Cyprus Problem as a Legal Problem Within Europe*, 12 Revue Européenne de Droit Public 1195–1214 (2000); A. Sepos, *The Europeanization of Cyprus: Polity, Policies and Politics* (Palgrave Macmillan 2008), A. Theophanous, *The Cyprus Question and the EU: The Challenge and the Promise* (Intercollege Press 2004).

Talat, in an attempt to find a solution to the Cyprus problem;[40] such negotiations failed to produce tangible results. Subsequent President Nicos Anastasiades also carried out lengthy negotiations with the representatives of the Turkish Cypriot Community; however, the negotiations reached a deadlock.

40. *See* A. Emilianides, M. Kontos & G. Kentas, *A Marked Deck: The Confidential Documents of the Negotiations between Christofias and Talat* (Power Publishing 2010, in Greek).

Chapter 2. Profile of the Form of Government

18. Based on the principle of bi-communality, Cyprus is a unitary state comprised of two communities;[41] the Greek community and the Turkish community. According to Article 2 of the Constitution, the Greek Community comprises all citizens of the Republic who are of Greek origin and whose mother tongue is Greek, or who share the Greek cultural tradition, or who are members of the Greek Orthodox Church. The Turkish Community comprises all citizens of the Republic who are of Turkish Origin and whose mother tongue is Turkish, or who share the Turkish cultural traditions, or who are Muslims. Citizens of the Republic, who did not fulfil any of the above criteria, opted to belong either to the Greek or to the Turkish Community, within three months of the date of the coming into operation of the Constitution. A citizen of the Republic must therefore belong, or opt to belong, either to the Greek or to the Turkish Community; however, no aliens may belong to either Community. Greek and Turkish are the official languages of the Republic.

19. As already noted, the principle of bi-communality permeates the whole constitutional structure, according, in many respects, an equal status to the Greek community, representing 82% of the population, with the Turkish community representing 18%.[42] It was therefore provided that a Greek Cypriot President should be elected by members of the Greek Community, while a Turkish Cypriot Vice-President should be elected by members of the Turkish Community. The President and the Vice-President would exclusively exercise the executive power on specific matters and retain broad powers of veto on decisions of the Council of Ministers concerning foreign affairs, defence and security. A similar veto right was accorded to the President and the Vice-President, with respect to the laws enacted by the House of Representatives. It was further provided that the Council of Ministers should comprise of seven Greek Cypriots appointed by the President of the Republic and three Turkish Cypriots appointed by the Vice-President. At the same time, the Public Service should be composed on the basis of a seven-to-three analogy, while the Public Service Commission – which had the power to appoint, promote, transfer and exercise disciplinary control over civil servants – should consist of ten members, out of which seven shall be Greek Cypriots and three Turkish Cypriots. If the issue concerned whether a vacant post should be filled by a Greek or a Turkish Cypriot, a minimum number of votes from either Community were needed for a decision to be reached.

---

41. C. Tornaritis, *The Constitution of Cyprus*, 6 Intl. Rel. 28–40 (1964); T. Tsatsos, *Observations on the Constitution of Cyprus* (A. Sakkoulas 1965); M. Dendias, 'L' Arrangement du Problème de Chypre: Regime Constitutionelle et International et Garanties de la Republique de Chypre', in *Festchrift für Prof. W. Schätzel* 88ff (1960).
42. G. Papademetriou, *The Constitutional Problem of the Republic of Cyprus*, 39 Cyprus L. Tribune 850–856 (1991) (in Greek); C. Yiallourides, *Minderheitenschutz und Volksgruppenrecht im 20. Jahrhundert unter besonderer Berücksichtigung der Verhältnisse auf Zypern* (1981); N. Antonopoulos, 'Les Tendances Constitutionelles des États Avant Accédé Récement à l' Independance: La Constitution de la République de Chypre' 15 Revue Hellénique de Droit International 307–326 (1962).

20. The House of Representatives would consist of fifty Representatives; once again, 70% of the members of the House of Representatives were to be elected separately by the members of the Greek Community, while 30% were to be elected separately by the members of the Turkish Community. The President of the House of Representatives would be a Greek Cypriot, elected from among the Greek Cypriot Representatives, while the Vice-President would be a Turkish Cypriot, elected from among the Turkish Cypriot Representatives. Any amendments to the electoral law, the passing of laws concerning municipalities and laws imposing taxes or duties, would require a separate majority among Greek and Turkish Cypriot representatives, present and voting. In addition, the amendment of non-fundamental constitutional provisions would require a two-thirds majority of the representatives of each Community, voting separately. The Constitution also provided for two communal chambers: a Greek communal chamber and a Turkish communal chamber, which should have legislative power in educational, cultural, religious and other matters of a purely communal nature.

21. It was further provided that the judicial power was to be exercised by the Supreme Constitutional Court, the Supreme Court and their subordinate courts. The Supreme Constitutional Court should be composed of a non-Cypriot citizen as President and two members, a Greek Cypriot and a Turkish Cypriot, all appointed jointly by the President and the Vice-President. The Supreme Court would consist of two Greek Cypriot judges and one Turkish Cypriot, while the President of the Court would also be non-Cypriot. The bi-communal element was evident in the judiciary. The composition of the security forces was also based on increased proportions: an army of 2,000 men should consist of 60% Greek Cypriots and 40% Turkish Cypriots, while the Police and Gendarmerie would be composed on the basis of a seven-to-three analogy.

22. Probably the most striking provision of the Constitution, which was a result of the need to safeguard bi-communality, was Article 159 of the Constitution. It provided that a court exercising civil jurisdiction in a case where the plaintiff and the defendant belonged to the same Community would be composed solely of a judge or judges belonging to that Community; where the plaintiff and the defendant belonged to different Communities, the Court would be composed of such judges belonging to both Communities as the Supreme Court would determine. Furthermore, a court exercising criminal jurisdiction in a case where the accused and the person injured belong to the same Community, or where there was no person injured, should be composed of a judge or judges belonging to that Community, where the accused and the person injured belonged to different Communities, the court would be composed of such judges belonging to both Communities as the Supreme Court may determine. It was further provided that a coroner's inquest where the deceased belonged to the Greek Community should be conducted by a Greek coroner and where the deceased belonged to the Turkish Community by a Turkish coroner. In case there were more than one deceased belonging to different Communities, the inquest would be conducted by such coroner as the Supreme Court may direct. In addition to the above, the execution of any judgment or order of a court exercising civil or criminal jurisdiction, if the court was composed of a

Greek judge or Greek judges, should be carried out through Greek officers of the court, if the court is composed of a Turkish judge or Turkish judges, should be carried out through Turkish officers of the court, and in any other case, such execution should be carried out by such officers as the court of trial shall direct.

23. Essentially, the structure provided by the Constitution aimed at assuring that each Community would enjoy partial administrative autonomy while, at the same time, the numerically smaller Turkish Community would effectively participate in the exercise and functions of government in such a way so as to avoid the supremacy of the larger Community. De Smith noted that the 1960 Constitution is a tragic and occasionally almost ludicrous document and that it is possibly the most rigid, detailed and complicated Constitution in the world, weighed down by checks and balances, procedural and substantive safeguards, guarantees and prohibitions which set daunting obstacles to the people who are called to abide by it. He concluded that:

> Unique in its tortuous complexity and in the multiplicity of the safeguards that it provides for the principal minority, the Constitution of Cyprus stands alone among the Constitutions of the world. Two nations dwell together under its shadow in uneasy juxtaposition, unsure whether this precariously poised structure is about to fall crushing about their ears. The Nicosia model will never attract enthusiastic emulators, but it must be judged as the only acceptable remedy for a situation in which the will of the local majority had to be subordinated to the interests of international peace.[43]

24. As a result of the Cyprus Problem and the abnormal constitutional situation prevailing in the island, a significant number of constitutional provisions which refer to the Turkish Cypriot community have not been in force for sixty years, even though they are considered to be fundamental and thus not subject to modification. A doctrine of necessity has been accepted by the Supreme Court of Cyprus so that the House of Representatives may enact laws, even contrary to those provisions of the constitution, which are temporarily not in force because of the Cyprus Problem. This has resulted in a fundamental differentiation between the written form of the 1960 Constitution and the living Constitution as applied in Cypriot case-law and practice since 1964. No analysis of the constitutional order of Cyprus might be accurate without an understanding of the importance of the doctrine of necessity in the perseverance, interpretation and function of the Constitution.

43. A.S. De Smith, *The New Commonwealth and Its Constitutions* 296 (Stevens & Sons 1964).

Chapter 3. State Territory and Trust or Other Non-self-governing Territories

§1. The Republic of Cyprus and the 'Turkish Republic of Northern Cyprus'

25. Following the Turkish invasion in 1974, the Turkish Cypriot leader Rauf Denktash announced the unilateral establishment of the so-called Turkish Cypriot Federal State.[44] The Security Council of the UN expressed, with Resolution 367/75, its dissatisfaction with the unilateral statement. On 15 November 1983, the Turkish-occupied area declared itself as the 'Turkish Republic of Northern Cyprus' ('TRNC'), although that entity is recognized only by Turkey. The Security Council of the UN has condemned the declaration of the so-called TRNC with Resolution 541/83, in which it declared that such declaration was legally invalid.[45] The Security Council called upon all Member States to abstain from recognizing any other state in Cyprus apart from the internationally recognized Republic of Cyprus. Similar was the reaction of other international organizations, including the European Community (Statement of the Commission of 16 November 1983, Statement of the Council of Ministers of 10 June 1985, Resolutions of the European Parliament of 17 November 1983 and 13 September 1985) and the Council of Europe (Decision of 24 November 1983, Resolution 816/84 of 21 March 1984).

26. The fact that the government of the Republic of Cyprus is the only internationally recognized government and that the occupied areas continue to form part of the Republic of Cyprus has also been recognized by various decisions of international Courts, such as the Court of Justice of the European Union (CJEU)[46] and the European Court of Human Rights (ECtHR),[47] as well as British[48] and US courts.[49]

---

44. *See* G. Kasimatis, *Observations on the Denktash Constitution*, 1 To Syntagma 856–870 (1975) (in Greek); C. Tornaritis, *The Alleged Constitution of the So-Called Turkish Cypriot Federal State* (1978, in Greek), *Ibid.*, *The Legal Effect of the Establishment of a Turkish Cypriot Federal State* (1975); Z. Nedjati & G. Leathers, *A Study of the Constitution of the Turkish Federated State of Cyprus*, 5 Anglo-Am. L. Rev. 67–92 (1976); *Hesperides Hotels Ltd and Another v. Muftizade* (1979) AC 508 HL.
45. *See also* L. Clerides, *The Legal Invalidity of the Unilateral Declaration of an Independent State from the Turkish Cypriot Leadership*, 7 Cyprus L. Rev. 1198–1203 (1984) (in Greek); K. Ioannou, *Observations on Certain Legal Aspects of the New Cyprus Crisis*, 3 Cyprus L. Rev. 491–497 (1983) (in Greek).
46. For the avoidance of confusion, I refer to the CJEU, although most of the judgments were issued by the European Court of Justice (ECJ) as it was then called. C-432/92, *R v. Minister of Agriculture, Fisheries and Food*, ex p. *S. P. Anastasiou (Pissouri) Ltd and Others* [1994] ECR I-3087; C-219/98, *R v. Minister of Agriculture, Fisheries and Food*, ex p. *S. P. Anastasiou (Pissouri) Ltd and Others* [2000] ECR I-5241; C-140/02, *R v. Minister of Agriculture, Fisheries and Food ex p. S.P. Anastasiou (Pissouri) Ltd & Others* [2003] ECR I-10635. *See* S. Laulhé-Shaelou, *The EU and Cyprus: Principles and Strategies of Full Integration* 20–83 (Brill 2010); N. Emiliou, *Cypriot Import Certificates: Some Hot Potatoes*, 20 European L. Rev. 202–210 (1995); P. Koutrakos, *Legal Issues of EC-Cyprus Trade Relations*, 52 Intl. & Comp. L. Q. 489–498 (2003).
47. *Loizidou v. Turkey*, App. 15318/89, Judgments of 23 Mar. 1995 and 18 Dec. 1996, *Cyprus v. Turkey*, App. 25781/94, Judgment of 10/5/2001.

The ECtHR has confirmed in both the *Loizidou* judgment and the interstate judgment of *Cyprus v. Turkey* that 'Turkish armed forces of more than 30,000 personnel are stationed throughout the whole of the occupied area of Northern Cyprus, which is constantly patrolled and has checkpoints on all main lines of communications.' In view of the above, it was held that 'TRNC' should be properly considered to be a subordinate administration to Turkey. It was observed that:

> It is obvious from the large number of troops engaged in active duties in northern Cyprus ... that her army exercises effective overall control over that part of the island. Such control, according to the relevant test and in the circumstances of the case, entails her responsibility for the policies and actions of the 'TRNC'.

27. On 1 May 2004, the Republic of Cyprus, including the occupied territory, joined the EU. However, the application of the *acquis communautaire* in the occupied areas has been suspended. In the landmark *Orams* case, the CJEU held that the suspension of the application of the *acquis* in the occupied areas should be interpreted restrictively and must be limited to what is absolutely necessary to attain its objectives. The suspension is therefore limited to the application of the *acquis* in the northern area of the Republic of Cyprus, which is currently not under the effective control of the Republic; the suspension, however, does not apply with respect to judgments of courts sitting in the government-controlled area, the recognition of which is sought, even if such judgments concern land situated in the occupied areas.[50] It was therefore considered that the British Courts should recognize and enforce, on the basis of Brussels I Regulation,[51] a judgment of the District Court of Nicosia according to which Linda and Charles Orams were ordered to demolish the villa which they had erected in Lapithos (an area not under the effective control of the Republic of Cyprus) and deliver to the rightful owner of the property Meletis Apostolides free occupation of the land and damages for trespass.[52] The *Orams* judgment confirms that the occupied areas continue to form part of the Republic of

48. *Caglar v. Billingham (Inspector of Taxes)* [1996] STC (SCD) 150; *Veysi Dag v. Secretary of State for the Home Department* (2002) 122 ILR 529; *R v. Secretary of State for Transport* (2010) EWCA Civ 1093.
49. *Autocephalous Greek – Orthodox Church of Cyprus and Another v. Goldberg and Another* 917 F 2d 278 (1990). *See* further *Kanakaria Mosaics: The Trial*, Cyprus L. Tribune (2d ed., 1994); M. Kyprianou, *Caveat Emptor: The Four Byzantine Mosaics and the Struggle to Good Title*, in *Proceedings of the 10th Commonwealth Law Conference* 659–670 (1993); W. Muir, 'La Revendication Internationale des Biens Culturels à Propos de la Décision Américaine Eglise Autocephale', 81 Revue Critique de Droit International Privé 1–34 (1992).
50. C-420/07, *Orams v. Apostolides* [2009] ECR I-3571.
51. Council Regulation (EC) No. 44/2001 of 22 Dec. 2000 on jurisdiction and the recognition and enforcement of judgments in civil and commercial matters. This has now been repealed and substituted by Regulation (EU) 1215/2012 of the European Parliament and of the Council of 12 Dec. 2012 on jurisdiction and enforcement of judgments in civil and commercial matters.
52. *Apostolides v. Orams* [2010] EWCA Civ 9.

Cyprus, whose government is the sole internationally recognized government, a position that has been reinforced following the accession of the Republic of Cyprus to the EU.[53]

§2. The British Sovereign Base Areas

28. According to Article 1 of the Treaty of Establishment, the areas referred to as the Akrotiri SBA and the Dhekelia SBA, which cover 250 sq. km of the land area of the island of Cyprus, would 'remain under the sovereignty of the UK'.[54] A further thirteen sites, most notably the listening post on Mount Olympus, the highest point on the island, were retained for use by the UK under a provision made in the Treaty of Establishment. According to Article 2 section 2 of the Treaty of Establishment, the Republic of Cyprus shall cooperate fully with the UK in order to ensure the security and effective operation of such military SBAs, as well as the full enjoyment by the UK of the rights conferred by the Treaty. The legal status of the SBAs was confirmed by Protocol 3 of the Treaty of Accession of the Republic of Cyprus in the EU,[55] entitled *On the Base Areas of the UK of Great Britain and Northern Ireland in Cyprus*, where it is provided that the Treaty shall not apply to the SBAs of Akrotiri and Dhekelia, except to the extent necessary to ensure the implementation of the agreements set out in the Protocol. Following Brexit, a new Protocol[56] was attached to the Withdrawal Agreement of the UK[57] in order to safeguard that the arrangements applicable to the relations between the EU and the SBAs after Brexit would continue to be defined within the framework of the Republic of Cyprus' EU membership; the SBAs thus remained part of the customs territory of the EU after Brexit.

29. The extent of the UK's sovereignty over the SBAs is disputable. The SBAs are clearly not a state, since they do not have autonomous powers and are completely dependent on the UK. Nor could it be accepted that the SBAs are a 'quasi-state',[58] since any authority exercised by the authorities of the SBAs derives exclusively from the UK sovereignty and the relevant provisions of the Treaty of

53. *See* S. Laulhé-Shaelou, *The EU and Cyprus: Principles and Strategies of Full Integration* 172–232 (Brill 2010).
54. J. Woodliffe, *The Peacetime Use of Foreign Military Installations under Modern International Law* 74–76, 114 (Martinus Nijhoff Publishers 1992) observes that the SBAs are a prominent example of the use of legal forms representing an earlier epoch, in order to establish a new foreign military base.
55. On the Base Areas of the UK of Great Britain and Northern Ireland in Cyprus.
56. Protocol relating to the Sovereign Base Areas of the UK of Great Britain and Northern Ireland in Cyprus.
57. Agreement on the Withdrawal of the UK of Great Britain and Northern Ireland from the EU and the European Atomic Energy Community.
58. As suggested by L. Papaphilippou, *The Legal Status of the British Base Areas in Cyprus: Nature and Extent of the Sovereignty of the British Authorities* (1993, in Greek). *See* K. Chrysostomides, *The Republic of Cyprus: A Study in International Law* 87 (Martinus Nijhoff Publishers 2000).

Establishment. Could then one conclude that the SBAs are a colony under international law? Article 2 (ii) of the Declaration by Her Majesty's Government, regarding the Administration of the SBA (Appendix O), provides that the Government does not intend to develop the SBAs for purposes other than military and does not intend to set up and administer colonies.

30. Despite such declaration, however, the position under British constitutional law seems to be that the SBAs constitute a *colony*, in the sense that in 1960 all Cyprus, apart from the SBAs became independent; therefore, the SBAs are what remains of the former Colony of Cyprus and are to be regarded *as constituting a Colony acquired by consent or cession, as from 5 November 1914*, which is the date of annexation of Cyprus by the UK.[59] Concluding, however, that the SBAs are a colony is not so simple, since the UK has never considered that the SBAs are a colony in the sense of Article 73 of the UN Charter and has refrained from transmitting reports to the UN on the SBAs, as it did for other of its colonies. If it is accepted that the presence of the SBAs in Cyprus is a form of colonization, then it should be concluded that such presence cannot be justified according to international law, since two Resolutions of the General Assembly of the UN, namely 2555/1969[60] and 2621/1970,[61] prohibit the continuation of colonization in whichever form.

31. Another approach would be to characterize the SBAs as sui generis servitudes in favour of the UK, which, therefore, represent the rights of the UK arising from the Treaty of Establishment. Therefore, it could be argued that the SBAs are foreign military bases, without any real sovereignty under international law, despite the use of the word *sovereignty* in the Treaty of Establishment. Such view is supported by the decision of the Supreme Court of Cyprus in *Preece v. Estia.*[62] In its aforementioned decision, the Supreme Court held that:

> there is no doubt that the Sovereign Bases are neither a state nor a colony, but areas of the island of Cyprus, in which the UK at the time of the establishment of the Republic of Cyprus, for military and defence purposes alone, maintained, sovereignty with the restrictions and definitions mentioned ... See also Appendix 'O' of the Treaty of Establishment which contains the Declaration of the Government of the UK in relation to the future of the Sovereign Base Areas. There the use of the Base is restricted only to military purposes. In Appendix 'P': exchange of official correspondence between the President and the Vice-President of Cyprus and the Representative of the UK Government,

---

59. This position was adopted in Halsbury's, *Laws of England* vol. 6, para. 1074 (3d ed.).
60. Resolution 2641 of the 14 Dec. 1969, entitled '*Implementation of the Declaration of the Granting of Independence to Colonial Countries and Peoples by the Specialized Agencies and the International Institutions Associated with the United Nations*'.
61. Resolution 2621 of the 12 Oct. 1970, entitled '*Programme of Action for the Full Implementation of the Declaration on the Granting of Independence to Colonial Countries and Peoples*'.
62. *Preece v. Estia Insurance and Reinsurance Company Ltd* [1991] 1 CLR 568 (in Greek). *See also Chimonas* [2016] 1 CLR 395 (in Greek), S. Theodoulou, *Bases militaires en droit international: le cas de Chypre* (Bibliopolis 2006).

in the letter on behalf of Cyprus to which the Representative of Britain agrees the following were contained: 'in the event, however, that the Government of the UK, in view of changes in their military requirements, should at any time decide to divest themselves of the aforesaid sovereignty or effective control over the Sovereign Base Areas, or any part thereof, it is understood that such sovereignty or control shall be transferred to the Republic of Cyprus'.

32. It is submitted that the view according to which 'sovereignty' over the SBAs equals effective control over military base areas is the correct one.[63] It could, therefore, be argued that the SBAs could not have a right to territorial sea, since only states can exercise such a right, according to international law.[64] While Article 3 of Annex A of the Treaty of Establishment provides that the Republic of Cyprus shall not claim as part of its territorial sea, waters lying between the four Lines described in the Annex, this has been interpreted as a sui generis right of the SBAs to control some part of the territorial sea, as well as a sui generis obligation of the Republic of Cyprus to accept certain restrictions to the extent of its right to territorial sea; the purpose of the aforementioned provision with regard to territorial sea was to safeguard free access to the territory controlled by the SBAs and under no circumstances to accept that the British Base Areas have a right to territorial sea. It is also suggested that the relevant provisions of the Treaty of Establishment do not recognize a right of the British Base Areas to continental shelf; such an argument is strengthened by the fact that the UK has not objected in any way to the agreement between Cyprus and Egypt, which recognizes the right of the Republic of Cyprus to the continental shelf in the area opposite to the SBAs.

33. A significant development which coincided with the accession of Cyprus to the EU was the decision of the British Government to extend the application of the European Convention on Human Rights (ECHR) (but not the Protocols of the ECHR) to the SBAs with effect from 1 May 2004; since the aforementioned development, all citizens of the Republic who live or go through the SBAs ought, in principle, to be able to enjoy the rights and freedoms that they would have elsewhere in the island. On 15 January 2014, the Republic of Cyprus and the UK signed an arrangement relating to the regulation of non-military development in the SBAs. The arrangement aims at allowing planning and zoning rules to apply to geographical areas situated in the SBAs that are not being used for military purposes so as to safeguard the interests of those resident or working in the SBAs who wish to develop and/or sell their properties at prices equivalent to those in the Republic of Cyprus.

63. *See* A. Pellet, *The British Sovereign Areas*, Cyprus Y.B. Intl. L. 57–72 (2012). *See also* S. Laulhé Shaelou, *Focus on Territorial Exclusion and Sui Generis Territories in the EU: The British Bases in Cyprus. A Special Case*, Cyprus Y.B. Intl. L. 73–110 (2012).
64. Article 3 of the 1982 Convention on the Territorial Sea. *See* the analysis of L. Loucaides, *The Legal Status of the British Base Areas and the Right to Territorial Waters*, 27 Cyprus L. Rev. 4175–4178 (1989) (in Greek). *See also* S. Theodoulou, *The Legal Status of the British Military Base Areas in the Territory of the Republic of Cyprus* (1995, in Greek).

34. On 30 July 2018, the UK Supreme Court issued its interim judgment in the case of *Bashir.*[65] A number of refugees, who had arrived in the SBA in 1998, were recognized as refugees under the 1951 Convention relating to the Status of Refugees and asked to be admitted to the UK. The Secretary of State refused entry. A main issue in the proceedings was whether the Refugee Convention and the 1967 Protocol extend to the SBA. The Supreme Court held that since the ECHR applied to the territory now comprising the SBAs prior to the Independence of Cyprus, and since the UK had never notified the Secretary General of the Council of Europe that it would no further apply in such territory, it followed that the ECHR continued to apply to the SBAs after 1960. It was accordingly held that:

> In the case of the SBAs the only change which occurred in 1960 was that whereas they had previously been part of the UK-dependent territory of Cyprus, they were thereafter the whole of it. The mere fact the UK lost 97% of the island of Cyprus did not alter the status of the 3% that it retained. The status of the SBAs vis-à-vis the rest of the world did not change, except in relation to the rest of Cyprus, and that was because of a change in the status of the rest of Cyprus and not because of a change in the status of the SBAs.

65. *R (on the application of Tag Eldin Ramadan Bashir & Others) v. Secretary of State for the Home Department and Sovereign Base Area Authority* [2018] UKSC 45.

Chapter 4. State Population

35. Since the Turkish invasion, providing precise figures with respect to the population of Cyprus has presented certain difficulties due to the abnormal situation prevailing in the island. The Statistical Service of the Republic of Cyprus has estimated, however, that by the end of 2006, the population of Cyprus was 867,600, out of which 660,600 (76.1%) belonged to the Greek community, while 88,900 (10.2%) belonged to the Turkish Community. The remaining 118,100 (13.7%) were foreign residents, including mainly Greek and British citizens, as well as citizens of Russia, Philippines, Sri Lanka, Romania, Bulgaria and other countries. Out of the members of the Greek community, 2,700 (0.4%) were Armenians, 4,800 (0.6%) were Maronites and 900 (0.1%) were Roman Catholics. According to the 2011 official census, the population of Cyprus was 840,407, out of whom 667,398 (79.41%) were Cypriots, 106,270 (12.64%) were European citizens and 64,113 (7.62%) were third-country nationals.[66] An official census was more recently carried out in 2021; the population seems to have increased to 923,381, out of whom 719,252 (77.9%) were Cypriots, 93,540 (10.1%) were European citizens, and 107,168 (11.6%) were third-country nationals. The slight increase in third-country nationals was mainly due to British citizens (2%) being considered as third-country nationals after Brexit.

36. It should be noted that the actual number of Turkish Cypriots residing in Cyprus is difficult to estimate with precision since, after the Turkish invasion of 1974, there has been an effort by Turkey to change the demographic character of the occupied Northern Cyprus through the implantation of settlers.[67] It is estimated that 57,000 Turkish Cypriots have emigrated from Cyprus following the invasion of 1974. The number of settlers currently residing in Cyprus is not known. It is estimated, however, that more than 100,000 settlers from mainland Turkey are currently residing in the occupied areas. While the Statistical Service of the Republic of Cyprus estimates that the number of Turkish Cypriots currently residing in the occupied areas reaches approximately 88,900, it is suggested that the actual number might be closer to 120,000, as estimated by Turkish Cypriot sources. Illegal settlers are not included in any estimation of the current population of Cyprus.[68]

---

66. The remaining 0.33% were unidentified. Source: Statistical Service of the Republic of Cyprus.
67. A. De Zayas, *The Annan Plan and the Implantation of Turkish Settlers in Northern Cyprus*, Cyprus Y.B. Int. Rel. 163 (2006); M. Stavrinos, *Settlements as a Crime in International Law* (Parga 2013, in Greek).
68. *See* Council of Europe, 2 May 2003, Doc. 9799, *Colonization by Turkish Settlers of the Occupied Part of Cyprus* (Rapporteur Mr Laakso); L. Loucaides, *Expulsion of Settlers from Occupied Territories: The Case of Turkish Settlers*, in *Essays on the Developing Law of Human Rights* 108–138 (Martinus Nijhoff Publishers 1995).

Part I. Sources of Constitutional Law

Chapter 1. Treaties

§1. The Zurich and London Agreements

37. As already noted, the establishment of the Republic was the outcome of the Zurich and London Agreements of February 1959, on which the fundamental provisions of the Constitution were based.[69] The Zurich Agreements were signed on 11 February 1959 by the then Prime Ministers of Greece and Turkey, Konstantinos Karamanlis and Adnan Menderes, respectively. The Agreements were then approved on 19 February 1959 in London by the then Prime Minister of the UK, Harold Mac Millan and the representatives of the Greek and Turkish Community of Cyprus, Archbishop Makarios and Fazil Kucuk respectively. Apart from the Basic Structure (which provides for the constitutional structure), two additional international treaties were signed, which became part and parcel of the package deal agreed upon in Zurich; those were the Treaty of Alliance, signed between Greece, Turkey and the newly established Republic of Cyprus, according to which Greek and Turkish contingents would be permitted to be stationed on the island,[70] and the Treaty of Guarantee, signed between the Republic of Cyprus, Greece, Turkey and the UK, according to which Greece, Turkey and the UK would act as the guarantor powers of the independence, territorial integrity and constitutional order of the Republic of Cyprus.

38. The Agreement on the Basic Structure, as agreed upon in London, consists of twenty-seven articles which correspond to the fundamental articles of the Constitution of the Republic of Cyprus, as such, are defined in Annex III of the Constitution.[71] The only provision of the Basic Structure which was not included in the Constitution is Article 26, which was a transitional provision according to which the new Republic ought to have been constituted as soon as possible and, in any event,

69. *See* G. Zotiades, *The Founding Treaties of the Republic of Cyprus*, Y.B. L. Sch. Aristotle U. Thessaloniki 1287–1317 (1966) (in Greek); A. Emilianides, *The Zurich and London Agreements and the Cyprus Republic*, in *Mélanges Seferiades*, vol. II, 629–639 (1961).
70. C. Tornaritis, *The Treaty of Alliance and the Agreement for Its Application*, in *Ibid.*, *Constitutional and Legal Problems of the Republic of Cyprus* 33–39 (2d ed., 1972).
71. *See* in detail A. Emilianides, *Beyond the Constitution of Cyprus* (Sakkoulas 2006, in Greek).

within three months from the date of signature of the Agreements. However, the initial three-month deadline was soon replaced by a twelve-month deadline; eventually, the Constitution entered into force eighteen months from the date of signature of the Agreements.

39. Following the entry into force of the 1960 Constitution, the Basic Structure is no longer in force.[72] The Courts may, however, refer to the Basic Structure in case of ambiguity of the Constitution in accordance with Articles 149 and 180 of the Constitution. The Treaty of Guarantee and the Treaty of Alliance were attached to the Constitution as Annexes I and II respectively; thus, they have constitutional force in accordance with Article 181 of the Constitution. On the contrary, the Treaty of Establishment, which determines the territory of the Republic and who were citizens of the Republic at its inception, was not attached to the Constitution and does not enjoy constitutional force.[73]

§2. The Cyprus Act, 1960

40. Despite the undeniable importance of the Zurich and London Agreements, the establishment of the Republic of Cyprus from an international law perspective was due to the transfer of sovereignty from the previous sovereign, namely the UK, to the new Republic.[74] Such sovereignty was transferred when the British Parliament enacted on 29 July 1960 the Cyprus Act, 1960, section 1 of which authorized the Queen of England to issue an Order in Council which would enter into force the Constitution of the Republic of Cyprus. On 16 August 1960, which was the date that the Order of Council 1368/1960[75] entered into force, an independent and sovereign Republic of Cyprus was established according to section 1 of the Cyprus Act, 1960 and the Queen of England no longer had any sovereignty upon Cyprus.

41. While the traditional notion of parliamentary sovereignty, as interpreted in the UK, provides that no parliament can bind a future parliament by passing a law that cannot be reversed by a future Parliament,[76] there remains little doubt that a potential future revocation of the Cyprus Act, 1960 by the British Parliament would have absolutely no effect whatsoever in the sovereignty and international status of the Republic of Cyprus. In *Blackburn,* Lord Denning concluded that it would be inconceivable to imagine that the Parliament could revoke the independence of a former colony, since freedom once conferred cannot be revoked.[77] Even if it could

72. T. Tsatsos, *Observations on the Constitution of Cyprus* 15 (A. Sakkoulas 1965, in Greek).
73. Ex p. *Samuel N. Samuel* 3 (1960–1963) RSCC 76.
74. *See* C. Tornaritis, *The Genesis of the Cypriot State and Its Form* (1974, in Greek); K. Chrysostomides, *The Republic of Cyprus: A Study in International Law* 69 (Martinus Nijhoff Publishers 2000).
75. Republic of Cyprus Order in Council, 1960, S.I. 1969, No. 1368.
76. *See* C. Munro, *Studies in Constitutional Law* 127–171 (Butterworths 1999), *Ellen Street Estates v. Minister of Health* [1934] 1 KB 590, *Vauxhall Estates v. Liverpool Corporation* [1932] 1 KB 733.
77. *Blackburn v. Attorney-General* [1971] 1 WLR 137. *See also British Coal Corporation v. The King* [1935] AC 500, *Ibralebbe v. R* [1964] AC 900, *Ndlwana v. Hofmeyr* [1937] AD 229, *Harris v. The*

be considered that the UK may, in accordance with its internal law, revoke the Cyprus Act, 1960, such a revocation would have no effect under international law and it would essentially amount to a law whereby the British Parliament would legislate that smoking in Paris is illegal,[78] namely a law with no practical effect which the remaining States will simply ignore. Following 1960, the UK is irrevocably no longer sovereign in Cyprus.

§3. International Treaties and Their Hierarchical Status

42. Article 169 section 1 of the Constitution provides that every international agreement with a foreign State or any International Organization relating to commercial matters, economic cooperation (including payments and credit) and modus vivendi shall be concluded under a decision of the Council of Ministers. Any other treaty, convention or international agreement shall be negotiated and signed under a decision of the Council of Ministers, in accordance with Article 169 section 2, and shall only be operative and binding on the Republic of Cyprus when approved by a law made by the House of Representatives whereupon it shall be concluded. The above is subject to the veto right of the President[79] provided for in Articles 50 and 57 section 13, if the decision of the Council of Ministers relates to foreign affairs, defence or security. An international treaty, convention or agreement that has been concluded in accordance with the procedure described above shall have as from its publication in the Official Gazette of the Republic, superior force to any municipal law on condition that such a treaty, convention and agreement is also applied by the other party thereto, in accordance with Article 169 section 3 of the Constitution.

43. In view of the above, the Constitution provides for a dualistic approach with respect to the relationship between national and international law. An international treaty, convention or agreement will therefore not become part of the Cypriot legal order unless and until it has been ratified by the Council of Ministers, approved by law by the House of Representatives and published in the Official Gazette of the Republic. It is only through publication in the Official Gazette that the international law instrument may be invoked before the Cypriot courts and applied in the Cypriot legal order. The international law instrument has superior force over any ordinary domestic legislation, not in the sense of repealing any inconsistent domestic law, but in the sense of having superiority and precedence in its application. International law, once incorporated in the national legal order and published in the Official Gazette, is superior to any other municipal law, irrespective of whether such law is prior or subsequent to the international law instrument; an international law instrument may not be impliedly repealed through the enactment of conflicting subsequent municipal legislation.

Minister of the Interior [1952] 2 SA 428, S. De Smith & R. Brazier, *Constitutional and Administrative Law* 81 (8th ed., Penguin 1998); G. Marshall, *Parliamentary Sovereignty and the Commonwealth* 139–250 (Clarendon Press 1957).

78. I. Jennings, *The Law and the Constitution* 171 (5th ed., U. London Press 1959).

79. Or the Vice-President of the Republic; however, the post of the Vice-President remains vacant since the 1963 withdrawal of Turkish Cypriots from the Government.

44. Thus, the international law instrument is superior not on the basis of the principle of *lex posterior derogat lex priori* but rather on the basis of the principle of *lex superior derogat lex inferiori.*[80] Hierarchically, the international law instrument is therefore placed above any other municipal legislation, with the exception of the Constitution. The Constitution, as the supreme law of the Republic, does not fall within the definition of municipal law of Article 169 section 3 of the Constitution. Consequently, an international law instrument, either treaty, convention or agreement, is inferior to the Constitution and the constitutional provisions prevail in case of any inconsistency between them and the provisions of the international law instrument.[81] It should be further noted that while an international law instrument has to be ratified and published in the Official Gazette in order to become part of the Cypriot legal order, its interpretation is governed by the principles and interpretation of international law and particularly those contained in the Vienna Convention on Treaties; the rules and principles of interpretation of ordinary statutes do not apply with respect to the interpretation of international law instruments.

45. Article 169 section 3 of the Constitution introduces the condition of reciprocity, namely the condition that the international law instruments, either treaties, conventions or agreements, have to be applied also by the other party thereto, in order to enjoy superior force over municipal legislation. The condition of reciprocity was considered by the Supreme Court in the leading case of *Malachtou v. Armefti*, which concerned the question of whether the Convention on the Legal Status of Children Born out of Wedlock, ratified by Law 50/1979, had superior force over municipal legislation.[82] The Court noted that conventions or treaties may be bilateral or multilateral. In bilateral conventions where objective rights are created or obligations are undertaken by one State towards the other or the nationals of the other State, reciprocity is essential, although according to Article 60 of the Vienna Convention, it is only a material breach of the Treaty that entitles the other party to invoke the breach as a ground for terminating the Treaty or for suspending its operation in whole or in part.

46. The Court further observed, however, that the nature, objective and function of certain international treaties and conventions are such so as to exclude the condition of reciprocity; these are multilateral conventions, the object of which is not to create any subjective or reciprocal rights for the contracting parties themselves, but rather to promote certain principles of law, moral and legal values and which a contracting party signs and ratifies only for the realization of this objective. Examples of such international conventions are those which protect human rights, or whose aim is the improvement and formulation of common rules and the achievement of social justice. The Court further clarified that for an international law instrument to be applicable, it must be self-executing in the sense that its provisions must

80. *Malachtou v. Armefti and Another* [1987] 1 CLR 207. *See also* C. Tornaritis, *The Introduction of International Law into the Legal System of Cyprus*, 3 Cyprus L. Tribune 460–474 (1990); *Ibid., The Treaty Making Power, Especially under the Law of the Republic of Cyprus* (1973).

81. *Malachtou v. Armefti and Another* [1987] 1 CLR 207; *Shipowners Union and Another v. The Registrar of Trade Unions and Others* [1988] 3 CLR 457.

82. *Malachtou v. Armefti and Another* [1987] 1 CLR 207.

be of such nature so that they may be applied by the organs of the State and be enforced by the Courts, or that they may create rights for the individuals, govern or affect directly relations of the internal life between the individuals, and the individuals and the State or the public authorities. Provisions which do not create by themselves rights or obligations of persons or interests and which cannot be justiciable or do not refer to acts or omissions of State organs are not self-executing. In view of the above, it was held that:

> It would be incomprehensible for a State not to secure the rights and freedoms defined in s.1 of the Convention of Human Rights on the ground that another party to the Convention violates the Convention even against a national of the first State ... Where there is any international mechanism of control or supervision: the condition of reciprocity again cannot validly be raised.

47. Consequently, the Court in *Malachtou v. Armefti* held that the condition of reciprocity is not applicable with respect to the Convention on the Legal Status of Children Born out of Wedlock, since the Convention does not create reciprocal rights for the Contracting Parties themselves; its objective is to improve the situation of children born of wedlock, the formulation of common rules concerning their status and the harmonization of the laws of the Member States of the Council of Europe in this field.[83] Similarly, the ECHR and its Protocols have, on the basis of the aforesaid Article 169 section 3 of the Constitution, superior force to any municipal law, either antecedent or subsequent to their ratification by Law and the condition of reciprocity is not applicable.

§4. The Position of EU Law

48. Following the accession of the Republic of Cyprus to the EU in 2004, questions arose as to the need for an amendment of the Constitution, so as to reflect the post-accession framework of the Republic, as well as the position of the EU law within the Cypriot legal order.[84] The CJEU has long considered that the EU Treaty is different from other treaties in that it has established a new legal order for the benefit of which the Member States have permanently limited their sovereign rights.[85]

---

83. *Ibid.*
84. *See* A. Emilianides, *The Constitution of Cyprus post-Accession*, in *Policy Proposals* 81–101 (A. Emilianides ed., Power Publishing 2005, in Greek); S. Laulhé-Shaelou, *The EU and Cyprus: Principles and Strategies of Full Integration* (Brill 2010); E. Venizelos, *The Constitutional Issue, the Constitutional Legal Order and the Prospect of Accession to the European Union*, 20 Hellenic Rev. European L. 287–306 (2000) (in Greek); E. Nicolaou, *The Accession to the European Union and the Constitutional Order of Cyprus*, 19 Hellenic Rev. European L. 23–33 (1999) (in Greek); S. Papasavvas, *Constitutional Aspects of the Accession of the Republic of Cyprus to the European Union*, 22 Hellenic Rev. European L. 89–91 (2002) (in Greek); C. Clerides & X. Xenofontos, *Accession Should Lead to Immediate and Radical Constitutional Amendments*, Cyprus L. Tribune 40–47 (2004) (in Greek).
85. Case 26/62, *Van Gend en Loos* [1963] ECR I, Case 6/64, *Costa v. ENEL* [1964] ECR 585.

The CJEU has therefore considered that the supremacy and primacy of EU law extends even against the provisions of the national constitutions of the Member States of the Union.[86]

49. In the case of *Constantinou*, the Appellant, the Attorney-General of the Republic, had petitioned for the delivery of the respondent to the authorities of the UK on the basis of the EC Framework Decision with respect to the European Arrest Warrant (EAW).[87] The respondent, a citizen of the Republic of Cyprus, who had been criminally prosecuted for offences against the Treasury in the UK, raised the issue that the Law incorporating the EC Council's Framework Decision with respect to the EAW ran contrary to the express provisions of Article 11 section 2(f) of the Constitution of Cyprus, according to which the extradition of citizens of the Republic was not permitted. The Attorney-General argued that EU law was superior to the law of the Member States and therefore the Framework Decision had to be applied, irrespective of the conflicting provisions of the Constitution.

50. The Full Bench of the Supreme Court held that the provisions of Law 133(I)/2004, which incorporated the Framework Decision on the EAW into the Cypriot legal order, ran contrary to the express provisions of the Constitution of Cyprus, according to which the extradition of Cypriot citizens was not permitted. Although the Supreme Court acknowledged that case-law of the CJEU considered Community law superior to national legal orders, it held that without an amendment of the Constitution, it could not apply the Law that incorporated the Framework Decision on the EAW to a citizen of the Republic of Cyprus. Article 169 section 3, as it stood at the time of the judgment, provided only for the supremacy of international law over ordinary municipal law, not over constitutional provisions.

51. Following the *Constantinou* judgment, the Constitution was amended with the Fifth Constitutional Amendment of 2006, 127(I)/2006, which aimed at facilitating the exercise of the rights and obligations of the Republic of Cyprus as a Member State of the EU. The newly added paragraph 4 of Article 169 provides that the Republic may exercise any option and discretion provided for in the Treaty establishing the European Community or the Treaty on EU and to any Treaties substituting or modifying them. Modified Article 179 section 2 provides that no law or decision of the House of Representatives or of any of the Communal Chambers and no act or decision of any organ, authority or person in the Republic exercising executive power or any administrative function shall in any way be repugnant to, or inconsistent with, any obligation imposed upon the Republic as a result of its participation as a Member State of the EU. Furthermore, the newly inserted Article 1A of the Constitution provides that no constitutional provision is considered to invalidate any laws, acts or measures which are deemed necessary due to the obligations of the Republic of Cyprus as a Member State of the EU or impede the legal effect

86. Case 11/70, *Internationale Handelsgesellschaft* [1970] ECR 1125.
87. *Attorney-General v. Constantinou* [2005] 1 CLR 1356 (in Greek).

and application of Regulations, Directives or other EU, or European Communities' legal instruments of a binding nature in the Republic.[88]

52. As a result, EU law now has an intra-constitutional effect, in the sense that it is considered to be an integral part of the Constitution, and no constitutional provision may invalidate any provision of a binding nature of EU law. It should be noted that it is the Constitution itself which provides for the facilitation of Community law within the Cypriot legal order and its specific primacy. EU law is therefore accorded a constitutional status by the Constitution itself, in the sense that no other provision of the Constitution may be invoked so as to declare the provisions of EU law unconstitutional. Such effect is purely intra-constitutional as far as the Cypriot legal order is concerned.

88. *See also* C. Lycourgos, *Cyprus Public Law as Affected by Accession to the European Union*, in *Studies in European Public Law* 101ff (C. Kombos ed., Sakkoulas 2010); *Ibid.*, *The Application of EU Law in Cyprus: Selected Aspects*, Cyprus Y.B. Intl. L. 43ff (2012); S. Laulhé Shaelou, *Back to Reality: The Implications of EU Membership in the Constitutional Legal Order of Cyprus*, in *Brave New World. Application of EU Law in the New Member States* 471–502 (A. Lazowski ed., TMC Asser Press 2010); C. Kombos, *The Impact of EU Law on Cypriot Public Law* (Sakkoulas 2015).

Chapter 2. Constitution

§1. Supremacy

53. The Constitution of Cyprus is a written and lengthy document consisting of 199 Articles and three Annexes. The Greek and Turkish texts of the Constitution are both originals and have the same authenticity by virtue of Article 180 of the Constitution. The Constitution is separated in thirteen distinct Parts as follows: Part I (Articles 1–5): General Provisions, Part II (Articles 6–35): Fundamental Rights and Liberties, Part III (Articles 36–60): The President of the Republic, the Vice-President of the Republic and the Council of Ministers, Part IV (Articles 61–85): The House of Representatives, Part V (Articles 86–111): The Communal Chambers, Part VI (Articles 112–121): The Independent Officers of the Republic, Part VII (Articles 122–128): The Public Service, Part VIII (Articles 129–132): The Forces of the Republic, Part IX (Articles 133–151): The Supreme Constitutional Court, Part X (Articles 152–164): The High Court and the Subordinate Courts, Part XI (Articles 165–168): Financial Provisions, Part XII (Articles 169–178): Miscellaneous Provisions, Part XIII (Articles 179–186): Final Provisions. Articles 187–199 of the Constitution consist of transitional provisions. Annex I is the Treaty of Guarantee, Annex II is the Treaty of Alliance, and Annex III is the list of the fundamental articles of the Constitution which may not be amended.

54. Article 179 section 1 of the Constitution provides that the Constitution shall be the supreme law of the Republic, while 179 section 2 provides that no law or decision of the House of Representatives or of any of the Communal Chambers and no act or decision of any organ, authority or person in the Republic exercising executive power or any administrative function shall in any way be repugnant to, or inconsistent with, any of the provisions of the Constitution. The Constitution of Cyprus is the supreme law of the Republic, its *grundnorm*,[89] its ultimate rule of recognition[90] and any ordinary laws, or international law instruments must not be inconsistent with the Constitution. Following the Fifth Amendment of the Constitution with Law 127(I)/06, the supremacy is subject to the application of Article 1A, which provides for the application of mandatory provisions of EU law. In addition, the principle of supremacy, as enshrined in Article 179 of the Constitution, has to be read in conjunction with the doctrine of necessity.

§2. The Doctrine of Necessity

I. The Origins of the Doctrine

55. As a result of the bi-communal violence that broke out in Cyprus in December 1963, there existed a state of armed rebellion against the established Government of the Republic, which led to armed clashes between organized groups

89. *See* in particular H. Kelsen, *General Theory of Law and State* (Russell & Russell 1961).
90. *See* in particular H.L.A. Hart, *The Concept of Law* 79ff (2nd ed., Clarendon Press 1994).

resisting the authority of the State, loss of life, damage to property, interruption of communications, and assertion of authority and actual physical control over areas of State territory by the insurgents and their political leaders. The Turkish Cypriot Vice-President, the three Turkish Cypriot Ministers, as well as the fifteen Turkish Cypriot members of the House of Representatives vacated their offices. Furthermore, the President of the Supreme Constitutional Court, a German citizen, and the President of the High Court, a Canadian citizen, both resigned.[91] In view of the above, the two highest tribunals of the Republic had ceased to function. No appeals, criminal or civil, could be adjudicated upon, and no constitutional jurisdiction or any revisional jurisdiction in administrative law matters could be exercised.

56. The administration of justice, as well as the very existence of the Republic of Cyprus, was in immediate danger.[92] In view of the aforementioned problems, the House of Representatives enacted the Administration of Justice (Miscellaneous Provisions) Law 33/1964, according to the provisions of which a newly established Supreme Court would exercise the jurisdiction and powers of the Supreme Constitutional Court and the High Court, 'until such time as the people of Cyprus may determine such matters'.[93] The remaining five members of the two former highest tribunals of the Republic (three Greek Cypriots and two Turkish Cypriots) would constitute the Supreme Court, with a Turkish Cypriot, Judge Zekia, holding the position of the President of the Court. The constitutionality of the said law was challenged before the Supreme Court itself in *Ibrahim.*[94] Undeniably, the law would be considered to be prima facie unconstitutional, unless it could be justified on the premises of the doctrine of necessity.[95]

57. The first argument raised before the Court concerned an objection to the legality of the proceedings. The respondent argued that since the Supreme Court was constituted by virtue of Law 33/64, which was prima facie unconstitutional, it had no legal existence, and thus, it had no power to deal with the matter of constitutionality. The Court rejected the argument by holding that once the Court has seized on the case, it must assume the competence and responsibility to deal 'with

---

91. Ernst Forsthoff, the President of the Supreme Constitutional Court, had actually resigned since May 1963.
92. *See, inter alia, The Attorney-General of the Republic v. Ibrahim* [1964] CLR 195.
93. Preamble of Law 33/64.
94. *The Attorney-General of the Republic v. Ibrahim* [1964] CLR 195.
95. On the doctrine *see* A. Emilianides, C. Papastylianos & C. Stratilatis, *The Republic of Cyprus and the Doctrine of Necessity* (Sakkoulas 2016, in Greek); P. Polyviou, *The Case of Ibrahim, the Doctrine of Necessity and the Republic of Cyprus* (Chryssafinis & Polyviou 2015); C. Kombos, *The Doctrine of Necessity in Constitutional Law* (Sakkoulas 2015); A. Emilianides, *Accession of the Republic of Cyprus to the EU, the Constitution and the Cypriot Doctrine of Necessity*, Cyprus Y.B. Intl. Rel. 65–82 (2007); L. Papaphilippou, *The Doctrine of Necessity and the Constitutional Order of Cyprus* (1995, in Greek); C. Tornaritis, *The Principle of Necessity and the Cypriot Legal System* (1978, in Greek); A. Eftychiou, *The Doctrine of Necessity and its Application on Cypriot Law*, 12 Cyprus L. Rev. 1951–1956 (1985) (in Greek).

all matters raised therein, including questions going to the legality of its existence'.[96] The Supreme Court should be given the opportunity to decide whether Law 33/64 was constitutional, even if a negative decision would mean that the Court should no longer function.

58. The second question to be answered was whether there truly was a state of emergency in Cyprus. The Supreme Court unanimously held that it could take judicial notice of the fact that there existed a state of emergency, which could not be met within the provisions of the Constitution.[97] The Court held that it would be unreasonable to declare that a state of emergency did not exist at a time when the Security Council of the UN dispatched an international force to Cyprus to assist in the return to normality. A third and more important question was whether the Government and the House of Representatives of the Republic of Cyprus were still functioning legally, since they were not constituted according to the relevant provisions of the Constitution, which provided for a bi-communal structure. It was accurately held that the existence of Cyprus as an independent state could not be deemed to be dependent on the fate of the operation of its constitution, since such existence is governed by the principles of international law, and in particular by the principle of recognition by other States. Bearing in mind that the existence of the Government of the Republic of Cyprus, as well as the existence of the Republic of Cyprus, had been affirmed by the Security Council of the UN,[98] the Court could take judicial notice of the fact that the constitutional organs of the Government of the Republic of Cyprus were still functioning in accordance to the law.

59. Eventually, the Supreme Court went on to discuss the nature of the doctrine of necessity, as it would be applied in Cyprus. Based on the legal principles of '*salus populi suprema lex esto*' and '*necessitas non habet legem*', the Court held that the doctrine of necessity was a direct result of the rigidity and narrow ambit of the Constitution of 1960 and that it would be inconceivable that a state should destroy itself because of its Constitution. It was, therefore, held that Article 179 of the Constitution, which states that the Constitution is the supreme law of the Republic, ought to be applied subject to the proposition that where it is not possible for a basic function of the state to be discharged properly, or where a situation has arisen which cannot be adequately met under the existing provisions of the Constitution, then the appropriate organ may take such steps within the nature of its competence as are required to meet the necessity.[99] It was, therefore, understood that the doctrine of necessity is not a supraconstitutional principle; on the contrary, it forms part of Article 179 of the Constitution as an implied principle.

---

96. *The Attorney-General of the Republic v. Ibrahim* [1964] CLR 195, at 204, Judgment delivered by Vassiliades J.
97. Article 183 of the Constitution provides for a state of emergency to be declared for certain limited purposes.
98. Security Council Resolution 186/64.
99. *The Attorney-General of the Republic v. Ibrahim* [1964] CLR 195, at 234, Judgment delivered by Triantafyllides, J.

60. In essence, the Supreme Court held that there are four prerequisites in order to determine whether the doctrine of necessity could be applied in a particular case, namely: (i) an imperative and inevitable necessity or exceptional circumstances, (ii) no other remedy to apply, (iii) the measure taken must be proportionate to the necessity, and (iv) it must be of a temporary character limited to the duration of the exceptional circumstances.[100] The Supreme Court is responsible for determining whether the aforementioned prerequisites are satisfied, taking into account that the doctrine of necessity is applied, so as to safeguard constitutional rights and freedoms. Based on the aforementioned principles, it was unanimously held that Law 33/64 was constitutional on the basis of the doctrine of necessity. The *Ibrahim* case forms the foundation of the subsequent case-law of the Supreme Court with regard to the doctrine of necessity and was cited with approval in a number of international cases, such as in Canada,[101] Pakistan,[102] Lesotho[103] and Grenada.[104]

II. The Nature of the Doctrine of Necessity

61. There are two principal theories with regard to the justification of the doctrine of necessity, which, however, essentially coincide in their essence. The political theory of justification argues that the doctrine of necessity is a political principle, which may legitimate any illegal measures, which are the direct result of the emerging necessity.[105] On the contrary, the legal theory of justification suggests that the doctrine of necessity is itself a legal principle according to which the executive ought to act in order to safeguard the Republic. While the Supreme Court of Cyprus has not considered the question of the status of the doctrine of necessity as a result of political or legal justification, it is suggested that while the doctrine of necessity in the Cypriot legal order is justified due to reasons of political necessity, it forms part of the constitutional order of the Republic of Cyprus as a legal principle. The aim of the doctrine of necessity is, therefore, to solve problems, which were not foreseen by the drafters of the constitutional order, and which threaten the existence of the Republic. The doctrine of necessity is accordingly neither an extra-constitutional nor a supraconstitutional principle; it is rather a constitutional principle per se, which indirectly forms a part of Article 179 of the Constitution of the Republic of Cyprus. Thus, the doctrine of necessity should be considered to be an indispensable part of the constitutional order.

---

100. *Ibid.*, p. 264, Judgment delivered by Josephides J.
101. *Re Manitoba Language Rights* [1985] SCR 721.
102. *Bhutto v. The Chief of the Army Staff and the Federation of Pakistan* PLD 1977 SC 710.
103. *Mokotso and Others v. King Moshoeshoe II and Others*, 5 Aug. 1988 (1992) 90 ILR 427.
104. *Mitschell and Others v. Director of Public Prosecutions and Another* 45 (1986) LRC 86. *See also* *Annual Survey of Commonwealth Law* 76–79 (1965) and 59 (1973).
105. *See also* C. Tornaritis, *Changeability of the Constitution*, in *Ibid.*, *Constitutional and Legal Problems of the Republic of Cyprus* 75 (1972).

III. The Limits of Proportionality

62. As already observed, one of the four main criteria in order to apply the doctrine of necessity is that the measure taken must be proportionate to the necessity. Therefore, the Supreme Court was called upon to apply the principle of proportionality according to the particular circumstances of each specific case. It is submitted that in its first judgment in *Ibrahim,*[106] it became evident that the Court was willing to accept a rather wide interpretation of the principle of proportionality. In *Ibrahim*, the Court held that merging by Law 33/64 the Supreme Constitutional Court and the High Court into a newly established Supreme Court was in accordance with the principle of proportionality, without considering whether it would be necessary to replace the neutral presidents of the two former Supreme Courts, who had resigned before the enactment of Law 33/64. It also held that the provision of Article 144 of the Constitution, according to which the Supreme Constitutional Court has exclusive jurisdiction to determine questions of constitutionality of laws, is no longer valid, since the enactment of Law 33/64 intended for any court of the Republic to determine the said questions of constitutionality of laws. Such provisions of Law 33/64 were held to be proportional.

63. Such a wide interpretation of the principle of proportionality is understandable. The doctrine of necessity, as applied in Cyprus, did not concern the exercise of legislative powers by the executive or the restriction of fundamental individual rights. Law 33/64 was enacted by the legislative organ of the Republic of Cyprus, which was deemed to be in a better position than the Court to appreciate which were the most appropriate measures in order to face the exceptional circumstances; it was not for the Court to turn itself into a legislative body, but only to consider whether the measures proposed should be considered to be arbitrary. The interpretation of the principle of proportionality with regard to the application of the doctrine of necessity was further disputed in subsequent cases.

64. According to Article 125 of the Constitution, the Public Service Commission has the exclusive competence to appoint, promote, transfer, retire and exercise disciplinary control over public officers. Since December 1964, the three Turkish Cypriot members of the Public Service Commission vacated their offices, while a Greek Cypriot member passed away and another resigned. As a direct consequence, a quorum could not be constituted. The Public Service Law 33/67 provided for the functioning of the Public Service Commission in view of the new circumstances. However, the aforementioned law differed in certain provisions from the constitutional mandates. Eventually, the Supreme Court was called upon to decide whether such different provisions could be justified on the grounds of the doctrine of necessity.

65. In *Hadjianastassiou,* the Court held that the Public Service Commission, which was created by Law 33/67, was not the Commission which was set up pursuant to Article 124 of the Constitution and which ceased to function due to the

106. *The Attorney-General of the Republic v. Ibrahim* [1964] CLR 195.

abnormal situation prevailing since 1963.[107] Therefore, the fact that Law 33/67 did not include the constitutional mandate according to which *no person shall be appointed as, or be, a member of the Commission who is, or within the preceding twelve months in the case of the Chairman or six months in the case of any other member, has been a public officer, or a member of the armed forces* was held to be justified on the grounds of the doctrine of necessity, since the aforementioned omission did not in any way undermine the independence of the Public Service Commission and thus, within the limits of the principle of proportionality. Accordingly, the doctrine of necessity could not only justify the substitution of members of the Turkish Community with members of the Greek Community[108] but also certain amendments which were held to be necessary, in order to safeguard the efficiency of the Public Service Commission. Such wide interpretation of the principle of proportionality was confirmed in the case of *Kyriacou*, where it was, however, held that the law regarding the new Public Service Commission must be as similar as possible to the constitutional provisions.[109]

66. A similar line of judicial thinking was also followed with regard to the constitutionality of the Cyprus Tourism Organization Law 54/69. According to Articles 122 and 125 of the Constitution, the Public Service Commission has the exclusive competence to appoint, promote or dismiss employees of the Cyprus Tourism Organization. However, Law 54/69 provided that such competence belongs to the Cyprus Tourism Organization. The Supreme Court held that the aforementioned law could be justified on the grounds of the doctrine of necessity.[110] Furthermore, the Cyprus Tourism Organization Law was not supposed to be identical to the constitutional provisions regarding the Public Service Commission, so long as they were proportional and could not be considered arbitrary.[111] It should therefore be clear that the principle of proportionality has been widely interpreted by the Supreme Court, since the Court is not a political organ and should not substitute the legislative organ of the Republic.[112] It is, therefore, submitted that so long as the enacted measures correspond to an actual necessity and are not arbitrary, they shall generally be considered justified on the grounds of the doctrine of necessity. On the contrary, the Court shall not allow the enactment of legislation which is arbitrary and does not correspond to an actual necessity.

67. In *Pastellopoulos*, the Supreme Court held that Articles 103 and 104 of the Military Penal Code and Procedure Law 40/64, which provided that the President of the Military Court would be appointed by the Council of Ministers, while the other two members of the Military Court would be appointed ad hoc for each particular case, were contrary to Article 157(2) of the Constitution which provides that

---

107. *Hadjianastassiou v. The Republic* [1982] 3 CLR 1173. *See also Coupepides v. The Republic* [1980] 3 CLR 256, *Louka v. The President of the Republic* [1983] 3 CLR 783.
108. This was the view of Pikis J. in *Solomou v. The Republic* [1984] 3 CLR 533, *Kazamias v. The Republic* [1982] 3 CLR 239, *Makrides v. The Republic* [1984] 3 CLR 677.
109. *The Republic v. Kyriacou* [1987] 3 CLR 1189.
110. *HjiGeorghiou v. The Cyprus Tourism Organisation* [1986] 3 CLR 1110.
111. *The Cyprus Tourism Organisation v. Hadjidemetriou* [1987] 3 CLR 780.
112. *See also Koumi v. Kortari* [1983] 1 CLR 856.

matters concerning judges are within the exclusive competence of the Supreme Judiciary Council and could not be justified on the grounds of the doctrine of necessity.[113] It is submitted that such narrow interpretation of the principle of proportionality in *Pastellopoulos* is due to the fact that the exercise of the competences of the Supreme Judiciary Council had not been affected by the constitutional crisis of 1963 and thus, any legislative act, which was contrary to Article 157(2) would be considered to be arbitrary. While in the case of the Public Service Commission, a new organ had been created due to the fact that the constitutional provisions relating to the Public Service Commission were no longer workable, in the case of *Pastellopoulos,* there was no plausible justification for overriding the existing constitutional provisions.

68. Similarly, the Supreme Court refused to justify on the grounds of the doctrine of necessity administrative acts of a final nature, such as dismissal or promotion, which were decided by the administrative organs without the enactment of a law conferring the relevant competences to such organs. It was, therefore, held that the fact that the Public Service Commission was unable to constitute a quorum could not justify the application of the doctrine of necessity with regard to administrative acts. Any urgent needs could be faced with temporary measures, until such law was enacted that would allow the Public Service Commission to constitute a quorum.[114] It is suggested that the justification for such narrow interpretation of the principle of proportionality with regard to administrative acts is due to the fact that administrative acts, unlike legislation, are not of a general character and thus there would exist a greater possibility that such acts were arbitrary. Administrative acts of a final nature could not themselves be justified on the grounds of the doctrine of necessity; however, administrative acts of a final nature which were based on a law, which was justified on the grounds of the doctrine of necessity, would also be justified.[115]

IV. State Organs and the Doctrine of Necessity

69. The Republic of Cyprus has followed two distinct methods in filling the Turkish Cypriot offices, which remained vacant since the constitutional crisis of 1963; offices which are the result of elections, such as the position of the Vice-President of the Republic, or the fifteen Turkish Cypriot seats in the House of Representatives have remained vacant,[116] while those offices which are the result of appointment, such as the offices of the three Turkish Cypriot Ministers, or the Deputy Attorney-General,[117] were mostly filled by Greek Cypriots. This should not, however, mean that a possible election of Greek Cypriot members of the House of

113. *Pastellopoulos v. The Republic* [1985] 2 CLR 165.
114. *Georghiades v. The Republic* [1966] 3 CLR 317, *Papapantelis v. The Republic* [1966] 3 CLR 515, *Hadji Georghiou v. The Republic* [1966] 3 CLR 504, *Iosif v. CYTA* [1970] 3 CLR 225, *Bagdassarian v. EAC* [1968] 3 CLR 736, *Poutros v. CYTA* [1970] 3 CLR 281.
115. *Mesaritou v. CYBC* [1972] 3 CLR 100, *Theodorides v. Plousiou* [1976] 3 CLR 319.
116. *See also Joannides v. Police* [1973] CLR 125, *The Republic v. Souleiman* [1973] 5 JSC 624.
117. *In Re Georghiou* [1983] 2 CLR 1.

Representatives, or a Greek Cypriot Vice-President, could not be justified on the grounds of the doctrine of necessity; it rather was a political choice on behalf of the Republic of Cyprus, in order to avoid any major alterations of the constitutional order in the hope that the constitutional crisis would soon be resolved. Such hope proved to be futile, since the Turkish invasion of 1974 only magnified the necessity.[118]

70. It was further accepted that the self-dissolution of the Greek Communal Chamber with Law 12/65 in view of the constitutional crisis of 1963 and the transfer of its competences to the newly established Ministry of Education and Culture, the House of Representatives and the Council of Ministers, could be justified on the grounds of the doctrine of necessity.[119] Thus, an eleventh ministry was added to the ten ministries provided for in the Constitution, namely the Ministry of Education (as it then was named), currently the Ministry of Education, Sports and Youth, which is a direct product of the doctrine of necessity.[120] A special status was further awarded on the grounds of the doctrine of necessity to the representatives of the three religious minority groups of the Republic, namely the Armenians, the Maronites and the Roman Catholics. According to Article 109 of the Constitution, each of the three *religious groups* of the Republic had the right to be represented by an elected member, or members of such group, in the Greek Communal Chamber, as provided by the relevant communal law. Ever since the self-dissolution of the Greek Communal Chamber, the members of the three religious groups, in addition to the right of electing and being elected in parliamentary elections, like every citizen of the Republic, also elected as members of their respective religious group, one member of each group, to represent such group in the House of Representatives. That member is in charge of all matters which concern the group but does not have the right to vote, as provided in the Religious Groups (Representation) Law 38/76.

71. Contrary to the above, the Supreme Court was understandably unwilling to legitimize any rare attempts to alter constitutional provisions despite the fact that no emergency seemed to exist. In *Sampson*, the Supreme Court held that the general amnesty announced by the President of the Republic, Archbishop Makarios, upon returning from his exile in 1974, could not be justified on the grounds of the doctrine of necessity, since the House of Representatives, which had the exclusive competence to enact laws, was functioning normally, and could, therefore, enact a law providing for general amnesty, if it so wished.[121] In another case, the Supreme Court unanimously held that the Coup (Special Provisions) Law of 1990, which amended the Coup Law 57/75 by providing that the members of the *Government* during the Coup of 1974 could not elect or be elected in presidential, parliamentary, or communal elections, was unconstitutional, since any impediments for election were

118. *Petroudes v. EAC* [1985] 3 CLR 2245.
119. *Cypiom Ltd v. Police* [2003] 2 CLR 459 (in Greek). *See also Georghiades v. The Republic* [1966] 3 CLR 252, *President of the Republic v. House of Representatives* [1985] 3 CLR 2801.
120. *See also President of the Republic v. House of Representatives* [1994] 3 CLR 167 (in Greek).
121. *The Republic v. Sampson* [1977] 2 CLR 1.

clearly provided for in Articles 40 and 64 of the Constitution.[122] The fact that the members of the said 'Government' were not criminally prosecuted after 1974 could not possibly mean that the House of Representatives had the competence to enact a law contrary to the provisions of the Constitution. The argument that the aforementioned Law could be justified on the grounds of the doctrine of necessity was accordingly rejected.

72. Following the above reasoning, the Supreme Court rejected three successive attempts of the House of Representatives to restrict the ambit of the competences of the President of the Republic. The Supreme Court held that the attempt of the House of Representatives to force the President of the Republic to vacate the office prematurely, in order for a by-election to take place, was contrary to Article 44 of the Constitution and could not be justified on the grounds of the doctrine of necessity.[123] Similarly, an attempt by the House of Representatives to define by name the ten ministries of the Republic was held to be unconstitutional, since it violated the provisions of Article 46 of the Constitution and could not be justified on the basis of the doctrine of necessity.[124] It is suggested that the aforementioned cases were extremely political in nature and had in reality nothing to do with the doctrine of necessity; the argument that the doctrine of necessity could justify such laws was simply a political argument and was rightly rejected by the Supreme Court.

V. Human Rights and the Doctrine of Necessity

73. The question of whether the doctrine of necessity could restrict fundamental human rights, which are protected in Part II of the Constitution, was first examined in *Chimonides*.[125] It was suggested that the Government of the Republic should have *reserved powers*, or *police powers*, so that it could interfere with the enjoyment of specific rights, such as the right to enter into contracts which is guaranteed in Article 26(1) of the Constitution. The approach of the *police powers* was adopted by two of the Judges of the Supreme Court in *Chimonides*;[126] it was also adopted by a different judge in *Apostolides*.[127] It was stressed, however, that such police powers should always correspond to the emerging necessity and should be of limited scope.

74. A different approach was suggested by two judges in *Chimonides*[128] and was eventually adopted by the majority of the Supreme Court in the subsequent case of *Alloupas*. It was held that such an implied right of the Government to exercise police powers in relation to the rights and liberties guaranteed in part II is neither

122. *President of the Republic v. House of Representatives* [1991] 3 CLR 252 (in Greek).
123. *President of the Republic v. House of Representatives* [1985] 3 CLR 2202. *See also President of the Republic v. House of Representatives* [1985] 3 CLR 1429.
124. *President of the Republic v. House of Representatives* [1985] 3 CLR 2801.
125. *Chimonides v. Manglis* (1967) 1 CLR 125.
126. *Ibid.*, decision of Josephides J, Hadjianastassiou J. concurring.
127. *Apostolides v. The Republic* (1982) 3 CLR 928, decision of Pikis J.
128. *Chimonides v. Manglis* (1967) 1 CLR 125, decision of Triantafyllides J., Stavrinides J. concurring.

needed nor possible because such right is expressly provided for in the Constitution, by appropriate exhaustive provisions in the several articles concerned, which provide for the conditions under which an individual right may be restricted.[129] Such conditions essentially correspond to those established by the ECHR. In view of such express provisions and in view of the responsibilities of the Republic of Cyprus as a contracting state of the ECHR, it was held that individual rights may not be further restricted. Constitutional rights may, thus, be restricted only on the basis of the relevant provisions of the Constitution and by applying the strictest possible criteria in assessing whether a state of necessity exists and whether such restrictions comply with the principle of proportionality.

75. It was, therefore, accepted that the temporary suspension of the right of creditors to collect the debts of debtors who became refugees and suffered as a result of the Turkish invasion in Cyprus in 1974, by Articles 3 and 4 of Law 24/79, could be justified on the grounds of the doctrine of necessity, since the aim of such measures was to reinforce the social structure and serve, in the long term, the maintenance of the constitutional order.[130] It was further accepted that successive orders of requisition of private property for the purpose of the defence of the Republic, which had arisen due to the Turkish occupation of part of the Republic of Cyprus by Turkey, could be justified on the grounds of the doctrine of necessity.[131]

VI. Turkish Cypriots and the Doctrine of Necessity

76. More recently, the doctrine of necessity has been used in order to safeguard the human rights of the Turkish Cypriot citizens of the Republic, who opted to reside in the non-occupied areas of the Republic of Cyprus. The first case where a Turkish Cypriot applicant argued that the doctrine of necessity should be applied with regard to Turkish Cypriots was the case of *Kemal Selim.*[132] According to Article 87 of the Constitution, matters concerning personal status and marriage of members of the Turkish Cypriot Community were governed by the relevant laws of the Turkish Communal Chamber. Since 1974, however, there were no Turkish judges in Cyprus in order to perform a civil marriage of members of the Turkish Community according to the Turkish Family Law, Cap. 339. Accordingly, section 34 of the Marriage Act, Cap. 279 did not provide the possibility for a Turkish Cypriot professing the Muslim faith to contact a civil marriage in Cyprus. Selim complained under Articles 8, 12 and 13 of the ECHR that he had been denied the right to marry and found a family. The ECtHR declared the application admissible, and

129. *Alloupas v. National Bank of Greece* (1983) 1 CLR 55.
130. *Ibid.*
131. *Adrian Holdings Ltd v. The Republic* [1999] 3 CLR 828 (in Greek) and *Koutsou v. The Republic*, Judgment of 10 Mar. 2000 (in Greek). *See also Aristides v. The Republic* [1983] 3 CLR 1507, *Kritiotis v. The Municipality of Paphos* [1986] 3 CLR 322, *Kitsis v. The Attorney-General*, Judgment of 20 Jul. 2001 (in Greek).
132. *Selim v. Cyprus*, App. 47293/99, Judgment of 16 Jul. 2002.

the Government of the Republic of Cyprus submitted a formal declaration accepting a friendly settlement of the case. Law 46(I)/02 provided for the temporary application of the Marriage Act 279 to members of the Turkish Community for as long as the abnormal situation prevailing on the island continued.[133] The application of the aforementioned Law was justified on the grounds of the doctrine of necessity.

77. A second case of extreme significance where the doctrine of necessity was used in favour of the Turkish Cypriots, who reside in the non-occupied areas, was the case of *Ibrahim Aziz.*[134] According to Article 63 of the Constitution, the members of the House of Representatives of each Community of the Republic of Cyprus are elected separately, and therefore, members of each Community are included in separate electoral lists. The applicant, who resided in the non-occupied areas, requested to be registered in the electoral roll in order to exercise his voting rights in the parliamentary elections. When the Minister refused to enrol the applicant, he complained that there was a violation of his rights under Article 3 of Protocol 1 of the ECHR, taken in conjunction with Article 14 of the ECHR. The ECtHR unanimously held that a violation had occurred.

78. Consequently, the Republic of Cyprus is now obliged to provide for the right of Turkish Cypriots who reside in the non-occupied areas to vote – and be elected – in parliamentary – and accordingly presidential, or municipal – elections in order to comply with the aforementioned judgment of the ECtHR. Such compliance could only occur on the grounds of the doctrine of necessity. A first step towards a unitary electoral list occurred during the elections for representatives of the Republic of Cyprus in the European Parliament in 2004, since Turkish Cypriots residing in the non-occupied area voted in the elections, and a Turkish Cypriot was a candidate for election. It is submitted that the application of the doctrine of necessity with regard to Turkish Cypriots reinforces the significance of the doctrine of necessity as a doctrine destined to preserve the constitutional order and the individual fundamental liberties of the people of Cyprus. In the 2019 European Parliament elections, Niyazi Kızılyürek, a Turkish Cypriot who had been residing in the areas controlled by the Republic and who was a Professor at the University of Cyprus, was elected as one of the six Cypriot Members of the European Parliament (MEPs), as a candidate with the left party Progressive Party of Working People (AKEL).[135]

§3. Amendment of the Constitution

79. According to the provisions of Article 182, those articles which have been incorporated from the Zurich Agreements and which are listed in Annex III of the Constitution are considered to be fundamental and, thus, they are not subject to

133. *See also* Law 104(I)/2003.
134. *Aziz v. Cyprus*, App. 69949/01, Judgment of 22 Jun. 2004.
135. E.g., 'Cyprus elects first Turkish Cypriot to European Parliament', Aljazeera, available in, https://www.aljazeera.com/news/2019/5/27/cyprus-elects-first-turkish-cypriot-to-european-parliament.

modification, a fact which confirms the rigid character of the Constitution.[136] On the contrary, the remaining non-fundamental constitutional provisions may be amended by a law passed by a majority vote comprising at least two-thirds of the total number of the Representatives belonging to the Greek Community and at least two-thirds of the total number of the Representatives belonging to the Turkish Community. Since the constitutional crisis of 1963, no constitutional provisions could be amended due to the absence of the Turkish Cypriot members of the House of Representatives.

80. Eventually, the House of Representatives enacted the First Amendment of the Constitution Law 95/1989, which amended Article 111 of the Constitution, which provides for the adjudication of family law disputes. Law 95/89 provided that all matters relating to divorce, judicial separation, or restitution of conjugal rights, or to family relations of the members of the Greek Orthodox Church and of the members of the three religious groups of the Republic would come under the jurisdiction of the newly established Family Courts, and Family Courts of Religious Groups, and also provided that members of the Greek Community may perform a civil marriage if they so wish. Such law was enacted with a majority vote comprising two-thirds of the Greek Cypriot Representatives, but no Turkish Cypriot Representatives had voted in favour of Law 95/89, since the Turkish Cypriot seats of the House of Representatives had been vacated since 1963.

81. The competence of the House of Representatives to amend the non-fundamental provisions of the Constitution, with a majority of its Greek Cypriot members only, on the grounds of the doctrine of necessity, was examined in the leading case of *Nicolaou.*[137] In *Nicolaou*, the Supreme Court was divided. Five judges of the Supreme Court held that Law 95/89 was constitutional on the grounds of the doctrine of necessity,[138] while five other judges of the Court held that the said Law was unconstitutional.[139] Thus, the aforementioned Law was held to be constitutional in view of the principle that any law is presumed to be constitutional unless it is proved to be unconstitutional beyond any reasonable doubt. The approach of

136. Without reproducing here Annex III, it is noted that fundamental Articles not subject to modification include either the entirety or various paragraphs of Arts 1, 3, 4, 5, 23, 36, 39, 42, 43, 44, 46, 50, 51, 52, 53, 57, 61, 62, 65, 78, 86, 87, 89, 92, 108, 112, 115, 118, 123, 126, 129, 130, 131, 132, 133, 137, 138, 139, 153, 157, 159, 160, 173, 178, 181, 182, 185. It is surprising that Art. 179 which provides for the supremacy of the Constitution is not itself fundamental.

137. *Nicolaou v. Nicolaou* [1992] 1 CLR 1338 (in Greek). For the different approach of previous case – law *see President of the Republic v. House of Representatives* [1985] 3 CLR 2224, *President of the Republic v. House of Representatives* [1986] 3 CLR 1439. *See also* S. Soulioti, *The Amendment of the Constitution and the Application of the Doctrine of Necessity*, 13 Cyprus L. Rev. 2063–2078 (1986) (in Greek); A. Manesis & G. Papademetriou, *The Doctrine of Necessity and the Amendment of the Constitution of the Republic of Cyprus*, 34 Rev. Pub. L. & Admin. L. 7–13 (1990) (in Greek); M. Christofides, *The Power of the House to Amend*, 28 Cyprus L. Rev. 4333–4344 (1989) (in Greek); C. Clerides, *The Power to Amend the Constitution of the Republic of Cyprus*, 26 Cyprus L. Rev. 1951–1956 (1989) (in Greek).

138. Stylianides J., Kourris J., Papadopoulos J., Poyadjis J. and Chrysostomis J.

139. Loizou P., Pikis J., Nikitas J., Artemis J. and Constantinides J.

the five judges holding that Law 95/89 was unconstitutional was relatively straightforward; they observed that the doctrine of necessity is by nature a temporary measure limited for the duration of the exceptional measures, while on the contrary, the amendment of constitutional provisions is a permanent measure. Thus, the doctrine of necessity could not be considered to be a sufficient justification for amending Article 111 of the Constitution with a majority of its Greek Cypriot Representatives only, since one of the four prerequisites of the doctrine was not fulfilled.

82. It is suggested that the aforementioned approach was unnecessarily formalistic. In 1989, the executive and the legislative branches of the Republic of Cyprus had already been exercising the full spectrum of their competences for more than twenty-five years, including the conclusion of international treaties, conventions and agreements, the enactment of laws and the appointment of public officers and civil servants. Could it ever be considered that all those laws, treaties and appointments were simply temporary measures in the sense that they would automatically cease to exist when the state of emergency ended? Would the Republic of Cyprus automatically resign from being a Member State of the EU?[140] The answer can be negative, and this is due to the fact that the state of emergency was not in itself temporary or static. Bearing in mind that the 1960 Constitution was never completely implemented even during the period 1960–1963,[141] the Turkish occupation of a great part of Cyprus, and the fact that continuing negotiations for the solution of the Cyprus problem have been going on for nearly sixty years, it would simply be inconceivable to suggest that a solution of the Cyprus problem would be found, by automatically implementing all the provisions of the original 1960 Constitution, without specific provisions which would deal with the consequences of the Turkish invasion, the acts of the internationally non-recognized 'TRNC' and the fact that the doctrine of necessity has been part of every single act of the executive, the legislative and the judicial organs of the Republic of Cyprus since 1963.

83. It is therefore suggested that the House of Representatives may modify the non-fundamental provisions of the Constitution by a majority of two-thirds of its Greek Cypriot members on the grounds of the doctrine of necessity, so long as any such amendments are not contrary to the international obligations of the Republic of Cyprus, and more importantly the ECHR and EU Law. This should not mean that the temporary character is no longer an element of the Cypriot doctrine of necessity; it should, however, imply that the doctrine of necessity should have as its primary purpose the stability of the Republic, in view of the degree and quality of the actual necessity. Such a view was also adopted by a majority of nine judges to four in the subsequent case of *Koulountis,*[142] which examined the constitutionality of the Third Amendment of the Constitution Law 115(I)/96, which amended Article 66 section 2 of the Constitution so that a vacant parliamentary seat would be filled as provided by law and not by a by-election.

---

140. In 1989, there existed a customs union between Cyprus and the European Economic Community, as it was then called.
141. Articles 123, 129 and 173(1) of the Constitution were never implemented.
142. *Koulountis v. The House of Representatives* [1997] 1 CLR 1026 (in Greek).

84. The power of the House of Representatives to amend the non-fundamental provisions of the Constitution by virtue of the doctrine of necessity was unanimously confirmed by the Plenary Bench of the Supreme Court in *Charalambides,*[143] where it was held that the amendment of Article 146 of the Constitution and the establishment of an Administrative Court to exercise the first-instance jurisdiction on administrative law issues, previously exercised by the Supreme Court, was constitutional. In *Charalambides,* the Supreme Court further confirmed that once a constitutional amendment has lawfully taken place in accordance with the doctrine of necessity, it is not possible to declare that the new constitutional provision is unconstitutional because its content conflicts with another constitutional provision. The Constitution is a unified whole and needs to be read and interpreted as such. So far, there have been eighteen amendments to the Constitution.[144]

143. *Charalambides and another v. Republic and another*, Administrative App. 99/2016, Judgment of 4 Apr. 2018 (in Greek).

144. Of Art. 111 with Law 95/89, of Art. 63 § 1 with Law 106(I)/96, of Art. 66 § 2 with Law 115(I)/96, of Arts 47, 118 § 3, 4 and 119 § 4 with Law 104(I)/02, of Arts 1, 11 § 2, 140, 169 and 179 with Law 127(I)/06, of Art. 17 with Law 51(I)/10, of Art. 11 with Law 68(I)/13, of Art. 146 with Law 130(I)/2015, of Art. 15 with Art. 69(I)/2016, of Arts 7 § 2, 11 § 3, 47, 48, 49, 53 § 4, 83 § 2 and 106 § 2 with Law 93(I)/2016, of Art. 167 with Law 100(I)/2019, of Arts 66 § 2 and 71 with Law 128(I)/2019, of Art. 40 with Law 160(I)/2019, of Art. 64 with Law 161(I)/2019, of Art. 146 § 3 with Law 135(I)/2020, of Art. 4 § 3 with Law 67(I)/2022, of Arts 136, 144, 146 and 155 with Law 103(I)/2022, and Art 111 with Law 3(I)/2023.

Chapter 3. Legislation and Equivalent Legislative Rules

85. There are certain ordinary laws which cover matters connected with constitutional law and thus, constitute a source of constitutional law. Such may be divided into four categories:[145]

a. Laws which deviate from the letter of the Constitution but have been justified by the doctrine of necessity; such laws, albeit ordinary ones, have in effect constitutional status in the sense that they govern matters which would otherwise be regulated by the constitutional provisions. The most important such laws are the Administration of Justice Law (Miscellaneous Provisions) 33/1964, which created a new Supreme Court with all the competences of the constitutionally provided Supreme Constitutional Court and High Court,[146] as well as Law 12/1965 which transferred the competences of the Greek Communal Chamber to the newly established Ministry of Education and Culture, the House of Representatives and the Council of Ministers.
b. Organic laws, namely laws whose existence is provided by the text of the Constitution itself, such as laws governing the function of the organs of the State. Typical examples of such laws are the electoral laws relating to the election of the President of the Republic and the members of the House of Representatives, as well as the Standing Orders of the House of Representatives, which have been enacted by virtue of Article 73 section 1 of the Constitution which provides that 'subject to the ensuing provisions of the Article, the House of Representatives by its Standing Orders regulates any matter of parliamentary procedure and of functions of its offices'.
c. Laws enacted in order to restrict the exercise of fundamental rights in a manner authorized by the Constitution. Many of the articles safeguarding human rights expressly provide that such rights may be restricted only for specific purposes and as 'prescribed by law'. A typical example is the law of libel which restricts the right of freedom of expression.
d. Ordinary laws which refer to matters of public law, such as the General Principles of Administrative Law Act 158(I)/1999, which govern administrative action.

145. *See also* A. Markides, *The Republic of Cyprus*, in *Constitutional Law of 10 EU Member States* I-17–18 (Kortmann et al. eds, Kluwer 2006).
146. Until the amendment of the relevant Articles of the Constitution with Law 103(I)/2022.

Chapter 4. Jurisprudence

86. The principles of common law and equity apply in the Republic of Cyprus.[147] Previous judgments of the Supreme Constitutional Court or the Supreme Court are binding for lower courts; thus, case-law is of great significance with regard to the interpretation of legal provisions.[148] The Supreme Constitutional Court or the Supreme Court may depart from their respective earlier decisions whenever they conclude that a previous decision is founded on an indisputably wrong principle of law, or a principle leading to manifest injustice or a principle which cannot be reconciled to changed legal or social circumstances. It is thus noted that previous case-law is only binding so far as a subsequent law with different content has not been enacted. The legal rule which must be applied is the *ratio decidendi,* or the legal principle on which the previous decision was founded. The ratio of the case is distinguishable from obiter dicta, which are statements on principles of law made in the course of a decision, but on which the decision does not depend. Having a substantially codified legal system, Cyprus applies common law principles where there is no Cypriot legislation in force and in so far as existing Cypriot legislation is not contradicted.[149]

87. With respect to constitutional and administrative law, however, the Supreme Court (prior to the recent re-establishment of a distinct Supreme Constitutional Court after sixty years) regularly cited judgments of continental law courts, such as the Greek Symvoulio tis Epikrateias and the French Conseil d' Etat.[150] It could therefore be argued that Cypriot constitutional justice forms an idiosyncratic osmosis between continental and common law.[151] Cypriot administrative law in particular is similar to Greek, French and German continental administrative law, and not to English administrative law; as a result, Greek and French authorities and

147. L. Loucaides, *The Dependence of Cypriot Law from Common Law*, in *Ibid.*, *Topics of Cypriot Law* vol. I, 36–77 (1982, in Greek); G. Pikis, *The English Common Law: The Rules of Equity and Their Application in Cyprus* (1981, in Greek).

148. C. Artemides, *The Principle of Commitment of Courts to Case-Law in English Common Law* in *Aspects of Cypriot Law* vol. I, 219–231 (Asselia 1981, in Greek); S. Nikitas, 'The Principle of Judicial Precedent in English Common Law' *Corpus de Jure Cyprii, v. I* (Legal Studies Council 1987, in Greek): 119–133.

149. S. Symeonides, *The Mixed Legal System of the Republic of Cyprus*, 78 Tulane L. Rev. 441–455 (2003).

150. From 1960–1963, while the President of the Supreme Constitutional Court was the German Ernst Forsthoff, the Supreme Court regularly cited German jurisprudence with respect to constitutional law cases.

151. *See* S. Papasavvas, *La Justice Constitutionelle à Chypre* (Economica/Presses Universitaires d' Aix – Marseilles, 1998); *Ibid.*, *The Osmosis of Continental Public Law and Common Law in Cyprus*, 28 Constitution 693–706 (2002). *See also* A. Emilianides, *Cyprus: Everything Changes and Nothing Remains Still*, in *A Study of Mixed Legal Systems: Endangered, Entrenched or Blended* 215 (S. Farran et al. eds, Ashgate 2014); N. Hatzimichail, *Reconstructing Mixity: Sources of Law and Legal Method in Cyprus* in *Mixed Legal Systems: East and West* 75 (V. Palmer et al. eds, Ashgate 2015).

jurisprudence have guided the evolution of Cypriot administrative law.[152] With respect to human rights, the Supreme Court was regularly guided by the case-law of the ECtHR. In addition, with respect to the interpretation of constitutional provision, the Supreme Court had been at times guided by the case-law of the Supreme Court of the United States of America (USA).

152. *See* M. Triantafyllides, *A Tabulation of Cases in Which the Supreme Court of Cyprus When Deciding Them Referred to Principles of Greek Administrative Law*, in *Proceedings of the First International Cyprological Conference* vol. III, 393–399 (T. Papadopoulos & M. Christodoulou eds, Socy. Cypriot Stud. 1973).

Chapter 5. Customary Law, Unwritten Law, General Principles of Law

§1. Unwritten Law

88. In view of the strict and detailed character of the Constitution of Cyprus, there does not seem to exist room to invoke unwritten or customary law in order to introduce, amend or repeal a constitutional provision. In any case, the question of whether the enduring and uniform application of a particular rule which is considered binding could acquire constitutional status or fill a constitutional vacuum (as a rule and not as mere constitutional practice) has never been examined in the constitutional legal order. As Markides notes, 'when one considers that finding parliamentary time to pass legislation has never been a problem in Cyprus, it is difficult to imagine a uniform and enduring application of any particular kind in order to meet a given set of circumstances'.[153]

§2. General Principles of Law

I. The Rule of Law and the Hierarchy of Laws

89. Several general constitutional principles may be derived from the Constitution, such as the principle of representative democracy which provides that people govern through elected representatives and the principle of bi-communality which has already been analysed in previous paragraphs. Furthermore, as already explained, the fundamental principle of supremacy of the Constitution implies that the courts have the power to examine the constitutionality of both laws and action of the administration and that no law, regulation or administrative act may be inconsistent with the Constitution. This also implies that the rule of law is a cardinal principle of the Constitution, as this is also evidenced by Part II of the Constitution which contains a Charter of Fundamental Rights based on the ECHR.[154]

90. There is a hierarchy of the rules of law in Cyprus, at the top of which is the Constitution. The hierarchical structure of legal rules in the Republic is essentially the following:[155]

a. Every provision of the 1960 Constitution, with the exclusion of provisions which have been lawfully repealed and the inclusion of provisions which have been lawfully added or amended in accordance with the procedure provided in Article 182 of the Constitution, taking into account that the doctrine of necessity and EU law is considered to be an integral part of the Constitution.

153. *See also* A. Markides, *The Republic of Cyprus*, in *Constitutional Law of 10 EU Member States* I-20 (Kortmann et al. eds, Kluwer 2006).
154. *See also* A. Loizou, *The Constitution of Cyprus* 6–7 (2001, in Greek).
155. *See* in detail A. Emilianides, *Beyond the Constitution of Cyprus* (Sakkoulas 2006, in Greek).

b. International treaties or conventions which have been ratified by law by the House of Representatives and which have been promulgated in the Official Gazette of the Republic in accordance with Article 169 section 3 of the Constitution and in so far as they are not inconsistent with or contrary to any provision of the Constitution.
c. Acts of the legislative power which have been enacted in accordance with the provisions of the Constitution and in so far as such are not inconsistent with or contrary to such provisions, or provisions of an International Treaty promulgated in accordance with Article 169 section 3 of the Constitution or Convention and so long as such have not been repealed.
d. Acts which have been enacted by organs of the Republic during the exercise of their right to enact subsidiary legislation, in so far as such an organ has been authorized to enact subsidiary legislation in accordance with a law which has not been repealed and in so far as such act has not been enacted ultra vires the authorizing legislation and is not inconsistent with or contrary to the Constitution or a provision of an International Treaty or Convention promulgated in accordance with Article 169 section 3 of the Constitution.
e. Legislation which was in force prior to the entry into force of the 1960 Constitution in so far as such has not been repealed by posterior legislation and in so far as such is not inconsistent with or contrary to the Constitution, in accordance with Article 188 of the Constitution and in so far as it is not inconsistent with a provision of an International Treaty or Convention promulgated in accordance with Article 169 section 3 of the Constitution.
f. Common law and the principles of equity in accordance with section 29(c) of the Courts of Justice Law 14/60 in so far as they are not inconsistent with or contrary to the Constitution, provisions of International Treaty or Convention promulgated in accordance with Article 169 section 3 of the Constitution, or legislation enacted in accordance with the Constitution, or legislation which remains in force in accordance with Article 188 of the Constitution.
g. Laws of the Parliament of the UK which were in force in Cyprus on the day prior to Independence, and in so far as such are not inconsistent with or contrary to the Constitution or International Treaties or Conventions promulgated in accordance with Article 169 section 3 of the Constitution or legislation enacted in accordance with the Constitution.
h. Judgments of the Supreme Court, the High Court or the Supreme Constitutional Court which form precedent, provided that the Supreme Court may in the appropriate case depart from its earlier case-law, and in so far as such judgments do not run contrary to (a)–(e) above.
i. Customary law in so far as it is not contrary to or inconsistent with (a)–(h) above.

II. Separation of Powers as a Constitutional Principle

A. The Separation of Powers Between the Executive and the Legislative

91. The principle of separation of powers has often been considered one of the most significant tools for maintaining the system of checks and balances enshrined in the Constitution of Cyprus. In accordance with the principle of separation of powers, each of the three powers of the State, the Legislature, the Executive and the Judiciary, 'is invested with power to act over the entire field of action covered by the corresponding domain of authority except to the extent that provision to the contrary is made to the Constitution'.[156] While the principle of separation of powers is not mentioned explicitly in the Constitution, several constitutional provisions confirm that the Constitution embodies such principle.[157] The Constitution itself has further introduced certain exception to the strict separation of powers.[158] The Council of Ministers may undertake preparatory legislative acts by drafting bills before they are introduced to the House of Representatives by a particular Minister in accordance with Article 54(f) of the Constitution,[159] and the Minister of Finance may submit the budget (Article 167 of the Constitution), Article 79 section 2 grants Ministers the right to follow the proceedings of the House of Representatives and to make statements to the House of Representatives, and Article 54(g) authorizes the Council of Ministers to issue subsidiary legislation in some circumstances.

92. The Supreme Court has repeatedly held that a law is unconstitutional if it runs contrary to the principle of separation of powers as this is enshrined in various constitutional provisions. Whereas the application of the principle is an effective tool for restricting abuse of power, the reasoning of the Supreme Court in applying the principle of separation of powers has not always been convincing; this might be due to the fact that no adequate criteria have been developed for distinguishing between legislative and executive power.[160] Furthermore, the manner in which the Supreme Court has interpreted the principle of separation of powers between the legislative and the executive may be considered to impede the exercise of control of the action of the executive by the legislative, thus leaving the executive unchecked by the legislative branch.

93. It has been repeatedly held that the House of Representatives cannot involve itself directly or indirectly in the appointment or termination of appointment of public service personnel. The Supreme Court has held that the House of Representatives may, in accordance with the Constitution, prohibit by legislation the engagement of temporary employees by the Republic, even if there has been approved for this purpose expenditure by means of the Budget of the Republic;[161]

---

156. G. Pikis, *Constitutionalism, Human Rights, Separation of Powers* 85 (Martinus Nijhoff 2006).
157. Such as Arts 46–49 and 54 which vest executive powers in the President of the Republic, or the Council of Ministers, Art. 61 which vests legislative power in the House of Representatives and Arts 133–164 which vest judicial power in the Supreme Constitutional Court, the Supreme Court and its subordinate courts.
158. *See* A. Markides, *The Republic of Cyprus*, in *Constitutional Law of 10 EU Member States* I-27 (Kortmann et al. eds, Kluwer 2006).
159. *See Police v. Hondrou* (1962) 3 RSCC 82.
160. As A. Markides, *The Republic of Cyprus*, in *Constitutional Law of 10 EU Member States* I-26 (Kortmann et al. eds, Kluwer 2006) correctly notes 'the definition which was once given-namely that whatever does not belong to the legislative sphere or to the judicial sphere belongs to the executive sphere-begs the question and is unsatisfactory'.
161. *President of the Republic v. House of Representatives* [1985] 3 CLR 1724, *President of the Republic v. House of Representatives* [1991] 3 CLR 746 (in Greek).

however, a provision whereby the procedure for the engagement of casual employees is subject to the approval of the House of Representatives is unconstitutional, since this would entail the House of Representatives interfering with the exercise of the administrative powers of the Council of Ministers in relation to the general direction and control of the government of the Republic under Article 54(a) of the Constitution.[162]

94. Similarly, it has been held that the House of Representatives may not enact legislation to provide for the permanent appointment to the public service of employees serving on a temporary basis, even if such a law is enacted with the concurrence of the Council of Ministers or the President of the Republic. This is due to the fact that the appointment of members of the public service is a matter outside of the legislative sphere and within the exclusive competence of the Public Service Commission. Appointment by legislation would not only violate the principle of separation of powers, but would also be inconsistent with the principle of equality, since it would not grant to everybody having the necessary qualifications an equal right to compete for appointment to the said positions in the public service. The Supreme Court has therefore repeatedly held that vacancies should be properly advertised affording everyone having the qualifications the opportunity to apply for appointment; personalized legislation aiming at transforming temporary employees as permanent ones cannot be tolerated.[163]

95. The rule that personalized legislation is not constitutionally permitted has been expounded upon in the *President of the Republic v. House of Representatives*, in which a law extending the tenure of the serving members of the Public Educational Service was held to be unconstitutional on the ground that it violated the principle of separation of powers; whereas, the House of Representatives could, in accordance with the Constitution, redefine the terms of service or tenure of the members of the Public Educational Service in an impersonal manner, it could not introduce personalized legislation aiming at extending the tenure of existing members.[164] In another case, the Supreme Court held that the participation of the executive in the appointment of the members of the Public Educational Services, by introducing the requirement that the House of Representatives should consent to the appointment of the said members, was unconstitutional.[165]

96. The principle that the House of Representatives may not interfere, either directly or indirectly, with the appointment of members of administrative bodies, was reiterated in subsequent cases of the Supreme Court. It was accordingly held that a provision which stipulated that the members of a Committee selecting Cypriots who contributed to the struggles of Cypriots for freedom and liberty would be appointed by the Executive subject to confirmation by the House of Representatives

162. *President of the Republic v. House of Representatives* [1985] 3 CLR 1724.
163. *Republic v. Yiallourou* [1995] 3 CLR 363 (in Greek), *Menelaou v. Republic* [1996] 3 CLR 370 (in Greek), *Elia v. Republic* [1999] 3 CLR 884 (in Greek).
164. *President of the Republic v. House of Representatives* [1992] 3 CLR 458 (in Greek).
165. *President of the Republic v. House of Representatives* [1985] 3 CLR 2165.

was unconstitutional, in so far as the confirmation by the House of Representatives was concerned.[166] The same was held with respect to a provision requiring the agreement of the House of Representatives to the appointment of members of a Committee which would recognize Cypriots who contributed to the struggles of Cypriots to resist the 1974 coup d'etat.[167]

97. Moreover, the requirement that the Council of Ministers consults and/or hears the views of a parliamentary committee prior to exercising its power to appoint the members of the Central Bank of Cyprus was held to amount to a violation of the principle of separation of powers. The fact that the role of the House of Representatives was of a consulting nature only and that the decisive powers remained to the Council of Ministers was immaterial, since the appointment of the members of the Central Bank of Cyprus fell under the exclusive powers of the executive organs of the Republic and accordingly the principle of separation of powers did not leave any room for interference in the exercise of such powers by the House of Representatives, even in an advisory role.[168]

98. The principle that the legislative power should not interfere with the constitutional powers of the executive has been further expanded in a case concerning the area of Agios Sozomenos.[169] The competent organs of the executive had decided that Agios Sozomenos would be an approved area for the dumping of refuse; the House of Representatives, however, enacted a law prohibiting the dumping of refuse in Agios Sozomenos. The Supreme Court held that the decision to choose where to dump refuse fell within the exclusive competence of the Executive in accordance with Articles 46, 54 and 58 of the Constitution and it was thus not permissible for the House of Representatives to overrule such a decision. Similarly, in the case of *Michael Theodosiou Ltd,* an attempt by the House of Representatives to reverse an order of acquisition of immovable property through the enactment of legislation was held to be unconstitutional, since the subject of such legislation was a purely administrative measure outside the competences of the House of Representatives.[170]

99. The Supreme Court subsequently held, by a majority of 7-6, that a law prohibiting and criminalizing fishing by the gri-gri method was inconsistent with the principle of separation of powers. The majority of the judges held that the issue was similar to the *Agios Sozomenos* case and held that the regulation of fishing methods fell under the powers of the organs exercising executive power, which should exercise its competences in order to determine whether a licence should be given in an appropriate case. Accordingly, it was held that the House of Representatives did not have the power to prohibit fishing by a specific method. The reasoning of the majority is hardly convincing and leads to an undue restriction of the powers of the House

166. *President of the Republic v. House of Representatives* [2000] 3 CLR 157 (in Greek).
167. *President of the Republic v. House of Representatives* [2001] 3 CLR 83 (in Greek).
168. *President of the Republic v. House of Representatives* [2013] 3 CLR 421 (in Greek). *See also President of the Republic v. House of Representatives*, App. 1/2017, Judgment of 5 Feb. 2018 (in Greek).
169. *President of the Republic v. House of Representatives* [1992] 3 CLR 109 (in Greek).
170. *Michael Theodosiou Ltd v. Municipality of Limassol* [1993] 3 CLR 25 (in Greek).

of Representatives. As the dissenting opinion correctly noted, the House of Representatives is the competent organ for legislation on any issue and enacting a general law prohibiting fishing by a given method that clearly falls within its powers. Contrary to the *Agios Sozomenos* case, the legislation was not personalized but referred in an impersonalized manner to a general prohibition of fishing by a specified method.[171]

100. The limits of legislative power were further considered in the case of the sixty-two dismissed persons. The Council of Ministers dismissed sixty-two public servants in 1980 on grounds of complicity or support of the 1974 coup d'etat. In 1993, the Council of Ministers, under a new Presidency, recalled the previous decision ex nunc, thus enabling the return of the sixty-two dismissed persons to the public service. The House of Representatives called upon the Council of Ministers to revoke their decision and amended the budget law in a manner designed to prohibit reemployment of the sixty-two dismissed persons. The Supreme Court held by majority that the decision of the House of Representatives was unconstitutional since one power of the state cannot dictate to another power the decisions it ought to take. Additionally, the amendment of the budget amounted to personalized legislation directly aiming at frustrating the execution of the decision of the Council of Ministers; such law was accordingly unconstitutional.[172]

101. Similarly, the Supreme Court held that the suspension of the application of the Regulation of Matters of Privatization Law 28(I)/2014 with regard to the Cyprus Telecommunications Authority (CYTA) violated the principle of separation of powers. The Council of Ministers had already exercised its competences by virtue of Law 28(I)/2014 and in accordance with Article 54 of the Constitution and had issued orders declaring CYTA as subject to privatization. Accordingly, it was held that the House of Representatives did not have the power to interfere with the powers of the Council of Ministers and, by suspending the legislation, effectively abolished the orders issued by the Council of Ministers.[173]

102. However, it was subsequently held by a majority of 6-5 that a bill repealing Law 28(I)/2014 was not inconsistent with the principle of separation of powers. The majority held that the House of Representatives had the inherent power to repeal legislation it had previously enacted, if it considered that the privatization legislation was no longer functional. The Council of Ministers does not have the exclusive power to administer state property, but only the executive powers. The House of Representatives is accordingly not precluded from exercising its own powers by enacting or repealing general legislation which is superior to the issuance of decrees by the Council of Ministers. Neither the existence of decrees issued by the Council of Ministers nor the existence of contracts signed pursuant to Law

171. *President of the Republic v. House of Representatives* [2014] 3 CLR 257 (in Greek).
172. *President of the Republic v. House of Representatives* [1994] 3 CLR 93 (in Greek). *See also President of the Republic v. House of Representatives*, App. 1/2022, Judgment of 12 Jun. 2023 (in Greek).
173. *President of the Republic v. House of Representatives* [2017] 3 CLR 429 (in Greek).

28(I)/2014 with third parties could restrict the exercise of the powers of the House of Representatives to repeal Law 28(I)/14.[174] It is submitted that the judgment of the majority is a correct one. However, it remains rather inexplicable why, on the basis of the above-mentioned reasoning, the House of Representatives has the power to repeal Law 28(I)/2014, but not, as per the prior judgment of the Supreme Court, the power to suspend its effect.[175]

103. The operation of shops on Sundays has sparked great controversy. The Minister of Labour, Welfare and Social Insurance (as she was then named) issued several decrees allowing for shops all over Cyprus to remain open on Sundays; the Minister maintained that the decrees have helped to reduce unemployment since a significant number of formerly unemployed persons were hired due to the increased sales and additional working hours of shops. The majority of the House of Representatives removed the power of the Minister to issue decrees by Laws 36(I)/15 and 55(I)/15 and enacted a new legislation which provided for shops, with the exception of some specific areas characterized as touristic, to be closed on Sundays; however, the legislation was unanimously held to be unconstitutional by the Full Bench of the Supreme Court as falling outside the competences of the House of Representatives and amounting to an interference with the powers of the executive. It was held that determining the working hours of shops was a matter for the executive power and accordingly could not be determined by general legislation but only by secondary legislation, either in the form of Regulations or decrees.[176]

104. Despite the ruling of the Supreme Court, the House of Representatives steadfastly refused to approve the Regulations submitted by the Minister for maintaining the shops open on Sundays and accordingly from 1 January 2016, Law 155(I)/06 provided that the shops should remain closed on Sundays. The shop owners, however, decided to keep their shops open on Sundays, maintaining that on the basis of the ruling of the Supreme Court, existing legislation preventing the shops from opening on Sundays should also be declared unconstitutional. It was eventually held that the relevant provision of Law 155(I)/06 preventing the shops from opening on Sundays was unconstitutional as falling outside the competences of the House of Representatives and, consequently, the criminal charges against the shop owners for failing to comply with the legislative prohibition were dismissed.[177] In view of the above-mentioned development, there has since been no regulation of the issue and accordingly shops remain open on Sundays.

---

174. *President of the Republic v. House of Representatives*, App. 2/2017, Judgment of 5 Feb. 2018 (in Greek). *See also President of the Republic v. House of Representatives* [1985] 3 CLR 2127.
175. The dissenting judgment in *President of the Republic v. House of Representatives*, App. 2/2017, Judgment of 5 Feb. 2018 (in Greek) raised this issue.
176. *President of the Republic v. House of Representatives* [2015] 1 CLR 662 (in Greek).
177. *Director of Department of Labour v. C.A. Papaellinas Commercial Ltd and others*, Criminal Case 4652/16, Judgment of 18 Mar. 2016 (District Court, in Greek).

B. The Emerging Functional Separation Between Political and Administrative Power

105. Of equal interest is the case-law of the Supreme Court concerning an emerging functional separation between political and administrative authorities.[178] In *Frangoulides*, the Supreme Court held that the participation of a Minister in the preparation of the annual confidential report of a public servant, au lieu of the Head of Department is not permissible, since the office of the Minister is one of a political nature and not one of a public servant.[179] It has further repeatedly been held that the Council of Ministers, or indeed any other political organ, may not exercise administrative competencies which are vested in other organs, such as the Public Service Commission.[180] The separation between the political and administrative wings of the public service is said to secure the overall political neutrality of the public service;[181] however, it is argued that the administrative wing of the public service cannot be entirely neutral, since the administration is called upon to promote the governmental policy as such is decided by the hierarchically supreme organ of the administration, namely the Council of Ministers. Accordingly, the well-intentioned aim for neutrality should not be exaggerated as implying that the administration can be completely neutral. Rather the aim should be for the administration to follow the governmental policy within the constraints of the Constitution, the law and the principles governing administrative action.[182]

106. One of the most important cases in this regard was *Karayiorges*.[183] The case concerned the constitutionality of a law providing for the presence of observers nominated by parliamentary political parties on the boards of public corporations and that the Council of Ministers should consult with the parliamentary political parties before appointing members of public corporations. The Supreme Court held by a 5-4 majority that the said law was unconstitutional, *inter alia*, because it ran contrary to Article 54 of the Constitution which entrusts to the Council of Ministers the exercise of the executive power and because it was inconsistent with the principle of separation of powers between the executive and the legislative by enabling parliamentary political parties to interfere with the process of appointment of members of the board of administrative organs. It was further held that the principle of equality was violated since the law discriminated between members of parliamentary political parties and citizens who are not members of such parties or

---

178. *See* A. Emilianides, *The Separation Between Political Power and Public Administration in Cypriot Law*, 1 Efimerida Dioikitikou Dikaiou 2–9 (2019) (in Greek).
179. *Frangoulides v. Republic* [1966] 3 CLR 676.
180. *Makrides v. Republic* [1984] 3 CLR 677, *Potamitou v. Council of Ministers*, Adm. App. 59/2020, Judgment of 7 Jun. 2021 (in Greek).
181. G. Pikis, *Constitutionalism, Human Rights, Separation of Powers* 88 (Martinus Nijhoff 2006).
182. A. Emilianides, *Public Servants and Separation of Powers in the Cypriot Legal Order*, in *Public Administration after the* Crisis 139–154 (X. Kontiades, A. Emilianides & C. Anthopoulos eds, Sakkoulas 2019, in Greek).
183. *CYBC v. Karayiorges* [1991] 3 CLR 159 (in Greek).

who are members of political parties which do not have parliamentary representation. It was held that every individual should have the opportunity to be appointed to a public post irrespective of political convictions or other preferences.

107. Whereas the intention of the majority in *Karayiorges* was self-evidently to safeguard neutrality in the appointment of members of the board of public bodies, it is questionable whether entrusting such power to the Council of Ministers without the need to consult anyone would actually lead to increased neutrality. Indeed, the practice of appointment of members of the board of public bodies has shown that the Council of Ministers regularly takes into account political convictions in order to appoint such members and regularly consults, albeit unofficially, with parliamentary political parties in order to hear their views before appointing such members. Even when there is no such unofficial consultation, the usual outcome is that the Government would appoint members who support the governmental policy. In another case, the Supreme Court further held that a law by virtue of which a technical committee would have the power to negotiate the terms of the contracts for the exploration of hydrocarbons and the Council of Ministers would merely have the right to approve, reject or refer back to the technical committee for re-negotiation, violated the principle of separation of powers between the political and administrative power. The competent Minister and the Council of Ministers should have the power to negotiate the terms themselves, if they so wish.[184]

108. A recent judgment of the Supreme Court showcases the problems associated with the so-called functional separation between political and administrative authorities. In *Pavlou*, the Supreme Court had held that a law rendering incompatible the holding of an office in the municipal council by a public servant was constitutional; accordingly, a public servant elected to a municipal council could only assume such office upon relinquishing the position held in the public service.[185] Subsequently, the House of Representatives enacted legislation repealing such incompatibility. It should be noted that whereas Articles 41, 58 and 70 of the Constitution expressly hold that it is incompatible for a public servant to become President of the Republic, Minister or member of the House of Representatives respectively, on the contrary, there is no provision in the Constitution introducing such incompatibility for elected members of the municipal council; this might well be attributed to the difference of importance between the office of a member of a municipal council and the officials of the central administration of the State. However, despite the fact that there was no provision in the Constitution prohibiting a public servant from being elected as a member of a municipal council, the Supreme Court held by majority that the functional separation between political and administrative authorities is an entrenched

184. *President of the Republic v. House of Representatives* [2013] 3 CLR 178 (in Greek).
185. *Pavlou v. General Registrar of Elections* [1987] 1 CLR 252.

principle of the Constitution and that accordingly the said law was unconstitutional because it violated the spirit of the Constitution.[186]

109. It was therefore held that the neutrality in substance of those taking administrative action implies that in the exercise of their duties, public servants ought to be free from every constraint, an aim which would not be achieved if public servants were allowed to be elected as members of the municipal council. The said majority judgment effectively ran contrary to a judgment of the Supreme Court in *Constantinides* which had correctly held that there is no general functional separation between political and administrative power enshrined in the Constitution.[187] It further ran contrary to the established case-law of the Supreme Court, holding that the spirit of the Constitution may be understood only in light of particular constitutional provisions and not in *abstracto*.[188] In essence, the majority of the Supreme Court, by holding that the election of a public servant as a member of a municipal council violates the spirit of the Constitution, transformed the principle of separation of powers from a general constitutional principle permeating the Constitution to an extra-constitutional principle which is not entrenched in specific constitutional provisions. With all due respect, such an interpretation is highly problematic.

110. It is submitted that the approach of the Supreme Court was much more in line with the principles governing constitutional review in a previous case where the Court examined the constitutionality of a law repealing the legislative impediment of public servants to belong to political parties. The Supreme Court held by majority that the law was constitutional and correctly held that the constitutionality of a law should be assessed by examining the compatibility of its content with the provision of the Constitution with which it is supposedly inconsistent. The fact that a person may potentially act in a partial manner when exercising his/her lawful administrative duties may not be taken into account when deciding whether a law is constitutional.[189]

C. The Judiciary and Separation of Powers

111. In the case of *Diagoras Developments Ltd*,[190] the Supreme Court was called upon to examine the constitutionality of the following amendment to the Debtors Relief (Temporary Provisions) Law: 'To remove any doubt as regards the interpretation of the term "stricken debtor," as set out in section 2 of the basic law, it is declared that the material time for evaluating the situation of a stricken debtor is, and always was, the time immediately after the Turkish invasion and not any other

186. *President of the Republic v. House of Representatives* [2011] 3 CLR 777 (in Greek). *See also* A. Emilianides, *Reviewing the Review of Constitutionality: A Commentary on Three Recent Judgments of the Supreme Court*, Y.B. Cyprus & European L. 50ff (2013, in Greek).
187. *Republic v. Constantinides* [1996] 3 CLR 207 (in Greek).
188. *Ibid., President of the Republic v. House of Representatives* [2009] 3 CLR 648 (in Greek).
189. *President of the Republic v. House of Representatives* [1991] 3 CLR 611 (in Greek).
190. *Diagoras Developments Ltd v. National Bank of Greece SA* [1985] 1 CLR 581.

time subsequent to it.' In the previous case of *Evangelou v. Ambizas*,[191] it was held that the material time for evaluating the situation of a debtor in order to determine the question whether he is able to respond to his/her contractual obligations is the time of the trial and not any other time anterior to the date of trial. The majority of the Supreme Court held that the law was unconstitutional because it violated the separation of powers between the legislative and the judiciary. It is submitted that the dissenting judgment, holding that the legislation was within the legislative power of the House of Representatives, is more convincing. The said section should essentially be considered an ordinary amending Law, which did not interfere with the rights of the parties in the *Evangelou* case but defined the rights of the public in general other than those dealt with in the said case.

112. Two of the judges in the majority accepted the position that there was no doubt that the legislature, instead of enacting the said section 2 as an interpretative provision, could have simply amended the definition of 'stricken debtor' in section 2 of Law 24/79 in a manner reversing the interpretation given to such definition in the *Evangelou* case. However, it was held that such a course was not adopted by the legislature and the said section 2 had been framed in such a way that it is impossible to speculate with any certainty what the legislative intention would have been, had it been in fact an amendment and not an interpretative provision. More problematic was the view of the remaining two judges of the majority who held that any attempt by the legislature to interpret its own laws is unconstitutional because the interpretation of laws is the exclusive province of the judiciary.[192] With all due respect, it is submitted that the House of Representative may of course interpret provisions in its own laws and indeed it does so regularly by interpreting the definitions used in such laws.[193] There can be no reasonable argument that the House of Representatives may not interpret its own laws through legislative amendments or otherwise. Indeed, in the end, the House of Representatives repealed the provision of the previous law and replaced it by a new provision with retrospective effect.[194]

113. Articles 135 and 163 of the Constitution form an exception from the principle of separation of powers, since they explicitly authorize the Supreme Court to exclusively issue procedural rules despite the fact that such power is of a legislative nature. The Supreme Court considers that the judiciary has the exclusive power to regulate procedural issues, i.e., to determine the ambit of powers exercised by it.[195] It was accordingly held that legislative provisions which stipulate that the court has the obligation to adjudicate specific kinds of applications by priority were inconsistent with the said power of the Supreme Court to exercise the judicial powers and to enact rules of procedure by virtue of Articles 152 and 163 of the Constitution and

191. [1982] 1 CLR 41.
192. A view elaborated in detail in G. Pikis, *Constitutionalism, Human Rights, Separation of Powers* 93ff (Martinus Nijhoff 2006).
193. Normally contained in s. 2 of a Law.
194. *See Papanicopoulos v. Morphou Co-Operative* [1986] 1 CLR 288.
195. *Mavrogenis v. House of Representatives* [1996] 1 CLR 49 (in Greek), *President of the Republic v. House of Representatives*, App. 2/2021, Judgment of 11 Oct. 2021 (in Greek).

section 69 of the Courts of Justice Law 14/60. It was similarly held that a legislative mandate that provided that an application for an order of suspension of the procedure of sale of the mortgaged land would automatically suspend the procedure of sale until the determination of the application by the court was inconsistent with the principle of separation of powers, since it automatically suspended the action without the exercise of judicial discretion and without hearing the other side.[196]

114. The Supreme Court further held that a bill pursuant to which the Supreme Court may publish rules of procedure in order to regulate the submission and change of the property assets of judges, their spouses and minor children, to the Supreme Judicial Council. The impugned legislation contained details which could be included in the rules of procedure and further provided that the Supreme Judicial Council could appoint auditors in order to verify the accuracy of the submissions made. The Supreme Court held that the impugned legislation effectively imposed to the Supreme Court the way in which to regulate an issue which falls under the Court's exclusive competence and accordingly violated the principle of separation of powers. It was held that the use of the 'may' was immaterial, since the substance of the issue was that the House of Representatives indirectly called upon the Supreme Court to act in a specific manner by pre-determining in detail the form and content of the submission. It was further held that the appointment of auditors to verify the accuracy of the submissions made by the judges would interfere with the independence of the judicial powers.[197] Admittedly, it is hardly convincing to argue that the appointment of independent auditors *by the Supreme Judicial Council itself* would undermine the independence of the judicial power; independence does not imply lack of accountability. Furthermore, it is rather unclear how the recognition of a discretionary power to the Court to act in a certain manner would effectively impose to the Court to do something. This becomes even more paradoxical, considering that the Supreme Constitutional Court subsequently held that the inclusion of the Attorney-General and the Deputy Attorney-General in the list of officials who are required to submit their property assets does not violate their independence; despite the fact that the said officials enjoy the same constitutional status as to their terms of employment as judges of the Supreme Court, the Supreme Constitutional Court held that the obligation to submit property assets does not refer to terms of employment.[198]

115. The question of separation of powers also arose with respect to section 3(b) of Law 68(I)/2008 which has recently amended section 38 section 2 of the Relationship between Parents and Children Law 216/90. The amended section 38 section 2 provides that the amount of the maintenance awarded shall automatically be increased by 10% every twenty-four months; the Court has the power to declare that

196. *President of the Republic v. House of Representatives* [2014] 3 CLR 499 (in Greek). *See also President of the Republic v. House of Representatives*, App. 1/2020, Judgment of 5 Oct. 2021 (in Greek).
197. *President of the Republic v. House of Representatives* [2017] 3 CLR 422 (in Greek).
198. *President of the Republic v. House of Representatives*, App. 3/2024, Judgment of 20 Nov. 2024 (in Greek).

such automatic increase shall not take force or be restricted, following an application by the debtor. The aim of providing for such automatic increase of the amount of maintenance every two years is to enable the beneficiary to receive an increased amount without the need to continuously resort to the Family Court in accordance with the principle that the needs of the children increase as they get older. The Supreme Court held by a majority of 8-4 that the law did not violate Article 30 § 2 of the Constitution safeguarding the right to due process, nor the principle of separation of powers.[199]

116. However, as the dissenting judgment correctly noted by providing for the automatic increase of an amount specified in a judicial order, without any action by the Court itself, the amended section 38 section 2 interferes in the judicial decision. While it is true that the Court might have the opportunity to consider whether such automatic increase ought to be restricted, this does not change the fact that such automatic increase constitutes an interference with a judicial decree and amends, by a legislative provision, the content of such judicial decree. Consequently, the legislator could provide that the Court itself may order for such an automatic increase of the amount of maintenance every two years. However, it is not consistent with the principle of separation of powers to provide that a judicial decree may be automatically amended, without any action by the Court itself.[200]

117. The distinction between administrative penalties and criminal proceedings has been considered in *Demand Shipping Co Ltd.*[201] The majority held that administrative fines or forfeitures are distinguishable from penalties imposed by a criminal court, since administrative sanctions aim at the effective application of administrative law and not at the punishment of the offender.[202] Accordingly, the imposition of administrative fines does not violate the principle of separation of powers between the executive and the judiciary; the view that only the judiciary may impose fines or forfeiture[203] was not upheld. The distinction between administrative and criminal proceedings was confirmed by the majority of the Full Bench of the Supreme Court in the subsequent case of *Sigma.*[204]

---

199. *Loizou-Christoforou v. Christoforou*, Legal Question 373, Judgment of 2 May 2017.
200. *See* A. Emilianides, *Family and Succession Law in Cyprus* 135ff (3d ed., Kluwer 2024).
201. *Republic v. Demand Shipping Co Ltd* [1994] 3 CLR 460 (in Greek).
202. This was also the view in the previous first-instance judgment *Istanbouli Brothers v. Director of Department of Customs & Excise* [1986] 1 CLR 465.
203. *See Chrysostomou v. Republic* [1986] 3 CLR 2666.
204. *Sigma Radio TV Ltd v. Radio and Television Authority* [2004] 3 CLR 134 (in Greek). A recourse before the ECtHR was rejected. *See Sigma Radio Television Ltd v. Cyprus*, App. 32181/04, Judgment of 21 Jul. 2011 and the detailed analysis in C. Stratilatis & A. Emilianides, *Media Law in Cyprus* (3d ed., Kluwer 2024).

Chapter 6. Administrative Regulations and Orders

118. The House of Representatives when enacting primary legislation may authorize the various organs of the administration to have the power to issue administrative regulations or orders in the form of secondary legislation. Such administrative regulatory acts set rules of a legislative nature, which are general and impersonal, and which could apply to cases irrespective of whether they actually exist or may exist in the future.[205] The authority to enact regulatory acts is usually delegated by the House of Representatives to the Council of Ministers; however, the House of Representatives may delegate such power to any other administrative organ. If the primary legislation has not explicitly specified the administrative organ to which it has delegated the authority to issue administrative regulations, the Council of Ministers shall have the authority to make any order or regulation for the carrying into effect of the primary legislation, in accordance with Article 54(g) of the Constitution.[206]

119. The power of the administration to issue administrative regulations or orders is not autonomous; it is always dependent upon the primary legislation which should explicitly authorize the administration to enact secondary legislation in the form of administrative regulations. It is normally for the House of Representatives to determine the issues which ought to be regulated with administrative regulatory acts, instead of primary legislation; the House of Representatives may well consider that it does not have sufficient time or expertise to regulate a specific issue, or it might well consider that the administration is better equipped to regulate specific aspects in accordance with some general guidelines provided by the legislator. It is often the case that the primary legislation provides certain guidelines or main rules, then authorizing the administration to regulate the matter in more detail. It should be noted that restriction of constitutional rights may normally occur only by legislation enacted by the House of Representatives and not by secondary legislation; the secondary legislation may, however, provide in more detail for the manner in which the restrictions set by the primary law are to be applied.[207]

---

205. N. Charalambous, *Cypriot Administrative Law Textbook* (3d ed., 2016, in Greek).
206. *Theodorides v. Central Bank of Cyprus* [1989] 3 CLR 1457, *Holy Archbishopric of Cyprus v. Republic* [1990] 3 CLR 1175 (in Greek).
207. *Spyrou v. The Republic* [1973] 3 CLR 627.

Chapter 7. Codification, Interpretation and Publication

120. In accordance with Article 188 of the Constitution, all laws in force on the date of the coming into operation of the Constitution shall, until amended, whether by way of variation, addition or repeal as the case may be, continue in force on or after that date and shall be construed and applied with such modification as may be necessary to bring them into conformity with the Constitution; no provision in such law shall continue to be in force, if it is contrary to, or inconsistent with, any provision of the Constitution (save as otherwise provided for in the Constitution itself). The Laws of Cyprus in force on 1 April 1959, before Independence, were compiled by former Attorney-General of the Republic Criton Tornaritis and are separated into six volumes and 354 Chapters (Caps) each Cap. corresponding to a single law. Laws which continue to be in force after Independence are referred to by their respective Cap. in the 1959 edition (e.g., Interpretation Law is Cap. 1, Advocates Law is Cap. 2).

121. Both the Greek and Turkish texts of the Constitution are originals and have the same authenticity and legal force. Articles 149(a) and 180 of the Constitution both provide that the Supreme Constitutional Court shall have exclusive jurisdiction to determine any conflict between the two original texts of the Constitution by reference to the text of the draft signed at Nicosia on 6 April 1960, in the Joint Constitutional Commission together with the schedule of amendments thereto signed on, by representatives of Greece, Turkey and the Greek and Cypriot Communities, due regard being had to the letter and spirit of the Zurich and London Agreements. Accordingly, the English text of the constitution shall guide the Supreme Court at reaching an authoritative interpretation of the text of the Constitution in case where there is conflict between the two original texts.[208] In case of ambiguity, due regard shall be had to the letter and spirit of the Zurich Agreement and of the London Agreement. The term 'conflict' has been interpreted as referring to both pending judicial proceedings,[209] as well as extra-judicial proceedings of constitutional and political importance, such as the election of a President of the House of Representatives.[210] There has been disagreement in the case-law whether it suffices for the conflict to exist subjectively, i.e., for the parties to disagree amongst themselves, or whether the criterion should be an objective one, i.e., it should be for the Court to determine that there is indeed a conflict.[211]

122. The main source for legislation, including constitutional amendments, is the Official Gazette of the Republic of Cyprus which has been published since Independence. Article 82 of the Constitution explicitly provides that a law or decision of the House of Representatives shall come into operation on its publication in the Official Gazette of the Republic, unless another date is provided by such law or

208. *Rodosthenous* [1961] CLR 127, *Ramadan v. EAC* (1961) 1 RSCC 49, *Stademos Hotels Ltd v. Improvement Board of Amathous* [1991] 4 CLR 2537 (in Greek).
209. *Republic v. Loftis* 1 RSCC 30.
210. *Ladas and others* [1985] 3 CLR 2823.
211. *Ioannidou and Others* [2012] 1 CLR 1442 (in Greek).

decision. Similarly, Article 57 of the Constitution provides that any enforceable decision taken by the Council of Ministers should be promulgated by the President of the Republic by publication in the Official Gazette of the Republic, unless the Council of Ministers otherwise states in that decision.

Part II. Form of Government

Chapter 1. General

§1. Introduction

123. Cyprus' system of government is a presidential democracy. The predominant bodies provided for in the constitution are the President, the Council of Ministers, the parliament, called the House of Representatives, and the Supreme Court. The President is the head of state and represents the Republic in all its official functions. The President belongs to the Greek Cypriot community and is elected for a five-year term directly, by universal suffrage and secret ballot. The President appoints and dismisses the members of the Council of Ministers and has vast executive powers. The Council of Ministers is composed of eleven Ministers who are chosen from outside the House of Representatives. The Council of Ministers exercises the executive power alongside the President. The House of Representatives exercises the legislative power of the Republic. The Representatives are elected for a term of five years in free, general and direct elections. The number of active representatives is currently fifty-six. The judiciary is independent from the executive and legislative organs and is a powerful factor both in legal and social life. The highest Cypriot courts are the Supreme Constitutional Court and the Supreme Court. Many of their decisions have been on the highest legal and political impact.[212]

§2. Political Parties, Lobbies and Interest Groups

I. The Political System and the Role of the Church

124. From 1960 until his death in 1977, Archbishop Makarios was not only the President of the Republic but also the most notable and influential political figure of the island.[213] In the '*Times*' editorial on the day following his death, Makarios was

212. *See* A. Emilianides, *The Constitution of Cyprus*, in *Encyclopedia of World Constitutions* vol. I, 240–243 (G. Robbers ed., Facts on File 2006).
213. On Makarios *see, inter alia*, P. Vanezis, *Makarios: Life and Leadership* (Abelard-Schuman 1979); S. Mayes, *Makarios: A Biography* (Palgrave MacMillan 1981); D. Assos, *Makarios. The Revolutionary Priest of Cyprus* (London: Tauris, 2018).

described as 'one of the most instantly recognizable figures of international politics'.[214] All parliamentary political parties supported, at least nominally, the policy of Makarios; even AKEL, the communist party of Cyprus,[215] while initially opposed to Makarios, it also provided after Independence overwhelming support to Makarios. The only major political coalition besides AKEL, from 1960 to 1969 was the Patriotic Front, which was not an organized political party, but rather a coalition of all politicians who supported Makarios.[216] When the first political parties were formed in 1969, Makarios' prior approval and blessing was provided.[217]

125. Ever since the death of Archbishop Makarios in 1977, however, the political system of Cyprus has been completely transformed.[218] To begin with, the political system has been completely secularized, since religious functionaries in principle refrain from participating actively in elections and are not appointed in public offices. Consequently, religious influence in political life has diminished substantially; no political party claims that it is guided by spiritual truths, or that it has the support of the Orthodox Church. In addition, the fact that the Archbishop or Metropolitans of the Church support a particular political party is of little significance to voters. For instance, while in the 1998 Presidential Elections, the former Archbishop Chrysostomos I supported the centrist candidate Paschalis Paschalides, this proved to be of little significance, as Paschalides was supported by only 18.65% of the voters and failed to qualify in the second round of the elections.

126. During the first round of the 2008 Presidential elections, Archbishop Chrysostomos II supported the former President Tassos Papadopoulos and during the second round, after Papadopoulos had been eliminated, he supported the candidate of the Democratic Rally (DISY) Ioannis Casoulides; both Papadopoulos and Casoulides lost the elections, despite enjoying the support of the Archbishop. During the second round of the Presidential elections, the great majority of the voters of Democratic Party (DIKO) voted for Christofias, who was supported by their party after the elimination of Papadopoulos, despite the fact that the Archbishop – also a supporter of DIKO – supported Casoulides. Other Metropolitans, or members of the clergy also support or express their preference towards a particular presidential candidate, without this dictating the results of any Presidential, parliamentary or municipal elections; the political parties exercise much more influence over their supporters with respect to the outcome of any political elections when compared to the Church.[219]

---

214. The Times, 4 Aug. 1977.
215. *See* T.W. Adams, *AKEL: The Communist Party of Cyprus* (Hoover Inst. Press 1971).
216. A. Emilianides, *Parliamentary Co-existence of Greek and Turkish Cypriots* (Epifaniou 2003, in Greek).
217. A. Emilianides, *Parliamentary History of the Republic of Cyprus 1964–1977* (Aigaion 2007, in Greek).
218. *See* G. Ioannides, *Political Parties and Tendencies of the Last 25 Years*, in *Cypriot Life and Society Before Independence and until 1984* 55–69 (Municipality of Nicosia 1993, in Greek), C. Yiallourides, *Cyprus*, in *The Political Parties of Western Europe: History, Programs, Practice* 159–205 (J. Raske & E. Katsoulis eds, Paratiritis 1992, in Greek).
219. *See* in more detail A. Emilianides, *Religion and Law in Cyprus* Ch. 5 (4th ed., Kluwer 2024).

II. A Pluralistic System of Political Parties

127. Following the death of Makarios in 1977, the political system which was dominated by his presence gave way to a modern system of government, whereby various and differing political parties aim to elect the President, secure seats in the House of Representatives and appoint their members in public offices.[220] Cyprus currently has a pluralistic system of political parties. Political parties are a fundamental element of public life and their function is an essential element of the constitutional order. It could even be argued that due to the small size of its population, Cyprus has emerged as a society which is to a large extent dependent upon the operation of its party system.[221] Appointments and promotions to the augmented public service, local administration and to the semi-governmental authorities including public universities, tenders of public procurement and governmental contracts, with the sole exception of appointments to the judicial authority, are often conceived by the public as being controlled by political parties.

128. The two largest political parties in Cyprus are the communist oriented AKEL, and the right-wing DISY. In the 2011 Parliamentary Elections, DISY received 34.28% and twenty seats, while AKEL received 32.67% of the votes and nineteen seats. However, in the 2016 Parliamentary Elections the power of both parties, while remaining dominant, decreased substantially; DISY received 30.69% and 18 seats, while AKEL received 25.67% and 16 seats. There was a further decrease in the 2021 Parliamentary elections, with DISY receiving 27.77% and 17 seats, and AKEL receiving 22.34% and 15 seats. The Communist oriented AKEL was founded in 1941 and is the successor of the Communist Party of Cyprus which was founded in 1926. AKEL is a member of the Party of the European Left in the European Parliament. The former Secretary General of AKEL, Dimitris Christofias, was elected in 2008 as President of the Republic of Cyprus and was during his five-year term the only communist head of state of an EU country. While Christofias was considered to be a communist President and AKEL is theoretically still a Leninist-Marxist political party, in practice AKEL functions within a free market economy and seems to have no intention of interfering with the free market; AKEL has, however, expressed from time to time reservations with respect to Cyprus' participation in the EU and often adopts communist rhetoric. It should be noted, however, that AKEL has supported many times non-communist Presidents of the Republic, including former President George Vasiliou (1988–1993), a successful businessman, who is a strong supporter of European integration and a liberal. Furthermore, the internal organization of AKEL is quite rigid. The current Secretary General of AKEL is Stefanos Stefanou.

129. The right-wing DISY was founded in 1976 by former President of the Republic Glafcos Clerides and is a member of the European People's Party. Its

220. For a development of political parties in Cyprus *see* S. Zavou, *The Political Parties of Cyprus in the Twentieth Century* (2d ed., Epifaniou 2011, in Greek).

221. *See also* G. Charalambous & C. Christophorou (eds), *Party-Society Relations in the Republic of Cyprus: Political and Societal Strategies* (Routledge 2015).

founder Glafcos Clerides was elected for two terms as President of the Republic (1993–2003), whereas a subsequent leader of DISY Nicos Anastasiades has also been elected for two terms as President of the Republic (2013–2023). Annita Demetriou, the President of the House of Representatives, is the current leader of DISY. Both DISY and AKEL have managed not only to overcome internal contradictions over the years but also to avoid being affected from the discharge of high profile party members who went on to form their own political parties.[222] While the success of DISY in avoiding these internal problems could be attributed to its open character, on the contrary, the success of AKEL ought to be attributed to its closed character. Undeniably, the two largest parties are also safeguarding the existence of the other party, by feeding upon perceived conflicts, which range from political figures such as Makarios to support for football teams. The need to safeguard the political structure of the two opposing poles and thus, the extent of political support that the two parties are enjoying, cause them to form coalitions and make concessions towards the centre, in order to safeguard that the current political structure and system will continue its course.

130. During the 2021 Parliamentary Elections, the centrist DIKO secured nine seats in the House of Representatives and 11.29% of the votes, while the Socialist Movement for Social Democracy (EDEK) secured four seats in the House of Representatives and 6.72% of the votes. DIKO was founded in 1976 by former President of the Republic (1977–1988) Spyros Kyprianou and is a member of the Alliance of Liberals and Democrats for Europe. Another former President of the Republic, Tassos Papadopoulos (2003–2008), was elected to Presidency while being the leader of DIKO. His son, Nicolas Papadopoulos, is the current leader of DIKO. DIKO has expressed the desire to gradually move to the Party of European Socialists, but this proved difficult, in view of the fact that another party, namely EDEK, which was founded in 1969 by former President of the House of Representatives Vasos Lyssarides, is a member of such Party. Marinos Sizopoulos is the current leader of EDEK. It should be noted that both DIKO and EDEK have been repeatedly faced in recent years with internal struggles which led to the ejection or withdrawal of former office-holders.

131. Other political parties that are currently represented in the House of Representatives are:

a. The far-right-wing National People's Front (ELAM) secured 6.78% of the votes and four seats in the House of Representatives;[223] ELAM is a nationalistic party

222. Like Adisok which was formed by former high profile AKEL members and European Democracy which was founded by high profile DISY members.

223. ELAM was associated with the Greek Golden Dawn, a political party that has been described as neo-Nazi and which has been convicted in 2020 by the Athens Court of Appeals as effectively a terrorist organization on charges of murder, attempted murder and violent attacks; the leadership of Golden Dawn was sent to prison.

which was founded in 2008 and which first secured parliamentary seats in 2016. The 2016 elections were the first time that a far-right-wing party secured seats in the House of Representatives.

b. The Democratic Alignment (DIPA), led by former President of the House of Representatives Marios Karoyian, secured 6.10% of the votes and four seats in the House of Representatives. DIPA mainly comprises of former members of DIKO; Marios Karoyian used to be the leader of DIKO before current leader Nicolas Papadopoulos.

c. The Ecological and Environmental Movement (Green Party) was supported by 4.41% of the voting population and has three seats in the House of Representatives. The Green Party was founded in 1996, comprising members of environmental, ecological, cultural and consumer organizations, as well as various pressure groups. It is a member of the European Green Party.

III. The Legal Position of Political Parties

132. The Constitution and the Rules of Procedure of the House of Representatives do not define the notion of political parties, nor do they provide for restrictions to the purposes of political parties, or for the possibility of judicial prohibition of the function of a political party. The elements that have to be fulfilled for a political party to exist were first set out by the Supreme Court in the case of *Modestos Pitsillos*.[224] The Justice Party, of which Pitsillos was the founder and the leader, was registered in 1969 pursuant to the provisions of the Clubs (Registration) Law, Cap. 112; the Appellant had been a candidate in the 1970 Parliamentary elections and polled 1250 votes, a negligible percentage of the vote cast. In 1981, the Cyprus Broadcasting Corporation (CYBC) announced its decision to organize a programme whereby the leaders of political parties would be invited to expound their views in light of the upcoming parliamentary elections of 1981. The Appellant and his party considered that their exclusion from the programme had been a violation of the right of equal treatment safeguarded by Article 28 of the Constitution and filed recourse to the Supreme Court, which was dismissed; Pitsillos filed an appeal.

133. The Supreme Court noted that section 19(3) of the CYBC Law, Cap. 300A, provided that the CYBC should at all times keep a fair balance in the allocation of broadcasting hours between political parties. The aforementioned provision aimed to ensure that effective opportunity be given to opposing viewpoints to be broadcasted, so that political parties have a proper platform for disseminating their views and the public at large has adequate information on political issues. The Court held that each political party is entitled to access, the discretion of the CYBC being limited to the determination of the broadcasting time each party is entitled to. The crucial question to be answered was thus, whether the 'Justice Party' should be considered a political party. The Court noted that what constitutes a political party

224. *Pitsillos v. CYBC* [1982] 3 CLR 208.

entails answering a mixed question of law and fact. The Court held that for a political party to be considered as such, it needs to have objectives consonant to the law and in accordance with the principle of democratic rule implanted in Cyprus' political system.

134. Furthermore, the Court noted that it is not enough for a political party to consist of a group of persons having the same political inclinations and who share common views and ideas; a political party should also pursue political power, since it is the element of aspiration of political power which distinguishes a political party from a mere pressure group. The test adopted by the Supreme Court in deciding whether an association is a political party is the following: would a reasonable man living in Cyprus and acquainted with the realities of the country and taking into account the practical and theoretical aims of the association, its institutions and organization, as well as the response of the public to it, identify the association as a political party? On the basis of the aforementioned test, the Court held that there was nothing to suggest that the 'Justice Party' evolved any concrete policies relevant to the issues that faced the electorate in the 1981 elections and that the participation of its leader in a past election was not sufficient to render the group into a contestant of political power. Thus, the 'Justice Party' could not properly be said to qualify as a political party.

135. Following the *Pitsillos* case, the Council of Ministers enacted the CYBC (Fair Treatment of Political Parties) Regulations of 1985 which defined a political party as either a political party with parliamentary representation, or as a political party which acquired at least 5% of valid votes in the most recent parliamentary elections. The definition provided by the 1985 Regulations was unreasonably narrow and excluded political parties who were not sufficiently established. On the contrary, Law 212/87 which amended section 2 of the CYBC Law, Cap. 300A, defined a political party as a party represented in the House of Representatives, or as an organization or association, or group of persons which would be considered a political party by an average reasonable man who is aware of the political realities of Cyprus and takes into account the group's organization, structure, aims and response of the public to it. The definition provided by Law 212/87 was completely in line with the case-law of the Supreme Court in the *Pitsillos* case and did not add the requirement of either parliamentary representation or a 5% of the votes in the most recent parliamentary elections.

136. In the case of the *Liberal Party and Another*, two non-parliamentary parties, the Liberal Party, led by former Minister of Foreign Affairs Nicos Rolandis and the Centre Union (Enosis Kentrou), led by former Minister and deputy and future President of the Republic, Tassos Papadopoulos, filed recourse against the decision of the CYBC to exclude them from political radio and television broadcasts.[225] The majority of the Supreme Court held that the 1985 Regulations which defined a political party as either a political party with parliamentary representation or as a

225. *The Liberal Party and Another v. The CYBC* [1989] 3 CLR 196 (in Greek).

political party which acquired at least 5% of the votes in the most recent parliamentary elections were invalid since they were contrary to the express definition provided in section 2 of the CYBC Law, Cap. 300A as amended by Law 212/87. Since there was manifest discrepancy between the two provisions, the Court held that the subsequent Law 212/87 had repealed the definition provided for in the 1985 Regulations. The decision of the CYBC was thus annulled.[226]

137. The test adopted by the Supreme Court and by Law 212/87, namely what the reasonable man considers, is quite vague and depends upon the factual circumstances of each given case; the criteria on the basis of which the reasonable man is supposed to evaluate whether a political party exists or not are therefore not sufficiently pre-determined.[227] It has even been suggested that the result of this approach is to turn the judge into the sole and ultimate interpreter of the way a reasonable man should apply the test;[228] however, the case of *Pakop* confirms that this is not an entirely accurate view.[229] The Pancyprian Party of Refugees and Suffered Persons (PAKOP) filed recourse against the decision of the CYBC not to consider them as a political party. The CYBC had decided that Pakop could not be considered a political party, since it had no history of participation in the political affairs of Cyprus. Moreover, it had not presented complete political positions on matters other than the Cyprus problem, it did not have sufficient organization and structure, and had only announced fourteen candidates for the parliamentary elections in only three electoral areas (out of fifty-six in six electoral areas).

138. The Supreme Court held that, similarly to any other administrative decision, the administration is to reach a decision on how the test is to be applied on the basis of the facts of the given case and the Court will only examine whether the administration has acted contrary to the law, or contrary to the principles of administrative law. Thus, it is not for the Court to engage in a fact-finding process;[230] it is for the CYBC to objectively identify whether a group of persons falls under the definition of a political party on the basis of what would generally be accepted by the average reasonable person and the Court will be the ultimate arbiter of whether the administrative decision has been reached legitimately and reasonably on the basis of the principles of administrative law.

139. The definition adopted in Law 212/87 was also adopted in the Political Parties (Acquisition, Possession, Disposal of Movable and Immovable Property) Law

---

226. The Court was unanimous in the decision to annul; however, three judges of the Supreme Court disagreed as to the reasoning and held that not only the Regulations were contrary to the subsequent law, but also ultra vires.
227. *See* the criticism of D. Melissas, *Political Parties in the Republic of Cyprus: The Development towards Institutionalisation* 37–41 (A. Sakkoulas, 1996, in Greek).
228. *Ibid.*, 39.
229. *Pakop and Others v. CYBC* [1992] 4 CLR 1992 (in Greek).
230. However, in the case of *Pitsillos v. CYBC* [1982] 3 CLR 208, it could be argued that the Court did just that.

199/89, albeit with one major difference: section 2 of Law 199/89 defined a political party as a party represented in the House of Representatives, or as an organization or association, or group of persons which would be considered a political party by an average reasonable man who is aware of the political realities of Cyprus and takes into account the group's organization, structure, aims and response of the public to it, and so far as it received at least 3% of valid votes in the most recent parliamentary elections. Thus, Law 199/89 introduced once again the requirement of receiving at least a percentage of valid votes in the most recent parliamentary elections for a group of persons to be considered as a political party, a requirement which undoubtedly restricts the definition of a political party for the purposes of Law 199/89. In *Diglis*, the Supreme Court held that providing funding to a political party on the basis of its political representation, as shown by the percentage of votes it received in the most recent parliamentary elections, is not arbitrary, nor does it amount to unequal treatment; the differentiation in treatment was based on objective and reasonable criteria.[231]

140. Two additional comments are in order. First of all, the definition of political parties provided for in Law 199/89 only applied to the purposes of Law 199/89; as far as any other legislative instrument or purposes are concerned, political parties should be defined on the basis of the criteria adopted by the Court in *Pitsillos*, without any additional restrictions. A different conclusion would violate the constitutional right to freedom of association, which includes the right to found political parties.[232] Second, it should be noted that the additional requirement of having received 3% of the votes in the most recent parliamentary elections, which is provided for in Law 199/89, only applies with respect to groups of persons, organizations or associations not already represented in the House of Representatives; parties represented in the House of Representatives, irrespective of how their deputies got elected (with a coalition of parties, with another party from which they later resigned, or with a party which elected deputies without having received 3% of the votes), are automatically considered political parties for the purposes of Law 199/89.[233]

141. Law 199/89 provided that political parties within the definition of such Law have the right to acquire, register, possess and dispose of movable and immovable property and are registered in a Register of Political Parties kept at the Ministry of Interior; no tax is imposed for the registration of immovable property transferred to

---

231. *Diglis and Others v. Ghalanos and Another* [1993] 4 CLR 2732 (in Greek). *See also President of the Republic v. House of Representatives* [1990] 3 CLR 4213 (in Greek).
232. D. Melissas, *Political Parties in the Republic of Cyprus: The Development Towards Institutionalisation* 23–24 (A. Sakkoulas 1996, in Greek).
233. *The Liberal Party and Another v. Republic of Cyprus* [1993] 4 CLR 1096 (in Greek), the appeal was dismissed on technical grounds *Republic of Cyprus v. The Liberal Party and Another* [1993] 3 CLR 583 (in Greek). However, an obiter dictum of Case 1183/06, *European Democracy v. House of Representatives*, Judgment of 12 Nov. 2008, which referred to deputy Prodromos Prodromou, supports the view that if a deputy got elected with another party from which he later resigned and then founded a new party, then this new political party should not be considered as a parliamentary political party.

a registered political party. Law 225/90 further provided that private donations to political parties up to CYP 3,000 for natural persons and up to CYP 10,000 for legal persons might be exempted for income tax purposes. The President of the Republic referred to the Supreme Court the question of whether the said Law was constitutional; the majority of the Supreme Court held that the funding of political parties by the State, or the grant of incentives for the funding of political parties by individuals is a legitimate aim and there is no violation of the principle of equality by the fact that the definition of a political party presupposes either parliamentary representation or receiving at least 5% of the votes in the most recent parliamentary elections, similarly to the provisions of Law 199/89. The aforementioned criteria are objective and reasonable.[234] Law 225/90 was, however, short-lived, since it was repealed by subsequent Law 226/90.

142. In 2011, the House of Representatives enacted the Political Parties Law 20/2011. Section 2 of Law 20/11 adopted a novel definition of political parties. In particular, it defined political parties as follows:

> a union or group of persons which participates in the formation of the political will of the people and participates in presidential, parliamentary, European and municipal elections or to some of these elections, with the aim to realise its political program and which functions within the legal framework set out by the Constitution and the laws of the Republic and including both parliamentary and non-parliamentary parties.
>
> Political parties which have elected at least one Member of the House of Representatives or of the European Parliament are considered as parliamentary parties. All political parties should be registered in the registry of political parties which is kept by the Permanent Secretary of the Ministry of Interior who acts as the Registrar. Section 3 of Law 20/11 provides that the exercise of the functions of political parties, while free, should respect the Constitution and its subordinate legislation; in addition, the internal organization of political parties should serve the free exercise of democratic principles.

143. Section 3 of Law 20/11 was judicially tested almost immediately following its enactment when DIKO decided to summarily expel its Deputy Chairman Georghios Kolokasides; Kolokasides had supported a decision of a deputy of DIKO Zacharias Koulias, who did not vote in favour of the President of DIKO Marios Karoyian to be re-elected as President of the House of Representatives, but instead voted in favour of another candidate. On 7/6/2011, the President of DIKO convened DIKO's executive committee, without inviting Kolokasides to participate or express his views; the executive committee decided to expel Kolokasides by twenty votes to seven. Kolokasides filed an action against DIKO and the District Court of Nicosia issued an interim order suspending the force of the decision to expel him,

234. *President of the Republic v. House of Representatives* [1990] 3 CLR 4213. In his dissenting opinion, Artemides J. held that the Law violated the principle of equality as enshrined in Art. 28 of the Constitution.

holding that since the internal organization of political parties should serve the free exercise of democratic principles, Kolokasides ought to have been given the opportunity to be heard and express his views before a decision for his expulsion is reached.[235]

144. Law 20/2011 was substituted by the Political Parties Law 175(I)/2012. The new law defines political parties as follows:

> a union or group of persons having a permanent character, constitutional structure and an organization of pancyprian ambit and having a political, ideological or programmatic connective tissue, which participates in elections or in other representative bodies provided in the legal order and which collaborates in the determination of the political will of the people with the aim to realise its political program. Its organization, function and structure are consistent with the legal framework set out by the Constitution and the laws of the Republic and in general its presence in the political life provides sufficient guarantees for the seriousness of its aims and intentions as a political party.

The novel definition adopted in Law 175(I)/2012 is undeniably a highly restrictive one, when compared to all previous definitions of the term, whereas it also refers to subjective criteria, such as seriousness of aims and intentions.

145. Section 3 of Law 175(I)/12 further provides that for a political party to be registered in the registry of political parties, it should support its application by three hundred signatures of registered voters and pay a fee of EUR 2,000; existing parliamentary parties are registered in the registry without application, so long as they submit their charter to the Registrar within six months from the date of operation of Law 175(I)/12. The new legislation no longer contains a reference that the internal organization of political parties should serve the free exercise of democratic principles. Initially section 9 of Law 175(I)/12 further provided that the decisions of the collective organs of a political party which are governed by their charters are not subject to judicial review, a provision which entirely negated democracy within political parties and enabled arbitrary decisions by their leaders. However, an amendment effected by Law 171(I)/2015 repealed such provision.

146. Political parties which are registered may receive State funding in order to carry out their activities; such funding is tax-free. Parliamentary political parties receive annual financing. The Council of Ministers decides on the amount of the annual financing which is included in the state budget; the financing is distributed mainly in proportion to the percentage that the political parties received during the last parliamentary elections; however, 15% of the overall financing is distributed equally amongst the parliamentary political parties. Financing is granted in five increments. Political parties may further receive additional funding in order to cover

235. App. 4844/11, *Kolokasides v. Democratic Party*, Judgment of 26 Jul. 2011 (District Court, in Greek).

part of their needs for parliamentary elections, funding being distributed in proportion to the percentage they received during the previous parliamentary elections. The Council of Ministers may decide that additional funding should be given for elections other than parliamentary ones. Representatives who have withdrawn from the party under which they were elected do not receive State funding until the end of their term. Non-parliamentary political parties are entitled to receive State funding to cover part of their needs prior to the elections, so long as they are registered, they have applied to the Registrar, i.e., the Permanent Secretary of the Ministry of Interior, prior to the announcement of the elections, have a list of candidates for at least 50% of the seats of the upcoming elections and have secured at least 3% in the last parliamentary elections, or in the elections for which the funding is requested.

147. In addition to State funding, political parties may receive private funding; such private funding is also tax-free. A natural or legal person who exercises lawful activities may donate up to EUR 50,000 per annum to a political party. Anonymous donations are not allowed. Political parties may not receive funding from legal persons of public law (with the exception of the Cyprus Youth Organization), state owned, or state controlled companies, illegal enterprises, or legal persons which are not registered in the Republic. No donation of more than EUR 5,000 is allowed, if the donor has not fulfilled their tax obligations, or has been disqualified from participating to public procurement, or has a criminal record, or controls a casino or betting agency, or if s/he is an alien who is not of Cypriot origin (in case of natural persons), or has not been situated in the Republic during the past three years (in case of legal persons).

148. The aim of the new legislative framework was to enhance transparency through a series of measures, including publicization of donors who offered more than EUR 500, the application of international accounting standards, the submission of detailed accounts of expenses and profits to the Registrar and the carrying out of detailed audits by the Auditor-General, the requirement that at least 90% of capital movement should take place through credit institutions and the imposition of administrative fines. However, serious concerns about the relationship between economic undertakings and political parties still exist. Whereas the legislative framework provides for an audit of the financial statements of political parties and of their income and expenses during pre-election campaigns, popular confidence in the transparency and accountability of political parties remains very low. It should be further noted that in addition to private funding, political parties with parliamentary representation enjoy public funding, a fact which undeniably increases the inequality between established political parties and new political parties; in practice, political parties receive an annual state grant, as well as additional funding before the presidential and parliamentary elections.[236]

236. *See also* Case 1183/06, *European Democracy v. House of Representatives*, Judgment of 12 Nov. 2008 (in Greek).

IV. Lobbies and Interest Groups

149. The Transparency in the Procedures for Reaching Public Decisions and Associated Matters Law 20(I)/2022 has introduced a detailed legislative framework specifically governing the operation of lobbies and interest groups in Cyprus.[237] The Independent Authority against Corruption, which was established by Law 19(I)/2022, is the competent authority for overseeing the implementation of Law 20(I)/22. Law 20(I)/22 applies with respect to any representative of a specific interest group (lobbyist) who wishes to engage in procedures for reaching public decisions. This includes any procedure for reaching decisions on matters pertaining to either executive or the legislative powers, and to which the targeted official or member of the wider public service has the authority to commence such procedure, or determine its content or its result.

150. All lobbyists falling within the ambit of Law 20(I)/22 have to be registered in a Registry prior to engaging with any kind of lobbying activities. Registration is personal and may not be either transferred or assigned to any other person; however, there is no obligation to register staff of the lobbyist. The lobbyist should have a clear criminal record, should not have been convicted for corruption, and should be over 18 years of age, if a natural person. The main details of lobbyists who have been registered in the Registry is publicized. Registered lobbyists may receive information from officials, participate in public consultations, and request meetings with public officials. Public officials should declare in writing any conflict of interests and refrain from the procedure. Violation of any provisions of Law 20(I)/22 amounts to a criminal offence and may lead to criminal sanctions or, depending on the case, administrative fines.

151. It should be noted that there are special interest groups which are not included in the ambit of Law 20(I)/22. Law 20(I)/22 does not apply, however, to matters governing the external relations of the Republic of Cyprus with another country or international organization, or its defence or external policy. It further does not apply to matters pertaining to the protection of human rights or to the application of public procurement procedures (with the exception of the stage preceding the application of the relevant public procurement legislation). Moreover, it does not apply to communications from representatives of trade unions or agricultural organizations regarding conditions of employment, or communication sent within the context of pending discussions before parliamentary committees, or within the context of a public consultation. Accordingly, trade unions or other pressure groups falling outside the ambit of Law 20(I)/22 can still aim to encourage or prevent changes in public policy. Many of these pressure groups are related to political parties. For instance, the two most important labour pressure groups, the Confederation of Cypriot Workers (SEK) and the Pancyprian Labour Federation (PEO) are associated with DISY and AKEL respectively. Similarly, the two larger youth organizations,

---

237. *See* V. Polyzoidou & A. Emilianides, *The Regulatory Framework of Lobbying and the Cypriot Legal System*, in *The Institution of the House of Representatives* 223–243 (A. Emilianides et al. eds, House of Representatives/UNIC School of Law 2022, in Greek).

Youth of DISY (NEDISY) (with their student branch Protoporia) and the United Democratic Organization of Youth (EDON) (with their student branch Proodeftiki) are controlled by DISY and AKEL respectively. The same is true with respect to other important pressure groups, such as those related to farmers, school teachers and professors, trade unions, and even professional pressure groups; the two larger political parties, as well as DIKO, control the most important lobbies and interest groups in Cyprus, while in many cases, the leaders of such pressure groups are prospective candidates for election to the House of Representatives with one of the major political parties in Cyprus.

152. However, two of the most important and successful pressure groups, namely the Pancyprian Trade Union of Public Servants (PASYDY) and the Cyprus Union of Bank Employees (ETYK) groups are not controlled by any political party and represent all the public servants and bank employees of Cyprus respectively. Similarly, the Cyprus Scientific and Technical Chamber (ETEK) which is the umbrella organization for all Cypriot engineers, as well as the Cyprus Bar Association and the Cyprus Medical Association are powerful professional organizations which routinely negotiate with the State without being directly controlled by any political party. As far as NGOs are concerned, they are rather a new phenomenon in Cyprus; a great number of Cypriot NGOs function on a voluntary basis and do not have the financial sustainability to ensure staff on payroll, necessary infrastructure or ongoing activities. Many NGOs are concerned almost exclusively with the Cyprus problem, either by organizing bi-communal activities, or by lobbying for a just and fair solution of the Cyprus problem.

§3. Miscellaneous

153. The Referendum Law 206/1989 provides that a referendum may take place upon the decision of the House of Representatives following a proposal by the Council of Ministers.[238] The referendum should refer to issues of special importance and of public interest. The Council of Ministers may propose at its own initiative to the House of Representatives that a referendum should take place, if such referendum refers to matters within the ambit of the executive power; otherwise, the House of Representatives may suggest to the Council of Ministers to propose a referendum. The decision of the House of Representatives should specify the question that has to be answered by citizens of the Republic over 18 years of age, as well as the date and procedure of the referendum; the question is to be answered either affirmatively or negatively. The Ministry of Interior is the competent authority to carry out the referendum. No referendum has yet taken place since the law was enacted, nor has a proposal ever been made by the Council of Ministers to the House of Representatives, a fact which might signify the unwillingness on behalf of the Cypriot authorities to refer to a referendum. It should be noted that the 2004 referendum

238. For the background to Law 206/89 *see* L. Papaphilippou, *The Referendum as a Democratic Ideal and Institution: The Possibility to Introduce it in Cyprus Within the Framework of the Constitutional Order*, 37 Nomiko Vima 410–425 (1989) (in Greek).

which resulted in the rejection of the Annan Plan was not carried out by the Republic of Cyprus, nor in accordance with the provisions of Law 206/89; such referendum was carried out by the Greek Cypriot and the Turkish Cypriot Community respectively under the auspices of the UN.

154. Pursuant to the European Citizens Initiative Law 59(I)/2013, the Permanent Secretary of the Minister of Interior has been appointed as the competent authority with regard to the facilitation at national level of the implementation of Community Regulation 211/2011 of 16 February 2011 on citizens' initiative. There is no national institutionalized citizens' initiative equivalent to the European Citizens Initiative or any other similar instrument in Cyprus. The Referendum Law 206/1989 contains no provision for a referendum to be initiated upon a citizens' initiative. Occasionally, signatures are collected in the course of civil society initiatives, albeit in a non-structured manner, but they are invariably ignored at political level.

Chapter 2. Head of State

§1. The Organ of State

155. The position of the Head of State is central in a presidential democracy.[239] Article 36 of the Constitution expressly provides that the President of the Republic is the Head of State and takes precedence over all persons in the Republic.[240] Article 39 of the Constitution further provides that the election of the President shall be direct, by universal suffrage and secret ballot. If there is only one candidate for election, then such candidate shall be declared as elected;[241] otherwise the candidate who receives more than 50% of the votes which have been validly cast shall be elected.[242] If none of the candidates attains the required majority, the election shall be repeated on the corresponding day of the following week between the two candidates who received the greater number of the votes validly cast; the candidate who receives at such repeated election the greatest number of the votes validly cast shall be deemed to be elected.[243] If the election cannot take place on the date fixed under the Constitution due to extraordinary and unforeseen circumstances such as earthquake, floods, general epidemic and the like, then such election shall take place on the corresponding day of the following week.

156. The Elections (President and Vice-President of the Republic) Law 37/1959 complements the constitutional provisions by providing for the administrative arrangements of presidential elections.[244] Section 3 of Law 37/59 provides that Cyprus shall be one electoral division, while section 8 provides that the Minister of Interior appoints the Returning Officer and any number of Assistant Returning Officers. In practice, the Returning Officer is the Permanent Secretary of the Ministry of Interior. Every candidate shall be nominated, in accordance with section 10 of Law 37/59, by a separate nomination paper signed by the candidate, one elector acting as a proposer and 100 seconders. Initially, only nine seconders were needed, but the number was considered very low for a presidential candidate and Law 91(I)/2016 raised the number of seconders needed to 100. Candidates should deposit with the Returning Officer the sum of EUR 2,000 for their nomination to be a valid one, in accordance with section 11 of Law 37/59; such deposit shall be repayable to the

239. C. Tornaritis, *The Presidential System as Opposed to the Parliamentary One*, 1 Cyprus L. Tribune 3–19 (1991) (in Greek).
240. It should be noted that in accordance with Art. 38 of the Constitution, the Vice-President of the Republic is the Vice-Head of State; however, due to the constitutional crisis the position of the Vice-President of the Republic has not been filed since 1963. Accordingly no analysis shall be undertaken with respect to the Vice-President of the Republic in this section.
241. This was the case in 1973 and 1978 with President Makarios and Kyprianou respectively being the only candidates for election.
242. In the elections of 1960 and 1968, President Makarios was elected in the first round of voting, as were Presidents Kyprianou in 1983 and Papadopoulos in 2003.
243. The following Presidents were elected in the second round of voting: Vasiliou (1988), Clerides (1993, 1998), Christofias (2008), Anastasiades (2013, 2018) and Christodoulides (2023).
244. Section 15 of Law 37/59 further provides for the eventuality of one of the candidates dying.

candidate, or personal representative in case of death, if there is no contested election, or if there is a contested election in case that the candidate obtains votes equal to not less than one-tenth of the total number of valid votes.[245]

157. Once elected, the President of the Republic is invested by the House of Representatives before which he makes the following affirmation: 'I do solemnly affirm faith to, and respect for, the Constitution and the laws made thereunder, the preservation of the independence and the territorial integrity, of the Republic of Cyprus', in accordance with Article 42 of the Constitution. The term of office of the President is for a period of five years commencing on the date of investiture until the next elected President is invested.[246] The election of a new President shall take place before the expiration of the five years period of office of the outgoing President so as to enable the newly elected President to be invested on the date such period expires. In practice, presidential elections are held on a Sunday in February, since the term of office normally expires on 28 February. In accordance with Article 43, the President of the Republic elected at a by-election due to a vacancy in the office of the President shall hold office for the unexpired period of office of the President whose vacancy he has been elected to fill.[247] Pursuant to the Thirteenth Amendment of the Constitution, Law 160(I)/19, a person may not stand for election if he has served as President of the Republic for the preceding two continuous terms.

158. A person shall be qualified to stand for election as President of the Republic, in accordance with Article 40 of the Constitution, if at the time of election such person: (a) is a citizen of the Republic, (b) has attained the age of thirty-five years, (c) has not been convicted of an offence involving dishonesty or moral turpitude or is not under any disqualification imposed by a competent court for any electoral offence, and (d) is not suffering from a mental disease incapacitating such person from acting as President of the Republic. In addition, and although not provided for in Article 40 of the Constitution, the President of the Republic should belong to the Greek Community, in view of the bi-communal structure of the Constitution which provided that the President of the Republic is a Greek Cypriot and the Vice-President of the Republic is a Turkish Cypriot.[248] The Supreme Court has held that the requirements for election set out by the Constitution are exhaustive and consequently no law may impose additional requirements or impediments to the election of a person as President of the Republic. An attempt by the House of Representatives to amend the Coup d' Etat Law 57/1975 in 1990 so as to impede the election of members of the 1974 coup Government was held to be unconstitutional; since

245. It is submitted that the constitutionality of such provision is dubious.
246. C. Tornaritis, *The Term of the President of the Republic*, Cyprus L. Rev. 2, 431–432 (1983) (in Greek).
247. This was the case with President Kyprianou from 1977 when he was elected at a by-election for the unexpired term of office of President Makarios until 1978.
248. *See also* s. 6 of Law 37/59. However, it is submitted that following the judgment of the European Court of Human Rights in *Aziz v. Cyprus*, App. 69949/01, Judgment of 22 Jun. 2004, Turkish Cypriots should also be allowed to stand for election for the position of President of the Republic.

the members of the 1974 coup Government had never been convicted or disqualified by a competent court, they had the right to stand for election.[249]

159. In the event of a temporary absence or a temporary incapacity to perform the duties of the President, the President of the House of Representatives and in case of his/her absence or pending the filling of a vacancy in any such office, the Representative acting for him/her under Article 72 of the Constitution, shall act, in accordance with Article 36 section 2 of the Constitution, for the President during such temporary absence or temporary incapacity. Admittedly, the said provision which effectively entails 'deputization for the President each time he has to go abroad for whatever reason, or even for one day in order simply to participate in a meeting of the European Council, appears strange, especially given modern communications'.[250] The person deputizing for the President has, in theory, and may exercise all the powers of the President in accordance with his/her own judgment and without reference to the President, including dismissing and replacing Ministers. As noted, the only real 'constraint on the person who deputizes for the president and often comes from a different political camp is, therefore, political common sense'.[251] However, it could be argued that a deputy should not be deemed as having the power to act in a manner that would effectively thwart the political programme of the elected President, such as permanent appointments. While in practice, deputies for the President have refrained from acting in a manner that would have abused their powers, a recent incident has proven to be highly controversial. At a time when both the President and the President of the House of Representatives would be abroad, MP Zacharias Koulias, as the senior MP, would temporarily act as President. Koulias warned that unless an Auditor-General was appointed prior to his temporarily acting as President, he would immediately proceed to appoint the Auditor-General himself. The 'warning' eventually led the President of the House of Representatives to cancel her trip, and the President proceeded to appoint a new Auditor-General immediately afterwards.

160. The office of the President of the Republic shall become vacant, in accordance with Article 44 of the Constitution: (a) upon his/her death, (b) upon his/her written resignation addressed to the House of Representatives through their President, (c) upon his/her conviction of high treason or any other offence involving dishonesty or moral turpitude, and (d) upon such permanent physical or mental incapacity or non-temporary absence, as would prevent him/her to effectively perform his/her duties. The decision whether the President has permanent physical or mental incapacity or absence that would prevent him/her from effectively performing his/her duties is to be decided by the Supreme Constitutional Court on a motion

249. *President of the Republic v. House of Representatives* [1991] 3 CLR 252 (in Greek).
250. A. Markides, *The Republic of Cyprus*, in *Constitutional Law of 10 EU Member States* I-31 (Kortmann et al. eds, Kluwer 2006).
251. *Ibid.*

by the Attorney-General and the Deputy Attorney-General of the Republic and upon a resolution of the Representatives carried by a simple majority.[252]

161. In the event of a vacancy, the President of the House of Representatives shall act as President of the Republic until such vacancy is filled by a by-election which shall take place within a period not exceeding forty-five days of the occurrence of such vacancy. The only case where a vacancy existed was the death of President Makarios in 1977, a few months before his term was to come to an end. All major political figures of the island agreed that it would be unreasonable to hold a by-election for such a brief term of service during a turbulent political period, and thus, the then-President of the House of Representatives Spyros Kyprianou was the sole candidate and was elected unopposed. However, in reality, there was another candidate, namely Modestos Pitsillos, who was the leader of an organization with a very negligible following called the Justice Party. Pitsillos started a pre-election campaign, but when he attended the office of the returning officer for the purpose of obtaining the necessary nomination papers, he was informed that his name was not included in the register of electors. As a result, he was prevented from being a candidate in the above election. Pitsillos filed an action against the Republic and the Supreme Court held that the register had been interfered with by officers of the Republic for the purpose of preventing the appellant from nomination as a candidate in the by-election for the presidency.[253]

§2. Legal Status

162. The office of the President of the Republic is incompatible, in accordance with Article 41 of the Constitution, with that of a Minister or a member of the House of Representatives, or a member of a Communal Chamber, or a Mayor, or a member of any municipal Council, or a member of the armed or security forces of the Republic or with a public or municipal office.[254] Furthermore, it is expressly stipulated that the President shall not, during term of office, engage either directly or indirectly, either for his/her own account or for the account of any other person, in the exercise of any profit or non-profit making business or profession. Accordingly, the office of the President of the Republic is one of near absolute incompatibility.[255] It should also be noted that the President of the Republic has an obligation to disclose, every three years, his/her property assets, as well as the property assets of his/her spouse and minor children, to a special parliamentary committee, pursuant to

252. The proposal for such resolution has to be signed by at least one-fifth of the total number of members of the House of Representatives.

253. *Pitsillos v. The Republic* [1984] 1 CLR 780. Pitsillos was awarded damages in the amount of Cypriot Pounds 3000.

254. For the purposes of Art. 41 '*public office*' means any office of profit in the public service of the Republic, or of a Communal Chamber, the emoluments of which are under the control either of the Republic, or of a Communal Chamber, and includes any office in any public corporation or public utility body.

255. *See also* The Incompatibility as to the Exercise of Duties of Certain Officials of the Republic to Certain Professional and other similar activities Law 7(I)/2008.

the President, Ministers and Representatives (Submission and Review of Property) Law 49(I)/2004. Submission of the property assets to the parliamentary commission should in any event take place within three months from assumption of duties and within three months from termination of duties.

163. The President of the Republic is not liable to criminal prosecution during his/her term of office, except in accordance with the provisions of Article 45 of the Constitution. Article 45 provides that the President may be prosecuted for high treason on a charge brought by the Attorney-General and the Deputy Attorney-General of the Republic before the Supreme Court upon a resolution of the House of Representatives carried by a secret ballot and a majority of three-fourths of the total number of Representatives.[256] In addition, the President may be prosecuted for an offence involving dishonesty or moral turpitude upon a charge brought by the Attorney-General and the Deputy Attorney-General of the Republic before the Supreme Court with the leave of the President of the Supreme Court. The President of the Republic, upon being prosecuted, shall be temporarily suspended from the performance of any of the functions of his/her office. Any prosecution of the President shall be tried by the Supreme Court; on conviction, the office of the President shall become vacant, while on acquittal, the President shall resume the performance of the functions of his/her office. Subject to the above, the President shall not be liable to prosecution for any offence committed by him/her in the execution of his/her functions, but he may be prosecuted for any other offence committed during his/her term of office after he ceases to hold office.

164. There have been no instances where a President has been prosecuted; however, there has been intense debate about the obligation of the Attorney-General to apply for leave of the President of the Supreme Court to initiate criminal proceedings against President Demetris Christofias. On 11 July 2011, ninety-eight containers holding munitions originating from Iran and bound for Syria self-detonated; the containers had been confiscated in 2009 and were being stored for 2.5 years in the Evangelos Florakis Naval Base. The resulting explosion killed thirteen people, including the Commander of the Navy and the Base Commander, while a further sixty-two people were injured. The explosion further damaged nearby buildings, including those of the island's largest power station, responsible for supplying over half of Cyprus' electricity. On 3 October 2011, Polys Polyviou, the independent state-appointed investigator released a 643-page document detailing his findings on the investigation; he concluded that President Christofias was the main one to blame for the events that led to the explosion, both institutionally, but also due to his personal role in the incident. The investigator called the Attorney-General to seriously examine the possibility of serious crimes, including involuntary manslaughter, having been committed by the President. However, the Attorney-General of the Republic refrained from applying for leave and declared that his decision was for the President not to be prosecuted.[257]

256. The proposal for such resolution has to be signed by at least one-fifth of the total number of members of the House of Representatives.
257. *See also Ioannidou and Others* [2012] 1 CLR 1442 (in Greek).

165. Moreover, no civil action may be brought personally against the President of the Republic in respect of any act or omission committed by him/her in the exercise of any of the functions of his/her office.[258] The President can therefore be sued on the basis of a cause of action, even during the duration of his/her term, so long as such cause of action is not in respect of an act or omission committed by him/her in the exercise of any of the functions of his/her office. An action may therefore be brought against the President under contract, or tort, or family, or succession law, or for any other reason which is not related to his/her functions as the President. Persons aggrieved by an act or omission of the Republic committed in the exercise of the functions of his/her office may file a civil action against the Republic of Cyprus.

166. The President is not politically or otherwise accountable to the House of Representatives, and thus, he is not obliged to resign if he does not enjoy the support of the majority of the House of Representatives, or indeed of even a single Representative. On 29 March 1985, the House of Representatives decided and called upon the President of the Republic to resign before the end of his term, and to proceed and proclaim a presidential election, because he did not comply with a Resolution of the House dated 22 February 1985 which related to the handling of the Cyprus Problem. The Supreme Court held that the said decision of the House of Representatives was not to be promulgated, since the decision constituted an expression of political will in relation to the Cyprus Problem, which is a subject outside the sphere of constitutional order.[259]

167. The structure of Presidential democracy also entails that the President of the Republic, while enjoying vast executive powers, does not necessarily control the majority of the House of Representatives. The President normally needs a coalition of political parties supporting him/her in order to be elected and to be able to fulfil his/her programme. This institutional peculiarity of Cyprus, if compared with other European countries, has played a pivotal role in the way political power is secured and exercised. It could be argued that no President of the Republic of Cyprus following the death of Makarios has had the opportunity to fully adopt and implement the policy he personally, or his party, believed to due to this institutional need to search for consensus and secure a majority in the House of Representatives. It is a fact that the two Presidents of the Republic who hailed from DIKO, namely Spyros Kyprianou and Tassos Papadopoulos, never fully implemented their proposed policy concerning the Cyprus problem, since they tried to make concessions to their coalition partners, most notably AKEL. Even during the time when either Kyprianou or Papadopoulos were not acting in coalition with AKEL, knowing that they did not enjoy a majority in the House of Representatives, their preferred policy had been to act with caution and seek solutions which might reflect wider political consensus.

---

258. *Ioannidou and Others v. Christofias*, Civil App. 492/2012, Judgment of 23 Apr. 2018 (in Greek).
259. *President of the Republic v. House of Representatives* [1985] 3 CLR 1429, *President of the Republic v. House of Representatives* [1985] 3 CLR 1501. *See also* P. Clerides, *The Presidential Succession, the Term and the Decision of the House of Representatives* (1985, in Greek).

168. The same approach was for the most part followed also by President Vassiliou, and divergence from this approach caused him to a large extent the elections and led to the coalition between Clerides and DIKO. Clerides, during his First Presidency also followed an approach of satisfying the concerns of other parties participating in his coalition, even adopting a very active foreign and defence policy, in collaboration with the Greek Government, during his First term, which might in reality be against his personal beliefs. It could be argued that the second term of Clerides was probably the only period during which a President of the Republic had the opportunity to adopt the policy he believed into with respect to the Cyprus problem; this policy was put to an abrupt end when Clerides lost the elections in 2003. Dimitris Christofias, while not really cooperating with his coalition partners, is a President in the post-Annan era, during which strong opposition and lack of support by the House of Representatives, especially after the tragic events of the explosion of Mari on July 2011, has affected to a degree his negotiating tactics and overall policy. Similarly, Nicos Anastasiades operated in a post-financial crisis era and had to secure support from a House of Representatives where the opposition controlled approximately two-thirds of the votes. The current President, Nicos Christodoulides, does not enjoy the support of either of the two major political parties, DISY and AKEL, who are in the opposition. He has been supported by DIKO, EDEK and DIPA who control only a minority of 17 out of the 56 elected Representatives.

§3. Competences

169. Article 37 of the Constitution provides that the President of the Republic as the Head of State: (a) represents the Republic in all its official functions, (b) signs the credentials of diplomatic envoys appointed under Article 54 and receives the credentials of foreign diplomatic envoys who shall be accredited to him/her, (c) signs the credentials of delegates appointed for the negotiation of international treaties, conventions or other agreements, or for signing any such treaties, conventions or agreements already negotiated in accordance with, and subject to the provisions of the Constitution, and further signs the letter relating to the transmission of the instruments of ratification of any international treaties, conventions or agreements approved as provided in the Constitution and (d) confers the honours of the Republic.

170. The President further ensures the exercise of the executive power of the Republic by designating all members of the Council of Ministers. While the executive powers vest, in accordance with Article 46 of the Constitution to the Council of Ministers, without the President having a right to vote, in practice, the President always has the power to replace Ministers who act contrary to his/her policy; such powers of the President are restricted only by the need to safeguard political alliances, or political common sense not to replace successful or popular Ministers. It should be noted that during the term of President Demetris Christofias, Minister of Commerce Praxoula Antoniadou Kyriakou filed a resource before the Supreme Court claiming that she had not resigned from her post as the President had claimed and that accordingly her replacement by Minister Neoclis Sylikiotis had been illegal. The recourse was rightly rejected by the Supreme Court, which held that the decision of a President to substitute Ministers is a government act and as such may not be judicially reviewed.[260]

171. The executive power exercised by the President consisted, in accordance with Article 47 of the Constitution, of powers which ought to be exercised by the President and the Vice-President of the Republic acting conjointly and, by virtue of Article 48 of the Constitution, of powers which could be exercised by the President acting by himself/herself.[261] In view of the fact that the position of the Vice-President has remained vacant since 1963, the President of the Republic exercises the executive power on all matters provided for in Articles 47 and 48 of the Constitution by himself/herself. Accordingly, the President has the power to: determine the design and colour of the flag of the Republic,[262] create and establish the honours of the Republic, institute compulsory military service as provided in Article 129 of the Constitution, reduce or increase the security forces of the Republic as provided in Article 130 of the Constitution.

172. The President further had the power to exercise the prerogative of mercy in capital cases, as provided for in Article 53 of the Constitution. In case the prerogative of mercy was exercised, the death sentence was commuted to life imprisonment. It should be noted that the Republic of Cyprus has officially abolished death penalty for all crimes since 19 April 2002, whereas capital punishment for murder has been abolished since 1983. The last executions carried out in Cyprus were on 13 June 1962. The Tenth Constitutional Amendment of the Constitution Law 93(I)/2016 deleted all references to capital punishment from the Constitution. However, the reference to the prerogative of mercy has not been repealed. The President of the Republic may also, on the unanimous recommendation of the Attorney-General and the Deputy Attorney-General of the Republic, remit, suspend or commute any sentence imposed by a court.[263] In any event, Article 53 does not imply under any circumstances that the President has the power to grant an amnesty with its full legal consequences, including suspension of the operation of the Criminal Code, Cap. 154.[264]

173. In addition to the above, the President has the power to appoint by designation members of the Council of Ministers and terminate the appointment of such

---

260. *Antoniadou v. President of the Republic*, Case 692/12, Judgment of 26 Nov. 2012 (in Greek).
261. Article 49 of the Constitution provides for executive powers vested to the Vice-President of the Republic; such Article is currently not applicable in practice, since there the position of the Vice-President is vacant since the resignation of the Turkish Cypriot Vice-President in 1963.
262. The national flag was adopted in 1960 by then-President Makarios and Vice-President Kutchuk as a result of a flag design competition; the flag was designed by a Turkish Cypriot, Ismet Guney and supposedly aimed to be neutral by design.
263. Former Attorney-General Solon Nikitas had suggested that pursuant to the doctrine of necessity, only the recommendation of the Attorney-General is required, since the Deputy Attorney-General is not currently a Turkish Cypriot. *See* e.g., *Attorney-General breakdown*, Simerini newspaper, 23 Dec. 2003 (in Greek). I do not subscribe to such view.
264. *The Republic v. Sampson* [1977] 2 CLR 1.

members. He has the right to convene the meetings of the Council of Ministers on his/her own motion, preside at such meetings, prepare the agenda of such meetings at his/her discretion, and take part in the discussions, albeit without a right to vote. The President also has the right to return any decision of the Council of Ministers for reconsideration; the decision has to be returned to the Council of Ministers for reconsideration within four days from the date when the decision had been transmitted to him/her in accordance with Article 57 of the Constitution. The Council of Ministers shall reconsider the matter and if they persist in such decision, the President shall promulgate such decision by promulgation in the official Gazette, unless the Council of Ministers otherwise states in such decision. If a decision relates to foreign affairs, defence or security as these terms are defined in Article 50 of the Constitution, the President may exercise the right to veto the decision within four days from the date when such decision had been transmitted to him/her.

174. The President also has the right to return any laws or decisions of the House of Representatives for reconsideration, as provided in Article 51 of the Constitution; such right has to be exercised within the period provided for the promulgation of laws and decisions of the House of Representatives pursuant to Article 52 of the Constitution, namely within fifteen days of the transmission of such law or decision to him/her. The President may also exercise the right to return the budget if, in his/her judgment, there is discrimination. The House of Representatives should reconsider and pronounce on the issue within fifteen days of such return (and in the case of the budget within thirty days of such return). If the House of Representatives persist in its decision, the President shall publish such law or decision or budget in the official Gazette of the Republic. Article 50 further provides that the President shall have the right of final veto on laws or decisions of the House of Representatives concerning foreign affairs, security or defence, a right which has to be applied within the fifteen-day period from the date that the law or decision is transmitted to him/her. The right of veto may be exercised either against the whole of a law or decision or against any part thereof; in the latter case, the law or decision shall be returned to the House of Representatives for a decision on whether the remaining part thereof will be submitted for promulgation. The President also has the power to address messages to the House of Representatives pursuant to Article 79 of the Constitution.

175. 'Foreign affairs' issues for which the President has a right to veto include: (a) the recognition of States, the establishment of diplomatic and consular relations with other countries and the interruption of such relations, the grant of acceptance to diplomat, representatives and of exequatur to consular representatives, the assignment of diplomatic representatives and of consular representatives, already in the diplomatic service, to posts abroad and the entrusting of functions abroad to special envoys already in the diplomatic service, the appointment and the assignment of persons, who are not already in the diplomatic service, to posts abroad as diplomatic or consular representatives and the entrusting of functions abroad to persons, who are not already in the diplomatic service, as special envoys; (b) the conclusion of international treaties, conventions and agreements; (c) the declaration of war and the conclusion of peace; (d) the protection abroad of the citizens of the Republic and of their interests; (e) the establishment, the status and the interests of aliens in the Republic; (f) the acquisition of foreign nationality by citizens of the Republic and their acceptance of employment by, or their entering the service of, a foreign Government. However, the term does not include the participation of the Republic in international organizations and pacts of alliance in which Greece and Turkey both participate.

176. 'Defence' issues for which the President has a right to veto include: (a) composition and size of the armed forces and credits for them,[265] (b) nominations des cadres and their promotions, (c) importation of war materials and explosives of all kinds, (d) cession of bases and other facilities to allied countries. 'Security' grounds for which the President has a right to veto include: nominations des cadres and their promotions, distribution and stationing of forces, emergency measures and martial law and police laws (not including those measures which concern the normal functioning of the police and the gendarmerie). The Vice-President of the Republic, Fazil Kucuk, exercised the right to veto with respect to the composition of the army of the Republic on 20 October 1961. The first, and so far only, time that the President of the Republic has exercised the right to veto was on 2 March 2011 against the decision of the House of Representatives to call him to submit an application for the participation of the Republic of Cyprus to the Partnership for Peace; such veto referred to 'foreign affairs'[266] and caused criticism from political parties that the right to veto was provided simply as a bi-communal safeguard for the Turkish Cypriot Vice-President of the Republic and that therefore its exercise by the President of the Republic against a decision of a House of Representatives composed by Greek Cypriots was not in accordance with the spirit of the Constitution.

177. Furthermore, the President has the right to appoint the Attorney-General and the Deputy Attorney-General of the Republic, the Auditor-General and the Deputy Auditor-General, the Governor and the Deputy Governor of the Issuing Bank of the Republic, the members of the Public Service Commission, the Accountant-General and the Deputy Accountant-General, the Heads and Deputy Heads of the army, the police and the gendarmerie of the Republic, the judges of the Supreme Constitutional Court and the Supreme Court of Cyprus,[267] a number of commissioners, as well as the advisory board provided for in cases of emergency in accordance with Article 184 of the Constitution. More controversial is whether the President of the Republic has the right to appoint Deputy Ministers. Specific legislation has granted to him/her such right, but it has been disputed whether such legislation is consistent with the constitutional provisions which provide only for explicit powers of the President to appoint public officials, whereas the remaining

265. *See* A. Emilianides, *Parliamentary Co-Existence of Greek and Turkish Cypriots* (Epifaniou 2003, in Greek).
266. It was, however, argued that the Partnership for Peace was an international organization or pact of alliance in which both Greece and Turkey participated, so that the subject matter did not relate to 'foreign affairs' in accordance with Art. 50 of the Constitution.
267. The President also has the power to appoint the advisory board provided for in cases of Emergency in accordance with Art. 184 of the Constitution, although this has never happened in practice.

power is vested in the Council of Ministers. The President also has the right of reference to the Supreme Constitutional Court, as provided for in Article 140 or 141 of the Constitution, the right of recourse to the Supreme Constitutional Court pursuant to Articles 137, 138, 139 and 143 of the Constitution; the President also publishes in the official Gazette of the Republic the decisions of the Supreme Constitutional Court, as provided for in Articles 137, 138, 139 and 143 of the Constitution.[268]

268. The President further has the power to refer to the Supreme Court laws and decisions of the Greek Communal Chamber; however, this is in practice inapplicable due to the self-dissolution of the Greek Communal Chamber.

Chapter 3. The Legislature

§1. The Organ of State

I. The House of Representatives: Number of Representatives and Elections

178. Whereas the Constitution provides for both a House of Representatives and two Communal Chambers, acting as the legislative bodies of the Republic, since the self-dissolution of the Greek Communal Chamber and on the basis of the doctrine of necessity, all the competencies of the Communal Chambers with respect to legislative power have been effectively transferred to the House of Representatives. Accordingly, the House of Representatives has been since 1965 the sole legislative organ of the Republic of Cyprus.[269] Article 62 of the Constitution provides that the number of Representatives in the House of Representatives shall be fifty, out of which 70% shall be elected by the Greek Community and 30% shall be elected by the Turkish Community, separately from amongst their members. The proportion of 70%–30% (thirty-five Greek Representatives and fifteen Turks) stipulated in the Constitution shall be independent of any statistical data. However, the participation of Representatives from the Turkish Community in the House of Representatives lasted only for three years, from 1960 to 1963;[270] since then, the House of Representatives has been composed of Greek Representatives only.

179. Article 62 of the Constitution further provides that the number of Representatives may be altered by a resolution of the House of Representatives carried by a majority comprising two-thirds of the Representatives elected by the Greek Community and two-thirds of the Representatives elected by the Turkish Community. On 20 June 1985, the House of Representatives passed a resolution on the basis of the doctrine of necessity which increased the number of Representatives to eighty (fifty-six Greek Representatives and twenty-four Turks). Since the elections of 8 December 1985, the House of Representatives is therefore composed of fifty-six Greek Cypriot Representatives and no elections are held for the twenty-four seats of the Turkish Cypriot Representatives. The increase in the number of Representatives was considered necessary in order to enable the House of Representatives to properly carry out its functions in light of the increase in the Parliament's activities and its participation in international parliamentary organizations.[271]

---

269. *See* generally D. Melissas, *The Organization of Political Power in the Cypriot State* (A. Sakkoulas, 1996, in Greek); C. Tornaritis, *The Republic of Cyprus and Its House of Representatives* (1978); *Ibid.*, *Issues Related to the Functionality of the House of Representatives*, 4 Cyprus L. Tribune 11–15 (1974); A. Michaelides, *The House of Representatives of the Republic of Cyprus*, 60 Parliamentarian 67–71 (1979).

270. *See* A. Emilianides, *The Parliamentary Co-Existence of Greeks and Turks in Cyprus* (Epifaniou 2003, in Greek).

271. *See also* L. Papaphilippou, *The House of Representatives: Analysis of Objects and Functionality* (1980, in Greek).

180. Article 66 of the Constitution stipulates that a general election for the House of Representatives shall be held on the second Sunday of the month immediately preceding the month in which the term of office of the outgoing House expires. If an election cannot take place on the date fixed by or under this Constitution owing to extraordinary and unforeseen circumstances such as earthquake, flood, general epidemic and the like, then such election shall take place on the corresponding day of the week following. It was initially provided that when a vacancy occurs in the seat of a Representative, such vacancy shall be filled by a by-election to be held within a period not exceeding forty-five days of the occurrence of such vacancy on a date to be fixed by the House of Representatives. After the adoption of the proportional system of electoral representation, the House of Representatives tried to abolish the institution of a by-election as the means of filling the vacant seat of a Representative by amending Article 66 section 2 of the Constitution. The law was, however, declared unconstitutional as this was prior to the judicial recognition that the Constitution may be amended by virtue of the doctrine of necessity.[272]

181. By a subsequent law, the Filing of a Vacant Parliamentary Seat Law 95/86, the House of Representatives provided for succession to a parliamentary seat of the first unsuccessful candidate of the political party to which the seat belonged in the electoral district where the Representative whose seat became vacant served. The law was held to be constitutional by the majority of the Supreme Court in *Angelides v. Peta.*[273] However, the subsequent judgment of the Supreme Court in *Mavrogenis v. House of Representatives*[274] overruled the precedent of *Angelides v. Peta* as having been wrongly decided and held that the said law was in violation of Article 66 section 2 of the Constitution. Accordingly, the House of Representatives amended the Constitution by the Third Amendment of the Constitution Law 115(I)/96 which provides that 'a vacant Parliamentary seat shall be filled within a period not exceeding forty-five days from the occurrence of such vacancy as provided by law'. A subsequent Law 118(I)/96 amended the Election of Members of the House of Representatives Law 72/1979 and reiterated that the first unsuccessful candidate of the political party to which the seat belonged in the electoral district where the Representative whose seat became vacant served would succeed to the vacant parliamentary seat. The law was held to be constitutional in *Koulountis.*[275]

182. At the parliamentary elections of 2016, the Chairwoman of the Solidarity Movement, following her declaration as an elected Member of the House of Representatives, decided to remain an MEP and accordingly decline the seat in the House of Representatives. In accordance with the electoral system, the first unsuccessful candidate of the Solidarity Movement, Giorgos Papadopoulos, was declared as a Member of the House of Representatives. A candidate from DISY challenged the election of the runner-up as a Representative. The Supreme Court held that the parliamentary term begins only with the assumption of duties pursuant to Article 69

272. [1986] 3 CLR 1439.
273. [1988] 1 CLR 173 (in Greek).
274. [1996] 1 CLR 315 (in Greek).
275. *Koulountis v. The House of Representatives* [1997] 1 CLR 1026 (in Greek).

of the Constitution. Whereas Law 72/79, as amended, provided that a vacant seat during the parliamentary term would be filled by the first unsuccessful candidate of the political party to which the elected Representative belonged, there was no provision with regard to the time prior to the beginning of the parliamentary term, i.e., from the day of election to the first meeting of the new House of Representatives.

183. It was accordingly held that the vacuum in Law 72/79 could not be filled by reasoning by analogy and accordingly by interpretation of the provisions of Law 72/79 as applying by analogy also to a vacant seat prior to the beginning of the parliamentary term. It was held that in the absence of an express legislative provision and authorization, it was not possible to declare that the runner-up of Solidarity would be elected as a Representative.[276] It is submitted that the judgment of the Supreme Court was not a correct one. Since there was a vacuum in Law 72/79, it was open to the General Commissioner for Elections to apply interpretation by analogy in order to fill the vacuum. The main objective of the electoral legislation is to apply a proportional electoral system, whereby each political party would safeguard parliamentary seats by virtue of the percentage of votes it has secured. The teleological interpretation of Law 72/79 could lead to the conclusion that the runner-up of the same political party should be elected in case of a vacant seat.

184. Following the judgment of the Supreme Court annulling the election of Papadopoulos, the majority of the House of Representatives enacted legislation by virtue of which the rule that a vacant seat would be filled by the runner-up of the political party to which the elected Representative belonged, would also apply to seats which became vacant prior to the beginning of the parliamentary term. By a majority of 7-6, the Supreme Court annulled the election of Papadopoulos once again and held that Articles 66 and 71 of the Constitution refer to a vacant seat and not to a seat which had never been filled, to begin with. It was thus held that following the decline of the seat by the Chairwoman of the Solidarity Movement, the seat never lawfully belonged to the Solidarity Movement and accordingly the House of Representatives could not be filled in the same manner as a vacant seat. It was further held that where there is no vacant seat, the Constitution imposes the application of the fundamental democratic principle of electing the Representatives by general elections by virtue of Articles 55 and 56 of the Constitution.[277]

185. With all due respect to the majority of the Supreme Court, the abovementioned judgment is incomprehensible. The Constitution does not distinguish between a vacant seat and a seat that has never been filled, to begin with. Nowhere in the Constitution is there a provision which refers to another method of filling a seat after the elections, other than in cases where there is a vacant seat. The majority acknowledges this fact but refers to Articles 55 and 56 of the Constitution which refer to the general elections. However, in this case, the general elections have

276. *Michaelides and another v. General Commissioner for Elections and others*, App. 2/2016, Judgment of 31 May 2017 (in Greek).

277. *Michaelides and another v. General Commissioner for Elections and others*, App. 1/2017, Judgment of 30 Apr. 2018 (in Greek).

already been held and accordingly this reference cannot lead to any solutions. Furthermore, pursuant to Law 72/79, the parliamentary seat was indeed secured by the Solidarity Movement. The electoral law first determines how many parliamentary seats are secured for each political party and in which electoral districts and then proceeds to fill the seats. There was no challenge to the Solidarity Movement securing the seat. Accordingly, the finding of the Supreme Court that the Solidarity Movement had not secured the seat is a wrong one. Following the new judgment of the Supreme Court, the House of Representatives enacted new legislation pursuant to which the seat would be given once again to Papadopoulos. The President of the Republic referred the law to the Supreme Court as unconstitutional; the Supreme Court once again held by majority that the Law was unconstitutional.[278]

186. The House of Representatives eventually amended Article 66 § 2 of the Constitution with the Twelfth Constitutional Amendment, Law 128(I)/2019. The amended Article 66 § 2 provided that seats which have not been filled or which have been declined are filled as provided by Law. The electoral law provided that such seats were filled by the first unsuccessful candidate of the same party. Law 128(I)/19 was intended to apply with regard to the Solidarity Movement seat. However, in an unprecedented decision, the majority of the Supreme Court held that Law 128(I)/19 was unconstitutional. Although the Court acknowledged that in order to annul once again the election of Papadopoulos, it would have to declare a constitutional provision, as amended, as unconstitutional, it did so relying on the Basic Structure Doctrine as applied in India.[279] The majority of the Court held that the constitutional amendment attempted to usurp the rights of the people to elect their Representatives and that, accordingly, they threatened the basic structure of the Constitution of Cyprus.[280]

187. The above-mentioned judgment has been harshly criticized.[281] The Constitution of Cyprus is an extremely rigid constitutional instrument, which explicitly provides a large list of constitutional provisions which are not subject to amendment. There is no room for introducing a 'basic structure' doctrine. Effectively, the Supreme Court has introduced additional constitutional provisions which are not subject to amendment contrary to the text of the Constitution itself. Moreover, as the minority of the Supreme Court also noted, the constitutional amendment aimed to rectify the problem created by the judgments of the Supreme Court itself which led to the House of Representatives not having the constitutionally prescribed fifty-six Representatives. The constitutional amendment and the organic law applying it simply applied the will of the people who had already expressed themselves in the general elections and who had already granted the seat to the Solidarity Movement

278. *President of the Republic v. House of Representatives*, App. 4/2018, Judgment of 19 Mar. 2019 (in Greek).
279. *Kesavanda Bharati v. State of Kerala* AIR 1973 S.C.1461Q (1973) 4 SCC 225.
280. *Michaelides and another v. General Commissioner for Elections and others*, App. 1/2019, Judgment of 29 Oct. 2019 (in Greek).
281. A. Emilianides, *The Judgment on the 56th Seat*, dikaiosyni, 30 Oct. 2020 (in Greek), available in https://dikaiosyni.com/katigories/arthra/iapofasi-gia-tin-56i-edra/. *See also* C. Kombos, *Cypriot Constitutional Law* 554ff (Nomiki Vivliothiki 2022, in Greek).

in accordance with the electoral legislation. The judgment of the majority of the Supreme Court effectively failed to comply with the electoral law and referred to the possibility of alternate elections despite the fact that these were not provided in the Constitution or the electoral law as an option.

II. The Right to Vote

188. Article 31 of the Constitution provides that every citizen has, subject to the provisions of this Constitution and any electoral law of the Republic, the right to vote in any election held under this Constitution or any such law.[282] Thus, the electorate is comprised of citizens of the Republic and is a direct organ of the State.[283] Article 63 section 1 of the Constitution further provides that every citizen of the Republic who has attained the age of 17 years and has such residential qualifications as may be prescribed by the Electoral Law shall have the right to be registered as an elector in either the Greek or the Turkish electoral list. Article 63 initially provided that a citizen ought to have attained the age of 21 years in order to have the right to be registered as an elector; however, the age limit was lowered to 18 by the Second Amendment of the Constitution Law 106(I)/2006, and further lowered to 17 by the Twentieth Amendment of the Constitution Law 67(I)/2025. Article 63 section 2 of the Constitution further specifies that no person shall be qualified to be registered as an elector who is disqualified for such registration by virtue of the Electoral Law. No other requirements, such as financial, social or educational criteria, may be constitutionally tolerated.[284]

189. The Election of Representatives of the House of Representatives Law 72/79,[285] as amended, qualifies the residential requirements for having the right to be registered as an elector, by providing that a person should have his/her ordinary (or habitual) residence in Cyprus for a period of six months immediately prior to a date set by the Minister of Interior as the date of possession of the relevant qualification, which is promulgated in the Official Gazette. Residence has, in general, been interpreted by the Supreme Court as denoting some degree of permanence; whereas this should not necessarily mean that the person concerned has a home of his/her own, it generally means that he has settled headquarters in Cyprus.[286] Residence thus implies actual physical presence in a particular place with a degree of

282. C. Tornaritis, *The Right to Vote and Its Exercise in Cyprus*, 1 Cyprus L. Rev. 100–103 (1983) (in Greek).

283. *Pingouras v. Police* [1987] 2 CLR 1. C. Tornaritis, *The Electorate as an Organ of the State* 5ff (1981, in Greek) correctly rejects the view that the electorate of each Community is a separate organ of the State. *See also Celaleddin v. Council of Ministers* 5 RSCC 108.

284. *See* D. Melissas, *The Organization of Political Power in the Cypriot State* 77 (A. Sakkoulas 1996, in Greek).

285. *See* A. Papacharalambous, *Cypriot Election Law for Members of Parliament*, 1 Paneuropean L. Rev. 141–145 (1997).

286. *Sayegh* [1990] 1 CLR 773 (in Greek), adopted by the Appellate Family Court in *Ajero* [2006] 1 CLR 1165 (in Greek). *See also Koraka v. Georghiou* [2004] 1 CLR 1935 (in Greek), *Antoniou v. Theodorou* [2004] 1 CLR 1944 (in Greek), *Razis v. Republic* [1979] 1 CLR 127, *Rossides v. Republic* [1984] 1 CLR 1482 interpreting the term in the context of electoral applications.

permanence; temporary sojourn or casual presence in transit, even for a substantial time, does not amount to residence. A person is ordinarily resident if they are normally residing in Cyprus, apart from temporary or occasional absences, and their residence has been adopted voluntarily and for settled purposes as part of the regular order of their life for the time being; decisions about whether a person is; ordinarily resident will need to be based on all the circumstances of the particular case.[287] A person can be ordinarily resident in more than one country; therefore, if a person divides their time between two different countries and can be said to live in both with a settled purpose, it shall be held as a matter of law that they are ordinarily resident in both.[288]

190. Whereas Article 63 of the Constitution provides that the members of the Greek Community shall only be registered in the Greek electoral list and the members of the Turkish Community shall only be registered in the Turkish electoral list, this is no longer the case. Following the case of *Ibrahim Aziz*,[289] the Law on the Exercise of the Right to Vote and be Elected by Members of the Turkish community with Habitual Residence in the Free Areas of the Republic (Temporary Provisions) 2(I)/2006 was enacted; this enabled Cypriot nationals who belong to the Turkish Cypriot community and had their habitual residence in the government-controlled areas of Cyprus to vote and to stand for election. Law 2(I)/2006 was enacted by virtue of the doctrine of necessity to effectively provide for a unitary electoral list. The provisions of Law 2(I)/2006 were challenged by two Turkish Cypriots, Ali Erel and Mustafa Damdelen. Before the parliamentary elections of 21 May 2006, the applicants submitted seventy-eight applications on behalf of other Turkish Cypriots and themselves to the Minister of the Interior of the Republic of Cyprus requesting to be placed on a separate electoral list, namely, a Turkish electoral list, in order to vote and stand for the parliamentary elections. The applicants claimed that Law 2(I)/06 was contrary to the Constitution.

191. Their applications were refused by the Minister, who noted that due to the irregular situation pertaining to Cyprus, the relevant Constitutional provisions concerning separate elections had become impossible to implement in practice. The applicants filed an application to the Supreme Court, which, however, dismissed it;[290] the Supreme Court noted that after the withdrawal of the Turkish community from the State organs in 1963 following a decision of its leadership, the relevant Articles of the Constitution providing for separate elections by the two communities had become impossible to implement in practice. The Supreme Court further noted that the applicants had their permanent residence in the northern part of Cyprus, which was occupied by and under the control of Turkish troops. They could not therefore claim a right to vote or to stand for election on the basis of the Court's ruling in the *Aziz* case and Law 2(I)/2006. The Applicants subsequently filed an

287. *Gout v. Cimitian* [1922] AC 105, *Lewis v. Lewis* [1965] 1 All ER 375.
288. *Ikimi v. Ikimi* [2001] EWCA Civ 873, [2002] Fam 72, *Armstrong v. Armstrong* [2003] EWHC 777 (Fam), [2003] 2 FLR 375, FD. *See*, however, *Marinos v. Marinos* [2007] EWHC 2047 (Fam) for the interpretation of habitual residence under the provisions of Brussels IIa Regulation.
289. *Aziz v. Cyprus*, App. 69949/01, Judgment of 22 Jun. 2004.
290. *Erel and Damdelen v. Republic* [2007] 3 CLR 186 (in Greek).

application before the ECtHR but such was also dismissed.[291] The ECtHR noted that the ECHR does not impose an obligation on States to set up separate electoral lists and carry out separate elections and recognized that in view of the irregular situation prevailing in Cyprus, the constitutional provisions requiring separate elections have been rendered ineffective. The ECtHR further reiterated that having to satisfy a residence or length of residence requirement in order to have or exercise the right to vote in elections does not constitute, in principle, an arbitrary restriction of the right to vote.

192. Law 72/79 provides that a person may be disqualified from voting by a decision of the court convicting him/her for a number of electoral offences.[292] In *Demetriades*, which, however, referred to disqualification on the basis of the pre-existing legal regime, the Supreme Court held that since, at all material times, the applicant was in prison serving a sentence of imprisonment after he had been convicted of a criminal offence, he could not be treated as an elector inscribed on the relevant electoral roll or a person claiming to have had the right to vote at the election concerned.[293] It is further noted that a person has to register in the electoral roll of a given electoral district in order to have the right to vote in accordance with section 7 section 1 of Law 72/79. Such requirement is formal rather than a substantive one.[294]

193. Section 7 section 2 of Law 72/79 used to provide that the exercise of the right to vote is obligatory. In *Pingouras,* the Appellant omitted to exercise his right to vote at the elections held for the election of Village Authorities and elected members of an Improvement Board, and as a result, he was convicted for failing to discharge his electoral right. He argued that compulsory voting was inconsistent with the right to vote safeguarded by Article 31 of the Constitution; however, such arguments were dismissed by the Supreme Court. The Court noted that in modern democracies, the representative system prevails. All citizens have the right to participate in the exercise of political power through the representatives whom they elect in accordance with the law. In this way, the electoral body constitutes the totality of the citizens and it is collectively a direct organ of the State. Since the right to vote is an exercise of a State function, compulsory voting is not unconstitutional.[295] With all due respect, it is submitted that Article 31 of the Constitution safeguards the right to vote; a right implies both positive and negative aspects, thus implying that the right not to vote should also be safeguarded. It is therefore submitted that, contrary to the above judgment of the Supreme Court, compulsory voting ought to have been considered unconstitutional. Compulsory voting was eventually repealed by Law 108(I)/2017.

---

291. *Erel and Damdelen v. Cyprus*, App. 39973/07, Judgment of 14 Dec. 2010.
292. Sections 6, 37, 42, 54 and 55 of Law 72/79.
293. *Demetriades v. Diglis* [1983] 1 CLR 575. *See also* L. Loucaides, *Do the Prisoners Have a Right to Exercise Their Right to Vote?*, in *Ibid.*, *Topics of Cypriot Law* vol. I, 149–151 (1982, in Greek).
294. D. Melissas, *The Organization of Political Power in the Cypriot State* 78 (A. Sakkoulas 1996, in Greek).
295. *Pingouras v. Police* [1987] 2 CLR 1, cited with approval in *Efthymiou* [1991] 3 CLR 299 (in Greek).

III. The Electoral System

194. While the Constitution does not specify electoral districts, the electoral law has, since the establishment of the Republic in 1960, divided the territory of the Republic into six electoral districts (Nicosia, Limassol, Famagusta, Larnaca, Paphos, Kyrenia); their size and boundaries correspond to those of the Republic's six administrative districts (section 3 of the Election of Representatives of the House of Representatives Law 72/79). The division into the aforementioned six electoral districts continues despite the Turkish occupation of the northern part of Cyprus in 1974. Currently, twenty out of the fifty-six Greek Cypriot seats are allocated to the district of Nicosia, twelve to Limassol, eleven to Famagusta, six to Larnaca, four to Paphos and three to Kyrenia. It has further been accepted that the Constitution does not provide for a specific electoral system. Accordingly, the choice of an electoral system is up to the House of Representatives, so long as the constitutional provisions are respected. The matter of political choices offered to the elector is, in principle, within the discretion of the legislator.[296] However, some fundamental principles, such as the secrecy of the ballot or the directness of the voting, have to be safeguarded. The House of Representatives initially introduced a majoritarian electoral system which gave the majority of the seats to the party which had the plurality of votes in each electoral district. Undeniably, such a system was not a fully democratic one if one considers the fact that Cyprus is a small country with only six electoral districts and which has a system of Presidential Democracy.

195. In the first parliamentary elections of 31 July 1960, AKEL, a political party which was represented by more than 30% of the overall voters of the Greek Cypriot Community, managed to elect five out of the thirty-five Greek Representatives, only because the dominant Patriotic Front restricted itself in nominating only thirty candidates for the thirty-five seats; this was in accordance with a political agreement between the then-President Makarios and AKEL.[297] The subsequent election of 5 July 1970 confirmed the problematic nature of the electoral system, which led to unjust and unequal allocation of seats which did not correspond to the actual power of political parties.[298] It was therefore correctly noted that the majoritarian system hindered the free and democratic expression of the will of the Cypriot people. In the elections of 5 September 1976, DISY did not elect a single Representative,

---

296. *See* for a discussion A. Pantelides, *Legal Opinion on the Question of the Constitutionality of the System for the Election of the Members of the House of Representatives*, 4 Cyprus L. Tribune 29–36 (1976, in Greek); *Ibid.*, *Electoral Systems*, in *Aspects of Cypriot Law* vol. II, 183–215 (Asselia 1982, in Greek); L. Clerides, *The Cypriot Current Electoral System and the Various Systems Abroad*, 1 Cyprus L. Tribune 8–16 (1977) (in Greek).
297. G. Clerides, *My Disposition* vol. I, 115ff (Alitheia 1988, in Greek); A. Fantis, *Cyprus Problem 1960–1974: In Search of the Truth* vol. A, 39ff (1999, in Greek).
298. *See* A. Emilianides, *Parliamentary History of the Republic of Cyprus 1964–1976* (Aigaion 2007, in Greek).

despite the fact that it had secured 27% of the overall votes. Law 72/1979 eventually replaced the majoritarian system and introduced a system of qualified proportional representation,[299] and subsequently, a system of effectively simple proportional representation by Law 11(I)/1996.[300]

196. The proportional representation system currently in force is a relatively straightforward one. Candidates may participate either individually or in a coalition; such coalition could be a one-party coalition, a multi-party coalition or even a coalition of independent candidates. Voters who intend to vote for an individual candidate simply vote for such candidate. On the contrary, voters who vote a coalition, first select the list of the political party or coalition of parties they prefer, and then, within the list, they can mark the individual candidates they wish.[301] Party leaders or other candidates heading a coalition do not require a preference mark to be elected. The electoral quota is found by applying a simple Hare quota, namely by dividing the number of valid votes cast in each constituency by the number of seats of such constituency. The number of seats per political party or coalition is found by dividing the number of valid votes of each party or coalition by the electoral quota (First Distribution).

197. The remaining seats are then distributed (Second Distribution) among the political parties which secured at least 2/56 of all valid votes in the Republic, namely at least 3.6% (for coalition of two parties, the requirement is for 10% of the total votes, whereas for the coalition of more than two parties, it is 20% of the total votes); such are distributed on the basis of the votes of each party or coalition which had not been used in order to secure a seat during the First Distribution. Any remaining seats are then distributed, one each, to each party or coalition on the basis of their votes which had not been used in order to secure a seat during the First or Second Distribution (Third Distribution); this is subject to the rule that a party should have secured at least 3.6% of all valid votes in the Republic in order to participate in the Third Distribution (the percentages required for coalitions of more parties remain the same as in the Second Distribution). Initially, the electoral threshold was set at 1.8%, i.e., 1/56 of the votes. However, the President of DISY proposed in 2015 that the electoral threshold be raised to 5%; following extensive debate, the political parties compromised on amending the electoral threshold to 3.6%, i.e., 2/56 of the votes. Accordingly, a political party which secures entry into the House of Representatives shall elect at least two Representatives. By virtue of Article 85 of the Constitution, any question with regard to the qualifications of candidates for election and election petitions shall be adjudicated by the Supreme Constitutional Court sitting in plenary.

299. Such system applied in the parliamentary elections of 24/5/1981, 8/12/1985, 19/5/1991.
300. Such system applied in the parliamentary elections of 26/5/1996 onwards.
301. They can mark one preference for every four seats to be filled in their constituency; if the constituency has less than four seats, then they can mark only one preference.

IV. The President of the House of Representatives

198. Article 72 of the Constitution provides that the President of the House of Representatives shall be a Greek and shall be elected by the Greek Representatives, whereas the Vice-President shall be a Turk elected by the Turkish Representatives. Since 1963 and due to the constitutional crisis, the seat of the Turkish Cypriot Vice-President of the House of Representatives remains vacant. The President of the House is elected at the beginning of each term for the whole period of the term of office of the House, irrespective of whether the parliamentary balance has, in the meantime, changed due to intervening events (e.g., the resignation of Representatives in order to be appointed as Ministers, death of Representatives, the fact that Representatives have switched political parties). The office of the President of the House of Representatives is an extremely important one. In accordance with Rule 8 of the Rules of Procedure of the House, the President of the House shall keep the order during the sittings of the House, shall ensure compliance with Rules of Procedure and shall conduct the proceedings in accordance with the Rules, shall put the matters under debate to the vote, shall announce the results of the voting, shall express the feelings of the House and generally, shall see that the deliberations of the House are smoothly carried out. Moreover, the President of the House shall speak from his/her chair when the subject of the debate is related to the Rules of Procedure, or in order to explain where the matter under debate stands, or to provide the necessary information, or to ask a speaker to keep to the subject under debate or to call to order those deviating from the Rules.

199. The President shall appoint and exercise supervision over the Clerks and Administrative Clerks in the performance of their functions and shall be the Head of the office of the House and shall order payments as provided in the budget of the House. Furthermore, he shall represent the House at official manifestations held within and outside the building of the House and at official ceremonies and receptions, either when the House is in session or after the end of the session. The President of the House shall also address, on behalf of the House, the President of the Republic and other Officers of the State. Finally, the President of the House deputizes for the President of the Republic in case of temporary absence or temporary incapacity to perform his/her duties, by virtue of Article 36 section 2 of the Constitution. The two Clerks and two Administrative Clerks of the House are elected from among the Representatives. The Clerks shall assist the President in conducting the proceedings of the House, shall read before the House any document deemed by the President that should be read, shall register in order to request the names of the Representatives asking for the right to speak, shall assist the President during voting and shall write down the decisions taken. The Administrative Clerks shall assist the President in the maintenance of order in the House and shall see that all directions of the President are carried out, especially those related to the maintenance of order during the meetings.

200. The Constitution and the Rules of Procedure of the House do not contain any provisions stipulating the procedure of electing the President of the House of Representatives. However, there have been occasions where no candidate has received a sufficient number of votes so as to secure the majority of the votes of the Representatives. The House has decided to resolve such deadlock by adopting the following procedure: each political party may nominate a candidate. The eldest Representative, acting as the presiding Representative, puts forward the name of each candidate in turn and asks who votes in favour of such candidacy and who votes against it; voting is done by open ballot. A candidate is elected if he secures the absolute majority of the votes of the Representatives who are present and voting. If no candidate secures such absolute majority, the election shall be repeated and the candidate who secures at least two-fifths of those present and voting shall be elected. If no candidate receives the required number of votes, then the election shall be held for a third time and the candidate receiving the relative majority of the votes of those present and voting shall be elected.

201. In the parliamentary elections of 1985, there were four candidates for the office of the President of the House of Representatives, namely Glafcos Clerides of DISY, George Ladas of DIKO, Ezekias Papaioannou of AKEL and Vasos Lyssarides of EDEK. During the first two rounds of voting, Clerides secured nineteen votes, Ladas secured sixteen votes, Papaioannou secured fourteen votes and Lyssarides secured six votes. Since no candidate was elected, the election was held for a third time. In the third round, each candidacy was put forward in turn: accordingly, Clerides secured nineteen votes, then Ladas secured sixteen votes, and then the Representatives of DIKO (who had already voted in favour of Ladas) voted in favour of Lyssarides, who thus secured twenty-two votes and was elected as President of the House. The Representatives of DISY questioned the election, arguing that the representatives of DIKO had effectively voted twice in a single election, once for their leader and once for Lyssarides. The matter came before the Supreme Court in *Ladas*.[302] It was held that the House of Representatives may regulate its own procedure not only by its Standing Orders but also, whenever this is necessary, by special decisions, which have the force of Standing Orders.

202. It was thus held that the House of Representatives may, when electing its President, prescribe, by a decision for this purpose, a special procedure for the election of its President in case none of the candidates secures the majority, which is required by Article 78 section 1 of the Constitution, provided of course that the decision of the House of Representatives regarding the special procedure will be passed by the majority which is required by Article 78 section 1 of the Constitution. It was accordingly held that the House of Representatives had the power to regulate its own procedure. The judgment has been criticized as tolerating a system which gave the Representatives the opportunity to exercise their right to vote more than once in the context of a single election.[303] It has been further suggested that the procedure for electing the President of the House ought to have been expressly provided for in the Rules of Procedure of the House.[304]

302. [1985] 3 CLR 2845.

303. A. Markides, *The Republic of Cyprus*, in *Constitutional Law of 10 EU Member States* I-41 (Kortmann et al. eds, Kluwer 2006).

304. D. Melissas, *The Organization of Political Power in the Cypriot State* 97ff (A. Sakkoulas 1996, in Greek).

203. The decision of 1985 regarding the procedure for electing a President of the House was followed in the elections for a President of the House of Representatives on 2 June 2011. Yiannakis Omirou, then Chairman of EDEK, was elected in the third round with twenty-eight votes, whereas Marios Karoyian, then Chairman of DIKO, secured twenty-seven votes; Yiorgos Perdikis of the Green Party who had received only his own vote in the first two rounds abstained in the third round. It should be noted that Representative of DIKO Zacharias Koulias voted against the candidate of his own party and in favour of Omirou and was subsequently expelled from his party. The procedure was also adopted during the elections for a President of the House of Representatives on 2 June 2016. Dimitris Syllouris from the Solidarity Movement was elected with twenty-one votes, as he was supported during the third round by the eighteen Representatives of DISY and the three Representatives of the Solidarity Movement. The eighteen Representatives of DISY had, during all three rounds of election, also voted for DISY President Averof Neophytou. The Chairman of EDEK, Marinos Sizopoulos, was supported during the third round by the Representatives of DIKO, EDEK, the Citizens Alliance and the Green Party and secured seventeen votes, whereas the Secretary General of AKEL, Andros Kyprianou, received sixteen votes from the Representatives of AKEL. The two Representatives of ELAM abstained.

204. An issue has arisen whether the order of voting should begin from the candidate supported by the smallest parliamentary party or from the candidate supported by the largest parliamentary party. For years, the order began from the largest party, but this changed in 2016, with the order beginning from the smallest party. In the 2021 elections for President of the House of Representatives, the order of voting was of significance. AKEL and DIKO had, in principle, agreed to vote for a common candidate during the third round of elections. However, in the second round, DIPA and ELAM supported the candidacy of Annita Demetriou, the candidate from DISY, who thus secured the required two-fifth of those present and voting. Since DISY was the largest parliamentary party, Annita Demetriou was the last candidate whose name was put forward in the second round, surprising AKEL and DIKO. If AKEL and DIKO had known in advance that DIPA and ELAM would support Demetriou in the second round, they would not have waited until the third round to vote for their common candidate, and they would have secured the relative majority in the second round of elections, instead of Demetriou.

205. In case of any vacancy of the office of the President of the House, Article 72 section 3 of the Constitution provides that an election should take place with all due speed and, if necessary, at an extraordinary session. In case of temporary absence or pending the filling of a vacancy, the functions of the President of the House are performed by the eldest Representative, unless the Representatives of such Community should otherwise decide. A question arose whether the Representatives could a priori decide that the President of the House shall be deputized by a given Representative (not being the eldest) in case of future temporary absence; it was submitted by AKEL that the issue should be decided each time the need to deputize the President of the House arose and not for an indefinite period of time. The Supreme Court held, by majority, that Article 72 section 3 of the Constitution properly interpreted did not restrict the House from deciding a priori that a Representative would deputize the President of the House if the need arose in the future.[305]

§2. Legal Status

206. Article 65 of the Constitution stipulates that the term of office of the House of Representatives shall be for a period of five years. The outgoing House shall continue in office until the newly elected House assumes office. The term of office of the first House of Representatives began on the date of the coming into operation of the Constitution. It should be noted that the term of office of the first House of Representatives was unconstitutionally renewed for additional five years; the term was successively renewed five times for a period of one year, each time on the ground that holding parliamentary elections at a time of a constitutional crisis would not be appropriate and that the Turkish side might take advantage of such elections in order to proceed with its aims to divide the island.[306] This effective doubling of the term of the House of Representatives, while justified on the basis of the doctrine of necessity, was highly irregular. The first House of Representatives eventually dissolved itself on 29 May 1970. The second House of Representatives also renewed its term for an additional year, citing the consequences of the Turkish invasion and the negotiations for a solution to the Cyprus problem.[307] Since 1976, the term of office of each House of Representatives has been five years, in accordance with the constitutional provisions.

207. Article 67 of the Constitution provides that the House of Representatives may dissolve itself only by its own decision carried by an absolute majority.[308] Any such decision shall provide for the date of the holding of the general election, which shall not be less than thirty days and not more than forty days from the date of such decision, and also for the date of the first meeting of the newly elected House which shall not be later than fifteen days after such general election and until such date the outgoing House shall continue to be in office. The term of office of the House of Representatives to be elected after dissolution shall be for the unexpired period of the term of office of the dissolved House. In case of dissolution within the last year of the five-year term of office, a general election for the House of Representatives shall take place both for the unexpired part of the term of office of the dissolved House, during which any session of the newly elected House shall be considered to be an extraordinary session and for the subsequent five years' term of office. In accordance with Article 68 of the Constitution, whenever a House of Representatives continues to be in office until the assumption of office by a newly elected

305. *Christofias and Others* [1996] 3 CLR 421 (in Greek).
306. Laws 45/65, 49/66, 50/67, 87/68, 58/69.
307. *See* A. Emilianides, *Parliamentary History of the Republic of Cyprus 1964–1976* (Aigaion 2007, in Greek).
308. It is further provided that such majority should include at least one-third of the Representatives elected by the Turkish Community, although such provision does not apply in practice in light of the abnormal situation prevailing in the island.

House, such House shall not have the power to make any laws or take any decisions on any matter except only in case of urgent and exceptional unforeseen circumstances to be specifically stated in the relevant law or decision.

208. A person shall be qualified to be a candidate for election as a Representative, in accordance with Article 64 of the Constitution, if at the time of the election that person: (a) is a citizen of the Republic, (b) has attained the age of twenty-one years,[309] (c) has not been convicted, on or after the date of the coming into operation of the Constitution, of an offence involving dishonesty or moral turpitude or is not under any disqualification imposed by a competent court for any electoral offence, and (d) is not suffering from a mental disease incapacitating such person from acting as a Representative. The office of a Representative shall be incompatible, by virtue of Article 70 of the Constitution, with that of a Minister or of a member of a Communal Chamber or of a member of any municipal council, including a Mayor or of a member of the armed or security forces of the Republic or with a public or municipal office[310] or in the case of a Representative elected by the Turkish Community, of a religious functionary. It should be noted that the incompatibilities referred to above do not relate to eligibility for election; accordingly, a Minister or a Mayor may well be candidates for election as a Representative so long as they resign from the post of Minister or Mayor if elected as a Representative.[311]

209. A Representative before assuming duties shall, in accordance with Article 69 of the Constitution, make the following affirmation, in the House of Representatives and at a public meeting thereof: 'I do solemnly affirm faith to, and respect for, the Constitution and the laws made thereunder, the preservation of the independence and the territorial integrity, of the Republic of Cyprus.' Article 71 of the Constitution further provides that the seat of a Representative shall become vacant upon his/her death, written resignation, conviction for an offence involving dishonesty or moral turpitude or imposition of disqualification by a competent court or the suffering of a mental disease incapacitating such person from acting as a Representative or upon his/her becoming a holder of an incompatible office. The immunities of the Representatives are specified in Article 83 of the Constitution. It is expressly provided that Representatives shall not be liable to civil or criminal proceedings in respect of any statement made or vote given by them in the House of Representatives. This corresponds to the idea that if Representatives were liable for the exercise of their parliamentary duties, then they would be unable to properly exercise their powers.

309. The age required to stand for elections was initially twenty-five years of age, but was amended pursuant to the Fourteenth Amendment of the Constitution, Law 161(I)/2019. *See*, however, A. Emilianides, *Do Minimum Age Requirements Violate the Right to Stand for Election under the European Convention on Human Rights?*, 5 European Human Rights L. Rev. 670–683 (2009).

310. Public office is defined for the purposes of this Article as any office of profit in the service of the Republic or of a Communal Chamber the emoluments of which are under the control either of the Republic or of a Communal Chamber, and includes any office in any public corporation or public utility body.

311. Correctly A. Markides, *The Republic of Cyprus*, in *Constitutional Law of 10 EU Member States* I-44 (Kortmann et al. eds, Kluwer 2006).

210. A Representative cannot be prosecuted, arrested or imprisoned, without the leave of the Supreme Court, so long as he/she continues to be a Representative. Such leave is not required in the case of an offence punishable with death or imprisonment for five years or more in case the offender is taken in the act. In such a case, the Supreme Court, being notified forthwith by the competent authority, decides whether it should grant or refuse leave for the continuation of the prosecution or detention so long as he/she continues to be a Representative. If the Supreme Court refuses to grant leave for the prosecution of a Representative, the period during which the Representative cannot thus be prosecuted shall not be reckoned for the purposes of any period of prescription for the offence in question. If the Supreme Court refuses to grant leave for the enforcement of a sentence of imprisonment imposed on a Representative by a competent court, the enforcement of such sentence shall be postponed until he/she ceases to be a Representative.

211. In *Georghiou*, the Supreme Court held that an application for leave to be granted should not be automatically granted in all instances; in deciding whether to grant it or refuse it, there must be taken into account the object of the relevant competence as well as the nature of the immunity from prosecution of a Member of the House of Representatives, the requirements of public interest in each particular case, the nature and seriousness of the offence in respect of which leave is sought to prosecute and the particular circumstances of each individual case. Furthermore, it has to be examined whether the prosecution is politically motivated, as this is a ground on which leave to prosecute may be refused. The Supreme Court shall not decide whether the evidential material is sufficient in order to establish the guilt of the Representative in respect of the offences concerned, since this is a task for the criminal court; rather, the Supreme Court should decide whether on the basis of the material placed before the Court, the prosecution of the Representative is prima facie warranted in law and in fact, in the sense that it is not arbitrary and not whether his/her conviction on the strength of such material should be warranted.[312] In a subsequent appeal by Georghiou against his criminal conviction on forgery, it was held that Article 83 section 2 properly interpreted, requires the police to seek leave of the Supreme Court before obtaining a statement under caution from a Representative, since such statement constituted an act of prosecution; accordingly, failure to secure the prior leave of the Supreme Court invalidated the statement which could not be presented as evidence.[313]

212. Following Georghiou's conviction, the Attorney-General applied before the Supreme Court for a decision that the conviction of the Representative had automatically caused the loss of the representative capacity so as to be possible to execute the sentence of imprisonment on him. The Supreme Court held, by majority, that since the respondent had been convicted of offences involving moral turpitude, his seat had become vacant upon conviction, and consequently, no leave by the Supreme Court was required in order to carry out his imprisonment; the fact that an appeal was pending against conviction and that the House of Representatives had

312. *Georgiou* [1983] 2 CLR 1.
313. *Georghiou v. Republic* [1984] 2 CLR 65.

never reached a formal decision that Georghiou had lost his seat were not considered material factors in the decision of the majority.[314] Furthermore, in *Sampson,* the Supreme Court held that the fact that Nicos Sampson had taken over the office of 'President of the Republic' during the 1974 coup had immediately and *ipso facto* deprived him of his seat as a Representative and accordingly, no leave of the Court was required for his leave and prosecution; since a Representative ceases to be a member of the House when lawfully becoming President of the Republic in accordance with Articles 70 and 71 of the Constitution, this applies *a fortiori* for a Representative who has taken over the office of President of the Republic unconstitutionally, as a result of a coup.[315]

213. In *Sarikas,* the Attorney-General of the Republic applied for leave to investigate and/or arrest and/or prosecute and/or imprison Representative Phidias Sarikas who was accused of crimes of corruption. Sarikas filed no objection; the Supreme Court held, however, that in applications of this kind, the Court should be satisfied that it should exercise its powers irrespective of whether there is an objection or not. The Supreme Court held by a majority of 7-4 that it could grant the leave for all stages of the investigation and prosecution that might be potentially needed with one single application and there was no need to separately apply for each stage of the procedure. The dissenting judgment noted that an application for leave for imprisonment ought to have been submitted only at the stage when the Supreme Court would have particular knowledge of the offences and imposed penalty; it was premature to determine whether the public interest would be served by granting a leave for execution of a penalty of imprisonment.[316]

214. The subsequent *Themistocleous* application differed from all previous similar cases because the alleged offences were not, individually considered, of a serious nature, since they all related to traffic offences. In case of conviction, the Representative would still maintain his seat. The Supreme Court, however, held that leave should be granted in all cases where there is no indication that the prosecution of the Representative is based on either political motive or motive unrelated to the offences. Since the application was based on genuine grounds and there were indications of repeated violation of the legislation by the Representative, there were no public interest grounds for not granting the leave. Accordingly, the leave was granted for all stages of the potential prosecution, including imprisonment, similarly to the ratio of the above-mentioned *Sarikas.*[317]

215. Article 84 of the Constitution stipulates that Representatives receive remuneration defined by law from the Public Revenue. However, it is expressly provided that any increase of such remuneration shall not become operative during the term of office of the House of Representatives in which such increase has been made.

---

314. *Attorney-General v. Georghiou* [1984] 2 CLR 251. *See also Rodosthenous v. Republic* [1961] CLR 382.
315. *Republic v. Sampson* [1977] 2 CLR 1.
316. *Sarikas* [2015] 1 CLR 233 (in Greek).
317. *Themistocleous* [2016] 1 CLR 358 (in Greek).

Accordingly, increase in the remuneration of Representatives may only take effect after new parliamentary elections have taken place and a new House of Representatives has been constituted. It should be noted that the House of Representatives tried to draw a distinction between remuneration and allowance expenses, increasing the latter with immediate effect in July 2005. Then Attorney-General Solon Nikitas opined that the decision to increase the allowances with immediate effect was unconstitutional as being contrary to Article 84 section 2 of the Constitution. The law was thus referred back to the House of Representatives by the President of the Republic and the House accepted the President's submission.[318] It should also be noted that all Representatives have an obligation to disclose, every three years, their property assets, as well as the property assets of their spouse and minor children, to a special parliamentary committee, pursuant to the President, Ministers and Representatives (Submission and Review of Property) Law 49(I)/2004. Submission of the property assets to the parliamentary commission should, in any event, take place within three months from assumption of duties and within three months from termination of duties.

§3. Competences

216. Article 61 of the Constitution provides that the legislative power of the Republic shall be exercised by the House of Representatives in all matters except those expressly reserved to the Communal Chambers under this Constitution; following the self-dissolution of the Greek Communal Chamber the whole of the legislative power of the Republic has been transferred to the House of Representatives. The House of Representatives may exercise its legislative power not only in relation to general matters but also in relation to matters of specific nature, such as loans, guarantees or similar legal obligations of the Government. Thus, the legislative power of the House includes the power to both enact general legislation which sets out rules of general application and which concerns specific cases. The exercise of the legislative power of the House is, however, subject to the application of the principle of separation of powers in the sense that the legislative power of the House of Representatives may not interfere with the powers of the executive or the judiciary.

217. Article 80 of the Constitution provides that the right to introduce bills belongs to the Representatives and the Ministers. However, Representatives may not initiate legislation by introducing a bill, if such bill results to an increase in budgetary expenditure;[319] thus, where the power of the executive to introduce bills is

318. *See* A. Markides, *The Republic of Cyprus*, in *Constitutional Law of 10 EU Member States* I-45 (Kortmann et al. eds, Kluwer 2006).

319. *President of the Republic v. House of Representatives* [1999] 3 CLR 859 (in Greek), *President of the Republic v. House of Representatives* [2001] 3 CLR 519 (in Greek), *President of the Republic v. House of Representatives* [2011] 3 CLR 72 (in Greek), *President of the Republic v. House of Representatives* [1990] 3 CLR 4435 (in Greek), *President of the Republic v. House of Representatives* [1994] 3 CLR 275 (in Greek), *President of the Republic v. House of Representatives* [1993] 3 CLR 16 (in Greek).

unrestricted, the power of Representatives to initiate legislation is significantly restricted. It has been held that the Constitution does not, however, prohibit a Representative from initiating legislation which reduces the revenues provided for in the budget. Accordingly, a law which reduced the rate of the Value Added Tax in specific cases was declared constitutional, despite the fact that it had been initiated by Representatives.[320] A bill introduced by a Representative amended the Immovable Property (Tenure, Registration and Valuation) Law, Cap. 224, in order to provide that any decisions of authorities pursuant to Cap. 224 and any court orders with respect to immovable property, which may substantially affect the value of any immovable property, should be notified by the competent authority to the owner of the affected immovable property. It was argued that the application of the legislation would unavoidably lead to administrative cost for the public service. The Supreme Court held that when a bill does not directly provide for increase of the budgetary needs, but merely leads to increased administrative cost, this does not amount to a violation of Article 80 § 2 of the Constitution.[321]

218. The House may undeniably restrict the power of the executive by amending or rejecting the bills introduced by the executive. During the Presidency of Dimitris Christofias, he repeatedly criticized the House of Representatives by claiming that it had become a so-called Governmental House, since it did not always enable the executive to enact the legislation it wanted. Whereas both the expression and its context were unfortunate, it shows the extent of the power that might be legitimately exercised by the House of Representatives. Furthermore, the House of Representatives may exercise parliamentary control over the executive through submitting questions to the competent Ministries and debating matters in plenary session; questions and debates may cover any aspect of the country's political, economic, social or cultural life. Such role of the House of Representatives to review the formulation and implementation of governmental policies is an important one and enhances the political importance of the House of Representatives. The House may further set up committees of enquiry in order to consider a matter of public interest, monitor the implementation of legislation by the executive and discuss the report of independent authorities, such as the Ombudsman.

219. The President of the Republic is invested in his/her office by the House of Representatives, before which he/she makes the affirmation of faith and respect for the Constitution and the laws, as well as to preserve the independence and territorial integrity of the Republic during the exercise of his/her duties in accordance with Article 42 of the Constitution. Furthermore, the House moves the procedure for the deposition of the President of the Republic from office on grounds of incapacity or high treason by a relevant resolution in accordance with Articles 44 and 45 of the Constitution respectively. The President of the Republic may address the House of

320. *President of the Republic v. House of Representatives* [2009] 3 CLR 648 (in Greek). *See*, however, *President of the Republic v. House of Representatives*, App. 1/2022, Judgment of 12 Jun. 2023 (in Greek).

321. *President of the Republic v. House of Representatives*, Case 1/2018, Judgment of 28 Jun. 2018 (in Greek). *See also President of the Republic v. House of Representatives* [1996] 3 CLR 462 (in Greek), *President of the Republic v. House of Representatives* [2000] 3 CLR 157 (in Greek).

Representatives by messages or transmit to the House of Representatives his/her views through the Ministers by virtue of Article 79 of the Constitution. Furthermore, the Ministers may follow the proceedings of the House of Representatives or any Committee thereof, and make a statement to, or inform, the House of Representatives or any Committee thereof, on any subject within their competence.

220. One of the most important functions of the House of Representatives is its participation in the formulation of the financial policy of the Republic. In accordance with Article 81 of the Constitution, the budget is introduced to the House at least three months before the day fixed by law for the commencement of the financial year and is voted by it not later than the day so fixed. Within three months from the end of the financial year, the final accounts should be submitted to the House for approval. If, for any reason, the budget has not been adopted by the commencement of the financial year, the House may authorize the meeting of any expenditure required for the continuance of public services by a resolution whose effect may not exceed one month; the sums so authorized by the House are called twelfth parts and may not exceed the proportion enacted for the same period in the Budget of the preceding year. Through the process of approving the budget, the House controls and evaluates all aspects of public expenditure and influences the formulation of the governmental financial policy.

221. The powers of the House regarding the budget were severely restricted by the preliminary agreement between the Republic of Cyprus and the Troika[322] for the signing of a Memorandum of Understanding in order to loan the bailout Cypriot economy following the 2012 Cypriot financial crisis; the House was obligated to enact legislation imposing austerity measures which formed part of the agreement without having the chance to consider it. Following a financial collapse in early 2013,[323] a Memorandum of Understanding (MoU) was signed with the Troika as a requisite in order to secure a bailout loan for the Cypriot economy; the agreement introduced a series of austerity measures in the island. The objectives of the MoU included fiscal consolidation by means of increasing efficiency and reducing spending in the country's public sector, as well as improving revenue collection. Structural adjustments included public spending cuts and tax increases, reform of the system of distribution of public benefits, as well as a privatization scheme for profitable semi-governmental organizations.[324] Improvement in the financial situation led to the completion of the financial support programme and exit from the MoU in 2016.

322. The tripartite committee composed by the European Commission, the European Central Bank and the International Monetary Fund.

323. C. Ioannou & A. Emilianides, *How the Cypriot Crisis Came to Be: The Real Causes and Responsibility*, 12 *Foreign Affairs: The Hellenic Edition* 41–51 (2013, in Greek).

324. *See also* O. Christou, C. Ioannou & A. Shekeris, *The Cypriot Welfare State in a Time of Crisis*, in *Challenges to European Welfare Systems* 79–104 (K. Schumbert et al. eds, Springer 2016); O. Christou & C. Ioannou, *The Cypriot Welfare State in the Memorandum Era* in *From Crisis to Development: In Search of New Developmental Models for Greece and the European South*

§4. WORKINGS

222. Article 73 of the Constitution authorizes the House of Representatives to regulate any manner of parliamentary procedure and functions of its offices by its Standing Orders, subject to the constitutional provisions. The House adopted its own Rules of Regulations on 19 December 1980.[325] It is provided in Article 73 section 2 that a Committee of Selection shall consist of the President of the House as Chairman, the Vice-President of the House as Vice-Chairman and eight other members elected by the House at its meeting after the election of the President and the Vice-President, out of who six shall be elected from amongst the Greek Representatives and two from amongst the Turkish Representatives. Following 1963, the provisions regarding the Vice-President of the House and the participation of Representatives hailing from the Turkish Community do not apply in practice. The Committee of Selection shall set up the Standing Committees and any other temporary, ad hoc or special Committee and shall appoint Representatives to be members thereof. There should be due regard to the proposals made by the political party groups of the House for such setting up and appointments. Furthermore, the political groups should be adequately represented on each of the Standing and of any other Committee of the House.[326]

223. The House of Representatives shall meet on the fifteenth day next following a general election and thereafter in each year on the corresponding day in such year without summons for its ordinary session. The ordinary session of the House of Representatives shall last for a period of three to six months in each year, as the House of Representatives may determine. The House of Representatives shall be summoned to an extraordinary session by the President of the House on the request of ten Representatives addressed to the President of the House. In accordance with Rule 7A of the Rules of Procedure of the House, the Representatives requesting the summons of an extraordinary session shall state in their request the topic to be debated and the reasons in brief for which it is necessary for the House to be summoned to an extraordinary session and they shall sign the request in person or through an authorized representative. After receiving the request, the President shall, within five days from the receipt of the request, fix the requested session of the House and the first sitting of this session which shall take place within eight days of the date of receiving the request. In practice, the House of Representatives holds its session throughout the year, with an ordinary session lasting 9–10 months.

119–130 (S. Valyrakis et al. eds, Papazisis 2015, in Greek); O. Christou & C. Ioannou, *The Restructuring of the Cypriot Welfare System*, in *Routledge Handbook of European Welfare Systems* 73–90 (S. Blum et al. eds, 2d ed., Routledge 2020).

325. For a detailed analysis *see* D. Melissas, *The Organization of Political Power in the Cypriot State* (A. Sakkoulas 1996, in Greek).

326. Article 73 § 4 further stipulates that the total number of the seats on such Committees distributed respectively to the Representatives elected by the Greek and the Turkish Communities shall be in the same proportion as that in which the seats in the House are distributed to the Representatives elected by the Greek and the Turkish Communities respectively. However, such provision no longer applies in practice in view of the non-participation of Turkish Cypriot Representatives since 1964.

224. The commencement and end of a meeting shall be declared by the President of the House by virtue of Article 76 of the Constitution. The meetings of the House of Representatives shall be open to the public and the minutes of its debates shall be published in accordance with Article 75 of the Constitution. However, the House may, if it thinks necessary, hold secret sessions on a resolution carried by a three-quarters majority vote of the total number of Representatives. At the end of the meeting, the President of the House shall announce the date and time fixed for the next meeting with the consent of the House and shall present the agenda of such meeting. The agenda shall be printed and distributed to the Representatives at least twenty-four hours prior to the meeting, but if such agenda relates to the topic already under debate, such distribution may be made at any time prior to the meeting. The agenda of the meetings of the House of Representatives shall be drawn up and presented to the House of Representatives by the President of the House in accordance with Article 73 section 6 of the Constitution. After the presentation of the agenda to the House of Representatives, any Representative may move any addition or amendment to such agenda, and such motion shall be decided upon by the House of Representatives. Rule 11 of the Rules of the Procedure stipulates that the agenda shall include the following chapters: (a) Chapter one: Legislative Work, (b) Chapter two: Introduction of Bills and Documents, (c) Chapter three: Questions and Answers, (d) Chapter Four: Matters entered for debate.

225. No Representative can speak at any meeting of the House of Representatives unless he/she registers his/her name in the proper Register or unless he/she obtains the permission of the person presiding at such meeting. By virtue of Article 73 section 6 of the Constitution, every Representative who has complied with such formality is entitled to be given reasonably sufficient time, having regard to the particular subject, to speak and to be heard at the relevant meeting. The speeches shall be made in order of the registration or of oral request, as the case may be, of those who desire to speak: Where there are opposite views held, a speaker shall, as far as practicable, follow another one who supports the opposite view. But Representatives speaking on behalf of the Committees or of the political party groups of the House of Representatives shall not be subject to such order of precedence. Representatives desiring to speak in connection with motions with regard to any matter relating to the agenda, the application of the Standing Orders or the closure of the debate shall be given precedence in time over the Representatives desiring to speak in connection with the subject of the debate; in such a case, two Representatives, one in favour and one against the motion, shall be allowed fifteen minutes each for their respective speeches.

226. All speeches in the House of Representatives shall be made from the rostrum of the House and addressed to the House of Representatives in accordance with Article 73 section 7 of the Constitution. Save as otherwise provided in the Standing Orders, interruptions of the speech of a Representative or personal attacks against any Representative unconnected with the subject under debate, both in the House and at the Committee meetings, are prohibited (Article 73 section 8 of the Constitution). The minutes of the debates in the House of Representatives shall comprise all proceedings fully. The minutes of the proceedings of the Committees shall be kept in a summary form. Upon objection to the minutes of a meeting of the House of Representatives through the oral submission of a Representative at the first following meeting or by a written objection sent to the President of the relevant meeting, the House of Representatives may decide to correct such minutes accordingly. Any political party which is represented at least by 12% of the total number of the Representatives in the House of Representatives can form and shall be entitled to be recognized as a political party group.

227. Article 73 section 5 of the Constitution stipulates that every Bill on being introduced in the House shall be referred for debate in the first instance before the appropriate Committee. Furthermore, with the exception of those which are considered to be of an urgent nature, no Bill shall be debated by a Committee before the lapse of forty-eight hours after its being distributed to the Representatives constituting such a Committee and no Bill which has passed the Committee stage shall be debated in the House before the lapse of forty-eight hours after it has been distributed to the Representatives together with the report of the Committee. By virtue of Article 78 of the Constitution, the laws and the decisions of the House of Representatives shall be passed by a simple majority vote of the Representatives present and voting. The quorum of the House shall consist of at least one-third of the total number of its members in accordance with Article 77 of the Constitution.

228. However, any modification of the Electoral Law and the adoption of any law relating to the municipalities and of any law imposing duties or taxes shall require a separate simple majority of the Representatives elected by the Greek and the Turkish Communities respectively. The rule concerning separate majority rule proved to be extremely problematic; as of 31 March 1961, the Republic of Cyprus no longer had tax laws, since whereas the majority of the Greek Cypriot Representatives had voted in favour of extending the effect of the existing laws, the majority of the Turkish Cypriot Representatives had voted against. The then-President of the Republic, Archbishop Makarios, ordered the authorities of the Republic to continue collecting taxes as if the effect of the laws had been extended, citing the doctrine of necessity as a justification for his decision.[327] Since 1964, the separate majority rule no longer applies in practice due to the non-participation of Representatives hailing from the Turkish Community. Constitutional amendment of non-fundamental Articles of the Constitution further requires a positive separate vote by two-thirds of the Representatives elected by the Greek and the Turkish majority, respectively. In this case also, the separate majority rule no longer applies since 1964. Confusion arose, however, during the recent enactment of the Nineteenth Constitutional Amendment. While the amendment was uncontroversial, there were not thirty-eight Representatives (i.e., two-thirds of fifty-six) present during the vote. The President of the House of Representatives, following advice by the parliamentary services, accepted that thirty-seven votes were sufficient to satisfy the two-thirds majority requirement and declared the amendment as a valid one. This was a procedural error, which was immediately corrected; the Attorney-General advised the President of the Republic to refer the constitutional amendment back to the House of

327. *See* in detail A. Emilianides, *Beyond the Constitution of Cyprus* (Sakkoulas 2006, in Greek).

Representatives pursuant to Article 51 of the Constitution, and the House of Representatives eventually approved the amendment with the required majority.[328]

§5. Miscellaneous

I. Legislation Having Retroactive Effect

229. The Constitution does not prohibit retrospective legislation with the exception of the imposition of tax, duties or rates of any kind (Article 24 section of the Constitution). Article 82 of the Constitution provides that a law or decision of the House of Representatives shall come into operation on its publication in the official Gazette of the Republic, unless another date is provided by such law or decision. However, retrospective legislation should, in principle, be discouraged, since it upsets certainty in the law. Section 10 of the Interpretation Law, Cap. 1 stipulates that legislation should be construed prospectively unless there is a clear indication to the contrary in the statute itself. Thus, the general rule is that except where there is a clear indication either from the subject matter or from the wording of the statute, the statute is not to receive a retrospective construction.

230. In *Papanicopoulos*,[329] the Supreme Court held that when Articles 61 and 82 of the Constitution are read together, it becomes clear that a statute is not unconstitutional merely because it was given retrospective alteration, unless it offends against a specific provision of the Constitution, excluding retrospectivity. Furthermore, it was held that a statute, which is given retrospective effect, is not unconstitutional merely because it interferes with vested rights. Indeed, the Constitution does not protect rights merely because they are vested. There is, however, a presumption against an intention to take away vested rights, unless this is clearly warranted by the wording of the retrospective legislation.[330] Furthermore, the legislature may interfere with vested rights only to the extent that such rights are not safeguarded by the Constitution itself, or the retrospective effect does not violate fundamental rights safeguarded in Part II of the Constitution. In any event, it has been clarified that legislation should not be considered retrospective merely because it changes existing law by reference to events or circumstances of the past; rather, the notion of retrospective legislation is the legislation which takes away or diminishes vested rights, namely rights which are accrued at a date prior to the promulgation of the law.[331]

231. The House of Representatives enacted legislation providing that a piece of legislation, Law 142(I)/2014, would not come into effect prior to the coming into

328. T. Kouspi & A. Emilianides, 'From Process Misstep to Environmental Milestone: Cyprus's New Constitutional Right' April *constitutionnet*, available at https://constitutionnet.org/news/voices/process-misstep-environmental-milestone-cypruss-new-constitutional-right.
329. *Papanicopoulos v. Morphou Co-Operative* [1986] 1 CLR 288.
330. *Republic v. Menelaou* [1982] 3 CLR 419, *Joannou & Paraskevaides Ltd v. Republic* [2009] 3 CLR 52 (in Greek).
331. *Republic v. Matthew* [1990] 3 CLR 2452 (in Greek).

operation of a set of legislations which were expected to be brought by the Council of Ministers to the House of Representatives within a specified time-frame. The Supreme Court held that the impugned legislation was inconsistent with the principle of separation of powers because it impliedly pressured the Council of Ministers to present bills to the House of Representatives within a given time-frame. Since the right to present bills to the House of Representatives falls within the powers of the executive, this amounted to a violation of the principle of separation of powers. Furthermore, the legislation was inconsistent with Article 82 of the Constitution, since it led to uncertainty as to the exact point in time when Law 142(I)/2014 would come into force.[332]

II. Communal Chambers

232. As already indicated, the Constitution also provides for two communal chambers: a Greek communal chamber and a Turkish communal chamber, which shall have legislative power in educational, cultural, religious and other matters of purely communal nature. Following the self-dissolution of the Greek Communal Chamber, Law 12/1965 transferred the competences of the Greek Communal Chamber to the newly established Ministry of Education and Culture, the House of Representatives, and the Council of Ministers. Despite the fact that the constitutional provisions concerning the Communal Chamber no longer apply in practice, they shall be briefly examined in this part for reference purposes only. Article 86 of the Constitution provides that the Greek and the Turkish Communities respectively shall elect from amongst their own members a Communal Chamber which shall have the competence expressly reserved for it under the provisions of this Constitution.

233. The Communal Chambers shall, in relation to their respective Community, have competence to exercise within the limits of this Constitution legislative power solely with regard to the following matters: (a) all religious matters; (b) all educational, cultural and teaching matters; (c) personal status; (d) the composition and instances of courts dealing with civil disputes relating to personal status and to religious matters; (e) in matters where the interests and institutions are of purely communal nature such as charitable and sporting foundations, bodies and associations created for the purpose of promoting the well-being of their respective Community; (f) imposition of personal taxes and fees on members of their respective Community in order to provide for their respective needs and for the needs of bodies and institutions under their control;[333] (g) in matters where subsidiary legislation in the

332. *President of the Republic v. House of Representatives* [2014] 3 CLR 518 (in Greek).

333. The power of imposing taxes shall be exercised, in accordance with Art. 88 of the Constitution, for the purposes of meeting the part of its expenditure provided in its budget in each financial year. Nothing in this subparagraph shall be construed as in any way curtailing the power of the House of Representatives to impose any personal taxes in accordance with the provisions of the Constitution.

form of regulations or by-laws within the framework of the laws relating to municipalities will be necessary to enable a Communal Chamber to promote the aims pursued by municipalities composed solely of members of its respective Community; (h) in matters relating to the exercise of the authority of control of producers and consumers cooperatives and credit establishments and of supervision in their functions of municipalities consisting solely of their respective Community, vested in them by this Constitution; (i) in such other matters as are expressly provided by this Constitution.

234. Article 87 section 3 of the Constitution further stipulates that no law or decision of a Communal Chamber shall in any way contain anything contrary to the interests of the security of the Republic or the constitutional order or the public safety or the public order or the public health or the public morals or which is against the fundamental rights and liberties guaranteed by this Constitution to any person. In addition to the imposition of personal taxes and fees on members of their respective Community (which may be collected on behalf of the Communal Chamber by organs of the Republic, if the Communal Chamber so requests by virtue of Article 88 section 3 of the Constitution), the House of Representatives shall, in respect of each financial year, provide in the Budget and make available for payment to both Communal Chambers in respect of their respective financial year for the purposes of their respective needs relating to matters within their respective competence. The amount to be paid shall be no less than CYP 2 million (EUR 3.4 million); such budget is to be allocated to the Greek and the Turkish Communal Chambers, in accordance with Article 88 section 2 of the Constitution, as follows: (a) to the Greek Communal Chamber an amount not less than the sum of CYP 1 million and CYP 600,000; and (b) to the Turkish Communal Chamber an amount not less than the sum of CYP 400,000. Provided that in the case of the increase of the minimum total amount payable to both Communal Chambers, the allocation to each of the Communal Chambers of such increased amount shall be made in such manner as the House of Representatives may decide.

235. The Communal Chambers shall further, by virtue of Article 89 of the Constitution, and in relation to their respective Community, also have competence: (a) to direct policy within their communal laws and to exercise administrative powers in the manner and through such persons as may be provided by a communal law, with respect to any matter on which they are competent to exercise legislative power under the provisions of Article 87 other than those provided in subparagraphs (g) and (h); (b) to exercise control on producers' and consumers' cooperatives credit establishments created for the purpose of promoting the well-being of their respective Community and which will be governed by the laws; (c) to promote the aims pursued by municipalities composed solely members of their respective Community and to supervise in their functions such municipalities to which the laws shall apply. Each Communal Chamber shall once a year prepare and adopt a budget of its revenue and expenditure for the ensuing financial year in accordance with Article 91 of the Constitution; such budget shall be voted by the Communal Chamber not later than the day fixed by a communal law for the commencement of the communal financial year.

236. Each Communal Chamber shall, by virtue of Article 90 of the Constitution, have power by or in its own communal laws to provide for the application of its laws and decisions. However, a Communal Chamber shall have no power to provide in any of its laws or decisions for imprisonment or detention for any violation thereof or failure to comply with any directions given by a Communal Chamber in exercise of any power vested in it under this Constitution. Furthermore, the Communal Chambers shall have no competence to use measures of constraint to secure compliance with their respective communal laws or decisions and the judgments of the Courts dealing with civil disputes relating to personal status and religious matters within their respective competence. Where it becomes necessary to use measures of constraint in compelling compliance with any law or decision of a Communal Chamber or with any matter connected with the exercise of the authority of control or supervision by a Communal Chamber, such measures of constraint shall, on the application by or on behalf of the Communal Chamber, be applied by the public authorities of the Republic which shall have exclusive competence to apply such measures of constraint. It is further provided that the execution of any judgment or order of a court in connection with any matter within the exclusive competence of a Communal Chamber shall be carried out through the public authorities of the Republic.

237. Article 96 of the Constitution provides that the term of office of the Communal Chambers shall be for a period of five years. A communal general election for a Communal Chamber shall be held, in accordance with Article 97 of the Constitution, at least thirty days before the expiration of the term of office of the outgoing Chamber. The number of members of each Communal Chamber shall be determined by a communal law carried by a two-thirds majority of the total number of the members of the Communal Chamber concerned in accordance with Article 92 of the Constitution. Either Communal Chamber may dissolve itself, in accordance with Article 98 of the Constitution, only by its own decision carried by an absolute majority. Article 93 of the Constitution provides that the elections for both the Communal Chambers shall be by universal suffrage and by direct and secret ballot. Every citizen of the Republic who has attained the age of twenty-one years and has such residential qualifications as may be prescribed by the respective communal electoral law shall have the right to be registered as an elector in the respective communal electoral list by virtue of Article 94 of the Constitution.

238. It is, however, provided that the members of the Greek Community shall only be registered in the Greek communal electoral list and the members of the Turkish Community shall only be registered in the Turkish communal electoral list. A person shall be qualified to be a candidate for election as a member of a Communal Chamber, by virtue of Article 95 of the Constitution, if at the time of the election, that person: (a) is a citizen of the Republic and is registered in the respective communal electoral list; (b) has attained the age of twenty-five years; (c) has not been, on or after the date of the coming into operation of this Constitution, convicted of an offence involving dishonesty or moral turpitude or is not under any disqualification imposed by a competent court for an electoral offence; (d) is not suffering from a mental disease incapacitating such person from acting as a member of a Communal Chamber. The office of a member of a Communal Chamber shall be incompatible with that of a Minister or a Representative or a member of any municipal council including a Mayor or a member of the armed or security forces of the Republic or with a public or municipal office and, in the case of that of a member of the Turkish Communal Chamber, with that of a religions functionary.

239. The meetings of the Communal Chambers shall be open to the public and the minutes of its debates shall be published by virtue of Article 103 of the Constitution. However, any Communal Chamber may, if it thinks necessary, hold secret sessions on a resolution carried by a two-thirds majority vote of the total number of its members. The Communal Chambers shall, by Standing Orders, make rules relating to all matters of procedure including the holding of ordinary and extraordinary meetings, the dates and duration of such meetings, the manner of voting and the transaction of business (Article 102 of the Constitution). Article 104 further provides that the laws or decisions passed by the Greek or the Turkish Communal Chamber shall be published in the official Gazette of the Republic immediately after being signed by the President or the Vice-President of the Republic respectively within fifteen days of the receipt by him/her of such laws or decisions.[334] A communal law shall come into operation on its publication in the official Gazette of the Republic unless another date is provided by such law.

240. Article 106 of the Constitution provides that a member of a Communal Chamber shall not be liable to civil or criminal proceedings in respect of any statement made or vote given by him/her in the Chamber. A member of a Communal Chamber cannot be prosecuted, arrested or imprisoned, without the leave of the Supreme Court, so long as he/she continues to be a member. Such leave is not required in the case of an offence punishable with death or imprisonment for five years or more in case the offender is taken in the act. In such a case, the Supreme Court, being notified forthwith by the competent authority, decides whether it should grant or refuse leave for the continuation of the prosecution or detention, as the case may be, so long as he/she continues to be a member. If the Supreme Court refuses to grant leave for the prosecution of a member of a Communal Chamber, the period during which such member cannot thus be prosecuted shall not be reckoned for the purposes of any period of prescription for the offence in question. If the Supreme Court refuses to grant leave for the enforcement of a sentence of imprisonment imposed on a member of a Communal Chamber by a competent court, the enforcement of such sentence shall be postponed until he/she ceases to be such member.

241. The seat of a member of a Communal Chamber shall become vacant, by virtue of Article 107, upon the death, written resignation, conviction of an offence involving dishonesty or moral turpitude or imposition of disqualification by a competent court for an electoral offence, or due to a mental disease incapacitating such person from acting as a member of a Communal Chamber, or if he/she ceases to be

---

334. Unless the President exercises the right to return such law or decision to the Chamber for reconsideration within fifteen days of the receipt.

qualified to be registered as an elector in the respective Communal electoral list, or upon his/her becoming the holder of an office which is incompatible with the position of a member of a Communal Chamber. Finally, Article 108 of the Constitution provides that the Greek and the Turkish Communities shall have the right to receive subsidies from the Greek or the Turkish Government respectively for institutions of education, culture, athletics and charity belonging to the Greek or the Turkish Community respectively. Also, where either the Greek or the Turkish Community considers that it does not have the necessary number of schoolmasters, professors or clergymen for the functioning of its institutions, such Community shall have the right to obtain and employ such personnel to the extent strictly necessary to meet its needs as the Greek or the Turkish Government respectively may provide.

Chapter 4. The Executive

§1. The Organ of State

242. Article 46 of the Constitution provides that the President and the Vice-President of the Republic, in order to ensure the executive power, shall have a Council of Ministers composed of seven Greek Cypriot Ministers and three Turkish Cypriot Ministers. It is further provided that either the Ministry of Finance, the Ministry of Foreign Affairs, or the Ministry of Defence shall be entrusted to a Turkish Minister. Following the resignation of the Turkish Cypriot Vice-President and the three Turkish Cypriot Ministers in 1963, all Ministers hail from the Greek Cypriot Community and are appointed by the President of the Republic. An eleventh Ministry, which is not provided in Article 46 of the Constitution, namely the Ministry of Education, Sports and Youth, was established pursuant to the Competence of the Greek Communal Chamber (Transfer of Exercise) Law 12/1965 and the doctrine of necessity in order to exercise the competences which constitutionally ought to be exercised by the self-dissolved Greek Communal Chamber.

243. Article 46 of the Constitution was considered by the Supreme Court in a reference to the President of the Republic concerning the constitutionality of the Council of Ministers and Ministries Law of 1985.[335] The Supreme Court held that from the construction of Article 46, it is derived that the Ministers and Ministries of the Republic are ten and that there is no power to appoint more than ten Ministers or create more than ten Ministries. The Ministry of Education and Culture (as it was then named), while not one of the ten Ministries envisaged by Article 46 of the Constitution, had been set up in accordance with the doctrine of necessity. Apart from the Ministry of Foreign Affairs, the Ministry of Defence and the Ministry of Finance, which are expressly named in Article 46 of the Constitution, and apart from the Ministry of Education, the remaining seven Ministries are specified exclusively by the President of the Republic. Accordingly, the law on the basis of which the House of Representatives specified the remaining seven Ministries had been enacted contrary to Article 46 of the Constitution and was outside the competence of the House of Representatives. It is therefore the President's prerogative to set up or name the seven ministries not named in the Constitution.[336]

244. Other than the Ministries named in the Constitution itself and the Ministry of Education, Sports and Youth, there are currently the following Ministries: Ministry of Interior; Ministry of Transport, Communications and Works; Ministry of Energy, Commerce and Industry; Ministry of Agriculture, Rural Development and Environment; Ministry of Labour and Social Insurance; Ministry of Justice and

335. *President of the Republic v. House of Representatives* [1985] 3 CLR 2801.

336. However, A. Markides, *The Republic of Cyprus*, in *Constitutional Law of 10 EU Member States* I-37 (Kortmann et al. eds, Kluwer 2006) correctly notes that: 'as the competences of various ministries are given to them by law, it can be argued that the President is not entirely free to replace at will one ministry by another because a law is necessary to define and regulate new competences and to repeal or re-assign existing competences'.

Public Order; and Ministry of Health. A Government Spokesman (and a Deputy Government Spokesman) and a Deputy Minister to the President are not part of the Council of Ministers but work closely with the President and the Council of Ministers in order to coordinate and promote the governmental work. During the Anastasiades Presidency, the following Deputy Ministries were also established: a) Shipping, b) Tourism, c) Research, Innovation and Digital Policy, d) Social Welfare, and e) Culture. Deputy Ministers (including the Deputy Minister to the President) are not members of the Council of Ministers and do not have a right to vote.

§2. Competences

245. The Council of Ministers is the most important organ of Government because it holds the bulk of executive power in accordance with Article 54 of the Constitution. Article 54 provides that subject to the executive power expressly reserved under Articles 47, 48 and 49 to the President and the Vice-President of the Republic acting either separately or conjointly, and the Council of Ministers shall exercise executive power in all other matters, including the following: (a) the general direction and control of the government of the Republic and the direction of general policy; (b) foreign affairs; (c) defence and security; (d) the coordination and supervision of all public services, I the supervision and disposition of property belonging to the Republic in accordance with the provisions of this Constitution and the law; (f) consideration of Bills to be introduced to the House of Representatives by a Minister; (g) making of any order or regulation for the carrying into effect of any law as provided by such law;[337] and (h) consideration of the Budget of the Republic to be introduced to the House of Representatives. The above is an indicative and not an exhaustive list.

246. A Minister is the Head of each of the Ministries and exercises executive power,[338] subject to the executive power reserved to the President and the Vice-President of the Republic, acting either separately or conjointly, and to the Council of Ministers. Article 58 of the Constitution provides that the executive power exercised by each Minister includes: (a) the execution of laws relating to, and the administration of all matters and affairs usually falling within, the domain of his/her Ministry; (b) preparation of orders or regulations concerning his/her Ministry for submission to the Council of Ministers; (c) the issuing of directions and general instructions for the carrying out of the provisions of any law relating to his/her Ministry and of any order or regulation under such law; and (d) the preparation for submission to the Council of Ministers of the part of the Budget of the Republic relating to his/her Ministry.

337. *See* N. Charalambous, *The Power of the Council of Ministers to Enact Subsidiary Legislation*, in *Aspects of Cypriot Law*, vol. II 115–152 (Asselia 1982, in Greek).
338. *See* C. Tornaritis, *The Legal Status of Ministers in the Republic of Cyprus*, 1 Cyprus L. Tribune 7–16 [1967] (in Greek).

§3. Workings

247. Article 46 of the Constitution provides that the decisions of the Council of Ministers shall be taken by an absolute majority and shall unless the right of final veto or return is exercised by the President or the Vice-President of the Republic or both, in accordance with Article 57, be promulgated immediately by them by publication in the official Gazette of the Republic. The meetings of the Council are convened by the President of the Republic who draws up the agenda. Article 60 of the Constitution further provides for a Joint Secretariat of the Council of Ministers headed by two Secretaries, one belonging to the Greek Community and the other belonging to the Turkish Community, who shall be public officers. Following 1963 and the resignation of the Turkish Cypriot Ministers, only one Secretary hailing from the Greek Community was appointed. The Secretary is in charge of the Council of Ministers Office, and in accordance with the instructions given by the Council of Ministers, he/she attends the meetings and keeps the minutes of such meetings and conveys the decisions of the Council of Ministers to the appropriate organ or authority or person.

§4. Miscellaneous

248. The qualifications for appointment to the office of a Minister are provided for in Article 59 of the Constitution. No person shall be appointed as a Minister unless he/she is a citizen of the Republic and has the qualifications required for a candidate for election as a member of the House of Representatives. The office of a Minister shall be incompatible with that of a Representative or of a member of a Communal Chamber or of a member of any municipal council including a Mayor or of a member of the armed or security forces of the Republic or with a public or municipal office or in the case of a Turkish Minister with that of a religious functionary. The Ministers shall hold office until their appointment is terminated by the President of the Republic; such termination is a governmental act not subject to judicial review.[339] Before entering office, appointees should make the following affirmation before the President of the Republic: 'I do solemnly affirm faith to, and respect for, the Constitution and the laws made thereunder, the preservation of the independence and the territorial integrity, of the Republic of Cyprus.'

249. An interesting question arose with respect to a Minister during Christofias' Presidency. Andreas Demetriou, a Professor at the University of Cyprus, was appointed as the Minister of Education and Culture but did not resign from his office as a Professor. Rather, he was given unpaid leave for a period of three years by the University. In light of the fact that the University of Cyprus is a legal person of public law, the Attorney-General opined that Mr Demetriou could not continue to be a Professor in a public University and simultaneously hold the office of a Minister, since the office of a Minister is incompatible with any public office. The fact that Mr Demetriou had been given unpaid leave was immaterial; the incompatibility

339. *Antoniadou v. President of the Republic*, Case 692/2012, Judgment of 26 Nov. 2012 (in Greek).

concerned the simultaneous occupation of two public offices and not the simultaneous payment of two salaries by public offices. Mr Demetriou was accordingly forced to resign from his position as a Professor at the University of Cyprus, in order to continue serving as a Minister.[340] The same principle was reiterated regarding the current President of the Republic at the time when he was Minister of Foreign Affairs of the Anastasiades Government, and he was appointed as a Lecturer at the University of Cyprus.[341]

250. The Government Spokesman and the Deputy Ministers are considered part of the Executive. However, as already indicated, they are not part of the Council of Ministers. The Supreme Court has repeatedly held that the Council of Ministers is an organ of the administration, and accordingly, the participation of the Government Spokesman and the Deputy Minister during the meeting of the Council of Ministers without them leaving prior to the deliberation for reaching a decision is unlawful and should lead to the annulment of the administrative act that the Council of Ministers has taken due to defects in its composition at the time of taking the decision.[342] It should also be noted that Ministers have an obligation to disclose, every three years, their property assets, as well as the property assets of their spouse and minor children, to a special parliamentary committee, pursuant to the President, Ministers and Representatives (Submission and Review of Property) Law 49(I)/2004. Submission of the property assets to the parliamentary commission should, in any event, take place within three months from assumption of duties and within three months from termination of duties.

251. The Incompatibility as to the Exercise of Duties of Certain Officials of the Republic to Certain Professional and Other Similar Activities Law 7(I)/2008 provides that Ministers shall not provide any consultancy services to the public or any person under public law, participate in undertakings tendering or carrying out public procurement contracts, or act as members of the board of directors of public companies, or media. A committee, presided by a retired judge, and comprised of the General-Auditor of the Republic, an Attorney from the office of the Attorney-General of the Republic and the Permanent Secretary of the House of Representatives, oversees the application of Law 7(I)/2008.[343] Furthermore, The Control of the Assumption of Work to the Private Sector by Former State Officials and certain Former Employees of the Public and Wider Public Sector Law 114(I)/2007 provides that Ministers have to apply to a committee in order to be allowed to undertake employment of any kind in the private sector, including self-employment, for

340. *See also Costi v. Republic*, Case 740/2011, Judgment of (in Greek).
341. *Christodoulides v. University of Cyprus*, Case 682/2019, Judgment of 5 Nov. 2021 (Administrative Court, in Greek). *See also* A. Emilianides, *Is the Incompatibility for University Faculty Anachronistic?*, dikaiosyni, 3 Dec. 2021 (in Greek), available in, https://dikaiosyni.com/katigories/arthra/einai-anaxronistiko-to-asimvivasto-gia-tous-panepistimiakous/.
342. *Akinita LAK Ltd v. Republic*, Case 1372/2011, Judgment of 5 Sep. 2013 (in Greek), *Andreou v. Republic*, Case 570/2009, Judgment of 15 Mar. 2012 (in Greek), *Christodoulou and others v. Republic*, Case 792/2009, Judgment of 14 Dec. 2012 (in Greek), *Afstralos and others v. Cyprus Tourism Organization*, Case 410/2011, Judgment of 17 Oct. 2013 (in Greek).
343. *See also President of the Republic v. House of Representatives* [2017] 3 CLR 364 (in Greek).

a period of two years following the termination of their public duties, or retirement. The committee is comprised of the three senior Attorneys from the office of the Attorney-General and considers all the circumstances in order to assess whether there is a conflict of interest. The committee may allow the former state official or employee to assume work in the private sector unconditionally, or to impose conditions relating to the duties to be undertaken, or the time when employment may be assumed.

Chapter 5. The Judiciary

§1. Judicial Organization

I. Ordinary Law Courts

252. The Constitution provides for the establishment of a Supreme Constitutional Court and a High Court. In accordance with Article 133 of the Constitution, the Supreme Constitutional Court was to be composed of a Greek Cypriot, a Turkish Cypriot and a neutral judge who would act as the President of the Court, whereas the High Court was to be composed of two Greek Cypriots, a Turkish Cypriot and a neutral judge (not a subject or citizen of the Republic of Cyprus, Greece, Turkey or the UK and its Colonies) who would act as the President of the Court. However, as already explained, from 1964 until July 2023, a newly established Supreme Court exercised the jurisdiction and powers of both the Supreme Constitutional Court and the High Court by virtue of the Administration of Justice (Miscellaneous Provisions) Law, 33/1964, which was enacted in accordance with the doctrine of necessity. As of 1 July 2023, there are once again two separate highest courts of the Republic, i.e., the Supreme Constitutional Court and the Supreme Court (as well as an Appellate Court), pursuant to the Seventeenth Amendment of the Constitution, Law 103(I)/22 and the amendment of Law 33/64 by virtue of Law 145(I)/22. The seats of the Supreme Constitutional Court, the Supreme Court, and the Appellate Court are in Nicosia.

253. The Supreme Court is the highest appellate court in the Republic and has jurisdiction, pursuant to Article 155 of the Constitution and section 9 § 3 of Law 33/64, to hear and determine civil and criminal appeals which are referred before it by the Appellate Court. The Appellate Court may refer the appeal to the Supreme Court if it relates to an issue of major public interest or public importance of general application or if there have been conflicting judgments of the Appellate Court and there is a need to achieve legal cohesion. The reference shall be based on an application determining precisely the issues which necessitate the case to be tried by the Supreme Court. If the Supreme Court determines that the reference is not justified, it shall inform the Appellate Court accordingly and the case shall be tried by the Appellate Court. The Supreme Court may further act as a court of third instance. For the Court to exercise such jurisdiction, either of the parties or the Attorney-General of the Republic should apply and request for leave to be granted accordingly. The Supreme Court shall exercise its jurisdiction if the judgment of the Appellate Court raises issues of divergence from previous case-law or if there is a need for proper interpretation of primary or secondary law, or if the issue relates to a major public interest or has public importance of general application, or if there have been conflicting judgments of the Appellate Court and there is a need to achieve legal cohesion. If the Court grants permission and hears the case in third instance, then its judgment shall substitute the judgment of the Appellate Court under appeal.

254. The Supreme Court may further decide whether a criminal case should be re-tried because of new facts or elements which may potentially justify vacating the original decision on conviction, which had been reached either by the trial court or on appeal. If the application for re-trial is accepted, then the Supreme Court shall refer the case to either the Appellate Court or to a trial criminal court, depending on the case. The Supreme Court may further determine applications to excuse judges of any court, other than the Supreme Constitutional Court, after the rejection of such applications by the said court. It further has the exclusive jurisdiction to grant the prerogative orders of habeas corpus, mandamus, prohibition, certiorari, and quo warranto. The Supreme Court may function in two distinct sections, i.e., the Criminal Law section and the Civil Law section. In civil and criminal appeals referred to by the Appellate Court, the Supreme Court is composed of a bench of at least three judges; other cases should be heard by the Plenary Bench of the Supreme Court.

255. The Supreme Constitutional Court shall have exclusive jurisdiction, by virtue of Article 149 of the Constitution, to determine any conflict between the two texts of this Constitution and to make, in case of ambiguity, any interpretation of this Constitution. In addition, the Supreme Constitutional Court shall have the exclusive jurisdiction to hear and determine recourse filed by virtue of Articles 137–139 and 143 of the Constitution and references for opinion filed by virtue of Articles 141–142 of the Constitution. It shall also have exclusive jurisdiction, by virtue of Article 145 of the Constitution, to adjudicate finally on any election petition, made under the provisions of the Electoral Law, with regard to the elections of the President (or the Vice-President of the Republic) or of members of the House of Representatives or of any Communal Chamber. The Supreme Court, sitting as the Supreme Constitutional Court, also used to have jurisdiction with regard to the election of members of the municipal and community councils; however, such jurisdiction has recently been transferred to the District Courts.[344] Furthermore, in accordance with Article 147 of the Constitution, the Supreme Constitutional Court shall have exclusive jurisdiction to adjudicate finally on a motion made by the Attorney-General and the Deputy Attorney-General of the Republic, in accordance with the provisions of paragraph 3 of Article 44, with regard to the question of the existence of such permanent or temporary incapacity, or absence, otherwise than temporary, of the President of the Republic, as would prevent him/her from performing effectively his/her duties as provided in subparagraph (d) of paragraph 1 of Article 44. It further determines issues of constitutionality of legislation by virtue of Article 144 of the Constitution.

256. In addition to its powers by virtue of the Constitution, section 9 of Law 33/64 provides that the Supreme Constitutional Court may act as the highest appellate court in the Republic with regard to administrative law appeals. The Court may hear and determine administrative law appeals which are referred before it by the Administrative Appellate Court. The Administrative Appellate Court may refer the

344. *See Kafkalias and others v. Nicolaides and others*, Civil App. 424/2017, Judgment of 23 Apr. 2018 (in Greek).

appeal to the Supreme Court if it relates to an issue of major public interest or public importance of general application or if there have been conflicting judgments of the Administrative Appellate Court and there is a need to achieve legal cohesion. The Supreme Constitutional Court may further act as a court of third instance. For the Court to exercise such jurisdiction, either of the parties or the Attorney-General of the Republic should apply and request for permission to be granted accordingly. The Supreme Constitutional Court shall exercise its jurisdiction if the judgment of the Administrative Appellate Court raises issues of divergence from previous case-law or if there is a need for proper interpretation of primary or secondary law, or if the issue relates to a major public interest or has public importance of general application, or if there have been conflicting judgments of the Administrative Appellate Court and there is a need to achieve legal cohesion. If the Court grants permission and hears the case at a third instance, then its judgment shall substitute the judgment of the Administrative Appellate Court under appeal. In all cases, the Supreme Constitutional Court sits as a Plenary Bench.

257. The Seventeenth Amendment of the Constitution Law 103(I)/22 initially established a single Appellate Court, which comprised of sixteen judges and would act as an appeal court at the second instance for all appeals, including appeals from specialized courts. The Appellate Court had sections for civil, criminal and administrative law and hears appeals in sections of three judges; however, a single judge may hear appeals of interlocutory judgments, with the exception of appeals on judgments regarding interim orders. A single judge may further hear interim applications or applications dealing exclusively with procedural issues. With the Twenty-First Amendment of the Constitution Law 130(I)/2025, a distinct Administrative Appellate Court was established, with jurisdiction to hear all administrative appeals. Article 158 of the Constitution further stipulates that a law shall provide for the establishment, jurisdiction and powers of courts of civil and criminal jurisdiction. Section 3 of the Courts of Justice Law has accordingly established the District Courts and the Assize Courts, which function as the lower courts of the Republic.[345] There are six District Courts, one for each administrative district of the Republic of Cyprus (Nicosia, Famagusta, Limassol, Larnaca, Paphos and Kyrenia). Since the 1974 Turkish Invasion, the District Court of Famagusta is located at Paralimni (and mostly operates in Larnaca) and the District Court of Kyrenia is located at Nicosia. The District Courts have jurisdiction to hear and determine at first instance all civil actions, with the exception of matters that fall within the exclusive jurisdiction of the Rent Control Tribunal, the Industrial Disputes Tribunal (IDT) and the Family Court, or the original jurisdiction of the Supreme Court in admiralty law cases. It should be further noted that section 2 of the Patents Law 16(I)/1998 inexplicably stipulates that the competent court for cases of patent infringement is the Supreme Court and not the District Court.[346]

---

345. *See* C. Clerides, *The Cypriot Legal System* (Nomiki Vivliothiki 2018, in Greek), P. Michaelides, *The Cypriot Courts of Justice Legislation*, in *Aspects of Cypriot Law* vol. I, 67–124 (Asselia 1981 in Greek).
346. *Andreou v. Colossos Signs Ltd* [2008] 1 CLR 580 (in Greek).

258. Cases before the District Courts are heard by a single judge, who may be, depending on the amount of the dispute, a District Court Judge, a Senior District Court Judge or a President of a District Court.[347] District Courts also have jurisdiction to hear and determine at first instance all criminal offences for which the accused is liable to imprisonment not exceeding five years or a fine of EUR 85,000 or both.[348] Assize Courts have jurisdiction to hear and determine criminal cases, and they normally hear criminal offences for which the accused may be liable to imprisonment exceeding five years. Assize Courts are constituted by three judges, one of whom has the rank of a President of the District Court.[349] Article 160 of the Constitution further provided for the establishment of courts of the Communal Chambers, having jurisdiction to deal with civil disputes relating to personal status and religious matters which are reserved for the competence of the Communal Chambers; however, since 1964, the jurisdiction of the Greek Communal Chamber has been transferred to the Supreme Court and its subordinate courts (District Courts, Family Courts).

259. In addition to the above, certain specific courts have been established in the Republic. Article 111 of the Constitution, as amended with Law 95/89, had established the Family Courts, the Family Courts of Religious Groups and the Appellate Family Court.[350] Article 111 section 2 A of the Constitution provided that the Family Court would be composed of three judges in divorce proceedings and of a single judge in any other trial. In divorce cases, the President of the Family Court would be appointed by the Orthodox Church of Cyprus and should be a ranked member of the clergy with legal education, while the other two judges are appointed by the Supreme Court and should be jurists of the highest professional and moral standards who belong to the Orthodox Church. If the Orthodox Church refused to appoint the President of the Family Court, as had been the practice since the establishment of the Family Courts, then such President would also be appointed by the Supreme Court and be a jurist of the highest professional and moral standards who belong to the Orthodox Church; thus, in practice, no member of the Family Court is a member of the clergy.

260. Article 111 of the Constitution was further amended with the Eighteenth Amendment of the Constitution, Law 3(I)/2023. It is no longer provided that the Family Court adjudicating the family relations of the members of the Orthodox

347. A person may be appointed as President of District Court or Senior District Court Judge if he/she is an advocate who has practised law for ten years and is of a high moral standard and as District Court Judge if he/she is an advocate who has practised for six years and is of a high moral standard.

348. However, the District Court may, as an exception and with the consent of the Attorney-General, hear and determine at first instance an offence for which the accused is liable to imprisonment exceeding five years if it is satisfied that this would be in the interests of justice on the basis of the circumstances of the case and provided that the sentence imposed by the District Court judge may not exceed five years of imprisonment (such as when the particular facts of the case do not disclose a serious offence).

349. The other two judges are normally a Senior District Court Judge and a District Court Judge.

350. A. Emilianides, *Family and Succession Law in Cyprus* (3d ed., Kluwer 2024).

Church is constituted of three members and presided over by a clergyman. The composition of the Family Courts shall be determined by a Law. Moreover, the Family Courts of the Religious Groups have been abolished and the Family Courts shall have jurisdiction over all family relations of the members of the three Religious Groups. The Appellate Family Court has also been abolished and appeals are heard by the Appellate Court. The Family Courts currently have first-instance jurisdiction for all marital or family law disputes, with the exception of the cases falling within the jurisdiction of the President of the District Court. The President of the District Court currently has the exclusive jurisdiction to adjudicate the matrimonial affairs of members of the Turkish Community who have celebrated their marriage in Cyprus.[351]

261. Three further special Courts, the IDT, the Rent Control Tribunal, and the Military Tribunal, were established by law. The IDT was established in 1973 and replaced the former Arbitration Tribunal. It has jurisdiction to hear and determine disputes arising out of industrial relations. It is composed of three members; the President of the IDT is a judge appointed by the Supreme Council of Judicature, whereas the other two members are not professional judges and represent the unions of the employers and the employees respectively.[352] The Rent Control Tribunal was established by law in 1983 and has jurisdiction to hear and determine disputes relating to the determination and adaptation of the rent of certain premises and the right to possession of such premises. It is composed of three members; the President of the Rent Control Tribunal is a judge appointed by the Supreme Council of Judicature, whereas the other two members are not professional judges and represent the unions of the owners of premises and of the tenants. Finally, the Military Tribunal has jurisdiction to hear and determine offences in violation of the Military Criminal Code, or criminal offences conducted by soldiers or military personnel. The Military Tribunal is composed of three members; the President of the Military Tribunal is a judge appointed by the Supreme Council of Judicature, whereas the other two members are military officers. The decision of each special Court is reached only by the professional judge, whereas the two other members have an advisory role only. Law 69(I)/2022 has further provided for the establishment of a Commercial and Admiralty Court; however, this new Court is not yet operational.

II. Administrative Court

262. Article 146 section 1 of the Constitution used to provide that the Supreme Constitutional Court shall have exclusive jurisdiction to adjudicate finally on a resource made to it on a complaint that a decision, an act or omission of any organ, authority or person, exercising any executive or administrative authority is contrary

351. Pursuant to the Marriage Law 104(I)/2003, or Cap. 279 for the brief period from the enactment of Law 46(I)/2002 until the entry into force of Laws 104(I)/2003 and 120(I)/2003.
352. *See* in detail A. Emilianides and C. Ioannou, *Labour Law in Cyprus* (3d ed., Kluwer 2024); P. Polyviou, *The Contract of Employment under Cypriot Law* (Chryssafinis & Polyviou, 2016, in Greek, v. I-II); P. Polyviou, *The Cypriot Labour Law: Theory and Practice* (Chryssafinis & Polyviou 2018, in Greek); S. Yiannikourou, *Cypriot Labour Law* (2d ed., Nomiki Vivliothiki 2022, in Greek).

to any of the provisions of the Constitution or of any law or is made in excess or in abuse of powers vested in such organ or authority or person. Jurisdiction to review administrative action was therefore vested exclusively to the Supreme Constitutional Court and, since 1964 the Supreme Court. However, the Eighth Amendment of the Constitution Law 130(I)/2015 amended 146 of the Constitution, so that a newly established Administrative Court would exercise the administrative jurisdiction at first instance. The Establishment and Function of the Administrative Court Law 131(I)/2015 established the Administrative Courts which function as of 2016. In 2018, the Establishment and Function of the Administrative Court for International Protection Law 73(I)/2018 further established a specialized administrative court for international protection. The Administrative Appellate Court hears all administrative law appeals, with the exception of cases which are referred to the Supreme Constitutional Court; the Supreme Constitutional Court further has jurisdiction to hear appeals in third instance.

263. No other Court can review the legality of administrative action either directly or indirectly. A Court exercising civil or criminal jurisdiction has no jurisdiction to question the validity of an administrative act or decision; accordingly, a District Court exercising civil or criminal jurisdiction or even the Supreme Court while exercising such jurisdiction shall accept any administrative act as valid and shall not, under any circumstances, question the validity of such administrative act.[353] It has accordingly been held that a person who violates the conditions of a building licence may not impugn the validity of the licensing decision before the District Court, in a prosecution for a building contrary to the provisions of the permit; similarly, a person may not question the validity of an administrative act on the basis of which he/she is liable to pay taxes before a District Court in a civil action to collect such taxes.[354] If such administrative act has been taken contrary to the Constitution or any law or the principles of administrative law, this should be examined by the Administrative Court and provided that the applicant has filed a resource in accordance with the provisions of Article 146 of the Constitution.

III. Legal Status of the Judges

264. The Supreme Court is currently composed of seven Greek Cypriot judges, one of whom is appointed as the President of the Court, whereas the Supreme Constitutional Court comprises nine Greek Cypriot judges, one of whom is appointed as the President of the Court. The judges of the Supreme Court and the Supreme Constitutional Court are appointed by the President of the Republic, amongst lawyers of high professional and moral standards. Section 5 of Law 33/64 further clarifies that for a person to be appointed as a Supreme Court judge, he/she should be an advocate, who has practised for at least twelve years and who is of a high moral

353. G. Pikis, *Constitutionalism, Human Rights, Separation of Powers* 114–115 (Martinus Nijhoff 2006).

354. *EOE Tourist Enterprises Ltd v. Sewerage Board of Limassol-Amathous* [2000] 1 CLR 441 (in Greek), *Kyriacou v. Director of Customs* [2000] 1 CLR 589 (in Greek).

standard.[355] Law 145(I)/2022 introduced a new qualification pursuant to which wide knowledge and experience in handling cases of constitutional and administrative law are taken into account for the appointment of a judge of the Supreme Constitutional Court, whereas wide knowledge and experience in the handling of cases of civil and criminal law are taken into account for the appointment of a judge of the Supreme Court. Knowledge and experience in EU law or human rights law can be taken into account for the appointment of a judge of either highest court.

265. Formerly, the President of the Republic used to have seemingly unlimited power to choose any lawyer who had such high professional and moral standards as a judge of the Supreme Court and a practice had emerged pursuant to which the President of the Republic sought (and regularly followed) the advice of the Supreme Court prior to the appointment of a new member of the Court. The advice of the Cyprus Bar Association was also taken into account. With one exception,[356] all Presidents of the Republic had appointed Supreme Court justices from amongst senior lower court justices and, in particular, from amongst Presidents of the District Courts.

266. Law 145(I)/2022 amended section 4 of Law 33/64 and introduced an Advisory Council of Judicature which determines the suitability of candidates for the position of a judge of either the Supreme Constitutional Court or the Supreme Court. For the appointment of judges of the Supreme Court, the Advisory Council of Judicature comprises the President and judges of the Supreme Constitutional Court, whereas, for the appointment of judges of the Supreme Constitutional Court, the Advisory Council of Judicature comprises the President and judges of the Supreme Court. The Attorney-General of the Republic, the President of the Cyprus Bar Association, and two advocates of high professional and moral standards always participate in the composition of the Advisory Council of Judicature but do not have the right to vote. The Advisory Council of Judicature prepares a list of candidates suitable for appointment; the list should include candidates at least three times the number of the available seats, to the extent that there are suitable candidates, and include justification with regard to the decision for the suitability of each candidate. The President may then appoint judges from the list in order to fill the vacant positions.

267. Supreme Court and Supreme Constitutional Court justices are permanent members of the judicial service of the Republic and hold office until they attain the age of sixty-eight.[357] The remuneration and other conditions of service of the Supreme Court, Supreme Constitutional Court and other judges are provided by law and may not be altered to their disadvantage after their appointment. In *Fylaktou*, it

355. Practice in the permanent judicial service or the legal service of the Republic is also considered as 'practice'.

356. Former President of the Republic Glafkos Clerides appointed in 1997 Judge Rallis Gavrielides, a senior member of the legal service of the Republic.

357. Whereas the Constitution provides that the President of the Supreme Constitutional Court and the President of the High Court were to appointed for a period of six years only, the President of the Supreme Court is appointed under the same terms as all other judges of the Supreme Court.

was held any adverse change of the terms of service of judges following their appointment is prohibited pursuant to Article 158 § 3 of the Constitution. It was further held that the intention of the Constitution was to safeguard the independence of the judiciary and accordingly any measures which restrict the compensation of judges were held to be unconstitutional.[358]

268. A judge may be forced to retire on account of mental or physical incapacity or infirmity as would render him/her incapable of discharging the duties of his/her office either permanently or for such period of time as would render it impracticable for him/her to continue in office.[359] Furthermore, a judge may be dismissed on the grounds of misconduct. The exclusive competence to determine all matters relating to the retirement or dismissal of any of the judges of the two highest courts lies with the Council; the Council is composed in matters relating to the retirement or dismissal of any Supreme Court judge by all the Supreme Constitutional Court Justices (Article 153 § 8 of the Constitution), and by all the Supreme Court judges in matters relating to the retirement or dismissal of any Supreme Constitutional Court judge (Article 133 § 8 of the Constitution) The proceedings of the Council shall be of a judicial nature and the judge concerned shall be entitled to be heard and present his/her case before the Council. It is provided that the decision of the Council, taken by a majority, shall be binding upon the President of the Republic.[360] This rule is consistent with the principle of the independence of the judiciary from the executive. In addition to the above, a judge may at any time resign his/her office by addressing a written resignation letter to the President of the Republic.

269. In case the seat of a Supreme Court or Supreme Constitutional Court justice is vacant, the President of the Republic has to appoint a new judge within forty-five days. Prior to the assumption of his/her duties, a judge should sign, before the President of the Republic, the official affirmation of faith towards the Republic. All judges of the Supreme Court and the Supreme Constitutional Court enjoy, in principle, equal power and jurisdiction, unless otherwise provided in the Law. The seniority of each judge (with the exception of the President who is ex officio considered the most senior judge) is determined on the basis of the date of the promulgation of their appointment in the official Gazette of the Republic; if the promulgation of the appointment of two judges was effected in the same date, their seniority shall be determined on the basis of their previous judicial service, or in case they had no judicial service, on the basis of the priority of the document appointing them.

358. *Fylaktou and others v. Republic* [2013] 3 CLR 565 (in Greek). *See also Laoutas v. Republic* [2001] 3 CLR 40 (in Greek), *Kronides v. Republic* [2009] 3 CLR 669 (in Greek).

359. A judge so retired shall be entitled to all benefits and emoluments provided by any law in force for the time being.

360. *Deputy Attorney-General of the Republic* [2015] 3 CLR 484 (in Greek). *See also Lawrence v. The Attorney-General (Grenada)* [2007] UKPC 18, *Chief Justice of Gibraltar* [2009] UKPC 43, *The Governor of the Cayman Islands – Justice Levers* [2010] UKPC 24. *See also Kamenos*, Decision of the Supreme Council for the Judiciary of 19 Sep. 2006 (in Greek), *Kamenos v. Cyprus*, App. 147/07, Judgment of 31 Oct. 2017.

270. By virtue of Article 157 of the Constitution and section 10 of Law 33/64, the appointment, promotion, transfer, termination of appointment, dismissal and disciplinary matters of judicial officers, other than Supreme Court and Supreme Constitutional Court judges, fall exclusively within the competence of the Supreme Council of Judicature which is composed of Supreme Court judges. Pursuant to Laws 145(I)/22 and 163(I)/22, which amended section 10 of Law 33/64, the Attorney-General of the Republic, the President of the Cyprus Bar Association, and two advocates of high professional and moral standards may participate in proceedings regarding appointment, promotion or transfer of judges (but not with regard to dismissal and disciplinary matters), but without a right to vote. No judicial officer shall be retired or dismissed except on the same grounds and manner as a judge of the Supreme Court. Accordingly, the Constitution aims at safeguarding both the institutional and functional independence of the judiciary by assigning to the judiciary itself the power to regulate the judicial profession; in accordance with the principle of strict separation of powers, neither the executive nor the legislative may interfere with issues pertaining to the legal status of judges. Furthermore, judges enjoy immunity for any act done or words spoken in their judicial capacity and no action may be brought against them for any acts related to the exercise of their judicial functions. No judicial recourse is used to lie against a decision of the Supreme Council of Judicature.[361] However, since 1 July 2023, decisions of the Supreme Council of Judicature are subject to an objection before the Supreme Constitutional Court, which acts as an Appellate Council of Judicature exercising a review jurisdiction. If an objection is filed, the decision of the Supreme Council of Judicature is suspended until the determination of the objection by the Supreme Constitutional Court. Following the Twenty-First Amendment of the Constitution Law 130(I)/2025, the judges of the Administrative Appellate Court, the Administrative Court, and the Administrative Court for International Protection fell under the jurisdiction of a newly formed Supreme Constitutional Council of Judicature, instead of the Supreme Council of Judicature. The Supreme Constitutional Council of Judicature is composed of the judges of the Supreme Constitutional Court, while the Attorney-General of the Republic, the President of the Cyprus Bar Association, and two advocates of high professional and moral standards may participate in proceedings regarding appointment, promotion or transfer of judges (but not with regard to dismissal and disciplinary matters), but without a right to vote. Decisions of the Supreme Constitutional Council of Judicature are subject to review before the Supreme Court.

IV. Judicial Proceedings

271. Articles 134 and 154 of the Constitution stipulate that the sittings of the Supreme Constitutional Court and the Supreme Court respectively for the hearing

361. *Stylianides v. Supreme Council of Judicature and another*, Administrative App. 83/2016, Judgment of 5 Feb. 2018 (in Greek), *Kourris v. Supreme Council of Judicature* [1972] 3 CLR 390, *Karatsis v. Supreme Council of Judicature* [2001] 3 CLR 220 (in Greek), *Varosiotou*, Civil App. 99/2022, Judgment of 13 May 2022 (in Greek).

of all proceedings shall be public, but either Court may hear any proceedings in the presence only of the parties, if any, and the officers of the Court if it considers that such a course will be in the interest of the orderly conduct of the proceedings or if the security of the Republic or public morals so require. As an exception, it is provided in Article 134 section 2 that where a recourse filed before the Supreme Constitutional Court appears to be prima facie frivolous, the Court may, after hearing arguments by or on behalf of the parties concerned, dismiss such recourse without a public hearing if satisfied that such recourse is in fact frivolous. This is also reiterated in rules of procedure enacted by the Supreme Court. In practice, the Supreme Court had not often used its powers to dismiss recourses as frivolous without a public hearing.

272. One of the most important powers of the Supreme Constitutional Court and the Supreme Court is the power to make their own rules of procedure, in accordance with Articles 135, 163 and 164 of the Constitution and section 17 of Law 33/64, for regulating their practice and procedure; the Supreme Court may further issue rules of procedure to regulate the procedure of any other court established in accordance with the Constitution.[362] The power of the Supreme Court to effectively legislate in so far as rules of Court and procedure are concerned is very wide; such rules may relate to the regulation of the sittings of the courts and the selection of judges, the prescription of forms and fees in respect of proceedings in the courts and the regulation of costs of, and incidental to, any such proceedings, the prescription and regulation of the composition of the registries of the courts and the powers and duties of officers of the courts, the prescription of time within which any requirement of the Rules of Court is to be complied with, and the prescription of the practice and procedure to be followed by the Supreme Council of Judicature in the exercise of its competence with regard to disciplinary matters relating to judicial officers. Furthermore, the Court may provide in the rules of procedure for the summary determination of any appeal or other proceedings which appear to the Supreme Court or such other court before which such proceedings are pending to be frivolous or vexatious or to have been instituted for the purpose of delaying the course of justice.

§2. Judicial Review

I. Constitutional Review of Legislation

273. Article 140 of the Constitution provides for a form of preventive constitutional review of laws. In particular, Article 140 of the Constitution provides that the Supreme Constitutional Court has exclusive jurisdiction to hear and determine a reference by the President (or Vice-President) of the Republic, for the opinion of the Court as to whether a law or decision of the House of Representatives or any specified provision thereof, is repugnant to or inconsistent with any provision of the Constitution, otherwise than on the ground that such law or decision or any provision

362. With the exception of communal courts, which, however, do not function in practice.

thereof discriminates against either of the two Communities; such reference may be made at any time prior to the promulgation of such law or decision of the House of Representatives. The Supreme Constitutional Court shall consider every question referred to it and, having heard arguments on behalf of the President (or Vice-President) of the Republic and on behalf of the House of Representatives, shall give its opinion on such question and notify the President of the Republic and the House of Representatives accordingly. In case the Supreme Court is of the opinion that such law or decision or any provision thereof is repugnant to or inconsistent with any provision of this Constitution, such law or decision or such provision thereof shall not be promulgated by the President of the Republic.

274. The mechanism provided in Article 140 may also be used in order to determine whether legislation enacted by the House of Representatives is inconsistent with the EU law, either the Treaties or secondary legislation; this is due to the fact that EU law is considered part of the Cypriot constitutional order. The Supreme Court (exercising then jurisdiction as Supreme Constitutional Court) has held that a bill amending the Radio and Television Organizations Law 7(I)/1998[363] was inconsistent with Article 49 of the Treaty for the Functioning of the European Union (TFEU) providing for the right of establishment and Article 56 of TFEU providing for the right to provide services. The bill provided that the Radio Television Authority would not grant new television licences if, in accordance with the study of registered auditors, the new licence would hinder the financial viability of the existing television licensees. It further provided that the audiovisual services hailing from other Member States or third countries and which are retransmitted in the Republic would be retransmitted without advertising or commercial announcements aimed at the territory of the Republic.[364]

275. Repressive Constitutional Review of Legislation is governed by Article 144 of the Constitution which originally provided that the Supreme Constitutional Court had exclusive jurisdiction to decide on any questions of constitutionality of any law of the Republic which are material for the determination of any matter at issue in judicial proceedings. Whenever such question would be raised before a court, the latter would reserve the question for the decision of the Supreme Constitutional Court and stay further proceedings until such question would be determined by the Supreme Constitutional Court. Any decision of the Supreme Constitutional Court would be binding on the court by which the question has been reserved and on the parties to the proceedings. Following the constitutional crisis of 1963, however, and the enactment of the Administration of Justice (Miscellaneous Provisions) Law 33/64, it was accepted that the concentrated review of constitutionality provided in Article 144 of the Constitution was no longer applicable; it was held that due to the merge of the Supreme Constitutional Court and the High Court into a single

---

363. *See* in detail C. Stratilatis & A. Emilianides, *Media Law in Cyprus* (3d ed., Kluwer 2024).
364. *President of the Republic v. House of Representatives* [2017] 3 CLR 635 (in Greek). *See also President of the Republic v. House of Representatives* [2017] 3 CLR 647 (in Greek).

Supreme Court, the conditions precedent of the operation of such a provision of concentrated review of constitutionality by a single court could no longer be deemed to be necessary.[365]

276. In light of the above, since 1964, any court in the Republic had jurisdiction to hear questions on the constitutionality of laws without having to resort to the procedure provided for in Article 144 of the Constitution, or having to refer the question to the Supreme Constitutional Court. Thus, any lower Court (subject to appeal), or the Supreme Court in the exercise of its appellate jurisdiction, could hear and decide on any questions concerning the constitutionality of laws.[366] The Seventeenth Amendment of the Constitution, 103(I)/2022 amended Article 144 of the Constitution. It is now provided that any party at any stage of the procedure, including on appeal, can raise a question of constitutionality of legislation or decision that is substantial for the determination of the pending dispute. The court before which the dispute is pending may refer the case to the Supreme Constitutional Court, in which case the court suspends its proceedings until the determination of the question by the Supreme Constitutional Court. The Supreme Constitutional Court may, however, decide to dismiss the reference and not adjudicate the question, in which case the trial court determines the question itself. If the question of constitutionality is raised before the Supreme Court, the Supreme Court is obliged to refer the case to the Supreme Constitutional Court and suspend its proceedings until the determination of the question. Accordingly, where lower courts have discretion, the Supreme Court must refer: the mechanism was inspired by the mechanism for preliminary reference before the CJEU. Section 9 § 2 of Law 33/64 provides that references to questions of constitutionality before the Supreme Constitutional Court should set out clearly the factual background and the legal question that needs to be determined and identify the relevant legal provisions and the grounds that led the trial court to refer the question to the Supreme Constitutional Court.

277. It should be noted that a declaration of unconstitutionality shall not abrogate the unconstitutional law or automatically delete it from the statute books; the effect of such declaration is binding only on the parties of the proceedings and accordingly the law shall be inapplicable to the case in hand only (Article 144 § 3 of the Constitution). A judgment of the Supreme Constitutional Court declaring a law as unconstitutional, however, shall effectively 'abrogate' such law, in light of the principle of binding precedent, unless there is a subsequent amendment of the said constitutional provision or a new approach in case-law. An interesting illustration is sections 4 and 5 of the Law providing for the Retention of Telecommunication Data with the intention of investigating serious criminal offences 183(I)/

365. *Attorney-General v. Ibrahim* [1964] CLR 195. *See also Charalambides and another v. Republic and another*, Administrative App. 99/2016, Judgment of 4 Apr. 2018 (in Greek).

366. C. Tornaritis, *Constitutional Review of Laws in the Republic of Cyprus* (1983); E. Venizelos, *The Judicial Control of the Constitutionality of Laws in Greece and Cyprus: A Parallel Overview*, 39–40 Cyprus L. Rev. 5845–5856 (1992) (in Greek); E. Nicolaou, *The Control of Constitutionality of Laws and Distribution of Competences of the Organs of the State in Cyprus* (A. Sakkoulas 2000, in Greek); A. Loizou, *The Judicial Control of Unconstitutionality of Laws and Legality of Administrative Acts*, 27 Cyprus L. Rev. 4161–4173 (1989) (in Greek).

2007, which were declared unconstitutional as inconsistent with Article 17 of the Constitution by the Full Bench of the Supreme Court (exercising its jurisdiction as Supreme Constitutional Court) in *Matsias*.[367] However, Article 17 of the Constitution was subsequently amended with the Sixth Amendment of the Constitution Law 51(I)/10, so that sections 4 and 5 of Law 183(I)/2007 are now consistent with the Constitution.

278. This mechanism for incidental review of constitutionality of laws, which was introduced with Law 33/1964, did not apply with respect to family law disputes.[368] Consequently, the Supreme Court had exclusive jurisdiction with respect to questions of constitutionality of laws in family law affairs in accordance with Article 144 of the Constitution. The decision of the Family Court or the Family Court of Religious Groups to refer should occur whenever a question of constitutionality of any law which is material for the determination of the dispute is raised; the opinion of the lower court on whether the law is prima facie constitutional or unconstitutional is not a factor on the basis of which it may decide whether to refer the question to the Supreme Court or not.[369] It has been held that in divorce proceedings, for a valid reference to take place, this should be referred and signed by the three-judge panel and not by any single judge of the Family Court.[370] Pursuant to the Seventeenth Amendment of the Constitution, 103(I)/2022, the mechanism for the review of constitutionality is now the same for all lower courts in the Republic, including the Family Court.

279. The Supreme Court has formulated certain general principles which govern the constitutional review of legislation. The principles, which effectively derive from the jurisprudence of the Supreme Court of the USA, were stated in the leading case of *Kyriakides*[371] and have been adopted by the case-law of the Supreme Court ever since. A cardinal rule of precautionary nature is that no law and no legislative provision shall be declared as unconstitutional, unless they are unconstitutional beyond all reasonable doubt. Accordingly, there is a presumption that the law is constitutional, unless the Court is satisfied beyond any reasonable doubt that such is inconsistent or repugnant with any provision of the Constitution. The Court should try, if possible, to construe the legislative provision in question in a manner consistent with the Constitution and should only, as a last resort, declare such provision as unconstitutional. Another maxim of constitutional interpretation is that the courts are concerned only with the constitutionality of legislation and not with its motives, policy or wisdom, or with its concurrence with natural justice, fundamental principles of government or spirit of the Constitution.[372] It is not for the Court to make a value judgment on the desirability of a law, or its importance, but rather to decide whether such law is inconsistent with a constitutional provision.

---

367. *Matsias and Others* [2011] 1 CLR 152 (in Greek).
368. *Nicolaou* [1991] 1 CLR 1045 (in Greek).
369. *Zeniou v. Zeniou* [2002] 1 CLR 1175 (in Greek).
370. *Paikkou v. Paikkou* [1994] 1 CLR 610.
371. *The Board of Registration for Architects and Civil Engineers v. Kyriakides* [1966] 3 CLR 640.
372. *President of the Republic v. House of Representatives* [1989] 3 CLR 1931.

280. Moreover, the Court shall not decide abstract questions of a constitutional nature, unless this is absolutely necessary for the decision in the case at hand. The Court shall not determine questions of constitutionality, if the dispute may be properly settled without the need to determine such questions. This is also why the Court shall not formulate a rule of constitutional law broader than is required by the *precise* facts to which it is to be applied. In cases involving statutes, portions of which are valid and other portions invalid, the Courts will separate the valid from the invalid and throw out only the latter unless such portions are inextricably connected. The test of severability of the unconstitutional part from the constitutional part of the law is to be determined by considering whether severance would leave unaffected the nucleus of the law.[373] Furthermore, with regard to the power of the State to regulate the right to exercise a profession or carry on any trade or business, it has been held that the power to impose reasonable conditions on such right excludes those who cannot meet those conditions.

II. Other Forms of Constitutional Review

281. The Supreme Constitutional Court has exclusive jurisdiction to hear and determine a recourse filed by the President (or Vice-President) of the Republic, by virtue of Article 137 of the Constitution, on the ground that any law or decision of the House of Representatives discriminates against either of the two Communities.[374] The recourse shall be made within seventy-five days of the promulgation of any such law or decision. Notice of the filing of such recourse shall be published in the official Gazette of the Republic within a period of twenty-four hours from such filing and shall suspend the operation of such law or decision until the Supreme Court determines such recourse. The Supreme Constitutional Court may confirm or annul such law or decision or any provision thereof, or return it to the House of Representatives for reconsideration, in whole or in part, provided that in the case of annulment of a law or decision or any provision thereof, such annulment shall operate from the date of the publication of the decision of the Supreme Constitutional Court without prejudice to anything done or left undone under such law or decision or provision thereof. The decision of the Court shall be notified to the President of the Republic and published in the official Gazette of the Republic.

282. Moreover, the Supreme Constitutional Court has exclusive jurisdiction to hear a recourse filed by the President (or Vice-President) of the Republic, by virtue of Article 138 of the Constitution, on the ground that there is discrimination in the budget adopted by the House of Representatives; such recourse is filed if the President has exercised his/her right to return the budget to the House of Representatives

373. *President of the Republic v. House of Representatives* [2000] 3 CLR 157.
374. Such recourse is in practice obsolete due to the non-participation of the Turkish Cypriot Community in the political power of the Republic.

on the ground that there is discrimination, but the House has persisted in its decision.[375] Such recourse shall be made within the period fixed by the Constitution for the promulgation of the laws or decisions of the House of Representatives, namely within fifteen days of the transmission of such law or decision to the President. Upon such recourse, the Court may annul or confirm the Budget or return it to the House of Representatives, in whole or in part. The decision of the Court shall be notified to the President of the Republic and published in the official Gazette of the Republic.

283. It is further provided that the Supreme Constitutional Court has exclusive jurisdiction to hear and determine a recourse made in connection with any matter relating to any conflict or contest of power or competence arising between the House of Representatives and the Communal Chambers, or any one of them and between any organs of, or authorities of the Republic, by virtue of Article 139 of the Constitution. Recourse by virtue of Article 139 may be made by the President (or Vice-President) of the Republic, the House of Representatives, one or both the Communal Chambers, or any other organ of, or authority in, the Republic, if involved in such conflict or contest. It has been held that the Deputy Governor of the Central Bank is not an organ or authority of the Republic in accordance with Article 139 of the Constitution, since the organ or authority of the Republic is the Central Bank and the Deputy Governor is merely part of the Central Bank.[376] Such recourse shall be made within thirty days of the date when such power or competence is contested. Upon such a recourse, the Court may declare that the law or the decision or the act, the subject or the recourse, is void, either from the time when the conflict or contest arose, or *ab initio*, and without any legal effect whatsoever, either in whole or in part, on the ground that such law or decision or act was made or taken or done without power or competence, and in either case the Court may give directions as to the effect of anything done or left undone under such law or decision or act. The decision of the Court shall be notified to the President of the Republic and published in the official Gazette of the Republic.

284. The President of the Republic and the Council of Ministers applied to the Supreme Court by virtue of Article 139 of the Constitution requesting a declaration that the decision of the House of Representatives to reject the Regulations submitted by the Council of Ministers regarding the holidays and working hours of shops was inconsistent with the principle of the separation of powers. The Supreme Court held that any conflict of powers between the executive and the legislative powers arose at the time when the House of Representatives enacted legislation which provided that the powers of the executive to determine the holidays and working hours of shops would be determined with Regulations; which, by virtue of the Submission before the House of Representatives of Regulations issued in accordance with Legislative Authorization Law 99/1989, have to be submitted before the House of Representatives for approval. Accordingly, the conflict of powers had not arisen at

375. Such recourse is in practice obsolete due to the non-participation of the Turkish Cypriot Community in the political power of the Republic.
376. *Deputy Governor of the Central Bank v. President of the Republic* [2013] 3 CLR 731 (in Greek).

the time when the House of Representatives rejected the Regulations but beforehand. Since the recourse had not been filed within the mandatory deadline of thirty days from the time when the issue arose, it was rejected as being out of time.[377]

285. In another case, the House of Representatives enacted legislation through the budget of the Republic, mandating the termination of employment of indefinite duration of a specific group of employees in the public sector. The said employees were initially hired under a contract for the provision of services as consultants to the President of the Republic, but the Director of Social Insurance held that they were actually working as employees. Having worked continuously for the Presidency for more than thirty months, they were held to be employees of indefinite duration pursuant to Law 98(I)/2003. Because the Constitution did not provide for the possibility to refer for preventive constitutional review specific provisions of the budget, the President opted not to refer to the budget as a whole for constitutional review, since otherwise the State would be left without a budget. He then applied to the Supreme Court, by virtue of Article 139 of the Constitution, alleging that the specific provision of the budget mandating the termination of employment of his consultants was unconstitutional. The Supreme Court, however, held that since the President had opted to publish the budget, thus affirming its constitutionality, it was not permissible to subsequently refer to specific aspects of the budget by virtue of a recourse under Article 139 of the Constitution. The application was not examined on the merits.[378] Eventually, however, the affected employees applied themselves before the IDT, which held that the legislation in question violated the principle of separation of powers and Articles 25, 26 and 28 of the Constitution safeguarding the right to work, the right to enter into a contract and the principle of equality.[379]

286. In another case, the Municipality of Aglantzia filed a recourse pursuant to Article 139 of the Constitution challenging the constitutionality of the new Municipalities Law 52(I)/2022, by virtue of which it would no longer be recognized as a distinct municipality. The Supreme Court, however, declined to hear the recourse, holding that it had not been filed within the mandatory deadline of thirty days from the time when the issue arose. The judgment of the Supreme Court was highly controversial since it held that the time the issue arose was the enactment of the new legislation by the House of Representatives and not its subsequent promulgation in the Official Gazette by the President of the Republic.[380] However, this is inconsistent with the previous case-law of the Supreme Court which clearly provides that the conflict arises at the time of publication of the legislation and not at the time of

377. *President of the Republic v. House of Representatives* [2016] 3 CLR 167 (in Greek). *See also Council of Ministers v. House of Representatives* [1986] 3 CLR 1176.
378. *President of the Republic v. House of Representatives*, App. 1/2022, Judgment of 20 Jul. 2022 (in Greek).
379. *Ataliotou and others v. Attorney-General*, App. 385/2022, Decision of 12 May 2023 (IDT, in Greek).
380. *Municipality of Aglantzia v. House of Representatives*, App. 2/2022, Judgment of 2 May 2023 (in Greek).

its enactment by the House of Representatives: pursuant to Article 82 of the Constitution legislation comes in force as of its publication in the Official Gazette.[381] It is submitted that it is incorrect to hold that a conflict may arise when the legislation has not been published and accordingly remains incomplete since it is not yet in effect.

287. The Supreme Constitutional Court has exclusive jurisdiction to hear and determine a reference by the President (or Vice-President) of the Republic, by virtue of Article 141 of the Constitution, for the opinion of the Court as to whether any formalities, conditions or restrictions on the right guarantees by Article 25, which are imposed by law, are not in the public interest or are contrary to the interests of either Community; such reference may be made at any time prior to the promulgation of such law of the House of Representatives. The Supreme Constitutional Court shall consider such question and, having heard arguments on behalf of the President (or Vice-President) of the Republic and on behalf of the House of Representatives, shall give its opinion and notify the President of the Republic and the House of Representatives accordingly. In case the Supreme Constitutional Court is of the opinion that such formality, condition or restriction is not in the public interest or is contrary to the interests of such Community, such law or any provision thereof prescribing such formality, condition or restriction shall not be promulgated by the President of the Republic.

288. In addition to the above, the Supreme Constitutional Court has jurisdiction to hear and determine a reference by the President of the Republic, by virtue of Article 142 of the Constitution, with regard to any law or decision of the Greek Communal Chamber or by the Vice-President of the Republic with regard to any law or decision of the Turkish Communal Chamber, for its opinion as to whether such law or decision or any specified provision thereof is repugnant to or inconsistent with any provision of this Constitution; the reference may be made at any time prior to the publication of such law or decision.[382] The Supreme Constitutional Court shall consider every question referred to it and, having heard arguments on behalf of the President or the Vice-President of the Republic, as the case may be, and on behalf of the Communal Chamber concerned, shall give its opinion on such question and notify accordingly the President or the Vice-President of the Republic, as the case may be, and the Communal Chamber concerned. In case the Supreme Constitutional Court is of the opinion that such law or decision or any provision thereof is repugnant to or inconsistent with any provision of this Constitution, such law or decision or such provision thereof shall not be published by the President or the Vice-President of the Republic, as the case may be. Article 142 of the Constitution is, in practice, inapplicable due to the self-dissolution of the Greek Communal Chamber and the non-existence of the Turkish Communal Chamber.

---

381. *President of the Republic v. House of Representatives* [2016] 3 CLR 167, *Council of Ministers v. House of Representatives* [1986] 3 CLR 1180.
382. Such reference is in practice obsolete due to the non-participation of the Turkish Cypriot Community in the political power of the Republic and the self-dissolution of the Greek Communal Chamber.

289. Article 143 of the Constitution further provides that the Supreme Constitutional Court has exclusive jurisdiction to hear and determine a recourse filed by the President (or Vice-President) of the Republic or Representatives consisting of at least one-fifth of the total number of a newly elected House of Representatives, on the question whether there exist such urgent and exceptional unforeseen circumstances as to justify a House of Representatives which continues to be in office until the assumption of office of a newly elected House, to make any laws or take any decisions as provided in Article 68 of the Constitution. Such recourse, if made by the President of the Republic, shall be made within the period provided by the Constitution for the promulgation of the laws and decisions of the House of Representatives, namely within fifteen days of the transmission of such law or decision to the President; if made by such Representatives, it shall be made within fifteen days of the date when the new House first meets. The decision of the Court shall be notified to the President of the Republic and to the President of the House of Representatives and shall be published in the official Gazette of the Republic.

III. Prerogative Orders

290. Article 155 section 4 of the Constitution stipulates that the Supreme Court shall have exclusive jurisdiction to issue orders in the nature of habeas corpus, mandamus, prohibition, quo warranto and certiorari.[383] Such writs are collectively called prerogative orders and have their origin in English common law; the jurisdiction of the Supreme Court to issue the prerogative writs is a significant one, since it enables the Court to review the action of lower courts or organs. The two most important forms of prerogative orders are habeas corpus and certiorari. Habeas corpus is a writ which demands that a prisoner be taken before the Supreme Court in order to determine whether there is a lawful authority to detain such person; the writ is of extreme importance in cases of wrongful detention of persons. Certiorari is an order by the Supreme Court which may review a judgment, order or decision of a lower court in cases where there is manifest illegality, or mistaken application of the Constitution or of a Law, or excess of jurisdiction, or where the repugned order was issued due to collusion between the parties or misleading the Court.

291. The remaining prerogative orders are mandamus, prohibition and quo warranto. Mandamus is a writ issued by the Supreme Court to compel or direct a lower court or a government officer to perform mandatory duties, whereas conversely, prohibition is a writ directing a subordinate to stop doing something the law prohibits. Finally, quo warranto is a writ which requires a person to show by what authority they exercise power. In view of the exclusive jurisdiction of the Administrative

---

383. P. Artemis, *Prerogative Orders* (Larnaca 2004, in Greek); C. Clerides, *Prerogative Orders*, 3 Cyprus L. Tribune 297–312 (1994) (in Greek); L. Clerides, *Prerogative Writs*, 14 Cyprus L. Rev. 2195–2208 (1986) (in Greek); C. Tornaritis, *The Prerogative Orders under the Constitution and the Law of the Republic of Cyprus*, in *Proceedings of the Second International Cyprological Conference* 641–650 (T. Papadopoulos & G. Ioannides eds, Socy. Cypriot Stud. 1987).

Court to consider administrative decisions by virtue of Article 146 of the Constitution, the prerogative writs cannot be used against decisions, acts or omissions of the administration. Thus, habeas corpus may not be invoked if a person is detained on the basis of an administrative act, even if such act is allegedly unlawful; the legality of the administrative act may be reviewed only by a recourse filed in accordance with Article 146 of the Constitution.

IV. Contempt of Court

292. Article 162 of the Constitution provides that the Supreme Court shall have jurisdiction to punish for any contempt of itself, and any other court of the Republic shall have power to commit any person disobeying a judgment or order of such court to prison until such person complies with such judgment or order and in any event for a period not exceeding twelve months. The power of contempt has always been regarded as an inherent power of the courts, a power, which is founded upon immemorial usage.[384] The power of a Court to punish any person disobeying its judgments or orders is one of the most significant ones. However, in administrative cases, the Supreme Court has interpreted this provision in a manner which has weakened its effect. It was held that punishment for contempt for disobeying an order of the Court presupposes an order of a prohibitory or mandatory nature; judgments which annul an administrative act or decision by virtue of Article 146 of the Constitution are of a declaratory character and accordingly the Administrative Court and the Supreme Court when exercising its jurisdiction in administrative law cases has no power to punish for contempt if the decision is not complied with.[385] The remedy in case of non-compliance or refusal to abide by the decision would be either a new recourse or an action for damages.

293. The notion of contempt is further expanded in Article 44 of the Courts of Justice Law 14/60 where, *inter alia*, acts of disrespect, obstruction or disturbance of any judicial proceedings, including publications which are capable of prejudicing the fair trial of such proceedings, are penalized and wrongdoers are liable to imprisonment up to six months.[386] The judgment of the Grand Chamber of the EctHR in *Kyprianou v. Cyprus*[387] led to a re-evaluation of the principles governing the most straightforward and notorious cases of contempt, those where the offence is committed in the face of the court and in particular by advocates. Section 44 of the Courts of Justice Law 14/60 was amended by Law 36(I)/2009 in order to conform

384. For a general introduction to the problem of contempt of court *see Arlidge, Eady and Smith on Contempt* (5th ed., Sweet & Maxwell 2017).

385. *Republic v. Thalassinou* [1991] 3 CLR 203 (in Greek), *Vyronas v. Republic* [1999] 3 CLR 77 (in Greek); *Epameinonda and Others v. Municipality of Limassol* [2016] 3 CLR 203 (in Greek).

386. S. Stavrinides, *Contempt of Court in Cyprus*, 2 Cyprus L. Tribune 167–178 (1991) (in Greek).

387. *Kyprianou v. Cyprus*, App. 73797/01, Judgment of 15 Dec. 2005. *See* A. Emilianides, *Contempt in the Face of the Court and the Right to a Fair Trial*, 13 European J. Crime, Crim. L. & Crim. J. 401–412 (2005).

to the findings of the *Kyprianou* judgment.[388] The amended provision 44 stipulates that while Cypriot courts still have the power to punish for contempt committed in the face of the court, if the act constituting the contempt is committed against the person of the judge, they cannot adjudicate the matter personally, but they have to refer the matter, including the minutes of the Court, to the President of the Supreme Court who may appoint another judge to adjudicate the matter.

294. The Court referring the matter to the President of the Supreme Court should inform the alleged perpetrator of the act or words which constitute contempt and of the penalties provided in the law; if the alleged perpetrator has apologized in a satisfactory manner, the Court may refrain from referring the matter. If the judge appointed by the President of the Supreme Court in order to adjudicate the offence, holds that an offence has been committed, before imposing penalty, he/she shall balance between the need to safeguard the integrity of the judiciary on the one hand and the right of freedom of expression on the other. Especially with regard to advocates, section 44 section 9 provides that words or behaviour by an advocate who appears before the Court and examines or cross-examines witnesses, or expresses statements or arguments on behalf of the party he/she represents, do not constitute a criminal offence, but could only constitute a disciplinary offence; such provision aims at safeguarding both the freedom of expression of the advocate, as well as the right to a fair trial of his/her client.

295. In the *Loucaides* case,[389] the former Cypriot ECtHR judge and thereafter advocate, Loukis Loucaides, was considered by a Superior District Court Judge to have behaved and expressed words in a manner giving rise to contempt in the fact of the court; in particular, it was argued that Loucaides had expressed the opinion that the Superior District Court Judge was not a person fit to act as a member of the judiciary and that he then left the court chambers without permission having been given by the Court. The aggrieved Judge referred the case to the President of the Supreme Court who appointed the President of the District Court to adjudicate the case. Loucaides argued that the President of the District Court had no jurisdiction to adjudicate contempt proceedings against him; however, his objections were dismissed. Loucaides then filed an application for a writ of certiorari before the Supreme Court of Cyprus. A judge of the Supreme Court granted a certiorari and quashed the contempt proceedings. It was held that since Loucaides was representing a client in the proceedings before the District Court, section 44 section 9 of Law 14/60 precluded the application of criminal proceedings of contempt; the matter should have been examined by the Disciplinary Board of the Cyprus Bar Association. Accordingly, the District Court lacked jurisdiction on the matter.

---

388. *See also* K. Ebeku, *Revisiting the Acquittal of 10 Policemen: Issues of Judicial Independence, Trial by Media and Fair Trial in Cyprus*, 18 European J. Crime, Crim. L. & Crim. J. 1–42 (2010).

389. *Loukis Loucaides Advocate*, Application 45/2011, Judgment of 16 May 2011 (in Greek). *See also* A. Emilianides, *Reflections on the Law of Contempt in Light of Recent Cypriot Jurisprudence*, 2 Cyprus Human Rights L. Rev. 221–226 (2012).

296. It was further considered that section 44 section 8 of Law 14/60 explicitly provides that the President of the Supreme Court may appoint a judge to adjudicate the alleged contempt in accordance with the procedure provided for in a procedural regulation issued by the Supreme Court; since the Supreme Court had never issued such procedural regulation, it was held that the appointment of the President of the District Court by the President of the Supreme Court was not legally permitted. Accordingly, the President of the District Court lacked jurisdiction to adjudicate the matter. In the initial decision to grant leave for an application of certiorari, the Supreme Court had also considered additional parameters of the case, which, in view of its conclusions, were not finally pronounced upon in the final judgment.[390] It was noted that there is no prosecutor in contempt proceedings and that the judge essentially acts as both prosecutor and judge contrary to the fundamental principles governing a criminal trial. In addition, the trial was to be held in accordance with the minutes prepared by the aggrieved judge, minutes which had been disputed by the accused. Furthermore, the accused did not have the right to cross-examine witnesses with respect to the facts supporting the case against him. It is considered that these are serious issues which might influence the manner in which the law of contempt is exercised by the courts, also in cases which do not concern advocates.

390. Application 37/2011, *Loucaides*, Judgment of 23 Mar. 2011 (in Greek).

Chapter 6. Independent Non-political Bodies in the Legislative or Executive Branch with an Advisory or Supervisory Task

§1. The Attorney-General

297. The Attorney-General of the Republic is the single most important independent officer of the Republic.[391] The Attorney-General and the Deputy Attorney-General of the Republic are appointed by the President of the Republic and are members of the permanent legal service of the Republic. They serve on the same terms and conditions and may not be removed from office except on the same grounds and manner as judges of the Supreme Court; thus, the Attorney-General and the Deputy Attorney-General hold office until they attain the age of sixty-eight and may be dismissed only by a decision of the Council on the ground of misconduct, or on account of mental or physical incapacity or infirmity as would render them incapable of discharging the duties of their office either permanently or for such period of time as would render it impracticable for them to continue in office.[392] Whereas the Constitution stipulates that the Attorney-General and the Deputy Attorney-General shall not hail from the same Community, by virtue of the doctrine of necessity, both the Attorney-General and the Deputy Attorney-General are Greek Cypriots.[393]

298. The Attorney-General of the Republic is, by virtue of Article 112 of the Constitution, the Head of the Law Office of the Republic; the Law Office is an independent office of the Republic, which shall not be under any Ministry. The Deputy Attorney-General acts as the Deputy Head of the Law Office. He/she has the right to audience in any court and shall take precedence over any other persons appearing before it. One of the most important powers of the Attorney-General is the power to institute, conduct, take over, continue or discontinue any proceedings for an offence against any person in the Republic; such power may be exercised by him/her in person or by officers subordinate to him/her acting under and in accordance with his/her instructions.[394] The Attorney-General has the power to direct the police, oversee the investigation of any offence and decide whether there is a case justifying prosecution. Furthermore, such power shall be exercised in accordance with his/her discretion in the public interest, by virtue of Article 113 of the Constitution. In the exercise of his/her powers, the Attorney-General is not subject to control from any executive or judicial authority; his/her decision to prosecute or discontinue any

391. L. Loucaides, *The Institution of the Attorney-General in Cyprus* (Nicosia, 1974, in Greek), A. Pantelides, *Der Attorney-General in England, der Attorney-General in Zypern und die Staatsanwaltschaft in Deutschland* (München, 1975).
392. A person so retired shall be entitled to all benefits and emoluments provided by any law in force for the time being.
393. A Turkish Cypriot Deputy Attorney-General, Orhan Feridun, served until 1963; the office remained vacant until 1975, when a Greek Cypriot, Loukis Loucaides, was appointed.
394. D. Kyprianou, *The Role of the Cyprus Attorney-General's Office in Prosecutions: Rhetoric, Ideology and Practice* (Heidelberg 2010); C. Tornaritis, *The Constitutional Power of the Attorney-General to Institute, Conduct or Discontinue any Criminal Proceedings*, 2 Cyprus L. Rev. 203–224 (1983) (in Greek).

prosecution by a *nolle prosequi* is absolute and not subject to judicial control.[395] Moreover, it is not permissible for the House of Representatives to interfere with the constitutional decisions of the Attorney-General.[396]

299. In light of the above, the Attorney-General is both the general prosecutor and the legal advisor of the State. He/she represents the President of the Republic before the Supreme Court in recourses or references and he/she represents the Republic in civil actions and administrative resources before the Cypriot courts; civil actions by or against the Republic are instituted or defended in the name of the Attorney-General by virtue of section 57 of the Courts of Justice Law 14/60. Furthermore, the Attorney-General acts as the agent of the Republic before the CJEU and the ECtHR. Furthermore, he/she is the Chairperson of the Legal Council, the Disciplinary Board and the Pension Fund of Advocates and an honorary Chairperson of the Cyprus Bar Association. The Deputy Attorney-General exercises all the powers and performs all the functions and duties vested in the Attorney-General, subject to the directions of the Attorney-General by virtue of Article 114 section 2 of the Constitution, and acts in lieu of the Attorney-General, by virtue, in case of his/her absence or his/her temporary incapacity to perform his/her duties. The dual role of the Attorney-General as the general prosecutor, as well as the legal advisor of the State, has proved extremely controversial in recent years. The Council of Ministers has submitted a bill before the House of Representatives, which is currently pending, aiming for the establishment of a new independent officer, a Prosecutor-General, who would undertake all powers regarding prosecutions, with the Attorney-General retaining all other existing powers.

300. The Supreme Court has held that whereas the Attorney-General is the legal consultant of the President of the Republic, this does not imply that the President is required to accept the legal opinion of the Attorney-General in cases where this would have the effect to deprive the President of the right to exercise his/her constitutional rights, such as the right to petition the Supreme Court by virtue of Article 140 of the Constitution. The Supreme Court held that in a case where the Attorney-General considered the impugned legislation as constitutional and accordingly declined to file a petition and to represent the President before the Supreme Court, the President had a right to appoint a private advocate of his choice in order to exercise his constitutional rights.[397] It is moreover noted that the Attorney-General may appoint private advocates to represent him/her, instead of being represented by advocates of his/her office, if he/she considers that there are grounds which justify doing so.[398]

---

395. *Police v. Athienitis* [1983] 2 CLR 194, *Chomatenos v. Police* [1979] 2 CLR 119, *Ellinas v. Republic* [1989] 1 CLR 17.
396. *Attorney-General of the Republic v. House of Representatives*, Case 4/21, Judgment of 24 Jan. 2022 (in Greek).
397. *President of the Republic v. House of Representatives* [2013] 3 CLR 178 (in Greek).
398. *Deputy Attorney-General of the Republic* [2015] 3 CLR 236 (in Greek).

301. The application of the Attorney-General of the Republic to remove the Deputy Attorney-General of the Republic from office for misconduct is of significance. The Attorney-General of the Republic Costas Clerides had announced that an independent investigator had concluded that the Deputy Attorney-General had received a bribe from a major Cypriot law firm in order to be persuaded to act in their interest in a multi-million euros case. He further announced that the issue would have to be carefully assessed in order to determine whether prosecution should take place against the Deputy Attorney-General. Immediately following the announcement, the Deputy Attorney-General held a press conference, which was broadcasted live and accused the Attorney-General of acting in a conspiracy against him and of having received himself bribes.

302. Referring to a number of commonwealth cases regarding the notion of 'misconduct' by judges or public officials, the Supreme Court acting as Council, held that the behaviour of a judge or a public official should reaffirm the people's faith in their integrity, dignity and impartiality. It was held that the conduct of the Deputy Attorney-General fell far short of the minimum standard of behaviour expected from a public official and was unacceptable. He had accused without cause the Attorney-General of having committed serious criminal offences in a manner which showed serious lack of right judgment and self-control[399] Accordingly the Council decided to remove the Deputy Attorney-General from office. The Deputy Attorney-General was eventually convicted of bribery by the Assize Court and was sentenced to 3.5 years imprisonment.[400] In a subsequent judgment the Supreme Court acting as Council clarified that whereas the President of the Republic, or the Attorney-General had a right to submit an application to remove a judge or an independent official from office for misconduct, no such right existed for members of the public at large. Accordingly, an application by a citizen to fire the Attorney-General for misconduct was struck out as inadmissible.[401]

§2. The Auditor-General

303. The Auditor-General and the Deputy Auditor-General are appointed by the President of the Republic, by virtue of Article 115 of the Constitution, and act as the Head and Deputy Head of the Audit Office of the Republic respectively. Whereas, the Constitution stipulates that the Auditor-General and the Deputy Auditor-General shall not hail from the same Community, by virtue of the doctrine of necessity both the Auditor-General and the Deputy Auditor-General are currently Greek Cypriots. The Audit Office is an independent office which is not under any Ministry.[402] The Auditor-General and the Deputy Auditor-General are members of the permanent public service of the Republic and shall not be retired or removed

399. *Ibid.*

400. *Kyprizoglou and others v. Republic*, Criminal Apps. 53, 64, 66, 68/2017, Judgment of 15 Dec. 2017 (in Greek).

401. *Tryfonos* [2017] 3 CLR 21 (in Greek), *Loi*, App. 1/2017, Judgment of 20 Sep. 2017 (in Greek).

402. C. Tornaritis, *The Legal Position of the Auditor-General*, in *Ibid.*, *Constitutional and Legal Problems in the Republic of Cyprus* 64–68 (2d ed. 1972).

from office except on the like grounds and in like manner as a judge of the Supreme Court. In a highly publicized and controversial case, the Supreme Constitutional Court acting as the Council decided to remove the popular Auditor-General Odysseas Michaelides from office. It was held that the conduct of the Auditor-General fell well below the minimum standards expected from a public official and that he was therefore guilty of a misconduct. The Court referred to a number of instances, effectively noting that the Auditor-General lacked self-control and engaged in continuous bickering with other State officials, without any respect for the institutions of the State, and showing a complete lack of exercise of good judgment. His behaviour against the Attorney-General and the Deputy Attorney-General was specifically singled out.[403]

304. The functions of the Auditor-General are of particular importance, since, by virtue of Article 116 of the Constitution, he/she controls, on behalf of the Republic, all disbursements and receipts and audit and inspect all accounts of moneys and other assets administered, and of liabilities incurred, by or under the authority of the Republic; he/she has for this purpose, the right of access to all books, records and returns relating to such accounts and to places where such assets are kept. The Auditor-General may exercise his/her powers in person or by subordinate officers acting under and in accordance with his/her instructions. The Auditor-General submits annually a detailed report on the exercise of his/her functions and duties to the President of the Republic, which shall be laid before the House of Representatives. The Fiscal Responsibility and Fiscal Framework Law 20(I)/2014 and the Submission of Data and Information to the Auditor-General of the Republic Law 113(I)/2002 further reinforce the powers of the Auditor-General to carry out audits and reviews and to request documents and other relevant information.

§3. The Governor of the Central Bank

305. The Governor of the Central Bank is appointed by the President of the Republic and is, by virtue of Article 118 of the Constitution, the Head of the Central Bank of the Republic, which is an independent office not under any Ministry. The Governor of the Central Bank is, in practice, appointed under the terms and conditions laid down to the instrument of his/her appointment and is appointed for a fixed term. The power of dismissal and any disciplinary matter in connection with the exercise of the functions of the Governor of the Central Bank lies with the Council. The Governor of the Central Bank administers the currency laws of the Republic and is in charge of the management of the Central Bank of the Republic; furthermore, he/she exercises all other functions and duties within the domain of the Central Bank of the Republic. The Governor shall, by virtue of Article 119 section 4 of the Constitution, consult and be guided by the advice of the Minister of Finance, with regard to the financial policy relating to his/her office and shall carry out the decisions of the Council of Ministers in this respect. The Governor shall submit half-yearly reports on the state of currency, funds and securities of the Republic

403. *Auditor-General of the Republic*, App. 1/2024, Judgment of 16 Sep. 2024 (in Greek).

to the President of the Republic which shall be laid before the House of Representatives. Despite the fact that the Constitution provides for the existence of a Deputy Governor, no such Deputy Governor had been appointed from 1963 until February 2013, when a Greek Cypriot was appointed as Deputy Governor.

§4. The Accountant-General

306. Article 126 of the Constitution provides that the President of the Republic shall appoint the Accountant-General and the Deputy Accountant-General of the Republic. Whereas the Constitution stipulates that the Accountant-General and the Deputy Accountant-General shall not hail from the same Community, by virtue of the doctrine of necessity, both the Accountant-General and the Deputy Accountant-General are currently Greek Cypriots. The Accountant-General and the Deputy Accountant-General are members of the permanent public service of the Republic and respectively act as the Head and Deputy Head of the Treasury of the Republic; their disciplinary control, including dismissal and removal from office, fall within the competence of the Public Service Commission. The Accountant-General, in accordance with Article 127 of the Constitution, manages and supervises all accounting operations in respect of all moneys and other assets administered and of liabilities incurred, by or under the authority of the Republic and receives and makes all the disbursements of moneys of the Republic.

§5. The Public Service Commission

307. According to Article 125 of the Constitution, the Public Service Commission has the exclusive competence to appoint, promote, transfer, retire and exercise disciplinary control over public officers. The Public Service Commission was to be composed, by virtue of Article 124 of the Constitution, of ten members, seven Greek Cypriots and three Turkish Cypriots. However, the Public Service Commission, as provided in the Constitution, has ceased to function due to the abnormal situation prevailing since 1963 and has been substituted by a new Public Service Commission established by Law.[404] The new Public Service Commission was initially established by the Public Service Law 33/67 and is currently governed by the provisions of the Public Service Law 1/90. It is comprised of five members, one of whom acts as President of the Public Service Commission, who are appointed by the President of the Republic for a six-year period; they cannot be dismissed from office except for the same reason and in the same manner as judges of the Supreme Court. The Public Service Commission has competence over public servants but not over employees of the wider public service or public corporations; the matters concerning the latter fall under the competence of the board of the respective corporation. It has been held that the law regarding the new Public Service Commission must be as similar as possible to the constitutional provisions.[405]

---

404. *Hadjianastassiou v. The Republic* [1982] 3 CLR 1173.
405. *The Republic v. Kyriacou* [1987] 3 CLR 1189.

§6. Independent Organs Established by Law

308. Whereas the Constitution provides for the establishment of only four independent officers of the Republic and their Deputies (Attorney-General, Auditor-General, Governor of the Central Bank, Accountant-General), additional independent officers have been established by ordinary legislation. The Office of the Ombudsman (Commissioner for Administration) was established in 1991 by virtue of the Ombudsman Law 3/1991, with the general duty of overseeing the proper function of the administration.[406] The Ombudsman is appointed for a six-year term by the President of the Republic, following a proposal by the Council of Ministers and with the consent of the majority of the House of Representatives.[407] He/she may examine individual complaints against the action, inaction or decisions of administrative organs and may submit proposals for the institutional and operational improvement of the system of administration of the Republic. The Ombudsman thus seeks to redress administrative action which has been unlawful and to prevent its repetition. Moreover, the Combating of Racism and Other Discrimination (Commissioner) Law 42(I)/2004 vests the Ombudsman with special competences, duties and powers for combating and eliminating discrimination in both public and private sectors. Any person or group of persons may lodge a complaint to the Ombudsman for having been subjected to discrimination. The Ombudsman is therefore authorized with the supervision of the implementation of the human rights instruments which the Republic has ratified. The Ombudsman may also carry out investigations *ex proprio motu* into incidents of discrimination, and prepare codes of practice concerning specific public authorities or persons in the private sector, obliging them to follow practical measures aimed at promoting non-discrimination and equality of treatment.

309. Another significant independent officer established by legislation is the Law Commissioner who is appointed by the President of the Republic for a six-year term. He/she has the competence to submit proposals for amendments in the legislation and for harmonization with EU legislation or international treaties. Another Commissioner is the Commissioner for the Rights of the Child whose role is to safeguard the interests of children in accordance with the Commissioner for the Protection of the Rights of the Child Law 74(I)/2007; the Commissioner for the Rights of the Child is appointed by the Council of Ministers for a five-year term. The Commissioner for Personal Data Protection is also appointed by the Council of Ministers for a four-year term and has the power to oversee the application of the Processing of Personal Data (Protection of the Individual) Law 138(I)/2001 and, since 25 May 2018, the General Data Protection Regulation.[408] The Commissioner for Personal Data Protection further acts as an Information Commissioner and is

---

406. E. Nicolaou, *Ombudsman: The First Decade*, 2 Cyprus L. Tribune 29–33 (2001) (in Greek).
407. The participation of the House of Representatives in the appointment of the Ombudsman may well be unconstitutional, in view of the interpretation given by the Supreme Court to the principle of separation of powers.
408. General Data Protection Regulation (EU) 2016/679 of the European Parliament and of the Council.

responsible for applying the legislation on access to public documents. Two additional independent officers established by Law are the Office of the Commissioner for State Aid Control and the Office for the Commissioner for Internal Audit of the Republic; both are appointed by the Council of Ministers for a six-year term. Other presidential commissioners are the Commissioner for Environment, the Commissioner for Overseas Cypriots, the Commissioner for Gender Equality, the Financial Ombudsman, the Agricultural Payments Commissioner, the Communications Commissioner, and the General Health System Supervision Commissioner.

310. Several independent collective organs have also been established by ordinary legislation.[409] The Educational Service Committee is an important organ with similar competences as the Public Service Commission but with respect to the appointment, promotion, transfer, retirement and disciplinary control of public educational officers. The Commission for the Protection of Competition is an Independent collective organ with the power to implement anti-trust legislation in the Republic of Cyprus. Several collective organs have the role of reviewing acts of the administration in given fields by exercising quasi-judicial authorities: such include the Tender Review Authority, the Refugees Review Authority, the License Review Authority, the Taxation Board, the Commission for the Investigation of Incompatibilities and the Review Board of the Central Agency for Equal Distribution of Burdens.

409. *See* V. Georgiou, *Public Administration in Cyprus* (En Typois 2012, in Greek).

Part III. The State and Its Subdivisions

Chapter 1. State Form

311. It has been suggested that the Republic of Cyprus cannot be characterized as a unitary state in view of the bi-communal nature of its Constitution.[410] Such views were mostly political ones, complemented by the Turkish argument that the dualistic nature of the Constitution should lead to a separate right of self-determination for each of the two Communities of the island and are not really convincing.[411] Irrespective of the bi-communal nature of the Constitution, there is little doubt that the Republic of Cyprus is a unitary State.[412] Article 185 section 1 of the Constitution explicitly states that the territory of the Republic is one and indivisible, whereas Article 185 section 2 of the Constitution prohibits the integral or partial union of Cyprus with any other State or the separatist independence. Moreover, the State organs exercise their executive, legislative or judicial powers in a unitary manner in the entire territory of the Republic and for all the people of the Republic, irrespective of the Community to which they belong. The public service, the military forces, the police and the gendarmerie are also unified. There were no federal or self-controlled entities in the territory of the Republic and accordingly no division of power between the central government and the (non-existing) administrations of component states or entities, as would be the case in a federal system.

312. The constitutional provision for the institution of the Communal Chambers does not put into question the unitary character of the State, as the Communal Chambers had limited competences on matters of a purely communal nature (religious, family and educational matters), which do not relate to the exercise of State power. There is no doubt that the competences of the Communal Chambers are not those of a federal entity.[413] Similarly, the constitutional demand for the establishment of separate municipalities in the five largest towns of the Republic related to the establishment of a system of local administration and not to the establishment

---

410. *See* e.g., Z. Necatigil, *The Cyprus Question and the Turkish Position in International Law* 15 (2d ed., Oxford U. Press 1993); A. Gazioglu, *Cyprus: A Few Facts and the Rule of Law* (2001); A. Søzen, *The Cyprus Conflict and the Negotiations: A Political and International Law Perspective* (1998); N. Ertekon, *The Status of the Two Peoples in Cyprus: Legal Opinions* (2d ed., 1997); N. Ertekon & Z. Necatigil, *The Right of the Turkish Cypriot People to Self-Determination* (1996).
411. *See* in detail A. Emilianides, *Beyond the Constitution of Cyprus* (Sakkoulas 2006, in Greek).
412. *See* C. Tornaritis, *The Genesis of the Cypriot State and Its Form* 13ff (1974, in Greek); K. Chrysostomides, *The Republic of Cyprus: A Study in International Law* (Martinus Nijhoff 2000).
413. *See* De Smith, *The New Commonwealth and Its Constitutions* 292 (Stevens & Sons 1964).

of federal entities. Accordingly, the Republic of Cyprus remains a unitary State, despite the peculiarities of its bi-communal structure.

313. It should, however, be noted that the federation was accepted as a basis for the solution of the Cyprus problem in 1977. Until 1974, Greek Cypriots had passionately rejected the Turkish proposal for federation, arguing that Cyprus lacked all of the necessary elements, either social, economic, geographical, demographical, or political, for the adoption of such a system of government.[414] Indeed, when federation was accepted as a basis for the solution of the Cyprus problem in 1977, the aim was to reach, by accepting federation, a quick solution to the Cyprus problem, so as to avoid the detrimental effects of maintaining the status quo. However, Turkey wilfully did not enter into an immediate agreement and as a result, federation became ever since 1977 the basis for solution. There is little doubt that the Greek Cypriot political leaders had not realized what they had accepted in 1977.[415] The official position of the Greek Cypriot Community concerning the agreement of 1977, as expressed, for instance, by the former Attorney-General of the Republic Criton Tornaritis, provided that the accepted federation should provide for the complete safeguard of human rights throughout the island, without any provisions for majority of land or population in either federal unit, as well as the safeguard of the unity of the state and the economy.[416] This remains the official position of the Government of the Republic of Cyprus until this day.[417]

314. However, it would emerge that the understanding of the UN and the Turkish side, as far as the interpretation of the term 'federation' is concerned, was quite different. Starting with the American-British-Canadian Plan of 1978 and culminating in the Annan Plan, all proposals for a solution to the Cyprus problem following the acceptance of federation interpreted the term, not in the sense officially accepted by the Greek Cypriot side,[418] but as reproducing the effects of the Turkish occupation of the island through a separationist structure.[419] The Greek Cypriots, faithful to their quest for a quick agreement, gradually adopted terminology which coincided with the terminology initially proposed by Turkey. Thus, the 'bi-communal federation'[420] became a 'bizonal, bi-communal federation' and ultimately a 'bizonal, bi-communal federation with political equality'.[421] The Greek Cypriot point of departure of transforming the 1960 Constitution into a federated state

414. *See* C. Tornaritis, *Cyprus and Federalism* (1974); P. Polyviou, *Cyprus in Search of a Constitution: Constitutional Negotiations and Proposals* (1976).
415. *See*, *inter alia*, the analysis of P. Polyviou, *Makarios: The Three Errors* 52–79 (Kastaniotis 2009, in Greek).
416. *See* C. Tornaritis, *The Legal Aspects of the Cyprus Problem* 17ff (1983, in Greek).
417. *See* for instance, the unanimous Resolution of the Cypriot National Council dated 18 Sep. 2009.
418. *See* the analysis of N. Christodoulides, *The Plans for the Solution of the Cyprus Problem* (Kastaniotis 2009, in Greek).
419. *See* in more detail A. Emilianides, *Beyond the Servant State Paradigm: The Cyprus Problem Revisited*, Inst. Intl. Rel. Panteion U. Y.B. 107–126 (2003–2004).
420. Provided for in the 1977 Agreement.
421. As provided for in the Agreement between Christofias and Talat of 23 May 2008.

became the 'virgin-birth' state of affairs, whereby each side (namely the Republic of Cyprus and the 'TRNC') can claim elements of continuity.[422]

315. The framework above essentially negated any possibility of an immediate solution to the Cyprus problem. The decision to adopt the Annan Plan as a framework for the solution of the Cyprus problem was the culmination of the failed experiment to reach a settlement and there was little doubt that the Plan would be rejected, as it eventually happened.[423] The first version of the Annan Plan was entitled 'Basis for a Comprehensive Settlement of the Cyprus Problem' and was submitted on 11 November 2002. The Plan was twice revised on 10 December 2002 and 26 February 2003, before being revised two more times in Bürgenstock, Switzerland, on 25 and 31 March 2004. The fifth and final version of the Plan was entitled 'The Comprehensive Settlement of the Cyprus Problem.' As has been correctly noted, the constitutional structure was based on division and discrimination and not upon democracy or the protection of fundamental rights.[424] Essentially, the viability of the intended United Cyprus Republic would be explicitly interwoven with the process of Greco-Turkish relations and the EU accession process of Turkey.[425]

---

422. As provided for in the Annan Plan.
423. C. Palley, *An International Relations Debacle* (Hart 2005); A. Syrigos, *The Annan Plan: The Legacies of the Past and the Prospects of the Future* (Patakis 2005, in Greek).
424. *See, inter alia,* L. Loucaides, *The Legal Support of an Illegal UN Plan by a UN Lawyer*, Cyprus Y.B. Intl. Rel. 19–64 (2007).
425. For an analysis of the main aspects of the Plan *see* A. Emilianides, *Constitutional Study of Annan V*, in A. Varnava & H. Faustmann, *Reunifying Cyprus: The Annan Plan and Beyond* 95–106 (Tauris 2009); A. Emilianides et al., *The Annan Plan: Five Critical Essays* (Ypsilon/Aigaion 2003, in Greek).

Chapter 2. Decentralized Authorities

316. The Municipal Corporations Law, Cap. 240, which was in force prior to Independence, provided for the existence of unitary municipalities, whereas both Greek and Turkish Cypriots were living in the same towns, without separation. However, in 1958, during the EOKA struggle, the Turkish Community established separate municipalities in the five largest towns of the Republic (Nicosia, Limassol, Famagusta, Larnaca and Paphos); such separate municipalities were vested with certain limited powers in regard to the collection and recovery of revenue by the British by Law 33/1959. Article 173 of the Constitution provides for the establishment of separate municipalities in the five largest towns of the Republic by the Turkish inhabitants of such towns; provided that the President and the Vice-President of the Republic were to examine, within four years of the date of the coming into operation of the Constitution, the question whether or not this separation of municipalities should continue. The Municipal Councils of Greek municipalities were to be elected by the Greek electors of the town, whereas the Municipal Councils of Turkish municipalities were to be elected by the Turkish electors of the town. A coordinating body was to be set up, composed of two members chosen by the Greek Municipal Council, two members chosen by the Turkish Municipal Council and a President chosen by agreement between the two Municipal Councils. Such coordinating body would provide for work which needed to be carried out jointly and would concern itself with matters which require a degree of cooperation.

317. The constitutional demand for the establishment of separate municipalities was considered an unfortunate innovation by the Greek Cypriots. The duplication of municipalities in the five largest towns would effectively lead to the duplication of services, elected officials and staff and would lead to an important increase in expenses. More importantly, the separation of municipalities was considered a deeply separationist provision. On the contrary, the Turkish Cypriots considered the separate municipalities as an important mechanism granting increased autonomy and power.[426] Despite intense negotiations between then-President Makarios and then Vice-President Kucuk, Article 173 of the Constitution was never implemented and separate municipalities were never established. The effect of Cap. 240 and Law 33/59 was prolonged by the House of Representatives, until 31 December 1962, when no further prolongation was enacted by the House of Representatives. As of 1 January 1963, the Republic no longer had in effect laws with regard to Municipalities.

318. In *Celaleddin*, the Supreme Constitutional Court held, by majority, that the constitutional provision regarding the establishment of separate municipalities in the five largest towns was part of the legislative programme in Articles 173–177 for the establishment of such municipalities; accordingly, such separate municipalities could only be established through legislation, something which had never

426. D. Markides, *Cyprus 1957–1963. From Colonial Conflict to Constitutional Crisis: The Key Role of the Municipal Issue* (U. Minn. 2001); S. Kyriakides, *Cyprus: Constitutionalism and Crisis Government* (U. Pennsylvania Press 1968).

occurred.[427] In *The Turkish Communal Chamber v. The Council of Ministers*,[428] the Supreme Constitutional Court further held, by majority, that the Council of Ministers had no power or competence to effectively establish unitary municipalities in the five largest towns of Cyprus, by creating an alternative means of local administration by virtue of the Villages (Administration and Improvement) Law, Cap. 243. Articles 173–177 of the Constitution continue to remain ineffective.

319. Cyprus is a very small State and accordingly its administration remains primarily centralized. The competences of local authorities, while not extensive, are, however, important since they relate, *inter alia*, to urban development, building permits, hygiene, cleaning garbage, protection of the environment, public health, regulation and issue of licences for shops, restaurants, cinemas, theatres, municipal markets, museums, traffic regulation, organization of cultural and other activities, sewerage, etc.[429] The Municipalities Law 111/85 regulates the establishment, abolition and functions of Cypriot municipalities. There are currently thirty municipalities functioning in the areas controlled by the Republic of Cyprus and nine additional municipalities which, while situated in the areas controlled by the Republic of Cyprus, may not exercise their competencies in the territories of their municipalities because of the Turkish occupation. Every Municipal Council is elected for a five-year term and consists of the Mayor and Councillors, whose number shall be no less than eight and no more than twenty-six. In addition to the Municipalities, there are also Improvement Boards and Village Authorities, as well as Sewerage Boards, Water Boards and School Boards. Local authorities are considered administrative organs when exercising administrative power. As of 2024, there will be a new Municipalities Law in effect (Law 52(I)/2022), pursuant to which there shall be twenty municipalities instead of thirty; the number of municipalities nominally situated in the occupied areas is not affected.

---

427. *Celaleddin v. The Council of Ministers* (1963) 5 RSCC 102. *See also The House of Representatives v. The Turkish Communal Chamber* (1963) 5 RSCC 123, *The Mayor, Deputy Mayor, Councillors and Citizens of Famagusta v. Petrides* (1962) 4 RSCC 71.

428. *The Turkish Communal Chamber v. The Council of Ministers* 5 RSCC 59.

429. *See* C. Tornaritis, *The Concept of Local Government within the Framework of a Unitary State* (1971); *Ibid., Local Administration in Cyprus* (1972, in Greek); A. Emilianides, *The Evolution of Administration in Cyprus* (1967, in Greek); L. Loucaides, *Local Administration in Cyprus*, in *Lectures of Popular University n. 2* 63–76 (1986, in Greek), V. Georgiou, *Public Administration in Cyprus* 357ff (En Typois 2012, in Greek).

Part IV. Citizenship and the Administration of Justice

Chapter 1. Rules Concerning Nationality and Relevance of Nationality

§1. Introduction

320. From 1878 until 1914, Cypriots were considered Ottoman subjects. Following the Cyprus Annexation Order in Council of 1914, however, and a subsequent Order in Council of 27 November 1917, it was provided that any person who was habitually resident in Cyprus on 27 November 1917 would automatically become a British subject; persons born in Cyprus who did not have their habitual residence in Cyprus could apply to the British High commissioner in order to become British subjects.[430] Following the establishment of the Republic, Annex D of the Treaty of Establishment[431] provided that any citizen of the UK and its Colonies who, on the date of the entry into force of the Treaty of Establishment (namely 16 August 1960), possessed any of the qualifications specified in section 2 of the Treaty shall become a citizen of the Republic if he/she was ordinarily resident in Cyprus at any time in the period of five years immediately before 16 August 1960. The qualifications specified in section 2 of the Treaty of Establishment were that the person concerned: (i) became a British subject under the Cyprus Annexation Orders in Council of 1914–1943, (ii) was born in Cyprus on or after 5 November 1914, or (iii) descends in the male line from any of the persons referred to in (i) and (ii) above.

321. Any citizen of the UK and its Colonies born between 16 August 1960 and 16 February 1961 shall become a citizen of the Republic at the date of his/her birth if his/her father becomes a citizen or would, but for his/her death, have done so. In accordance with section 4 of the Treaty of Establishment, any person who was a citizen of the UK or its Colonies before 16 August 1960 and possesses the qualifications specified in section 2 of the Treaty but did not become a citizen of the Republic

430. A. Emilianides, *The Issue of Citizenship of Cypriot from British Rule until Today*, in *Symmikta Streit* 299ff (1939, in Greek).

431. Annex D is extremely detailed; only an overview of its main provisions shall be included in this section. For an overview *see* C. Tornaritis, *The State Law of the Republic of Cyprus* 35ff (Cyprus Research Ctr 1982, in Greek).

shall be entitled to apply to the appropriate authority of the Republic to be granted citizenship of the Republic if he/she was immediately before 16 August 1960 ordinarily resident in the UK, or in a colony, protectorate, protected State or UK trust territory or in the territory of any country within the British Commonwealth of Nations, or Greece or Turkey, or elsewhere if he/she became or may become stateless.

322. A person of Cypriot origin (namely a person who was on 5 November 1914 an Ottoman subject ordinarily resident in Cyprus or who descended in the male line from such a person) who immediately before 16 August 1960 was not a citizen of the UK and its Colonies shall be entitled to apply to the appropriate authority of the Republic in order to be granted citizenship by virtue of section 4 subsection 2 of the Treaty. A woman who was married before 16 August 1960 to a person who is both entitled to and applied for citizenship of the Republic shall be entitled to also apply, so long as the marriage is still valid, to be granted citizenship of the Republic by virtue of section 4 subsection 3 of the Treaty; the same right is granted under certain conditions for a woman who was married before 16 August 1960 to a person of Cypriot origin or a person possessing the qualifications specified in section 2 subsection 2 of the Treaty, if their marriage was terminated by death or divorce (section 4 subsections 4 and 5 of the Treaty).

323. The Citizen of the Republic Law 43/67 governed all questions regarding the status of a citizen of the Republic until such law was abolished by the Population Registry Law 141(I)/02.[432] It is submitted that the provisions of Law 141(I)/02 regarding citizenship remain unnecessarily complicated. Citizenship of the Republic may be acquired by birth or descent, registration or naturalization. Section 108 of Law 141(I)/02 provides that a person is considered to be a citizen of the Republic if he/she had either acquired or is entitled to acquire citizenship at the entry into force of Law 141(I)/02, or who acquire citizenship following the entry into force of Law 141(I)/02 in accordance with the provisions of such Law or under the provisions of Annex D of the Treaty of Establishment. An overview of the provisions of Law 141(I)/02 with respect to citizenship shall be presented in the subsequent paragraphs.[433]

§2. Citizenship by Birth or Descent

324. Citizenship by birth is established by virtue of section 109 of Law 141(I)/02. Section 109 section 1 of Law 141(I)/02 provides that a person born in Cyprus on or after 16 August 1960 (the date the Republic of Cyprus was established) shall

432. C. Christoforou & C. Vezouvios, *Immigration Law and Policy* in *Introduction to Cyprus Law*, 132ff (Andreas Neocleous & Co LLC ed., 3d ed., Limassol 2010).

433. *See also* A. Emilianides & C. Papastylianos, *Citizenship and Nationality. Cyprus* in *Constitutionalism in Context* 330–350 (D. Law ed., Cambridge University Press 2022).

be a citizen of the Republic, if either of his/her parents was a citizen of the Republic at the time of birth; if neither parent was alive at the time of birth, then the person shall be a citizen of the Republic if either parent would have been entitled to become a citizen of the Republic, had he/she not died. The above provisions do not apply if the entry into or stay in the Republic of either parent was illegal. By virtue of section 109 section 2 of Law 141(I)/02, a person born in any foreign country at or after 16 August 1960 shall be a citizen of the Republic under the same conditions, as those provided for persons born in Cyprus, namely if either of his/her parents was or would be entitled (had he/she not died) to become a citizen of the Republic at the time of birth. The above provisions do not apply to a person who is a permanent resident of a foreign country, unless his/her birth was registered in accordance with the provisions of Law 141(I)/02.

325. Section 109 section 3 of Law 141(I)/02 introduces an exception to the general rule; it is provided that the relevant provisions of section 109 sections 1 and 2 do not apply to any person born between 16 August 1960 and 11 June 1999 who would have been entitled to become a Cypriot citizen by virtue of the fact that his/her mother was a citizen of the Republic or was entitled to become a citizen of the Republic at the time of death. Such a person has to be registered as a citizen of the Republic by applying to the Minister of Interior in the manner provided in Law 141(I)/02; if the person is a minor, the application should be made by either parent. If a person was born on or after 18 June 1960 and is descended from a person who either became a British national on the basis of the Annexation of Cyprus Orders in Council of 1914–1943 or was born in Cyprus between 5 November 1914 and 16 August 1960, during which time his/her parents were habitually resident in Cyprus, is entitled to be registered as a citizen of the Republic by submitting an application to the Minister of Interior and so long as he/she has made an affirmation of loyalty to the Republic.

§3. Citizenship by Registration

326. In accordance with section 110 section 1 of Law 141(I)/02, a citizen of the UK or its Colonies or of a member of the Commonwealth, who is of Cypriot origin (namely a person who was born in Cyprus while his/her parents were habitually residing in Cyprus), may register as a citizen of the Republic by submitting an application to the Minister of Interior and by making an affirmation of loyalty to the Republic, so long as he/she: (i) resides or has resided in Cyprus for a continuous period of twelve months prior to the submission of his/her application or is a member of the Public Service of the Republic; the period of twelve months may be reduced at the discretion of the Minister, if there are special circumstances; (ii) is a person of good character; (iii) intends to continue residing in the Republic, or depending on the case, serving at the Public Service of the Republic; (iv) is a person of sound mind and over 18 years of age.

327. The Minister of Interior may further register as a citizen of the Republic, by virtue of 110 section 2 of Law 141(I)/02 and following the submission of an application and an affirmation of loyalty to the Republic, any person who: (i) is the spouse or widower/widow of a citizen of the Republic or who would have become or would have a right to become a citizen of the Republic, but for his/her death; (ii) has resided with such spouse in Cyprus for a period of at least three years; provided that the period may be reduced by the Minister to a period of at least two years, but only so long as the spouse does not reside permanently or temporarily abroad. The period of three (or two) years need not be continuous; if the persons resided in Cyprus for at least six months a year and an aggregate of two years in the last three years, this shall be considered sufficient; (iii) is of a good character; (iv) intends to continue residing in the Republic; (iv) is a person of sound mind and over 18 years of age. No person may be registered if he/she entered or stays in the Republic illegally. The Minister of Interior may further register the minor child of any citizen of the Republic by virtue of section 110 section 3 of Law 141(I)/02. A person who has denounced or who has been deprived of citizenship may also register, but only with the approval of the Minister of Interior.

§4. Citizenship by Naturalization

328. The Minister may grant a certificate of naturalization, in accordance with section 111 of Law 141(I)/02, to any alien who is of sound mind and over 18 years of age, following the submission of an application and an affirmation of loyalty to the Republic. The qualifications for naturalization are provided in the Third Schedule of Law 141(I)/02 and are the following: (i) residence in the Republic for a period of twelve continuous months prior to the submission of the application; (ii) residence in the Republic or being a member of the Public Service for a period of at least five years in total during the eight years preceding the submission of the application; the ambit of such provision is heavily restricted by the highly confusing proviso that students, visitors, self-employed persons, athletes, coaches, sports technicians, domestic assistants, nurses, as well as persons employed by Cypriot or foreign employers or by offshore companies who reside in the Republic in order to work, or their spouses, or children, should reside in Cyprus for at least seven years in total during the last seven years, the last twelve of which must have been continuous. Admittedly, the proviso makes no sense; (iii) good character; (iv) intention to reside in the Republic, or become or continue to be a member of the Public Service of the Republic or international organization to which the Republic is a member, or association, or company, or body which was established in the Republic.

329. The Council of Ministers may at its discretion: (a) consider a period of twelve continuous months which occurred not more than six months prior to the submission of the application, as having occurred immediately prior to the submission of the application; (b) consider the residence of a person of Cypriot origin in a foreign country, or the residence in the former Colony of Cyprus or service at the Government of the former Colony of Cyprus prior to 16 August 1960, as residence in the Republic; (c) take into account periods of residence or service prior to the eight years before the submission of the application; (d) allow a person who has denounced Cypriot citizenship to acquire citizenship by naturalization irrespective of the time of residence; or (e) allow the naturalization of an alien irrespective of the time of residence, if there are exceptional cases of providing services of the highest standard to the Republic and for the public interest, so long as the House of Representatives is informed in advance.

330. In 2007, the Council of Ministers introduced a scheme for granting citizenship to investors from third countries. There was a limited number of 141 such naturalizations between 2007–2012, the legal basis being that they were exceptional cases that had provided, through the investment, services for the public interest of the Republic. This was a controversial legal basis, but faced with the ongoing financial crisis, the Anastasiades Government introduced a more ambitious citizenship investment scheme in 2013. Law 36(I)/2013 amended section 111A of Law 141(I)/2002 to recognize explicitly the power of the Council of Ministers to naturalize alien investors. The Council of Ministers interpreted this provision as enabling it to also naturalize the spouse and/or children of the investor, although there was no legal basis for this in the Law. Law 113(I)/2020 did explicitly provide for the power to naturalize members of the family of the investors. There followed extensive naturalizations on the basis of the scheme, which was unofficially described as a 'Golden Passport Scheme': 3.517 investors and 3.810 members of their families were naturalized.

331. The citizenship investment scheme was highly criticized by the European Commission, which argued that such schemes violated EU law. In October 2020, the Commission started an infringement procedure against Cyprus for its investor scheme. The Council of Ministers decided to terminate the scheme and not to receive any further applications as of 1 November 2020 after an Al Jazeera investigation led to turmoil and the resignation of the President of the House of Representatives, Demetris Syllouris. The Council of Ministers continued, however, to examine pending applications. As a result, the Commission sent to Cyprus a reasoned opinion on 9 June 2021. A four-member committee of enquiry was appointed by the Attorney-General to probe the implementation of the scheme; the Committee published its opinion on 7 June 2021, determining that naturalizations of members of the family of the investors lacked a legal basis until 2020 and were unlawful. It further suggested revoking a number of particular cases that did not fulfil the requirements.[434] The Council of Ministers has since revoked a number of citizenships. There is little doubt that the citizenship investment programme undermined confidence in Cypriot procedures, both domestically and externally.

434. Republic of Cyprus, *Report of the Committee of Inquiry for the Exceptional Naturalization of Alien Investors and Entrepreneurs*, 7 Jun. 2021 (in Greek), available in https://www.pio.gov.cy/assets/pdf/newsroom/2021/06/REPORT-NICOLATOU%20COMMITTEE_220621.pdf. *See also* Audit Service of the Republic, Audit of the Cyprus Investment Scheme, 22 Aug. 2022, available in, https://www.brief.com.cy/sites/default/files/2022-08/2022%2008%2022%20%CE%84%CE%88%CE%BB%CE%B5%CE%B3%CF%87%CE%BF%CF%82%20%CF%84%CE%BF%CF%85%20%CE%9A%CE%95%CE%A0.pdf.

§5. Denunciation and Deprivation of Citizenship

332. Section 112 of Law 141(I)/02 provides that any citizen of the Republic who is of sound mind and over 18 years of age and further has citizenship of another country may denounce citizenship of the Republic. The person is no longer considered a citizen of the Republic from the time that such denunciation is registered by the Minister of Interior; however, the Minister may suspend the effects of such denunciation if it occurs during wartime, or if the Minister considers that the aim of such denunciation is to avoid an obligation of military service, or any criminal prosecution.

333. A person who acquired citizenship by registration or naturalization may be deprived of such citizenship by an Order of the Council of Ministers in accordance with section 113 of Law 141(I)/02, as amended by Law 113(I)/2020. If a person is deprived of citizenship, members of his/her family may also be deprived of their citizenship if this had been acquired due to their status as members of the family of such person. If a person is deprived of citizenship, there is no return of the investment, or any donations or contributions made by such person. A three-member Independent Committee of Examination of Citizenship Deprivation advises the Council of Ministers on individual cases. This Committee is chaired by a representative of the Legal Services of the Republic and is further constituted by the Auditor-General and the Permanent Secretary of the Ministry of Justice and Public Order or their respective representatives. The Committee should provide the opportunity to the person affected to express their views prior to reaching an opinion.

334. If such registration or naturalization was achieved by fraud, false pretences, or disclosure of any material facts, a person shall be deprived of such citizenship. A person may further be deprived of such citizenship if he/she: (i) showed lack of loyalty to the Republic either verbally or by his/her actions; (ii) acts in a way that shows approval of, or holds an office in, the unlawful administration in the areas not controlled by the Republic, or has unlawfully entered or interfered or caused damage to any immovable property in such areas which is owned by another; (iii) was communicating or dealing with the enemy or knowingly participated in any activities which were assisting the enemy during wartime; (iv) was sentenced to imprisonment in any country for a particularly abominable offence or for an offence showing moral turpitude within ten years of naturalization, in so far as it is also an abominable offence or an offence showing moral turpitude and providing for the penalty of imprisonment under Cypriot law; (v) within ten years from registration or naturalization has become a person wanted by either EUROPOL or INTERPOL for a serious office punishable by imprisonment of five years or for an offence showing moral turpitude, in so far as it is also an offence punishable by imprisonment under Cypriot law; (vi) within ten years from registration or naturalization has been sanctioned or has repeatedly failed to abide by the requirements set out in Regulations; or (vii) resided in foreign countries for a continuous period of seven years, and if during such time, he/she did not notify every year the consular authorities of the Republic of his/her intention to remain a citizen of the Republic, or was not at any time a member at the service of the Republic or at the service of an international organization to which the Republic is a member.

§6. Relevance of Citizenship

335. The status of a Cypriot citizen is of extreme importance for the application of Cypriot constitutional law. Only citizens of the Republic comprise the Greek or Turkish Community of the island in accordance with Article 2 of the Constitution. Only citizens of the Republic may be qualified to be elected as President or Vice-President of the Republic in accordance with Article 40 of the Constitution, as a member of the House of Representatives in accordance with Article 64 of the Constitution, or as a member of either the, now self-dissolved, Greek or the Turkish Communal Chamber in accordance with Article 94 of the Constitution. Furthermore, Article 31 of the Constitution, which safeguards the fundamental right to vote in elections, safeguards such right only for citizens of the Republic. Only citizens of the Republic have the right to vote in elections for President or Vice-President (Article 1 of the Constitution), members of the House of Representatives (Article 63 of the Constitution), or members of the Communal Chambers (Article 94 of the Constitution).

336. With respect to municipal and community Elections, the Municipal and Community Elections (National of Other Member States) Law 98(I)/2004 has implemented Council Directive 94/80/EC of 19 December 1994 and Council Directive 96/30/EC of 13 May 1996 in the Cypriot legal order. In accordance with the provisions of Law 98(I)/2004, nationals of other Member States of the EU have the right to vote in municipal and community elections as long as they are at least 18 years old and they have been habitually residing in the Republic for a period of at least six months immediately prior to the date they became eligible to vote. Eligible voters who are nationals of other Member States are registered in a special electoral roll, which is kept by the Ministry of Interior. Nationals of other Member States who have attained the age of 21 and have registered in an electoral roll have the right to stand for election, albeit not for the post of mayor, or deputy mayor, or community president, or community vice-president. The House of Representatives rejected on October 2011 two bills regarding the extension, under certain conditions, of the right to vote in municipal and community elections to immigrants who are non EU-citizens.

337. Only citizens of the Republic may be appointed as a Minister in accordance with Article 59 of the Constitution, as a member of the Supreme Court of Cyprus in accordance with Articles 133 and 153 of the Constitution,[435] or as a member of the Public Service Commission in accordance with Article 124 of the Constitution and section 4 of the Public Service Law 1/1990. Furthermore, only citizens

435. With the exception of the (no longer existing) neutral Presidents of the High Court or the Supreme Constitutional Court.

of the Republic may be appointed as independent officers of the Republic.[436] It used to be that only citizens of the Republic could be appointed as members of the Public Service of the Republic in accordance with Article 123 of the Constitution. The accession of the Republic of Cyprus to the EU has affected the absolutism of such requirements. Section 31 of the Public Service Law 1/1990, as modified by section 3(a) of Law 128(I)/2003, provides that only citizens of the Republic may be appointed as members of the Public Service of the Republic; however, if the position does not imply direct or indirect participation in the exercise of public power and the preservation of the general interests of the State, members of Member States of the EU or the European Economic Area or Switzerland may be appointed. Section 31(f) further provides that the Council of Ministers may, in exceptional circumstances, and for the public interests, permit a person who is not a citizen of the Republic to apply for appointment to the Public Service.

338. In accordance with Article 130 of the Constitution, only citizens of the Republic can be appointed as members of the security forces of the Republic (police and gendarmerie). Furthermore, Article 129 of the Constitution provides that only citizens of the Republic can be appointed to the army of the Republic; however, the army of the Republic provided for in Article 129 has effectively never existed. Section 10 of the Army of the Republic Law 33/1990 provides that, in certain exceptional circumstances, the Council of Ministers may appoint non-citizens of the Republic as members of the Army of the Republic, although in view of the sensitive nature of the subject, this might in practice apply only for the case of Greek citizens. Section 14 of Law 33/90 further provides that only Cypriot citizens may be appointed as Volunteer Sub-Officers, whereas only Cypriot and Greek citizens may be appointed as Volunteer Sub-Officers of a Five-Year Term.

339. Only citizens of the Republic may be subject to compulsory military service in accordance with the provisions of the National Guard Law 20/1964. The issue was considered by the Supreme Court in the case of *Kalligeros*.[437] The Applicant was born in Cyprus in 1994; his father was a Greek citizen, whereas his mother was a Cypriot citizen. In accordance with section 109 section 3 of Law 141(I)/02 analysed above, any person born between 16 August 1960 and 11 June 1999 who would have been entitled to become a Cypriot citizen by virtue of the fact that his/her mother was a citizen of the Republic has to be registered as a citizen of the Republic by applying to the Minister of Interior in the manner provided in Law 141(I)/02. The Applicant never applied for citizenship by registration and accordingly never acquired Cypriot citizenship. It was therefore considered that the Applicant was not subject to compulsory military service in the National Guard and the decision of the Minister of Defence to the contrary was annulled.

436. This is due to the combined effect of Arts 112 and 153 of the Constitution (with respect to the Attorney-General and the Deputy Attorney-General), Arts 155 and 123 of the Constitution (with respect to the Auditor-General and the Deputy Auditor-General) and Arts 118 and 123 of the Constitution (with respect to the Governor and the Deputy Governor of the Central Bank of Arts 118 and 123 of the Constitution).

437. *Republic v. Kalligeros* [2013] 3 CLR 379 (in Greek).

340. In principle, the fundamental rights and liberties provided in Part II of the Constitution are safeguarded for all persons, irrespective of their citizenship.[438] However, there are certain rights which are restricted only to citizens, and predominant amongst those is the right of free movement within the Republic. Article 14 provides that no citizen shall be banished or expelled from the Republic, therefore not extending such protection to aliens, whereas Article 11 section 2(f) provides that the arrest or detention of a person to prevent him/her from effecting an unauthorized entry into the territory of the Republic or of an alien against whom action is being taken with a view to deportation or extradition may amount to a lawful deprivation of liberty. Pursuant, however, to the Seventh Amendment of the Constitution Law 68(I)/2013, it was provided that citizens of the Republic may also be deported or extradited pursuant to an EAW or an international convention which is binding upon the Republic and to the extent that the other party applies the principle of reciprocity. Furthermore, Article 32 of the Constitution explicitly provides that nothing contained in Part II precludes the Republic from regulating by law any matter relating to aliens in accordance with international law; the Aliens and Immigration Law, Cap. 105 sets out, by virtue of Article 32 of the Constitution, the requirements that have to be fulfilled in order for an alien to be allowed entry to or residence in the Republic of Cyprus.

438. *Municipal Council of Aghios Dometios v. Christoforou and Others* [1994] 3 CLR 434 (in Greek).

Chapter 2. Fundamental Rights and Liberties

§1. General (Domestic and International Sources, General Rules)

I. The General Characteristics of Part II of the Constitution

341. A detailed list of the constitutionally safeguarded fundamental rights is included in Part II of the Constitution of Cyprus (Articles 6–35) under the heading 'Fundamental Rights and Liberties.'[439] Legislation which is contrary to the provisions of the constitution safeguarding individual human rights may be declared unconstitutional by the trial court. It has been held that the fundamental rights and liberties safeguarded by the Constitution have to be narrowly construed and, in case of doubt, should always be interpreted in favour of the individual protected, rather than in favour of the State.[440] It is further noted that the Constitution safeguards minimum rights; the legislator may always opt to afford wider protection of a right or establish a new right; however, in the latter cases, such right shall not enjoy a constitutional level of protection but shall only be protected by ordinary legislation. Protection of fundamental rights has been considered a primary principle of the Cypriot State despite the continuous crises that Cyprus has faced, both political and financial. The Covid-19 crisis led to a re-evaluation of the manner in which constitutional rights are safeguarded. Whereas Cypriot authorities did not declare a state of emergency, they still introduced extensive lockdowns and severe restrictions on constitutional rights without specific legislative action or effective judicial review. The executive relied on the Quarantine Law, Cap. 260, in order to impose significant temporary restrictions on constitutional rights, including the right to movement, the right to private life, freedom of religion and freedom of assembly.[441]

342. Article 33 of the Constitution explicitly provides that the fundamental rights and liberties guaranteed by the Constitution shall not be subject to any other limitations or restrictions other than those provided in Part II of the Constitution. Such limitations may further only be introduced by legislation enacted by the House

---

439. *See* in general, C. Tornaritis, *The State Law of the Republic of Cyprus* (Cyprus Research Ctr. 1982, in Greek); *Ibid.*, *The Legal Aspects of Human Rights* (1977, in Greek); *Ibid.*, *The Human Rights as Recognized and Protected by Law, with Special Reference to the Law of Cyprus* (1967); P. Evangelides, *The Republic of Cyprus and Its Constitution, with Special Regard to the Constitutional Rights* (Difo-Druck GmbH 1996); A. Loizou, *Constitution of the Republic of Cyprus* (2001, in Greek), C. Paraskeva, *Cypriot Constitutional Law: Fundamental Rights and Freedoms* (Nomiki Vivliothiki 2015, in Greek).

440. *Fina (Cyprus) Ltd v. Republic* (1962) 3 RSCC 26.

441. *See* C. Stratilatis, *The Covid-19 Pandemic in Cyprus: A Problematic Legal Regime, and the Potential of Rule of Law in Emergencies*, in *Democracy after Covid. Challenges in Europe and Beyond* 91–109 (K. Chrysogonos & A. Tsiftsoglou eds, Spring 2022); C. Kombos, *Covid-19 and the Cypriot Example: A Constitutional Paradox*, UK Constitutional Law Association, 7 May 2020, available in https://ukconstitutionallaw.org/2020/05/07/constantinos-kombos-covid-19-and-the-cypriot-example-a-constitutional-paradox/, *Ibid.*, *Constitutional Improvisation and Executive Omnipotence: The Cypriot Handling of the Pandemic*, Verfassungsblog, 2 Mar. 2021, available in https://verfassungsblog.de/constitutional-improvisation-and-executive-omnipotence-the-cypriot-handling-of-the-pandemic/.

of Representatives or legislation deemed to be part of Cypriot law under Article 188 of the Constitution[442] or, since the accession of the Republic of Cyprus to the EU, legislation which forms part of EU law. It is further stipulated in Article 33 section 2 that limitations or restrictions to the fundamental rights safeguarded by the Constitution should be interpreted strictly and should not be applied for any purpose other than those for which they have been prescribed. Interference with constitutional rights should never be given wider effect than what clearly and beyond doubt is warranted by their context.

343. Authorities of the Republic, legislative, executive and judicial, are duty bound, in accordance with Article 35 of the Constitution, to secure within the limits of their respective competence, the efficient application of the provisions of Part II of the Constitution. The manner in which the Supreme Court approaches Part II, and in particular Article 35 of the Constitution, was elaborated in the leading case of *Georghiades*.[443] In the course of the trial of a psychologist, on charges of perjury and related counts, the trial Court ruled as admissible a conversation between the accused and his client that took place in the course of a medical examination overheard by the use of an electronic listening and recording device, preceded by the installation of a transmitter unknown to either the accused or his client, carefully hidden in the room where the examination would take place. The Supreme Court unanimously held that the overhearing by the prosecution witness concerned, by means of an electronic device (a transmitter and ear-phones), of a conversation between the accused and his client, without the knowledge of either of them, was an act incompatible with the protection of the right of privacy, as safeguarded by Article 8 of the ECHR, and Article 15 of the Constitution. It was also held that such act amounted to a violation of Article 17, safeguarding the right to respect for the secrecy of correspondence and other communication.

344. Consequently, the Supreme Court held that the trial Court could not have treated as admissible the evidence adduced regarding the overhearing of the conversation between the accused and his client, as there is no room for exercising any discretion in accordance with the principles governing the admissibility of evidence which has been obtained in violation of constitutional provisions. As stated in the oft-cited judgment of Pikis J:

> Any suggestion, that a discretion vests in Cyprus Courts to admit evidence obtained in defiance to the right guaranteed by the Constitution, is untenable in view of the provisions of Articles 34 and 35 of the Constitution. Article 34 denies to everyone any liberty to destroy any of the rights and liberties safeguarded by Part 11 of the Constitution, ruling out thereby discretion to admit evidence obtained in contravention of the provisions of Part II of the Constitution. The acknowledgment of any discretion to the Courts would also run counter to the duty cast upon all authorities of the State, including the Courts, to ensure the efficient application of Part II of the Constitution (Article 35).

---

442. *Police v. Hondrou and Another* (1962) 3 RSCC 82.
443. *Police v. Georghiades* [1983] 2 CLR 33.

> Admission of evidence obtained in breach of fundamental rights, would be incongruous with the efficient application of the provisions of this part of the Constitution. To our judgment, there is no discretion to admit evidence obtained or secured by contravention of the fundamental rights and liberties safeguarded by Part II of the Constitution.[444]

345. In addition, the Court effectively held in *Georghiades* that constitutional rights protect the individual not only from State interference but also from interference by other private individuals. In its leading subsequent judgment of *Yiallouros v. Nicolaou*,[445] the Supreme Court impliedly adopted the legal concept of *drittwirkung*, in accordance with which an individual plaintiff can rely directly on the constitutional provisions safeguarding fundamental rights in order to sue another individual or the government for the violation of those rights. Yiallouros, the Director of the Sewerage Board of Nicosia, had, during a whole year, taped and monitored the telephone conversations of Nicolaou, an employee of the Sewerage Board; in addition, Nicolaou was put on probation in light of the content of his telephone conversations.

346. Nicolaou sued Yiallouros before the District Court, requesting compensation for the violation of his constitutional rights, namely his right to privacy safeguarded by Article 15 of the Constitution and secrecy of communications safeguarded by Article 17. The District Court held that Yiallouros was liable to pay compensation to his employee. Yiallouros appealed, arguing that there is no direct right to sue for violation of constitutional rights, when such violations do not also constitute torts in accordance with the Torts Law, Cap. 148. The Supreme Court held that the violation of constitutional rights vests to the victim the right to invoke legal remedies for the vindication of his rights. The effective application of fundamental rights presupposes the right of a person whose constitutional rights have been violated to receive compensation for any damage suffered because of the violation. Consequently, the violation of constitutional rights is directly actionable before District Courts.

347. In *Doros Georghiades*, the Supreme Court considered the issue of whether a person may waive a human right; the accused had agreed, in light of the nature of charges, namely sexual offences, that part of the proceedings should be held in camera, thus waiving the right to a public hearing.[446] The majority of the Supreme Court correctly held that the accused could waive, under the circumstances, his right to a public hearing.[447] One judge of the Supreme Court, however, expressed the opinion

444. *Police v. Georghiades* [1983] 2 CLR 33, at 66.
445. [2001] 1 CLR 558. *See* P. Constantinides, *The Drittwirkung of Fundamental Rights in the Cypriot Legal Order* (Hippasus 2016, in Greek); S. Papasavvas, *There Is Drittwirkung of Human Rights in the Cypriot Legal Order: Comments and Thoughts on the Judgment of the Supreme Court in Civil Appeal 9931 Yiallouros v. Nicolaou*, 15 Dikaiomata tou Anthropou 837–861 (2002) (in Greek).
446. *Georghiades* [2002] 1 CLR 1455 (in Greek).
447. *See also Hakansson and Sturesson v. Sweden*, App. 11855/85, Judgment of 21 Feb. 1990, *Poitrimol v. France*, App. 14032/88, Judgment of 23 Nov. 1991.

that there is no room for compromise or relinquishment of human rights and that, accordingly, no person may waive, under any circumstances, his fundamental rights.[448] It is submitted that there are indeed provisions in Part II of the Constitution, which are inalienable under any circumstances, for example, prohibition of slavery; however, there are fundamental rights which may be waived if the person protected so wishes.[449]

II. The Significance of International Human Rights Instruments

348. Part II of the Constitution is modelled on the ECHR; however, the provisions of the ECHR have been extended and enlarged in some respects with a number of social and economic rights added in order to meet the basic requirements of a modern society.[450] Consequently, to the extent that it has been incorporated in constitutional provisions and to the degree that its provisions have not been altered during incorporation, the ECHR enjoys limited constitutional status.[451] It should be further observed that the Cypriot courts are invoking the case-law of the ECtHR, not only with respect to the interpretation of the ECHR but also with respect to the interpretation of the corresponding constitutional articles. Therefore, the courts will try, wherever possible, to interpret the relevant constitutional provisions in a manner which is consistent with the interpretation adopted by the ECtHR.[452]

349. The ECHR first became applicable to Cyprus during the British rule of the island. The UK, by its declaration n. 61/48/53 of 23 October 1953, made under Article 63 of the ECHR, extended it to various territories for the international relations of which it was held to be responsible, including the then colony of Cyprus.[453]

---

448. *Georghiades* [2002] 1 CLR 1455 (in Greek). *See also Cleanthous v. Cyprus Telecommunication Authority* [1991] 4 CLR 297 (in Greek).
449. *See*, however, G. Pikis, *Constitutionalism, Human Rights, Separation of Powers* 66–67 (Martinus Nijhoff 2006).
450. Acknowledged in several judgments of the Supreme Court of Cyprus, such as *Attorney-General v. Ibrahim* [1964] CLR 195: 225, *Attorney-General v. Afamis* 1 RSCC 121: 125–126. *See* further C. Tornaritis, *The Human Rights as Recognized and Protected by Law, with Special Reference to the Law of Cyprus* (1967); *Ibid.*, *The Social and Economic Rights under the Law of the Republic of Cyprus*, in *Melanges Bridel* 533–556 (Imprimeries Réunies 1968).
451. *See* A. Emilianides, *Beyond the Constitution of Cyprus* (Sakkoulas 2006, in Greek).
452. *See* further A. Loizou, *Cyprus and the European Convention on Human Rights* (Sakkoulas 2003, in Greek); C. Tornaritis, *The Operation of the European Convention for the Protection of Human Rights in the Republic of Cyprus*, 3 Cyprus L. Rev. 455–464 (1983); C. Clerides, *The Operation of the European Convention on Human Rights in the Civil Courts of Cyprus*, 39–40 Cyprus L. Rev. 6029–6043 (1992) (in Greek).
453. *See* for its application to the island during the turbulent years of 1955–1959 the first interstate application of *Greece v. UK*, n. 176/1956, as well as the second interstate application of *Greece v. UK*, 299/1957, 18 Human Rights Law Journal 348ff (1997); *The Reports of the European Commission of Human Rights with Respect to Cyprus. App. 176/1956 & 299/1957* (A. Emilianides ed., Ministry Educ. & Culture 2008, in Greek). Also E. Lauterpacht, *European Convention on Human Rights: Suspension of Its Application to Cyprus*, 6 Intl. & Comp. L. Q. 432–434 (1956).

Following the declaration of independence of the Republic of Cyprus, the application of the ECHR in Cyprus ceased.[454] On 24 May 1961, the Republic of Cyprus became a member of the Council of Europe,[455] and on 16 December 1961, it acceded to the ECHR. The ECHR was ratified in the internal legal order by the European Convention for the Protection of Human Rights (Ratification) Law n. 39/1962. The instrument of ratification was deposited with the Secretary of the Council of Europe on 6 October 1962. The International Covenant on Civil and Political Rights (ICCPR) and the International Covenant on Economic, Social and Cultural Rights of 16 December 1966 were also ratified by the Republic of Cyprus with Law 14/1969.[456] The ECHR and its Protocols, as well as the UN International Covenants, have, on the basis of Article 169 section 3 of the Constitution, superior force to any municipal law, either antecedent or subsequent to their ratification by Law. However, neither the ECHR nor the Covenants are superior to the Constitution; thus, the constitutional provisions shall prevail in case of any inconsistency between them and the provisions of the ECHR or the Covenants.[457]

§2. Civil and Political Rights

I. Right to Life

350. Article 7 of the Constitution stipulates that every person has the right to life and corporal integrity; Article 7 corresponds to Article 2 of the ECHR which safeguards the right to life but additionally safeguards the right to corporal integrity. Article 7 of the Constitution, similar to Article 2 of the ECHR, used to provide that no person shall be deprived of his/her life except in the execution of a sentence of a competent court following his/her conviction of an offence for which death penalty is provided by law.[458] The capital punishment exception was eventually repealed by the Tenth Constitutional Amendment Law 93(I)/2016.

351. The last executions for capital punishment in Cyprus occurred in 1962;[459] since there was an informal moratorium on executions sentence until 1983 when Cyprus formally abolished the death penalty for premeditated murder with Law

454. *See also* C. Tornaritis, *The European Convention on Human Rights in the Legal Order of the Republic of Cyprus* 6 (1975).
455. *See* C. Tornaritis, *Council of Europe and the Republic of Cyprus* 42 (1978); A. Loizou, *Cyprus*, in R. Blackburn & J. Polakiewicz, *Fundamental Rights in Europe: The European Convention on Human Rights and Its Member States, 1950–2000* 219 (Oxford U. Press 2001).
456. *See* M. Triantafyllides, *A Comparison of the Provisions for Civil and Political Rights in the Cyprus Constitution with Relevant Internationally Adopted Provisions*, 6 Cyprus L. Tribune 3–7 (1967), 1 Cyprus L. Tribune 5–10 (1968); O. Ozgur, *Implementation of International Human Rights Norms in the Republic of Cyprus: Some Problem Areas* in *10th Commonwealth Law Conference* 261–269 (1993).
457. *See* T. Hadjanastassiou, *The European Convention on Human Rights Applicable in Cyprus*, 3 Cyprus L. Tribune 97–113 (1976).
458. *The Republic v. Loftis* (1961) 1 RSCC 30.
459. On 13 Jun. 1962 Hambis Zacharia, Michael Hileticos and Lazaris Demetriou were hanged.

86/1983. On 19 January 2000, Cyprus ratified Protocol 6 of the ECHR which abolished death penalty for all offences in peacetime. On 12 March 2003, Cyprus further ratified Protocol 13 of the ECHR which abolishes the death penalty in all circumstances. Also, on 20 June 2003, Cyprus informed the Secretary General of the UN that it had decided to withdraw its reservation made upon accession to the Second Optional Protocol to the ICCPR to apply the death penalty in time of war pursuant to a conviction for offences of a military nature committed during wartime. Therefore, since 2003, Cyprus has fully abolished the death penalty in order to comply with its international obligations.

352. Article 7 section 3 of the Constitution stipulates that deprivation of life shall not be regarded as inflicted in contravention of Article 7 when it results from the use of force which is no more than absolutely necessary: (a) in defence of person or property against the infliction of a proportionate and otherwise unavoidable and irreparable evil, (b) in order to effect an arrest or to prevent the escape of a person lawfully detained, or (c) in action taken for the purpose of quelling a riot or insurrection when and as provided by law. The exceptions to the right to life should be narrowly and strictly construed.[460] The ECtHR has held that in determining whether the force used was no more than absolutely necessary, a stricter and more compelling test of necessity must be employed from that normally applicable when determining whether state action is 'necessary in a democratic society', under paragraph 2 of Articles 8–11 of the ECHR. The foremost criterion shall be the proportionality of the force used to the achievement of the aims.[461] The Court will consider, however, not only the actions of the agents of the state who actually administer the force but all the surrounding circumstances, including such matters as the planning and control of the actions under examination. In particular, the Court will consider whether the security forces' operation has been planned and conducted in such a way as to avoid or minimize to the greatest possible extent any risk to the lives of people[462] and possible recourse to lethal force.[463]

353. The case of *Andronicou and Constantinou* is of specific importance in determining whether the force used was no more than absolutely necessary.[464] On the morning of 24 December 1993, following a domestic dispute between Lefteris Andronicou and Elsie Constantinou, the police were called by neighbours to the flat which they shared. Mr Andronicou was said to be armed and was apparently holding Ms Constantinou against her will. There ensued a lengthy period of negotiations. Eventually, it was concluded on the basis of Andronicou's past behaviour and his current statements that he intended to kill Ms Constantinou and commit suicide shortly after midnight. At around 11.30 pm, the Chief of Police decided to approve a rescue plan. As a result of the operation, Andronicou was killed by members of the police, whereas Constantinou was severely wounded and eventually died, her

460. *McCann and others v. UK*, Judgment of 27 Sep. 1995, Series A, No. 324; (1996) 21 EHRR 97, para. 146.
461. *Ibid.*, para. 149.
462. *Andronicou and Constantinou v. Cyprus*, Judgment of 9 Oct. 1997; (1998) 25 EHRR 491.
463. *Gül v. Turkey*, Judgment of 14 Dec. 2000; (2002) 34 EHRR 719.
464. *Andronicou and Constantinou v. Cyprus*, Judgment of 9 Oct. 1997; (1998) 25 EHRR 491.

death being inadvertently caused by a shot. The ECtHR held that the rescue operation had been planned and organized in a way which minimized to the greater extent possible any risk to the lives of the couple. There were valid reasons in the circumstances for the police's conclusion that it was necessary to kill the young man to save the young woman's life as well as their colleagues' lives. The use of lethal force in the circumstances did not exceed what was absolutely necessary for the purposes of defending the life of the young woman and the lives of the officers. It was accordingly decided by a majority of 5-4 that there had thus been no violation of Article 2 of the ECHR.

354. The State has an obligation to refrain, through its agents, from deliberate unjustified killing. It further has an augmented responsibility to protect the life of individuals who are in custody, since they are in an extremely vulnerable condition. Thus, the ECtHR has held that the state could be liable, even for the failure to provide timely medical care to the detainee,[465] or the failure to protect a detainee by a dangerous, mentally ill prisoner, who was placed in the same cell.[466] As the EctHR observed in the McCann judgment: *any general legal prohibition of arbitrary killing by the agents of the State would be ineffective in practice if there existed no procedure for reviewing the lawfulness of the use of lethal force by State authorities.*[467] The ECtHR thus held that the right to life, read in conjunction with the State's general duty under Article 1 to secure to everyone under their jurisdiction the rights and freedoms defined in the ECHR, lead to the conclusion that there exists procedural protection of the right to life. Therefore, there should be some form of effective official investigation, when individuals have been killed as a result of the use of force, capable of leading to a determination of whether the force used was not justified under the circumstances.[468]

355. This obligation is not confined to cases where it has been established that the killing was caused by agents of the State, nor is it necessary that the deceased's family or others have lodged a formal complaint to the relevant investigative authorities. The mere knowledge of the killing on the part of the authorities could give rise to an obligation to carry out an effective investigation.[469] The authorities must thus act on their own motion once the matter has come to their attention.[470] It is highly important that the authorities who carry out the investigation are independent. This means not only a lack of hierarchical or institutional connection but also practical independence.[471] In addition to the principles stated above, the Court has recognized that Article 2 of the ECHR enjoins the State not only to refrain from the intentional and unlawful taking of life but also to take appropriate steps to safeguard the lives of those within their jurisdiction.[472] Such an obligation must not be

465. *Anguelova v. Bulgaria*, Judgment of 13 Jun. 2002.
466. *Edwards v. UK*, Judgment of 14 Mar. 2002; (2002) 35 EHRR 487.
467. *McCann and others v. UK*, Judgment of 27 Sep. 1995, Series A, No. 324; (1996) 21 EHRR 97.
468. *Kaya v. Turkey*, Judgment of 19 Feb. 1998; (1998) 28 EHRR 1.
469. *Ergi v. Turkey*, Judgment of 28 Jul. 1998; (2001) 32 EHRR 388.
470. *Jordan v. UK*, Judgment of 4 May 2001; (2003) 37 EHRR 52.
471. *Ergi v. Turkey*, Judgment of 28 Jul. 1998; (2001) 32 EHRR 388.
472. *LCB v. UK*, Judgment of 9 Jun. 1998; (1998) 27 EHRR 212.

interpreted though in a way, which would impose a disproportionate burden on the authorities. It must therefore be established that the authorities knew or ought to have known, at the time of the existence, of a real and immediate risk to the life of an identified individual from the criminal acts of a third party and that they failed to take measures within the scope of their powers.[473]

II. Prohibition of Torture, Inhuman or Degrading Treatment

356. Article 8 of the Constitution provides that no person shall be subjected to torture or inhuman or degrading punishment or treatment. Article 8 corresponds to Article 3 of the ECHR and provides for an absolute right, with no exceptions under any circumstances. The distinction between torture on the one hand and inhuman or degrading treatment on the other is primarily one of intensity of the suffering inflicted;[474] torture constitutes an aggravated and deliberate form of cruel, inhuman or degrading punishment or treatment. Inhuman or degrading is punishment or treatment which grossly humiliates, or degrades the dignity of the person, or causes the person to act against his/her will or conscience.[475] The State has both a negative obligation to refrain from acts of torture which amount to inhuman or degrading treatment or punishment, as well as a positive obligation to take appropriate measures to safeguard those within its jurisdiction. It has been held that the decision to extradite a person when there is a real risk that such person may be subject to inhuman or degrading treatment might give rise to a violation of Article 3 of the ECHR and accordingly Article 8 of the Constitution.[476]

III. Prohibition of Slavery or Servitude

357. Article 10 of the Constitution stipulates that no person shall be held in slavery or servitude. Article 10 corresponds to Article 4 of the ECHR and provides for an absolute right; the prohibition of slavery is further of public order and accordingly, slavery may not be imposed even if a person consents to become a slave. Section 2 of Article 10 further provides that no person shall be required to perform forced or compulsory labour; the term 'forced or compulsory labour' shall not include the following: (a) any work required to be done in the ordinary course of detention imposed according to the provisions of Article 11 or during conditional release from such detention; (b) any service of a military character if imposed or, in case of conscientious objectors, subject to their recognition by a law, service exacted instead of compulsory military service; or (c) any service exacted in case of an emergency or calamity threatening the life or well-being of the inhabitants. Contrary to Article 4 of the ECHR, Article 10 of the Constitution does not provide for

473. *Osman v. UK*, Judgment of 28 Oct. 1998; (1998) 29 EHRR 245.
474. *Ireland v. UK*, Judgment of 18 Jan. 1978, Series A, n. 25.
475. C. Tornaritis, *State Law of the Republic of Cyprus* 76ff (Cyprus Research Ctr. 1982, in Greek).
476. *Soering v. UK*, Judgment 7 Jul. 1989, Series A, n. 161.

an exception for 'any work or service which forms part of normal civic obligations'. It could thus be argued that in view of such omission, the imposition of 'work or service which forms part of normal civic obligations' might well fall under the notion of prohibited forced or compulsory labour.

358. The imposition of military service on conscientious objectors was considered in the leading case of *Pitsillides*.[477] The two appellants were convicted and sentenced by the Military Court to twelve months and ten months imprisonment, respectively, for the offence of not joining the National Guard of the Republic, that is, the national army, when called up, contrary to the National Guard Law 20/1964 as amended. On being formally charged in respect of the offence, the appellants had replied that the reason for not enlisting was due to their being Jehovah's witnesses and that their conscience did not allow them to take up arms. The appellants argued that their religious belief and conscience constituted a reasonable cause that absolved them from any criminal liability and that compulsory military service ran contrary to Article 18 of the Constitution, violating their freedom of religion and conscience.

359. The Supreme Court held that 'reasonable' is a relative term and for the cause to be reasonable, it must be objectively fair, with good faith and not contrary to, or incompatible with the Law. It was thus held that the religious beliefs and grounds of conscience of the appellants do not by themselves constitute a reasonable cause, so long as the Law does not otherwise absolve them from criminal liability due to such beliefs. The court concluded that *so long as the National Guard is used for the defence and security of the country, the Law imposing the obligation for military service on the citizens of Cyprus, irrespectively of whether the right to religion and conscience is restricted, is not unconstitutional*.[478] However, the Court noted that the appropriate authorities of the Republic ought to consider in the future the exemption of conscientious objectors from compulsory military service and/or the imposition of alternative service. Law 2/1992 amended the National Guard Law 20/1964 so that the right of conscientious objectors to choose civilian service has been since recognized.[479]

IV. The Right of Liberty and Personal Security

360. Article 11 of the Constitution provides that every person has the right to liberty and security of person;[480] such provision corresponds to Article 5 of the ECHR. No person shall be deprived of his/her liberty save in the following cases

477. *Pitsillides v. The Republic* [1983] 2 CLR 374. *See also Christou v. The Republic* [1982] 2 CLR 365.
478. *Pitsillides v. The Republic* [1983] 2 CLR 374.
479. For a detailed analysis of the evolution of legislation on conscientious objection in Cyprus *see* A. Emilianides, *Religion and Law in Cyprus* (4th ed., Kluwer 2024). *See also* T. Christodoulidou, *Religious Conscientious Objection in Cyprus*, 2 Cyprus & European L. Rev. 324–330 (2006).
480. S. Drakos, *The Right to Liberty and Security of Person. Article 11 of the Constitution*, 54–56 Cyprus L. Rev. 8019–8026 (1996) (in Greek).

when and as provided by law: (a) the detention of a person after conviction by a competent court; (b) the arrest or detention of a person for non-compliance with the lawful order of a court; (c) the arrest or detention of a person effected for the purpose of bringing him/her before the competent legal authority on reasonable suspicion of having committed an offence or when it is reasonably considered necessary to prevent his/her committing an offence or fleeing after having done so; (d) the detention of a minor by a lawful order for the purpose of educational supervision or his/her lawful detention for the purpose of bringing him/her before the competent legal authority; (e) the detention of persons for the prevention of spreading of infectious diseases, of persons of unsound mind, alcoholics or drug addicts or vagrants; (f) the arrest or detention of a person to prevent him/her effecting an unauthorized entry into the territory of the Republic or of an alien against whom action is being taken with a view to deportation or extradition. The Seventh Amendment of the Constitution Law 68(I)/2013 provided that citizens of the Republic may also be deported or extradited pursuant to an EAW or an international convention which is binding upon the Republic and to the extent that the other party applies the principle of reciprocity.

361. The executive power can therefore restrict the right of liberty only in accordance with the provisions of a law which has been enacted for any of the six grounds provided in Article 11; detaining or arresting a person *sine lege* is unconstitutional. Similarly, the legislative power cannot enact a law which provides for the arrest or detention of a person for any grounds other than those expressly provided for in Article 11 of the Constitution; such a law would be unconstitutional, as would any arrest or detention on the basis of such a law. Furthermore, detention may not be used abusively. In the case of *Parpas*, the appellant was arrested by virtue of a judicial warrant as a suspect for possessing explosive substances. During his detention, the Police obtained handwriting specimens from him. Such specimens were adduced in evidence against the appellant in respect of charges concerning forgeries of various cheques. The Supreme Court reached the conclusion that, in the circumstances of the case, the detention of the appellant as a suspect for possessing explosive substances was resorted to in order to enable the police to obtain the specimens needed for the purpose of investigating the offences for which the appellant was convicted. Accordingly, the Court held that the way in which the appellant's right to liberty was interfered with, when he was arrested and detained on suspicion of possessing explosives, was incompatible with Articles 33 and 34 of the Constitution and, consequently, his detention was rendered unconstitutional as being inconsistent with Article 11 of the Constitution because the obtaining of such specimens was completely unrelated to the reason of his arrest and detention.

362. Article 11 section 3 of the Constitution provides that no person shall be arrested save under the authority of a reasoned judicial warrant issued according to the formalities prescribed by the law. The only exception is the case of flagrant offences punishable with death or imprisonment, whereby the law may provide for the arrest of a person even without a judicial warrant; a flagrant offence has been defined as one whereby the commission of the offence and the arrest of the offender should follow each other directly in point of time and sequence.[481] In view of the express provision of Article 11 section 1(c) of the Constitution, the judicial warrant for arrest of a person may be issued only when there is reasonable suspicion that a person has committed an offence or when it is reasonably considered necessary to prevent his/her committing an offence or fleeing after having done so.

363. In accordance with Article 11 section 4 of the Constitution, every person arrested shall be informed at the time of his/her arrest in a language which he/she understands of the reasons for his/her arrest and shall be allowed to have the services of a lawyer of his/her own choosing. The person arrested shall, as soon as is practicable after his/her arrest, and in any event not later than twenty-four hours after the arrest, be brought before a judge, if not earlier released (Article 11 section 5 of the Constitution). Thus, an arrested person, either in accordance with a judicial warrant or in the case of a flagrant offence, has to be brought before a judge within twenty-four hours at the very latest. The judge before whom the person arrested is brought shall, in accordance with Article 11 section 6 of the Constitution, promptly proceed to enquire into the grounds of the arrest in a language understandable by the person arrested and shall, as soon as possible and in any event not later than three days from such appearance, either release the person arrested on such terms as he/she may deem fit or where the investigation into the commission of the offence for which he/she has been arrested has not been completed remand him/her in custody and may remand him/her in custody from time to time for a period not exceeding eight days at any one time. It is further provided that the total period of such remand in custody shall not exceed three months of the date of the arrest on the expiration of which every person or authority having the custody of the person arrested shall forthwith set him/her free. Decisions are subject to appeal.[482]

364. It has been held that in an application for remand order, the first question to be considered by the Judge is whether balancing public interest in the detection of crime as presented to him/her at the time, against a person's constitutional right to his/her liberty, the Judge finds sufficient justification for the making of a remand order. The trial Judge has to determine whether there is a reasonable suspicion that a person has committed an offence permitting the detention of such person, regarding the circumstances of the case as they appear at the material time. It is clear that the persistence of such suspicion is a condition sine qua non for the validity of the continued detention of the person concerned. Whereas the notion of 'reasonable suspicion' could not be extended to mean commission of the offence, the judge should be satisfied that the evidence presented before him/her shows the existence of such reasonable suspicion.[483]

---

481. *Kyriakides v. Republic* [1961] RSCC 66.
482. *See* generally L. Loucaides, *The Constitutional Safeguard of Human Rights During Arrest and Detention*, in *Ibid.*, *Topics of Cypriot Law* vol. I, 131–140 (1982 in Greek).
483. *Aeroporos and Another v. Police* [1987] 2 CLR 232, *Vassiliou v. Police* [1964] 2 CLR 64, *Stamataris and Another v. Police* [1983] 2 CLR 107, *Re Polycaprou* [1991] 1 CLR 207 (in Greek), *Tsirides v. Police* [1973] 2 CLR 204.

365. Every person who is deprived of his/her liberty by arrest or detention shall be entitled to take proceedings by which the lawfulness of his/her detention shall be decided speedily by a court and his/her release ordered if the detention is not lawful (Article 11 section 7 of the Constitution). The Supreme Court has held that a judicial order can only be reviewed in either of two ways: (1) by way of appeal when a right of appeal is bestowed by it or (2) by way of a prerogative order, such as an application for certiorari. Both the appellate jurisdiction and the jurisdiction to issue prerogative order vests exclusively in the Supreme Court. Accordingly, the Supreme Court held that proposed legislative amendments, which provided that a judicial warrant for arrest may be reviewed by an Assize Court or a District Court, were unconstitutional, since it is only the Supreme Court which has jurisdiction to review the legality of judicial orders in accordance with the Constitution. Furthermore, Article 11 section 8 of the Constitution provides that every person who has been the victim of arrest or detention in contravention of the provisions of this Article shall have an enforceable right to compensation.

V. The Rights of the Accused

366. Article 12 of the Constitution introduces the well-known legal maxim *nullum crimen nulla poena sine lege*. In particular, Article 12 section 1 of the Constitution stipulates that no person shall be held guilty of any offence on account of any act or omission which did not constitute an offence under the law at the time when it was committed, and no person shall have a heavier punishment imposed on him/her for an offence other than that expressly provided for it by law at the time when it was committed. *Nullum crimen nulla poena sine lege* is a fundamental principle of Cypriot criminal law. There can be no punishment unless the act constitutes an offence in accordance with a pre-existing law; accordingly, criminal legislation may not apply retroactively. In addition, customary law should not properly be considered a source of criminal law, since the constitutional requirement is that no punishment may be imposed without a law (law necessarily defined as legislation rather than custom). It is further not permissible to apply criminal legislation in an analogous manner against the interests of the accused.

367. Article 12 section 2 of the Constitution introduces the rule against double jeopardy by stipulating that a person who has been acquitted or convicted of an offence shall not be tried again for the same offence. No person shall be punished twice for the same act or omission except where death ensues from such act or omission. In the case of *Vassiliou,* the accused was convicted for drug offences and the Court imposed the sentence of imprisonment;[484] however, such sentence was suspended in light of the particular facts of the case. Subsequently, the Court imposed a heavy monetary fine on the accused in view of the fact that the penalty of imprisonment had been suspended. The Supreme Court held that the imposition of a fine was inconsistent with the principle enshrined in Article 12 section 2 of the Constitution since the accused had already been sentenced to imprisonment; suspension

484. *Attorney-General v. Vassiliou* [2003] 2 CLR 21.

had not changed the character of imprisonment as a punitive measure. In *Pernell*, the Supreme Court rejected the application of the Attorney-General of the Republic to adduce further evidence on appeal in support of the conviction, which was collected or adduced after the trial; the Court held that admitting such evidence would run contrary to the principle of double jeopardy safeguarded by the Constitution.[485]

368. The rule that punishment should not be disproportionate to the gravity of the offence is introduced in Article 12 section 3 of the Constitution. The rule is not intended to state that the 'punishment of crime is the exclusive territory of the judiciary',[486] or to interfere with the judicial individualization of a sentence through sentencing;[487] rather, the aim is to safeguard that legislation may not provide for a punishment which is disproportionate to the gravity of the offence; the constitutional rule therefore restricts the legislator in providing for either minimum or maximum sentence in a manner which is subjective or arbitrary. In *HadjiYianni*, the Supreme Constitutional Court held that a penal provision of a mandatory nature providing for a serious punishment to be imposed in all cases of a certain class or category, irrespective of the circumstances or merits of each particular case, when in such class or category there are bound to arise cases where the imposition of such punishment would be disproportionate to the gravity of the offence in view of its trivial or technical nature, is a provision contravening paragraph 3 of Article 12.[488] The rule is supplemented by Article 12 section 6 of the Constitution which provides that a punishment of general confiscation of property is prohibited; Article 12 section 6 is binding upon both the legislator and the judge.

369. The presumption of innocence is safeguarded in Article 12 section 4 of the Constitution which provides that every person charged with an offence shall be presumed innocent until proved guilty according to law. The trial judge, in fulfilling their duties, should accordingly not start with the conviction or assumption that the accused committed the act with which he/she is charged, since the onus to prove guilt falls upon the prosecution, and any doubt is to the benefit of the accused. The prosecution is obliged to prove at the trial every fact or circumstance stated in the indictment which is material and necessary to constitute the offence charged. The burden of proof of guilt lies upon the prosecution and it is not for the defence to prove innocence.[489] The constitutional presumption of innocence further implies that the accused has a right to silence and a right against self-incrimination;[490] no inferences concerning the guilt of the accused may be drawn from the exercise of

485. *Pernell v. Republic* [1998] 2 CLR 177.
486. As G. Pikis, *Constitutionalism, Human Rights, Separation of Powers* 52 (Martinus Nijhoff 2006) *seems* to imply.
487. *Milliotis v. Police* [1973] 2 CLR 116.
488. *District Nicosia Officer v. Hadji Yianni* [1961] 1 RSCC 79, at 82.
489. *Ioannou v. Police* [2012] 2 CLR 111 (in Greek).
490. *President of the Republic v. House of Representatives* [1994] 3 CLR 1 (in Greek).

the right to silence.[491] The prosecuting authority has to prove its case beyond any reasonable doubt in order to satisfy the Court that the accused should be convicted.[492]

370. As held in *Kyriakides*, the Constitution provides that the judiciary is the sole arbiter of the criminal responsibility of a person who is charged with having committed a criminal offence. The presumption of innocence is a fundamental guarantee of the freedom of a person and the constitutional protection of such a right admits no qualifications. No public authority may state or even imply that a person is guilty, unless such person has been convicted by a competent court. Article 12 section 4 of the Constitution shall be violated even if a public authority insinuates that a person is guilty following his/her declaration of innocence by a competent court. It was therefore held that administrative decisions which attribute criminal acts to a person violate the constitutional guarantee of the presumption of innocence and are consequently unconstitutional.[493]

VI. Free Movement

371. Article 13 section 1 of the Constitution stipulates that every person has the right to move freely throughout the territory of the Republic and to reside in any part thereof subject to any restrictions imposed by law and which are necessary only for the purposes of defence or public health or provided as punishment to be passed by a competent court.[494] Furthermore, Article 13 section 2 of the Constitution provides that every person has the right to leave permanently or temporarily the territory of the Republic subject to reasonable restrictions imposed by law. The Supreme Constitutional Court had clarified that the right to move freely throughout the territory of the Republic cannot in any way be interpreted as rendering unconstitutional laws or regulations which are reasonably necessary in every modern society in order to ensure that such right shall be exercised reasonably, with safety and with due regard for the enjoyment of by others of the same right, as well as of the right to life and corporal integrity. Accordingly, laws and regulations which have been enacted for the regulation of traffic are not inconsistent with Article 13 of the Constitution.[495]

372. In *Mamas Elia*, the Supreme Court considered the constitutionality of an Order issued by the Council of Ministers, by virtue of which the circulation of private motor vehicles was prohibited, subject to certain exceptions, on alternate weekends depending on whether their registration numbers were even or odd respectively. The Court observed that the use of a private motor car is normally

491. *Charalambous v. Republic* [1985] 2 CLR 97.
492. *Charitonos and Others v. Republic* [1971] 2 CLR 40.
493. *Kyriakides v. Republic* [1997] 3 CLR 485 (in Greek).
494. C. Tornaritis, *The Right to Freedom of Movement and Residence, Especially under the Law of the Republic of Cyprus*, 1 Cyprus L. Tribune 3–6 (1974), 2 Cyprus Law Tribune 3–12 (1974), 3 Cyprus Law Tribune 3–9 (1974).
495. *Gendarmerie of Morphou v. Michael* [1961] 2 RSCC 103.

indispensable for a citizen to move freely from one area of the Republic to another, in so far as distances which cannot be reasonably expected to be covered on foot, or by other means of private conveyance, are concerned. It was further considered that an average citizen cannot afford financially to have two private motor cars, one with an even registration number and one with an odd registration number, or to use, except in cases of urgent need, a taxi for the purpose of moving from one area of the country to another. Accordingly, the Court held that the operation of the Order of the Council of Ministers amounted to a restriction of the right to move freely as safeguarded by Article 13 of the Constitution, which was not necessary for the purposes of defence or of public health; the Order was declared unconstitutional.[496]

373. Article 14 of the Constitution further provides that no citizen shall be banished or excluded from the Republic under any circumstances. The protection afforded by Article 14 is restricted to citizens of the Republic and does not extend to aliens. Such Article was considered by the Supreme Court in the case of *Afamis*,[497] which noted that the Greek and Turkish text of the Constitution differed somewhat when compared to the English text; the Court held the following:

> It is true that the literal meaning of the relevant Greek and Turkish expressions might be more akin to the English term 'exiled' but for the purposes of the object of Article 14 of the Constitution it is clear that whether the precise phrase used is 'exile' or 'banishment', they connote one and the same idea, namely, a compulsory expulsion from the Republic of a citizen with a prohibition of his return to the Republic for a limited or unlimited period of time.

VII. The Right to Respect for Private and Family Life

374. Article 15 of the Constitution stipulates that every person has the right to respect for his/her private and family life. There shall be no interference with the exercise of this right except such as is in accordance with the law and is necessary only in the interests of the security of the Republic or the constitutional order or the public safety or the public order or the public health or the public morals or for the protection of the rights and liberties guaranteed by this Constitution to any person. Article 15 corresponds to Article 8 of the ECHR. Therefore, each individual has a right to privacy, which includes, *inter alia*, religious, philosophical or moral beliefs, family and emotional life, friendship, or personal health, activities of professional and business nature, as well as the right to establish and develop relationships with other human beings.[498] The notion of 'private life' or 'family life' should not be interpreted narrowly, since their aim is to safeguard fundamental rights; such rights may be restricted only in accordance with the law, so far as it is necessary for one of the reasons specified in Article 15 and in addition, in so far as the restriction is justified in a European democracy.

496. *Elia* [1980] 2 CLR 118.
497. *The Attorney-General v. Afamis* [1961] 1 RSCC 121.
498. *Niemetz v. Germany*, Judgment of 16 Dec. 1992; (1993) 16 EHRR 97.

375. The Supreme Court has held that a law obliging high State officials to reveal and submit information about their property and the property of their family members is inconsistent with Article 15 of the Constitution.[499] Article 15 of the Constitution was amended by the Ninth Amendment of the Constitution Law 69(I)/2016 which provided that the right may also be restricted for the protection of transparency and for measures against corruption in public life. Following such amendment, the House of Representatives enacted legislation which stipulated that all high-ranked public servants, public educational servants, employees of legal persons of public law, military and police officers, as well as their spouses and minor children, had to disclose and publicize their property assets and any change thereof. The Supreme Court noted that the property assets of persons are part of their private life and accordingly any interference needs to be absolutely necessary and proportional. In this case, there was drastic potential interference with the right to private life which was based on the high rank of the said persons and extended to their spouses and children. The Supreme Court held that there was not sufficient justification which could justify why the legislative measures were absolutely necessary and proportional to the need to tackle corruption in public life and held that the impugned legislation was inconsistent with Article 15 of the Constitution.[500]

376. The Supreme Court further held that a bill extending the obligation to publicize the property assets of the President of the Republic, Ministers and Members of the House of Representatives provided in the President, Ministers and Representatives (Submission and Review of Property) Law 49(I)/2004 to the officials' spouses and minor children, was inconsistent with Article 15 of the Constitution. The aim of protection of transparency and taking measures against corruption was sufficiently achieved through the submission of the property data to the appropriate commission and it was neither necessary, nor proportional to the stated need, to impose publication of the property assets of either the spouse or the minor children of the governmental officials.[501] It has similarly been held that the publicization, without distinction, of the business names of legal persons which contributed to the Independent Social Support Body, headed by the First Lady, violated the right to privacy since it would potentially allow the identification of the natural persons who control the said legal persons. It was further reasoned that the publicization violated the principle of proportionality and that the intended objective of securing transparency in public life regarding the Body's resources was not fulfilled.[502]

377. Of particular importance with respect to Article 15 is the case of *Modinos* which concerned the criminalization of private homosexual acts between consenting adults.[503] The Supreme Court of Cyprus considered the constitutionality of the

499. *President of the Republic v. House of Representatives* [2000] 3 CLR 238.
500. *President of the Republic v. House of Representatives*, App. 11–12, 14–16/2016, Judgment of 16 Mar. 2017 (in Greek).
501. *President of the Republic v. House of Representatives* [2017] 3 CLR 501 (in Greek), *President of the Republic v. House of Representatives* [2017] 3 CLR 513 (in Greek).
502. *President of the Republic v. House of Representatives*, App. 6/2024, Judgment of 11 Apr. 2025 (in Greek).
503. *Modinos v. Cyprus*, Judgment of 22 Apr. 1993, Series A, No. 259; (1994) 16 EHRR 485.

criminalization of private homosexual acts between consenting adults in the case of *Costa.*[504] The Court observed that in ascertaining the nature and scope of morals and the degree of the necessity commensurate to their protection, the case-law of the ECtHR and the European Commission of Human Rights has already held that the conception of morals changes from time to time and from place to place and that there is no uniform European conception of morals. It was therefore held that the authorities of each Country are in a better position than an international Judge to give an opinion as to the prevailing standards of morals in their Country. Consequently, the Supreme Court opted to adopt the dissenting opinion of Judge Zekia and not to follow the majority view in the *Dudgeon* case because:

> It is convinced that it is entitled to apply the Convention and interpret the corresponding provisions of the Constitution in the light of its assessment of the present social and moral standards in this Country; that, therefore, in the light of the aforesaid principles and viewing the Cypriot realities this Court is not prepared to come to the conclusion that section 171(b) of our Criminal Code, as it stands, violates either the Convention or the Constitution, and that it is unnecessary for the protection of morals in our country; accordingly the appeal against conviction should fail.[505]

378. In *Modinos*, the ECtHR held that an interference had occurred, regardless of the fact that the Attorney-General had followed a consistent policy of considering the law with regard to private homosexual conduct between consenting adults as a dead letter; the ECtHR observed that such policy did not preclude the possibility that the law might be enforced in the future, especially in view of the opinion of the Supreme Court expressed in the case of *Costa*. In essence, the ECtHR established that the criminalization of private homosexual adults between consenting adults cannot be considered necessary in a democratic society within the meaning of Article 8 and, thus, constitutes a violation of Article 8 of the ECHR.[506] Until 1998, various draft laws had been proposed before the House of Representatives with a view to lifting the criminalization, but each time, the legislation was blocked following opposition by the Orthodox Church. Eventually, section 171 of the Criminal Code, Cap. 154 was amended in 1998 so that homosexual acts between consenting adults no longer constituted a criminal offence.[507]

---

504. *Costa v. The Republic* [1982] 2 CLR 120.
505. *Ibid.*
506. *See also Dudgeon v. UK*, Judgment of 22 Oct. 1981, Series A, No. 45; (1982) 4 EHRR 149, *Norris v. Ireland*, Judgment of 26 Oct. 1988, Series A, No. 142; (1991) 13 EHRR 186.
507. *See* in general A. Emilianides, *The Decriminalisation of Homosexuality*, in *History of the Republic of Cyprus* vol. 4, 108–111 (P. Papapolyviou ed., Phileleftheros 2011, in Greek); *Ibid.*, *Homosexuality and Human Rights in the Cypriot Legal Order*, in *Sexualities: Views, Studies and Experiences in the Cypriot and Greek Space* 130–151 (C. Phellas et al. eds, Polyxromos Planitis 2014, in Greek); A. Tryfonidou, *The Legal Position of LGBT Persons and Same-Sex Couples in Cyprus*, 29 Cyprus Rev. 183–213 (2017).

379. Article 16 of the Constitution further stipulates that every person's dwelling house is inviolable. The protection afforded by Article 16 is not restricted to *domicilium* but is also extended to *domus*. The police or any other authority or person may not enter, or search the home of a person, irrespective of whether such home is of a permanent or temporary nature, unless such entry or search is in accordance with a duly reasoned judicial order as provided by law, or when the entry is made with the express consent of its occupant or for the purpose of rescuing the victims of any offence of violence or of any disaster. In the case of *Djirkalli*, the Supreme Constitutional Court held that forcible entry of a dwelling house in order to collect taxes under section 8 of the Tax Collection Law, Cap. 329, without a judicial warrant for which no provision is made in the said section 8, would be unconstitutional.[508]

380. Article 17 of the Constitution provides, in particular, the right to respect for the correspondence and other communication of a person. In particular, Article 17 section 1 of the Constitution stipulates that every person has the right to respect for, and to the secrecy of, his/her correspondence and other communication if such other communication is made through means not prohibited by law. The initial wording of paragraph 2 of Article 17 provided that there shall be no interference with the exercise of this right except in accordance with the law and only in cases of convicted and unconvicted prisoners and business correspondence and communication of bankrupts during the bankruptcy administration. As already stated, the Supreme Court held in *Georghiades* that the overhearing of a conversation between the accused and his client without the knowledge of either of them amounted to a violation of Article 17 of the Constitution.[509] In subsequent case-law, the Supreme Court further held that any information which arises out of constitutionally protected communication may not be admissible as evidence.[510] With respect to telephone conversation, Article 17 of the Constitution safeguards not only the privacy of the content of the telephone communication but also the numbers of the telephone calls, namely the external characteristics of communication.[511]

381. The EU Data Retention Directive[512] was transposed by the Law providing for the Retention of Telecommunication Data with the intention of investigating serious criminal offences 183(I)/2007. Sections 4 and 5 of the Law which provide for the access of police officers to telecommunications data were considered to be beyond the intention of the data retention directive and accordingly unconstitutional in the decision of the Full Bench of the Supreme Court of Cyprus in *Christos*

508. *Djirkalli v. Republic* [1961] 1 RSCC 36.
509. *Police v. Georghiades* [1983] 2 CLR 33.
510. *Police v. Yialllourou* [1992] 2 CLR 147 (in Greek), *Republic v. Aeroporou* [1998] 2 CLR 87 (in Greek), *Republic v. Symianou* [1999] 2 CLR 537 (in Greek).
511. *See also* A. Constantinou, *The Monitoring of Private Communication of a Person with Electronic or Other Means*, 3 Cyprus L. Tribune 9–38 (1998) (in Greek); N. Papaefstathiou, *The Right of Communication: Wiretapping as a Violation of a Constitutional and Right and of the Law*, 2 Cyprus L. Tribune 42–49 (2001) (in Greek).
512. Directive 2006/24/EC.

Matsias and Others.[513] The Full Bench of the Supreme Court of Cyprus held that sections 4 and 5 of Law 183(I)/2007, providing for the access of police officers to telecommunication data with the intention of investigating serious criminal offence, were not enacted for the purposes of harmonization with the data retention directive.[514] In particular, it was held that the aim of the data retention directive is to harmonize Member States' provisions concerning the obligations of the providers of publicly available electronic communication systems or of public communication networks with respect to the retention of certain data which are generated or processed by them in order to ensure that the data are available for the purpose of the investigation, detection and prosecution of serious crime, as defined by each Member State in its national law. Nowhere in the data retention directive is it provided that the Member States are obliged to enact legislation enabling access of the police to such telecommunications data.

382. Consequently, sections 4 and 5 of Law 183(I)/2007 were not covered by the provisions of the data retention directive and were, accordingly, inconsistent with Article 17 of the Constitution safeguarding the right of communication and prohibiting interferences with such right.[515] It should be noted, however, that *Matsias* was decided on the basis of the legal status prior to the amendment of Article 17 of the Constitution with the Sixth Amendment of the Constitution Law 51(I)/2010. Article 17 section 2 (C) of the Constitution, as amended, now provides that a Court may issue a judicial decree granting access to the telecommunications data (external aspects of communication) for the purpose of investigating serious criminal offences which provide in case of conviction a sentence of imprisonment of at least five years; such access may be granted only to the extent necessary for identifying the user or subscriber of such data. Following the annulment of the Data Retention Directive by the CJEU,[516] the Supreme Court considered whether this had any effect on the validity of Law 183(I)/2007. The Supreme Court held by majority that Law 183(I)/07 had been promulgated as domestic legislation and accordingly could not be affected by the annulment of the Data Retention Directive.[517]

383. The Sixth Amendment of the Constitution further amended Article 17 section 2 of the Constitution, so as to provide for the possibility of interfering with the internal aspects of correspondence or communication in specific cases. The amended text of Article 17 section 2 (B) of the Constitution provides that there shall be no interference with the exercise of this right except in accordance with the law in the following cases: (a) in cases of convicted and unconvicted prisoners, (b) pursuant to a judicial order which has been issued in accordance with the law, following a petition by the Attorney-General of the Republic and in so far as the

513. *Matsias and Others* [2011] 1 CLR 152 (in Greek).

514. *Ibid.*

515. *See* C. *Markou, Cyprus Highest Court Not Rejecting Data Retention Law, but Privacy Time Bomb Ticks On*, in *Law Across Nations: Governance, Policy & Statutes* 283–295 (S. Kierkegard ed., IAITL 2011).

516. Cases C-293/12 and 594/12, *Digital Rights Ireland v. Minister for Communications, Marine and Natural Resources and Others* EU:C:2014:238.

517. *Attorney-General v. Isaia* [2014] 1 CLR 1445 (in Greek).

interference is a measure necessary in a democratic society for the interests of the security of the Republic or the prevention, investigation or prosecution of the following serious criminal offences: (i) premeditated murder or homicide; (ii) trafficking of adults or minors, and offences related to child pornography; (iii) drug trafficking, supply, cultivation or production of drugs, psychotropic substances or dangerous pharmaceutical drugs; (iv) offences related to the currency of the Republic; or (v) offences of corruption which provide in case of conviction a sentence of imprisonment of at least five years.

VIII. The Right to Religious Freedom

384. Article 18 of the Constitution of Cyprus safeguards the right to religious freedom, including the freedom of religious conscience and freedom of worship.[518] The aforementioned Article corresponds in many ways to Article 9 of the ECHR, but it is more detailed, while its provisions cover sectors which are not recorded in Article 9. Article 18 section 1 provides that every person has the right to freedom of thought, conscience and religion. Such right is far-reaching and profound. Freedom of thought, conscience and religion is safeguarded for any person, either a believer or an atheist, a citizen or a non-citizen of the Republic of Cyprus. It is, therefore, not limited in its application to traditional religions or to religions and beliefs with institutional characteristics or practices analogous to traditional religions.[519] Until a person attains the age of sixteen, the decision as to the religion to be professed by him/her shall be taken by the person having the lawful guardianship of such person on the basis of Article 18 section 7 of the Constitution.

385. The Supreme Court has specified that Article 18 of the Constitution safeguards religious liberty, which is not to be confused with religious tolerance. It was held that:

> Tolerance as a legal concept is premised on the assumption that the State has ultimate control over religion and the churches, and whether and to what extent religious freedom will be granted and protected is a matter of state policy. The right of religious liberty is a fundamental right. The days that oppressive measures were adopted and cruelties and punishments inflicted by Governments in Europe and elsewhere for many ages, to compel parties to conform in their religious beliefs and modes of worship to the views of the most numerous sect, and the folly of attempting in that way to control the mental operations of persons and enforce an outward conformity to a prescribed standard, have gone. Mankind has advanced and the right to freedom of thought, conscience and religion is now a fundamental right.[520]

518. *See* A. Emilianides, *Law and Religion in Cyp*rus (4th ed., Kluwer 2024); *Ibid.*, *State and Church in Cyprus*, in *State and Church in the European Union* 281ff (G. Robbers ed., 3d ed., Nomos Verlagsgesellschaft 2019).
519. *Pitsillides v. The Republic* [1983] 2 CLR 374.
520. *Ibid.*

386. Article 18 section 4 guarantees the more particular manifestation of an individual's religious freedom, stipulating that every person is free and has the right to profess his/her faith and to manifest his/her religion or belief in worship, teaching, practice or observance, either individually or collectively, in private or in public, and to change his/her religion or belief. While religious freedom is primarily a matter of individual conscience, it also implies the freedom to manifest one's religion, since such freedom is intrinsically linked with the very existence of religious convictions.[521] The constitutional right to religious freedom further includes the negative aspects of such right, namely the right not to disclose one's religion. This was accepted by the Supreme Court in an obiter dictum in the case of *Elia*, where it was held that revealing in official documents the religion of a candidate for a position in the public service should be avoided in view of Article 18 of the Constitution. Thus, it was held that the fact that the official documents referred to the applicant as a Maronite was strictly prohibited by the Constitution.[522] While the above comments of the Supreme Court were only obiter, it is considered that they accurately reflect the position under Article 18 of the Constitution; a person has therefore a constitutional right not to disclose one's religion.

387. Any person has the right to replace one's current religion with another or to adopt atheistic views. It is immaterial why the person has chosen to change religion and whether such a choice was the result of that person acting in good faith or not, so long as it was the consequence of the exercise of the person's will and not, for instance, the result of duress, or psychological force. The issue was indirectly considered in the case of *Houssain*.[523] The petitioner, a Greek Cypriot and a member of the Greek Orthodox Church, had entered into a civil marriage in England with a Pakistani national of the Muslim faith. The respondent insisted both before and after the marriage that his wife ought to change her religion and become a Muslim; due to his wife's refusal to change her religion, he refused to consummate their marriage and maintained that he would not consummate their marriage, so long as she remained a Christian Orthodox. Eventually, she left England and returned to Cyprus, where she filed a petition for nullity of marriage on the ground of non-consummation due to the wilful refusal of the husband. The Court held that the wife's refusal to change religion *cannot be held as putting it out of the husband's power to request intercourse* and granted a decree of nullity after finding the husband guilty of a wilful refusal to consummate the marriage.

388. No limitations whatsoever are permitted with respect to the freedom of thought or conscience or on the freedom to have or adopt a religion or belief of one's choice; such freedoms are protected unconditionally and are considered to be absolute. However, the freedom to manifest one's religion can be restricted, by virtue of Article 18 section 6, so long as such limitations are prescribed by law and are necessary in the interests of: (a) the security of the Republic, (b) constitutional order, (c) public safety, (d) public order, (e) public health, (f) public morals, (g) the

521. *Kokkinakis v. Greece*, Judgment of 25 May 1993; (1994) 17 EHRR 397.
522. *Elia v. The Republic* [1985] 3 CLR 38.
523. *Houssain v. Houssain* [1979] 1 CLR 600.

protection of the rights and liberties guaranteed to every person by the Constitution. The interference has to be necessary for one of the constitutionally specified legitimate aims; a limitation which has been prescribed by law in order to facilitate interests other than those explicitly referred to in Article 18 section 6 of the Constitution shall not be considered to be legitimate. In addition to the conditions mentioned above, any limitations of the freedom to manifest one's religion must be considered to be necessary in a democratic society, under the mandate of Article 9 section 2 of the ECHR.

IX. The Right to Freedom of Expression

389. Article 19 of the Constitution stipulates that every person has the right to freedom of speech and expression in any form; such right includes freedom to hold opinions and receive and impart information and ideas without interference by any public authority and regardless of frontiers. The rights safeguarded by Article 19 of the Constitution are considered the cornerstone of democracy, since there can be no democracy without freedom of speech.[524] Article 19 corresponds to Article 10 of the ECHR. The exercise of the aforementioned rights may be subject to such formalities, conditions, restrictions or penalties as are prescribed by law and are necessary only in the interests of the security of the Republic or the constitutional order or the public safety or the public order or the public health or the public morals or for the protection of the reputation or rights of others or for preventing the disclosure of information received in confidence or for maintaining the authority and impartiality of the judiciary. In addition, any such restriction should be considered to be necessary in a democratic society.

390. In *Police v. Dias*, the Supreme Court unanimously held that Article 19 enumerates exhaustively the causes in respect of which freedom of speech and expression may be limited.[525] It further held that the Constitution extends to both true and false statements. Whereas, however, truth may be tolerated even where it appears to be damaging to, for example, state security, no such justification exists for suffering falsity in similar circumstances. Consequently, it was held that intolerance to false news or information, damaging to the causes for which freedom of speech and expression may be limited, is not intrinsically derogatory to the exercise of the right. The Court concluded that section 50 section 1 of the Criminal Code, Cap. 154, which criminalized the publication of false news or information which may impair public order or the confidence of the public in the state or its organs, was constitutional.

391. In *Cosmos Press*, the appellants were convicted at first instance for interfering with judicial proceedings, contrary to section 122 section 6 of the Criminal Code, Cap. 154.[526] The appellants had published in the newspaper *Kypros* a news

524. *Cyprus Sulphur and Copper Company Ltd v. Pararlama Ltd* [1990] 1 CLR 1051 (in Greek).
525. *Police v. Ekdotiki Eteria Inomeni Dimosiographiki Dias Ltd* [1982] 2 CLR 63.
526. *Cosmos Press Ltd v. Police* [1985] 2 CLR 73.

item which was considered calculated to obstruct or influence the proceedings in a criminal case pending before the District Court of Nicosia. The Supreme Court held that the legislative restriction of the freedom of expression was constitutional, since its aim was to maintain the authority and impartiality of the judiciary. However, it noted that any restriction on the right of expression must be applied in each particular case in a manner as favourable as possible to the freedom of the press. In light of the above, it was held that it was not safe in this particular case to hold beyond any reasonable doubt that the news item, in relation to which the appellants were convicted, was calculated or was likely to obstruct or influence the proceedings in the District Court.

392. The case of *Kyprianou* deserves special mention. Michalakis Kyprianou, an advocate and a former member of the House of Representatives, was defending two accused of murder before the Assize Court of Limassol. Kyprianou was conducting the cross-examination of a prosecution witness, when the Court interrupted his questioning, holding that his cross-examination went beyond the extent it could go at that particular stage of the main trial. In response, Kyprianou declared that he stopped his cross-examination, and he asked for leave to withdraw from the case on the basis that the Court seemed to consider that he was doing his job properly in defending the accused; his request was denied. At that point, Kyprianou protested that the Court prevented him from conducting his cross-examination in an efficient manner; Kyprianou alleged that while he was cross-examining the witness, the three members of the Court were talking to each other and sending '*ravasakia*' to each other.[527] The Assize Court considered that the words spoken by Kyprianou, and particularly the manner in which it was spoken, constituted contempt in the face of the court. Eventually, the Assize Court, by majority, sentenced Kyprianou to five-day imprisonment.

393. Kyprianou filed an appeal with the Supreme Court. However, his appeal was rejected, since it was considered that the power of courts to punish contempt is connected with the normal function of the courts, and its aim is the protection of judicial institutions, which is essential in order to safeguard a fair trial. Kyprianou eventually lodged an application with the ECtHR against the Republic of Cyprus, alleging violations of Article 6 and Article 10 of the ECHR in relation to his conviction and imprisonment for contempt in the face of the court. In addition to finding a violation under Article 6 of the ECHR, the ECtHR held that albeit discourteous, the Applicant's comments were aimed at and limited to the manner in which the judges were trying the case, in particular concerning the cross-examination of a witness, he was carrying out in the course of defending his client against a charge of murder. Accordingly, the ECtHR considered that the penalty imposed was disproportionately severe on the applicant and was capable of having a 'chilling effect' on the performance of lawyers of their duties as defence counsel. The ECtHR's finding of procedural unfairness in the summary proceedings for contempt served to compound that lack of proportionality. Thus, it was held that the

527. *Ravasakia* is a Greek word, which can define either a short and secret letter, or a love letter, or even a short written message with unpleasant results.

Assize Court failed to strike the right balance between the need to protect the authority of the judiciary and the need to protect the applicant's right to freedom of expression.[528]

394. One important provision with respect to freedom of the press is Article 19 section 4 of the Constitution which provides that seizure of newspapers or other printed matter is not allowed without the written permission of the Attorney-General of the Republic, which must be confirmed by the decision of a competent court within a period not exceeding seventy-two hours, failing which the seizure shall be lifted. Any restrictions to the freedom of the press should be interpreted as narrowly as possible. Article 19 section 5 of the Constitution further authorizes the Republic to require, if it so deems appropriate, the licensing of sound and vision broadcasting or cinema enterprises. Any requirements concerning licensing should be reasonable and non-discriminatory.[529]

X. The Right to Petition

395. Article 29 of the Constitution provides that every person has the right individually or jointly with others to address written requests or complaints to any competent public authority and to have them attended to and decided expeditiously;[530] an immediate notice of any such decision taken duly reasoned shall be given to the person making the request or complaint and in any event within a period not exceeding thirty days.[531] Where any interested person is aggrieved by any such decision or where no such decision is notified to such person within the period specified, such person may have recourse to the Supreme Court in the matter of such request or complaint. The aim of Article 29 is not just to promote correspondence between the citizens and public authorities but to ensure that requests or complaints by citizens are dealt with expeditiously by the competent authorities. It has been held that a non-competent public authority cannot be expected to deal with a request or complaint which has been addressed to it, if this is a matter outside its competence; however, in such cases, it has a duty to transmit such request or complaint to the competent authority or to inform the citizen of the competent authority.[532]

XI. The Right to Non-discrimination

396. Article 28 section 2 of the Constitution, implementing Article 14 of the ECHR, ordains that every person shall enjoy all the rights and liberties provided for

528. *Kyprianou v. Cyprus*, App. 73797/01, Judgment of 15 Dec. 2005.
529. *See* in detail C. Stratilatis & A. Emilianides, *Media Law in Cyprus* (3d ed., Kluwer 2024).
530. C. Tornaritis, *The Right to Petition the Authorities, Especially under the Laws of Cyprus*, 1 *Droit de l'Homme* 518–529 (1968); C. Paraskeva, *The Protection of the Right to Petition the Authorities in the Cypriot Legal Order*, Y.B. Cyprus and European L. 197–210 (2013, in Greek).
531. The thirty day period has to be interpreted by considering the circumstances of each particular case. *See Xenophontos v. Republic* (1961) 2 RSCC 89.
532. *Kyriacou v. CYBC* [1965] 3 CLR 482.

in this Constitution without any direct or indirect discrimination against any person on the grounds of his/her community, race, religion, language, sex, political or other convictions, national or social descent, birth, colour, wealth, social class, or on any ground whatsoever, unless there is express provision to the contrary in this Constitution. It should be noted, however, that Article 28 is autonomous and its application is not dependent upon a finding of violation of another article of the Constitution, contrary to Article 14 of the ECHR.[533] Article 1 of Protocol 12 of the ECHR, which has been ratified by the Republic of Cyprus, introduces a general and autonomous prohibition of discrimination, similar to Article 28 of the Constitution.

397. In addition to the principle of non-discrimination, Article 28 section 1 of the Constitution safeguards the complementing principle of equality, stating that all persons are equal before the law, the administration and justice and are entitled to equal protection thereof and treatment thereby. By virtue of paragraph 3 of Article 28, no citizen shall be entitled to use or enjoy any privilege of any title of nobility or of social distinction within the territorial limits of the Republic. Moreover, no title or nobility or other social distinction shall be conferred by or recognized in the Republic. A violation of fundamental rights is actionable and thus, an aggrieved person may file an action in civil courts against those perpetrating the violation, with the aim to recover just and reasonable compensation for any pecuniary or non-pecuniary damage that such person has suffered because of the discrimination; such discrimination may be either direct or indirect. The person may further demand that the Court holds that any discrimination inflicted upon him/her, on the basis of a Law, or an administrative act, is illegal and, thus, should be declared invalid and with no effect.

398. A difference in treatment is considered to be discriminatory, if it has no objective and reasonable justification;[534] thus, the courts will conclude that a law, or an act is discriminatory, if a difference in treatment does not pursue a legitimate aim, or if there is no reasonable relationship of proportionality between the means employed and the aim sought to be realized. The Republic of Cyprus has further enacted legislation in harmonization with EU law which prohibits discrimination. The Equal Treatment (Racial or Ethnic Origin) Law 59(I)/2004 harmonized Council Directive 2000/43/EC on the implementation of the principle of equal treatment irrespective of racial or ethnic origin, in both public and private sectors, in matters of social protection, health treatment, social services, education and access to goods and services. Furthermore, the Equal Treatment in Employment and Occupation Law 58(I)/2004 harmonized Council Directive 2000/78/EC and prohibits discrimination, specifically in the spheres of employment and occupation.

533. C. Tornaritis, *The Right of Equality of Treatment and Absence of Discrimination*, 3–4 Cyprus L. Tribune 5–6 (1973); G. Pikis, *Equality of Citizens Before the Law as a Requirement of Safeguarding Rule of Law* in *Aspects of Cypriot Law* vol. II, 217–239 (Asselia 1982, in Greek); L. Loucaides, *Guarantees Against Racial Discrimination under the Legal System of Cyprus*, 17 Cyprus L. Rev. 2659–2668 (1987).

534. *President of the Republic v. House of Representatives*, App. 1/2024, Judgment of 4 Sep. 2024 (in Greek).

399. In addition to the right to have access to courts, the Combating of Racism and Other Discrimination (Commissioner) Law 42(I)/2004 vests the Ombudsman, who is an independent officer of the Republic with special competences, duties and powers for combating and eliminating discrimination in both public and private sectors. Any person or group of persons may lodge a complaint to the Equality Authority of the Ombudsman's Office for having been subjected to discrimination prohibited by any law of the Republic, including legal instruments of EU origin, as well as the ECHR, the Framework Convention for the Protection of National Minorities (FCPNM), the International Convention for the Elimination of all forms of Racial Discrimination, the ICCPR, the Convention against Torture and Inhuman and Degrading Treatment or Punishment, the European Charter for Regional or Minority Languages, as well as any other international human rights instrument ratified by the Republic.[535]

400. The prohibition of discrimination refers to both direct and indirect discrimination. Indirect discrimination shall be taken to occur where an apparently neutral provision, criterion or practice would put persons at a particular disadvantage compared with other persons unless that provision, criterion or practice is objectively justified by a legitimate aim and the means of achieving that aim are appropriate and necessary. Indirect discrimination may occur where there is a failure to treat different individuals or groups differently, without any objective justification, in such a manner that an apparently neutral provision which theoretically applies to everybody, in essence, constitutes a disguised discriminatory provision which discriminates between the claimant and other persons. Thus, for an assessment of whether indirect adverse treatment exists, it is necessary to compare with a group of comparators and examine the hypothetically neutral provisions within the framework of the overall assessment of the particular age groups. Such difference in treatment will only constitute discrimination, however, so long as there is absence of justification or lack of proportionality.

401. In practice, the requirements to be met for both direct and indirect discrimination may well coincide, so that in many cases, it might be of theoretical value only to distinguish between the two forms of discrimination; indeed, the ECtHR does not use the terms direct, or indirect discrimination, but focuses on whether the differential treatment alleged has no objective and reasonable justification.[536] The assessment as to whether a less favourable treatment exists must be based on a comparator and thus, the notion of a 'comparable situation' is quite important; it should be proved that the claimant is treated less favourably than another person being in the same or essentially similar or comparable position as the claimant. The Supreme Court has repeatedly held that only persons in similar situations are entitled to equal treatment.[537] The principle of non-discrimination

535. *See* Second Report submitted by Cyprus pursuant to Art. 25, para. 1 of the Framework Convention for the Protection of National Minorities, 27 Oct. 2006, para. 22.

536. *Abdulaziz, Cabales and Balkandali v. UK*, Judgment of 28 May 1985; (1985) 7 EHRR 471.

537. *Serghides v. Republic* [1991] 1 CLR 119 (in Greek), *Yiasemidou v. Municipal Board* [1996] 3 CLR 491 (in Greek).

safeguards persons only when they are placed in analogous situations and accordingly deciding whether there has been a discriminatory difference of treatment that shall necessarily involve considerations of whether the groups of persons compared are indeed comparable.

402. In the case of *Zenonos v. The Republic*,[538] the Supreme Court held that there was a reasonable basis for differentiation between the applicants, whose services were lawfully terminated on 30 June 1968, before the enactment of Law 2/1969 providing for the increase of the salary of special constables, and the other special constables who were in service on the date of the enactment of Law 2/1969; the applicants were not in a similar situation as the other constables. Similarly, in *Tsinontas v. Cyprus Land Development Corporation*,[539] the Supreme Court held that reasonable differentiation in the remuneration of public officers on the basis of the length of their service was not arbitrary and did not violate Article 28 of the Constitution. Thus, equality of treatment might not always refer to exact arithmetical equality but only provides safeguards against arbitrary discrimination without excluding reasonable distinctions; the need for justification in cases of unequal treatment is thus considered to be of particular importance, in order to conclude whether the claimant is indeed treated less favourably.

403. The Supreme Court is, in general, reluctant to recognize affirmative action. It has held that legislation amending the Certain Legal Persons of Public Law (Appointment of Board of Directors) Law 149(I)/1988 so as to provide that at least a third of the members of the board of directors of any legal person of public law should be representatives of both sexes, violated the principle of equality and non-discrimination safeguarded under Article 28 of the Constitution. The Court rejected rather summarily arguments on affirmative action and held that the impugned legislation introduced an arbitrary and unreasonable discrimination which was not based on objective criteria.[540]

XII. The Right to a Fair Trial

404. Article 30 of the Constitution provides that no person shall be denied access to the court assigned to him/her by or under this Constitution. The right of access to court is subject to reasonable restrictions, such as prescription of periods of limitation for the exercise of such right; whether a limitation provided by law is reasonable has to be considered by the Court. In *Fekkas*, the Appellant claimed damages against the Electricity Authority Cyprus (EAC) for bodily injuries which he had suffered in the course of his employment. However, his claim was dismissed as being statute-barred, since the Law provided for a three-month limitation period. The Supreme Court recognized that the laying down of periods of limitation is a

538. [1973] 3 CLR 437.
539. [1987] 3 CLR 1766.
540. *President of the Republic v. House of Representatives* [2017] 3 CLR 604 (in Greek).

matter primarily within the sphere of competence of the Legislature and that different periods of limitation may be laid down in respect of different causes of action or different litigants depending on the nature of things. However, it held that the limitation period in question could not be reasonably justified and accordingly was unconstitutional. The Court concluded that:

> we see no conceivable justification or rational basis for the existence of a striking distinction in relation to periods of limitation (three months as against two years) as between an action for civil wrong against a public utility corporation, such as the respondent, and the same action against any other corporation.[541]

405. In *Phinikaridou v. Odysseos*, the Applicant had been born out of wedlock.[542] In December 1997, when the Applicant was fifty-two years old, her biological mother, just before dying, told her the name of her biological father. The Applicant lodged an application requesting judicial recognition of paternity on the basis of section 20 of the Children (Kinship and Legal Status) Law. The Respondent maintained that the Applicant's claim was time-barred. The Applicant argued that the three-year limitation period provided in the Law ran contrary to Article 30 of the Constitution. The majority of the Supreme Court held that the limitation period was reasonable and accordingly constitutional. The minority of the Supreme Court held, however, that determining the time limit for the exercise of the right to recognition of paternity, regardless and independently of the knowledge of facts that constitute it, effectively negates the right in question. In the case of *Phinikaridou v. Cyprus*, the ECtHR held that there was a violation of Article 8 of the ECHR and agreed with the minority of the Supreme Court that the application of a rigid time limit for the exercise of paternity proceedings, regardless of the circumstances of an individual case, and in particular, the knowledge of the facts concerning paternity, impairs the very essence of the right.[543]

406. It is not unconstitutional to regulate the right of access to court through the provisions of procedural legislation to the extent that the said legislation is not arbitrary or unreasonable.[544] Furthermore, it has been held that a legal provision stipulating that the internal disputes between the members of a cooperative society would be referred to arbitration did not violate Article 30 of the Constitution.[545] However, it was held that a law restricting the right to apply before the Court only to cases where the debtor has previously exhausted all efforts to secure an out-of-court settlement which has been institutionalized via either legislation or administrative act or other relevant provision, ran contrary to Article 30 § 1 of the Constitution because it unduly hindered access to courts. The Supreme Court held that not only the term

541. *Fekkas v. EAC* [1968] 1 CLR 173.
542. [2001] 1 CLR 1744 (in Greek). *See also Yiorgalla v. Hadjichristodoulou* [2000] 1 CLR 2060 (in Greek).
543. App. 23890/02, Judgment of 20 Dec. 2007.
544. *Georgadji and Another v. The Republic* [1971] 2 CLR 229, *Fatsita v. Fatsita and Another* [1988] 1 CLR 210.
545. *The Co-operative Grocery of Vasilia and Pirirou* (1962) 4 RSCC 19.

'other relevant provision' was vague, but a procedure introduced via an administrative act was uncertain since such acts do not need to be published even in the Official Gazette of the Republic.[546]

407. Article 30 of the Constitution further provides that the establishment of judicial committees or exceptional courts under any name whatsoever is prohibited. In the determination of his/her civil rights and obligations or of any criminal charge against him/her, every person is entitled to a fair and public hearing within a reasonable time by an independent, impartial and competent court established by law. Judgment shall be reasoned and pronounced in public session, but the press and the public may be excluded from all or any part of the trial upon a decision of the court where it is in the interest of the security of the Republic or the constitutional order or the public order or the public safety or the public morals or where the interests of juveniles or the protection of the private life of the parties so require or, in special circumstances where, in the opinion of the court, publicity would prejudice the interests of justice.[547]

408. The independence of the judicial power from the executive is a cardinal feature of the Cypriot legal system. The appointment, promotion, transfers and discipline of members of the judiciary, other than Supreme Court judges, rests exclusively within the power of the Supreme Court. In *Christoforou*, the Supreme Court held that the provisions of the Annual Holidays with Pay Law were unconstitutional to the extent that they envisaged the involvement of the executive in the appointment of the Chairman of the Arbitration Tribunal.[548] Similarly, in *Pastellopoulos,* it was held that the provisions of the Military Code and Procedure Law stipulating the appointment of the President of the Military Court by the Council of Ministers were unconstitutional.[549] Furthermore, the Court has to be objectively impartial. A judge should excuse himself/herself whenever he/she considers that this would be in the interests of justice, such as when he/she has a degree of connection with the case or the parties or an interest in the outcome of the case.[550] In the absence of valid reasons disqualifying a judge from sitting in the case, however, he/she should not be excused as this would be an abdication of duty and would acknowledge to the litigant a right to choose the judge who will try him/her.[551]

546. *President of the Republic v. House of Representatives* [2014] 3 CLR 499 (in Greek).
547. *See* C. Clerides, *The Access of Mass Media Communication to Court Proceedings*, 49–50 Cyprus L. Rev. 7157–7168 (1995) (in Greek).
548. *Keramourgia Aias Ltd v. Christoforou* [1975] 1 CLR 38.
549. *Pastellopoulos v. Republic* [1985] 2 CLR 165.
550. A. Emilianides, *Principles for the Disqualification of Judges*, 11 Cyprus & European L. Rev. 179–185 (2010) (in Greek).
551. *Autocephalous and Apostolic Orthodox Church of Cyprus v. House of Representatives* 3 CLR 54 (1990) (in Greek). *See also* A. Pantelides, *The Constitutional Guarantee about the Lawful Judge and the Cyprus Law*, 2 Cyprus L. Tribune 19–27 (1977), Cyprus L. Tribune 18–21 (1977).

409. One of the cardinal elements of a fair trial is that the judgment of the court must be reasoned.[552] A duly reasoned judgment presupposes an analysis of the evidence adduced in the light of the issues as arising and defined by the pleadings, concrete findings as to the facts of the case and a clear judicial pronouncement indicating the outcome of the case.[553] The Supreme Court may set aside judgments of the trial court if they lack due reasoning and do not reveal the reasoning of the court.[554] In the case of *Zervou,* the trial judge had effectively copied the text of the written submission of the Plaintiffs in his judgment, without anywhere in the judgment mentioning this fact, or explaining why he had so adopted it. It was held that this raised doubts about whether the trial court had exercised its own judicial discretion and whether the judgment could not be considered duly reasoned.[555]

410. Undeniably, one of the most significant problems of the administration of justice in Cyprus is delay.[556] Whereas the Supreme Court has repeatedly stressed that justice delayed is justice denied and that the timely administration of justice constitutes an element of justice itself,[557] in practice, there is a significant delay in the trial of cases. The House of Representatives has adopted the Law Providing for Effective Remedies for Exceeding the Reasonable Time Requirement for the Determination of Civil Rights and Obligations (Law 2(I) 2010). Law 2(I)/10 provides that individuals who consider that their right to determination of civil rights and obligations within a reasonable time has been violated may file a complaint, either when the relevant proceedings have been concluded court judgment, or while they are still pending. If it is held that there is an unreasonable delay, the applicant may have a right to receive compensation for the violation of his/her rights. In criminal trials, unreasonable delay may lead to the quashing of a conviction, if the delay has hindered the fairness of the trial.[558] On 27 March 2018, the Institute of Public Administration of Ireland officially presented before the Supreme Court their commissioned study for the reform of Cypriot courts so as to address delays. A committee has further been appointed in order to consider a revision of the Cypriot Civil Procedure Rules and submit proposals to the Supreme Court.

411. Articles 12 section 5 and 30 section 3 of the Constitution set out the minimum rights of litigants and correspond to Article 6 section 3 of the ECHR. It is therefore provided that every person has the right: (a) to be informed of the reasons why he/she is required to appear before the court, (b) to present his/her case before the court and to have sufficient time necessary for its preparation, (c) to adduce or

552. C. Georghiades, *The Reasoning of the Judgments of the Supreme Court as a Court of Second Instance*, 2 Cyprus L. Tribune 49–60 (2004) (in Greek).
553. *Pioneer Candy Ltd v. Tryfon and Sons* [1981] 1 CLR 540.
554. *Glyky v. Municipality of Limassol* [1998] 1 CLR 2319 (in Greek).
555. *Zervou v. Euroinvestment Finance Public Ltd* [2013] 1 CLR 688 (in Greek).
556. G. Pikis, *Report of the Committee on the Study of the Function of District and Other First Instance Courts* (1999, in Greek).
557. *Paporis v. National Bank of Greece* [1986] 1 CLR 578, *Victoros v. Christodoulou* [1992] 1 CLR 512 (in Greek).
558. *Christopoulos v. Police* [2001] 2 CLR 100 (in Greek), *Efstathiou v. Police* [1990] 2 CLR 294 (in Greek).

cause to be adduced his/her evidence and to examine witnesses according to law, (d) to have a lawyer of his/her own choice and to have free legal assistance where the interests of justice so require and as provided by law, (e) to have free assistance of an interpreter if he/she cannot understand or speak the language used in court.[559] The above requirements are considered fundamental elements of a fair trial and any breach of or deviation from them would invalidate the proceedings.

XIII. The Right to Marry

412. Article 22 of the Constitution safeguards the fundamental right to marry and found a family.[560] Article 22 section 1 provides that any person reaching the age of majority is free to marry and to found a family according to the law relating to marriage applicable to such person under the provisions of the Constitution. Such constitutional right is enjoyed by all natural persons, irrespective of whether they are citizens of the Republic or aliens. And it implies not only the right to marry but also the right not to marry; consequently, legislative provisions which imposed taxation on unmarried persons only were held to be unconstitutional.[561] Article 22 corresponds to Article 12 of the ECHR; however, it is more detailed and extensive due to the peculiarities of the Cypriot law of marriage. Such additional provisions are not inconsistent with Article 12 of the ECHR, since Article 12 specifically provides that the right is exercised in accordance with national laws. The right to marry is complemented by the right of respect for a person's private and family life safeguarded by Article 15 of the Constitution which corresponds to Article 8 of the ECHR.[562]

413. Marriage is, according to Cypriot law, a contract formally and willingly entered into conferring on the parties the status of husband and wife. It is thus a contractual agreement between a man and a woman to live together and to love one another as husband and wife to the exclusion of all others by recognizing mutual and reciprocal obligations involving sharing a common home and a common domestic life. However, marriage is a unique and peculiar contract. Special formalities need to be observed for a marriage to be concluded and such a contract cannot be discharged by agreement, but only by a formal legal act pronounced by a court of competent jurisdiction. Hence, marriage is also an institution creating a specific status, namely the condition of belonging to a particular class of persons to whom the law assigns certain peculiar legal capacities or incapacities. The mutual rights and duties of the parties are largely fixed by law and not by agreement; such a law is obligatory and cannot be derogated from with the consent of the parties. This is due to the fact that the State has a special interest in the institution of marriage.[563]

---

559. A. Loizou, *Constitution of the Republic of Cyprus* 181ff (2001, in Greek).
560. *See* A. Emilianides, *Family and Succession Law in Cyprus* (3d ed., Kluwer 2024). *See also* C. Tornaritis, *The Right to Marry and Found a Family, Especially under the Laws of Cyprus*, in *Mélanges Offerts à Polys Modinos* 320–330 (1968).
561. *Panayides v. The Republic of Cyprus* [1965] 3 CLR 107.
562. C. Tornaritis, *The State Law of the Republic of Cyprus* 128 (Ctr. Sci. Research 1982).
563. *See* A. Emilianides, *The Cypriot Law of Marriage and Divorce* (Sakkoulas 2006, in Greek).

414. The right to marry is exercised in accordance with the applicable law for each person as determined in the relevant constitutional provisions.[564] Article 111 of the Constitution applies with respect to marriages between members of the Greek Orthodox or the three religious groups, while marriages between members of the Turkish Community are governed by the constitutional provisions establishing the Turkish Communal Chamber. Article 22 section 2 of the Constitution further governs the applicable law in case of mixed marriages.[565] Article 22 does not safeguard a right to same-sex marriages or partnerships. The ECtHR has also held that Article 12 of the ECHR safeguarding the right to marry does not necessitate the Member States to recognize the right to marry or civil partnership for same-sex couples.[566] However, it has been held that once a State decides to recognize civil unions or registered partnerships as an alternative form to marriage, it would be a violation of the principle of non-discrimination if such was recognized for heterosexual partners only.[567] The right to celebrate a civil union instead of a marriage was eventually recognized by the enactment of the Civil Union Law 184(I)/2015. A civil union has the same legal validity and consequences as if a marriage, either religious or civil, had been celebrated,[568] with the exception of the right to adoption, which is precluded as it was deemed to be highly controversial. It should be noted, however, that the ECtHR has already recognized the right of adoption for single homosexual parents[569] and hence its exception from the ambit of Law 184(I)/2015 seems to be inconsistent with the principle of non-discrimination.

§3. Economic, Social and Cultural Rights

I. The Right to a Decent Existence and to Social Security

415. The Constitution does not specify a specific economic system. However, Part II of the Constitution guarantees to the individual certain social and economic rights which provide for a set of conditions that have to be met while structuring the economic system.[570] Article 9 of the Constitution stipulates that every person has the right to a decent existence and to social security. A law shall provide for the protection of the workers, assistance to the poor and a system of social insurance. The Constitution does not attempt to define the notion of a 'decent existence'; however, it is submitted that the State has an obligation to 'create and maintain such

564. *Venglis v. Venglis* [1982] 1 CLR 223.
565. G. Serghides, *Internal and External Conflict of Laws in Regard to Family Relations in Cyprus* (1988); A. Emilianides, *The Cypriot Law of Marriage and Divorce* (Sakkoulas 2006, in Greek); C. Tornaritis, *On the Applicable Law in Case of Mixed Marriages*, 19 Revue Hellénique de Droit International 293–294 (1966).
566. *Schalk and Kopf v. Austria*, App. 3014/04, Judgment of 24 Jun. 2010, *Gas and Dubois v. France*, App. 25951/07, Judgment of 15 Mar. 2012.
567. *Valianatos v. Greece*, Apps 29381/01 and 32684/09, Judgment of 7 Nov. 2013, *Oliari v. Italy*, Apps 18766/11 and 36030/11, Judgment of 21 Jul. 2015.
568. *See* S. Liasides, *Civil Union (Law 184(I)/2015). Legal Aspects* (2016, in Greek).
569. *E.B. v. France*, App. 43546/02, Judgment of 22 Jan. 2008.
570. *See* C. Tornaritis, *The Social and Economic Rights under the Law of the Republic of Cyprus*, in *Mélanges Bridel* 533–556 (Imprimeries Réunies 1968).

conditions of living, of work and of health as to enable every person to enjoy a standard of living adequate for the health and well-being of himself/herself and his/her family'.[571] The Republic further has a constitutional duty to enact legislation in order to provide for the protection of the workers, assistance to the poor and a system of social insurance. The right to social security is aimed at protecting the individual in the event of unemployment, illness, old age or other similar. Article 9 of the Constitution could be interpreted as a constitutional demand for the existence of some form of welfare state.

416. However, the right to a decent existence does not imply that there is a free licence for anyone to act as he/she deems fit, irrespective of the general interests of society, for the purpose of allegedly ensuring a decent existence. Any interpretation to the contrary would lead to absurd results, since it would negate the prerogative of the State to regulate, within reason and in order to safeguard the general welfare, social and economic life. In light of the above, the Supreme Constitutional Court dismissed the argument that section 16 of the Shop Assistants Law, Cap. 185, which regulated the exercise of the profession of a shopkeeper, was inconsistent with Article 9 of the Constitution.[572]

II. The Right to Work

417. Article 25 of the Constitution safeguards the right of every person to practise any profession or to carry on any occupation, trade or business. The exercise of this right may be subject to such formalities, conditions or restrictions as are prescribed by law and relate exclusively to the qualifications usually required for the exercise of any profession or are necessary only in the interests of the security of the Republic or the constitutional order or the public safety or the public order or the public health or the public morals or for the protection of the rights and liberties guaranteed by this Constitution to any person or in the public interest. Provided that no such formalities, conditions or restrictions purporting to be in the public interest shall be prescribed by law if such formality, condition or restriction is contrary to the interests of either Community.

418. As an exception, a law may provide, if it is in the public interest, that certain enterprises of the nature of an essential public service or relating to the exploitation of sources of energy or other natural resources shall be carried out exclusively by the Republic or a municipal corporation or by a public corporate body created for the purpose by such law and administered under the control of the Republic, and having a capital which may be derived from public and private funds or from either such source only; provided that where such enterprise has been carried out by any person, other than a municipal corporation or a public corporate body, the installations used for such enterprise shall, at the request of such person, be acquired on

571. C. Tornaritis, *The Human Rights as Recognized and Protected by the Law of the Republic of Cyprus* 15 (1974).
572. *Police v. Milliotis* [1961] 1 RSCC 113.

payment of a just price, by the Republic or such municipal corporation or such public corporate body, as the case may be. A law providing that the Administrative Commission for Natural Gas would be the owner and administrator of the network of transport and distribution of natural gas and the exclusive supplier of natural gas in the Republic was held to be inconsistent with Article 25 of the Constitution. Whereas Article 25 § 3 permits the Republic, or legal persons under public law under the control of the Republic, to exclusively exploit natural resources, the Administrative Commission for Natural Gas was not a legal person under public law but, on the contrary, a legal person under private law, i.e., a private company established in accordance with the Companies Law, Cap. 113.[573]

419. The right guaranteed by Article 25 of the Constitution is thus not unrestricted, but it might be subject to qualifications in accordance with the law. Furthermore, Article 25 safeguards only against direct and not indirect interference with the right safeguarded thereunder.[574] It was accordingly held that reasonable restrictions imposed on the right to practise the profession or trade of a driver or of an owner of a public vehicle are not unconstitutional, since they are necessary for public safety, for the protection of the rights and liberties guaranteed by the Constitution to any person and in the public interest.[575] However, it was held that section 3 of the Bakeries (Night Work) Law, Cap. 177, which prohibited night work in bakeries was not necessary for the protection of public health and accordingly ran contrary to Article 25 of the Constitution.[576]

420. In *Shistris*, it was held that nothing in Article 25 limits the right of the State to subject the exercise of a trade or profession to any number of licences for the public interest; so long as the conditions imposed are reasonable, the law will be upheld.[577] Control of the profession or trade which may be considered necessary for the exercise of such right is therefore not excluded by Article 25; a test of reasonableness should guide the Courts in deciding whether a restriction to the exercise of the rights safeguarded by Article 25 should be considered as legitimate.[578] In *Voyias*, it was held that the imposition of a licence fee does not infringe the right of the Applicant to practise his profession, since it is only imposed with a view to exact revenue for the Municipality and for assessing the tax and not a regulatory process of the activities constituting a profession. Moreover, in *Kyriakides,* it was confirmed that conditions or restrictions laid down to regulate the qualifications required for the exercise of a profession (such as an architect, engineer, doctor or advocate) are not, in principle, inconsistent with the provisions of Article 25.[579]

---

573. *President of the Republic v. House of Representatives* [2013] 3 CLR 96 (in Greek).
574. *Loizou v. Poullis* [1969] 1 CLR 17, at 24.
575. *Police v. Liveras* [1962] 3 RSCC 65.
576. *Nicosia Police v. Georghiou* [1962] 4 RSCC 36.
577. *Shistris v. Cyprus Tourism Organization* [1983] 2 CLR 72.
578. *President of the Republic v. House of Representatives* [1992] 3 CLR 165 (in Greek).
579. *The Board for Registration of Architects and Civil Engineers v. Kyriakides* [1966] 3 CLR 640. *See also Ioakeim v. Republic*, Adm. App. 190/2019, Judgment of 28 Jan. 2022 (in Greek).

421. In the case *of Lapertas Fisheries*, the Supreme Court held that section 3 section 1 of the Stock Exchange Law of Cyprus (Amendment) Law 42(I)/2000 which imposed on a company the obligation to proceed to initial public offering, irrespective of considerations about the damaging or even destructive effect of such obligation to the financial interests of the company or its members, was inconsistent with Article 25 of the Constitution. The Court held that the impugned legislation completely disregarded the financial interests of the company and its right to exercise a trade or profession and deprived them of the opportunity to act in the manner that they themselves consider as beneficial for their own interests. The obligation was so extensive so as to effectively negate the right safeguarded by Article 25 of the Constitution.[580] A similar conclusion was reached in *Pitsillides*; it was held that obligating an investment fund to invest 80% of its funds within a timescale of twelve months, irrespective of whether such investments would be considered financially sound by the management of the investment fund, was inconsistent with Article 25 of the Constitution.[581]

III. The Right to Enter into a Contract

422. Closely connected with the right to exercise a profession or carry out any occupation, trade or business is the freedom to contract which is guaranteed under Article 26 of the Constitution. Article 26 provides that every person has the right to enter freely into any contract subject to such conditions, limitations or restrictions as are laid down by the general principles of the law of contract. In *Chimonides v. Manglis*, the majority of the Supreme Court held that Article 26 safeguards only the right to enter into a contract and not the obligations arising out of an agreement resulting from an exercise of the right to contract.[582] Rights arising out of a contract were therefore not considered to be guaranteed by Article 26 of the Constitution as fundamental rights.

423. The Supreme Court, however, in a unanimous judgment, partly reversed the *Chimonides* majority ruling and held that the right safeguarded under Article 26 of the Constitution includes the right to determine the content of the contract in accordance with the free will of the parties. Accordingly, any subsequent interference by the legislator is not consistent with the freedom of contract, except under the circumstances provided for in the Constitution and to the extent that they do not prejudice the substance or core of the right. Accordingly, a law by virtue of which either the guarantors, or the mortgaged debtor, would be absolved from any further liability following the sale of a mortgaged land, irrespective of whether the profits of the sale sufficed to repay the entirety of the debt, was held to be unconstitutional.[583] In

580. [2002] 2 CLR 335 (in Greek).
581. *Pitsillides v. Cyprus Securities and Exchange Commission* [2004] 3 CLR 7 (in Greek). *See also Cyprus Securities and Exchange Commission v. Laser Investments Ltd* [2007] 3 CLR 224 (in Greek).
582. [1967] 1 CLR 125.
583. *President of the Republic v. House of Representatives* [2014] 1 CLR 487 (in Greek), *President of the Republic v. House of Representatives* [2014] 1 CLR 527 (in Greek). *See also President of the*

a subsequent judgment, the Supreme Court held that a bill by virtue of which, during the restructuring of a loan by a credit institution, the amount of the loan received would be set off with the nominal value of the securities of the debtor, minus the current value of said securities, was inconsistent with Articles 23 and 26 of the Constitution. It was held that the intended legislation restricted without justification the right that a credit institution might claim from the debtor and further limited the amount of contractual interest to be claimed by the credit institution, thereby interfering *a posteriori* to the contractual rights of the creditor contrary to Article 26 of the Constitution.[584]

424. Article 26 § 2 of the Constitution provides that a law may provide for collective labour contracts of obligatory fulfilment by employees and workers, with adequate protection of the rights of any person, whether or not represented at the conclusion of such contract. However, no such law has ever been enacted by the Republic.[585] Collective agreements are an important source of labour law; however, the general rule is that collective agreements between trade unions and employers are not legally binding to them.[586] Thus, their success rests on the willingness of the social partners to abide by them and the voluntary cooperation of the workers and the employers. Collective agreements which have not been incorporated into legislation do not, as a principle, create rights and obligations under public law.[587] Accordingly, a collective agreement may not amend the rights of the employee under public law, unless it has become part of the practice of the administrative organ.[588] However, their terms may be incorporated in individual employment contracts and so become binding on the parties thereto.[589] Moreover, a collective employment agreement may not prevail over an individual employment agreement, unless the terms of the collective agreement have been incorporated, expressly or impliedly, in the individual employment agreement.[590]

IV. The Right to Strike

425. The right to strike is safeguarded by virtue of Article 27 of the Constitution and its exercise may be regulated by law only for the purposes of safeguarding the

---

Republic v. House of Representatives, App. 9/2016, Judgment of 26 Jan. 2017 (in Greek), *President of the Republic v. House of Representatives* [2011] 3 CLR 683 (in Greek), *Republic v. Menelaou* [1982] 3 CLR 419.

584. *President of the Republic v. House of Representatives* [2017] 3 CLR 235 (in Greek). *See also President of the Republic v. House of Representatives* [2017] 3 CLR 226 (in Greek).
585. *See* in detail A. Emilianides & C. Ioannou, *Labour Law in Cyprus* (3d ed., Kluwer 2024).
586. C. Tornaritis, *Collective Employment Agreement*, 1–2 Cyprus L. Tribune 14–17 [1972].
587. *Kontemeniotis v. CyBC* [1982] 3 CLR 1027, *Papadopoulosand others v. CyBC* [1996] 3 CLR 1 (in Greek), *Evangelou and others v. CyBC* [1985] 3 CLR 1410, *Angelides v. CYTA*, Case 46/2011, dated 1/9/2014 (in Greek), *Mesaritis and others v. TEPAK*, Cases 1322–1333/2011, dated 11 Jun. 2015 (in Greek).
588. *DerParthogh v. CyBC* [1984] 3 CLR 635.
589. *Lanitis Bros Co Ltd v. Ioannides and others* [1979] 1 CLR 815.
590. *Hatzikonstanti v. Golden Coast Ltd* [2012] 1 CLR 65 (in Greek), *Loizou v. Stylson Engineering Co Ltd* [1998] 1 CLR 2077 (in Greek).

security of the Republic or the constitutional order or the public order or the public safety or the maintenance of supplies and services essential to the life of the inhabitants or the protection of the rights and liberties guaranteed by this Constitution to any person. A law cannot render the right to strike meaningless and accordingly regulation of the right to strike should be in accordance with the constitutional provisions; the right may be restricted only if it is absolutely necessary.[591] Accordingly, an employer may not fire employees because they exercise their right to strike. The members of the armed forces, of the police and of the gendarmerie shall not have the right to strike. It is further provided that a law may extend such prohibition to the members of the public service. No such prohibition has been extended to members of the public service; however, on the contrary, section 63 of the Public Service Law 1/90 safeguards the unhindered exercise of the freedom of association (and any related rights) of public servants.

V. Freedom to Assembly and Association

426. Article 21 of the Constitution corresponds to Article 11 of the ECHR and safeguards the right of every person to freedom of peaceful assembly and association. The right to freedom of association with others included the right to form and join trade unions for the protection of one's interests.[592] Subject to the provisions of any law regulating the establishment or incorporation, membership (including rights and obligations of members), management and administration, and winding up and dissolution, the provisions of this Article shall also apply to the formation of companies, societies and other associations functioning for profit. It is explicitly provided that no person shall be compelled to join any association or to continue to be a member thereof. It follows that Article 21 guarantees both the positive freedom of every person to form and join an association or trade union and the negative freedom not to join or continue to be a member of a trade union.

427. Restrictions may be placed on the exercise of these rights if they are prescribed by law and are absolutely necessary in the interests of the security of the Republic or the constitutional order or the public safety or the public order or the public health or the public morals or for the protection of the rights and liberties guaranteed by this Constitution to any person, whether or not such person participates in such assembly or is a member of such association. It is further provided

591. *See* A. Emilianides & C. Ioannou, *Labour Law in Cyprus* (3d ed., Kluwer 2024); C. Christodoulou, *Handbook of Cypriot Labour Law* 76–92 (Epifaniou 2009, in Greek); T. Eliades, *The Right to Strike* 2 Cyprus L. Tribune 28–30 (1970), A. Loizou, *Restriction of the Right to Strike under the Constitution of Cyprus and International Conventions*, 11 Lysias 23–30 (1995) (in Greek); C. Tornaritis, *Sympathy Strike in accordance with the Existing Law in Cyprus*, 4 Cyprus L. Tribune 3–8 (1969) (in Greek); L. Loucaides, *The Right of Strike and Sympathy or Solidarity Strike*, 5 Cyprus L. Review 831–838 (1984) (in Greek).

592. A. Emilianides, *The Freedom of the Worker to Organize in Cyprus*, in *Die Koalitionsfreiheit des Arbeitnehmers/The Freedom of the Worker to Organize* 1057–1069 (1980); L. Loucaides, *Legal Protection of the Freedom of Trade Unionism in Cyprus*, 15 Cyprus L. Review 2346–2359 (1986), A. Eftychiou, *The Law of Freedom of Trade Unionism*, 22 Cyprus L. Review 3455–3463 (1988) (in Greek), R. Prentzas, *Freedom of Trade Unionism* (Ermogenis 1997) (in Greek).

that a law may provide for the imposition of restrictions on the exercise of these rights by members of the armed forces, the police or gendarmerie. Whereas section 28A of the Army Law 33/1990 provides that no member of the armed forces may become or remain a member of any trade union, association or body affiliated to a trade union, or of any association or body the objects of which are to control or influence the conditions of employment in any trade or profession, or the pay, pensions or terms of service of the force, the only restriction set out by section 55 of the Police Law 73(I)/2004 is that members of the force may not protest in public, while in police uniform, for matters pertaining to their pay, pensions or conditions of service. There is no similar restriction for civil servants or other members of the administration. Any association of the object or activities which are contrary to the constitutional order is prohibited.

VI. The Right to Education

428. Article 20 of the Constitution provides that every person has the right to receive, and every person or institution has the right to give instruction or education subject to such formalities, conditions or restrictions as are in accordance with the relevant communal law and are necessary only in the interests of the security of the Republic or the constitutional order or the public safety or the public order or the public health or the public morals or the standard and quality of education or for the protection of the rights and liberties of others including the right of the parents to secure for their children such education as is in conformity with their religious convictions.[593] Similarly, Article 2 of the First Protocol of the ECHR provides that no person shall be denied the right to education and that in the exercise of any functions which it assumes in relation to education and teaching, the State shall respect the right of parents to ensure such education and teaching in conformity with their own religious and philosophical convictions.

429. It is further provided that free primary education shall be made available by the Greek and the Turkish Communal Chambers in the respective communal primary schools. The various legislative provisions have extended the right to free education to all levels of education, including the University level, as far as public schools or universities are concerned. Primary education shall be compulsory for all citizens of such school age as may be determined by a relevant law. Education, other than primary education, shall be made available by the Greek and the Turkish Communal Chambers, in deserving and appropriate cases, on such terms and conditions as may be determined by a relevant communal law. Following the constitutional crisis of 1963 and the self-dissolution of the Greek Communal Chamber, all competencies with respect to education have been transferred to the Ministry of Education and Culture. The Compulsory Education Law 24(I)/1993 provides that parents are

593. A. Emilianides & C. Hadjisoteriou, *Cyprus*, in *Balancing Freedom, Autonomy and Accountability in Education* 1–25 (J. deGroof and C. Glenn eds, John Hopkins School of Education and European Association for Education Law and Policy 2020).

obliged to register their children at a school within their educational region, independently of whether they reside in the island legally or not; education is compulsory and free in public schools for all citizens until the age of 15 (and starting from the age of 4 years and 8 months).

430. The stipulation that the parents have the right to secure for their children the education which conforms to their religious convictions, aims at safeguarding the possibility of pluralism in education. The State is forbidden to pursue an aim of indoctrination which might be considered not respecting the parents' religious convictions.[594] However, it should be noted that religious lessons given in primary and secondary schools follow the doctrine of the Eastern Orthodox Church. In secondary education, the courses are given by graduates of university schools of divinity, while in primary education, they are given by the class teacher. Attendance is compulsory for Orthodox pupils; atheists or members of other religions, however, may be excused. There is no possibility of religious education for members of other religions in public schools, with the exception of Maronites and Turkish Cypriots; the religious instruction of Maronite children who attend public schools is taught by Maronite priests who receive a monthly salary from the state. Similarly, where there is an adequate number, Turkish Cypriot pupils may be religiously educated in their mother language and in their own religion, even in Greek-speaking schools.

431. The fact that the State cannot offer religious education consistent with every single individual religion or creed is not of course surprising; the great majority of pupils in each non-Turkish public school adhere to the Orthodox Christian religion and thus, it would be practically unfeasible for the State to provide religious education which would meet the demands of all parents. This is why the State has opted to assist children belonging to religious groups to attend private schools of their choice, if they so desire, and further why non-Orthodox Christian pupils may request to be exempted from religious education, including collective worship. In any event, parents (or lawful guardians, as the case may be) have the right to request in writing that their children be exempted from religious education if they are not Orthodox Christians. In the case of *Arvanitakis*, the school had refused to exempt from religious education pupils who were Jehovah's Witnesses.[595] The applicants had stressed that in the textbooks used in the classes, Jehovah's Witnesses are referred to as an anti-Christian and anti-social sect and are generally presented in a negative manner; however, their arguments were rejected by the school, which declared that attendance to all classes is obligatory for all students irrespective of their religion. The Supreme Court had no difficulty in holding that the school had exercised its competences in an unlawful manner.

594. *Kjeldsen, Busk Madsen and Pedersen v. Denmark*, Judgment of 7 Dec. 1976; (1979–1980) 1 EHRR 711, *Valsamis v. Greece*, Judgment of 18 Dec. 1996; (1997) 24 EHRR 294.

595. *Arvanitakis v. The Republic* [1994] 3 CLR 859 (in Greek).

432. Exempting, however, only pupils who do not belong to the Orthodox Church might present certain problems; parents who belong to the Orthodox Christian religion might not wish for their children to receive doctrinal religious education. Furthermore, atheists or non-Orthodox might not wish to declare their religious beliefs to the school authorities in order to be exempted from religious education. Similarly to the principle that religion should not be referred to in public documents because it might lead to indirect discrimination on grounds of religion, revealing one's religious beliefs for the purpose of exempting one from religious education, might, in a predominantly Orthodox society, also lead to discrimination; the exercise of the right to opt out of religious activities, might entail significant discomfort or embarrassment for the students, or entrench religious differences at an early stage of the student's lives.[596]

VII. The Right to Property

433. Article 23 of the Constitution safeguards the right to property; whereas Article 23 corresponds to Article 1 of Protocol 1 of the ECHR, it is much more detailed and extensive. Paragraph 1 of Article 23 thus provides that every person, alone or jointly with others, has the right to acquire, own, possess, enjoy or dispose of any movable or immovable property and has the right to respect such right. The right of the Republic to underground water, minerals and antiquities is reserved.[597] It has been held that the object of the Immovable Property (Tenure, Registration, Valuation) Law, Cap. 224 relates strictly to the regulation of civil law rights in property and accordingly does not conflict with the provisions of Article 23 of the Constitution; it was not the aim of Article 23 to prohibit the regulation and management of the civil law rights of individuals in immovable property.[598]

434. No deprivation or restriction or limitation of any such right shall be made except where restrictions or limitations are absolutely necessary, by virtue of paragraph 3 of Article 23, in the interest of the public safety or the public health or the public morals or the town and country planning or the development and utilization of any property to the promotion of the public benefit or for the protection of the rights of others may be imposed by law on the exercise of such right. In cases of restriction or limitation of property, just compensation shall be promptly paid for any such restrictions or limitations which materially decrease the economic value of such property: such compensation is to be determined in case of disagreement by a civil court. With respect to compulsory acquisition, Article 23 section 4 explicitly provides that any movable or immovable property or any right over or interest in any such property may be compulsorily acquired by the Republic or by a municipal corporation or by a Communal Chamber for the educational, religious, charitable or sporting institutions, bodies or establishments within its competence and only from

596. *See* more detailed analysis in A. Emilianides, *Law and Religion in Cyprus* (4th ed., Kluwer 2024).
597. *See* the Unified Administration of Water Law 79(I)/2010, the Antiquities Law, Cap. 31 and the Mines and Quarries Law, Cap. 270.
598. *Ratip* (1962) 3 RSCC 102, *Evlogimenos v. Republic* (1961) 2 RSCC 139.

the persons belonging to its respective Community or by a public corporation or a public utility body on which such right has been conferred by law.

435. Compulsory acquisition may be effected only: (a) for a purpose which is to the public benefit and shall be specially provided by a general law for compulsory acquisition which shall be enacted within a year from the date of the coming into operation of this Constitution; (b) when such purpose is established by a decision of the acquiring authority and made under the provisions of such law stating clearly the reasons for such acquisition; and (c) upon the payment in cash and in advance of a just and equitable compensation to be determined in case of disagreement by a civil court. The law governing compulsory acquisition is Law 15/1962, which has been held to be constitutional despite the fact that it was enacted within two years from the date of the coming into operation of the Constitution, instead of within one year as provided in Article 23 section 4 of the Constitution.[599] The decision to compulsorily acquire immovable property has to be sufficiently justified by the public authority concerned and has to be necessary for the purpose of public benefit provided in the acquisition order.

436. Persons affected by the acquisition order have the right to object to the notification of the acquisition within thirty days. The public authority has to decide within a reasonable time whether to accept or reject the objections submitted and whether it still intends to proceed with the compulsory acquisition. The order for acquisition has to be issued within twelve months from the date of publication of the notification of acquisition in the Official Gazette of the Republic. The public authority should only order the compulsory acquisition of immovable property when the purpose of public benefit may not be achieved by any less restrictive means.[600] The public authority should negotiate with the owner of the property within a period of fourteen months from the notification of the acquisition in order to reach an agreement on the compensation to be awarded. If there is disagreement, the public authority ought to offer immediately the compensation it has determined and the owner may file a recourse before the District Court within seventy-five days and request for a determination of the amount of compensation to be awarded. Fair and just implies the full and perfect equivalent in money of the property taken.[601]

437. Any immovable property or any right over or interest in any such property compulsorily acquired shall, by virtue of paragraph 5 of Article 23, only be used for the purpose for which fit has been acquired. If within three years of the acquisition, such purpose has not been attained, the acquiring authority shall, immediately after the expiration of the said period of three years, offer the property at the price it has been acquired to the person from whom it has been acquired. Such person shall be

599. *Aspri v. Republic* (1962) 4 RSCC 57.
600. *Mestana v. Municipal Board of Athienou* [1991] 4 CLR 2288 (in Greek), *General Constructions Ltd v. Republic* [1991] 4 CLR 2694 (in Greek).
601. *Moti v. Republic* [1968] 1 CLR 102. *See also Serghides v. Republic* [1991] 1 CLR 191 (in Greek), *Serghides v. Republic* [1993] 1 CLR 339.

entitled within three months of the receipt of such offer to signify his/her acceptance or non-acceptance of the offer, and if he/she signifies acceptance, such property shall be returned to him/her immediately after his/her returning such price within a further period of three months from such acceptance. In *Zenon Efthymiades Estates Ltd*, it was held that the obligation of the administration to attain the purpose of the acquisition within three years should be considered objectively and not on the basis of the subjective intention of the administration.[602] If the purpose has been attained within the three-year period, no rights are created by a subsequent decision of the administration to change the original purpose.[603]

438. Paragraph 8 of Article 23 further provides that any movable or immovable property may be requisitioned by the Republic or by a Communal Chamber for the purposes of the educational, religious, charitable or sporting institutions, bodies or establishments within its competence and only where the owner and the person entitled to possession of such property belong to the respective Community, and only: (a) for a purpose which is to the public benefit and shall be specially provided by a general law for requisitioning which shall be enacted within a year from the date of the coming into operation of this Constitution; (b) when such purpose is established by a decision of the requisitioning authority and made under the provisions of such law stating clearly the reasons for such requisitioning; (c) for a period not exceeding three years; and (d) upon the prompt payment in cash of a just and equitable compensation to be determined in case of disagreement by a civil court. The law governing requisition is the Requisition of Property Law 21/1962.

439. Notwithstanding paragraphs 3 and 4 of Article 23, the right to property may be restricted by virtue of paragraph 7 of Article 23, in accordance with any law, for the purpose of levying execution in respect of any tax or penalty, executing any judgment, enforcing any contractual obligation or for the prevention of danger to life or property. However, by virtue of Article 23 section 9, there can be no deprivation, restriction or limitation of the right to property in respect of any movable or immovable property belonging to any. See, monastery, church or any other ecclesiastical corporation or any right over it or interest therein, except with the written consent of the appropriate ecclesiastical authority being in control of such property. It is explicitly provided that the provisions of paragraphs 3, 4, 7 and 8 of Article 23 shall be subject to the provisions of Article 23 section 9 of the Constitution and that the only exceptions are restrictions or limitations for the purposes of town and country planning. The same prerogative is provided in respect of any vakf movable or immovable property, including the objects and subjects of the vakfs and the properties belonging to the Mosques or to any other Muslim religious institutions, or any right thereon or interest therein; no deprivation, restriction or limitation shall be made except with the approval of the Turkish Communal Chamber and subject to the Laws and Principles of Vakfs.

602. *Zenon Efthymiades Estates Ltd v. Republic* [2006] 3 CLR 166 (in Greek).
603. *Zimpilos a.o v. EAC*, Adm. App. 71/2016, Judgment of 26 Jul. 2023 (in Greek).

440. Whereas the ambit of the near absolute prohibition of imposing restrictions or limitations to the property of religious organizations without their written consent is quite straightforward (exempting only restrictions and limitations for the purpose of town and country planning),[604] the recent judgment in *Holy Metropolis of Paphos v. Aristo Developers Ltd* concluded that not only restrictions and limitations for the purpose of town and country planning, but effectively all exceptions and limitations provided for in paragraphs 4, 7 and 8 of Article 23, citing the Greek text of the Constitution as proof of such an interpretation.[605] With all due respect to the Supreme Court, this is not only a misconceived interpretation of the Greek text of Article 23 section 9 which clearly exempts the property of religious organizations from the application of the said paragraphs, but it is also contrary to the clear interpretation of the Turkish text of the Constitution, as well as the English text of the Constitution.[606]

441. Due to the military occupation of northern Cyprus by Turkey, the violation of the right of property of Greek Cypriots by Turkey has been considered by the ECtHR. In *Loizidou*, the ECtHR held that Turkey exercises effective military control on the occupied areas and that 'TRNC' was essentially a puppet state. Accordingly, it was held that Turkey is liable for human rights violations occurring in the occupied territories of Cyprus.[607] The ECtHR held that as a consequence of the fact that the Applicant had been refused access to her immovable property since 1974, she had effectively lost all control over, as well as all possibilities to use and enjoy, her property. The continuous denial of access should therefore be regarded as an interference with her rights under Article 1 of Protocol No. 1 of the ECHR. The ECtHR concluded that there had been a continuous breach of Mrs Loizidou's right to property. In the subsequent Fourth Interstate Application of *Cyprus v. Turkey*, the ECtHR confirmed that Turkey was liable for the violation of the right to property of all Greek Cypriot displaced persons.[608] In the *Demopoulos* case, however, the

604. *The Holy Temple of Chryseleousis v. The Republic* [1989] 3 CLR 3074, *Holy Monastery of Kykkos v. Republic* [1996] 3 CLR 3362 (in Greek).

605. [2011] 1 CLR 1377 (in Greek).

606. *See also* A. Emilianides, *Reviewing the Review of Constitutionality: A Commentary on Three Recent Judgments of the Supreme Court*, Y.B. Cyprus & European L. 50ff (2013) (in Greek).

607. *Loizidou v. Turkey*, App. 15318/89, Judgments of 23 Mar. 1995 and 18 Dec. 1996. *See* further R. White, *Tackling Political Disputes Through Individual Applications*, European Human Rights L. Rev. 61–72 (1998); G. Cohen Jonathan, 'L' Affaire Loizidou devant la Cour Européenne des Droits de l' Homme: Quelques Observations' 46 *Revue Général de Droit International Public* 123–144 (1998); S. Perrakis, *The Importance of the Loizidou Case and the Consequences of the Judgments of the European Court of Human Rights in the International Legal Order*, Y.B. Inst. Intl. Rel. 169–180 (2000) (in Greek); H. Dipla, 'Responsabilité de l' état en Droits de l' Homme: L' Arrêt de la Cour de Strasbourg en l' Affaire Loizidou c. Turquie' 50 *Revue Hellénique de Droit International* 17–42 (1997). For a criticism *see* Z. Necatigil, *The Loizidou Case: A Critical examination* (Sam Papers 1999).

608. App. 25781/94, Judgment of 10 May 2001. *See* L. Loucaides, *The Judgment of the European Court of Human Rights in the Case of Cyprus v. Turkey*, 15 Leiden J. Intl. L. 225–236 (2002).

ECtHR held that the Greek Cypriot displaced persons should first exhaust the internal domestic remedies set up by Turkey prior to applying them for human rights violations.[609]

442. With respect to Turkish Cypriot properties, the Republic of Cyprus has enacted the Turkish Cypriot Properties (Administration and other matters – Temporary Provisions) Law 139/91; the aim of Law 139/91 is to regulate the administration of Turkish Cypriot properties in the Republic, pending the continuation of the Cyprus problem. The Law provides, *inter alia*, for the Minister of Interior to be appointed as a Custodian with the duty of administering all Turkish Cypriot properties, including the power to enter into contracts and leases with regard to such properties, the collection of rent or other sums to be held on behalf of the owner, and the carrying out of repairs. The Supreme Court has held that the law did not aim to either compulsory acquisition or requisition, but rather to the protection and temporary administration of Turkish Cypriot properties which had been deserted by their owners after the Turkish invasion of 1974.[610]

443. In *Koutselini,* the Supreme Court held that pension rights are property rights and are safeguarded by Article 23 of the Constitution. A legislative provision by virtue of which the pension rights of persons holding or assuming any state office or position would be suspended was inconsistent with Article 23 of the Constitution. The arguments that the system of pensions should be modernized so as to avoid people receiving multiple pensions, or both a salary from the State and a pension, or that the Government would save money were considered inadequate to justify interference with the property right of the Applicants.[611]

444. However, in *Charalambous*, the Supreme Court held by majority that the imposition of a special contribution from the salaries of public servants and employees of the wider public sector was not inconsistent with Article 23 of the Constitution. The Supreme Court held that whereas a salary is a property right, the right does not extend to the actual amount of the salary. In the particular case, the contribution amounted to no more than 1.5–3.5% of the monthly salary and accordingly it did not substantially reduce, nor affect the core of the right. Furthermore, the imposition of the contribution was not arbitrary. The fiscal measures aimed to improve the problematic financial situation of the State and accordingly were in the public interest. Taking into account the financial crisis that the State was faced with,

609. *See* P. Polyviou & L. Arakelian, *Fall of the Guardians: The European Court of Human Rights and the Case of Demopoulos* (U. Nicosia Press 2011); L. Loucaides, *Is the European Court of Human Rights Still a Principled Court of Human Rights after the Demopoulos Case*, 24 Leiden J. Intl. L. 435–465 (2011). *See also* C. Paraskeva, *The Relationship Between Domestic Implementation of the European Convention on Human Rights and the Ongoing Reforms of the European Court of Human Rights, with a Case Study on Cyprus and Turkey* (Intersentia 2010).

610. *Kitsis v. Attorney-General* [2001] 1 CLR 1077 (in Greek), *Korkut v. Georghiou* [2008] 1 CLR 905 (in Greek). *See* further A. Emilianides, *Turkish Cypriot Properties and Guardian: A Review of the Case-Law*, 9 Cyprus & European L. Rev. 457–501 (2009) (in Greek).

611. *Koutselini and others v. Republic* [2013] 3 CLR 361 (in Greek). *See also Afxentiou and others v. Republic*, Cases 5672 and others, Judgment of 15 Nov. 2016 (in Greek, Administrative Court).

a fair balance had been struck between the public interest and the need to safeguard the right to property. It was further held that the decision to impose measures aiming at the public servants was under the circumstances reasonable, since one of the main fiscal problems was the state payroll. There was thus no violation of the principle of non-discrimination and the Court would not examine the wisdom of the legislator, but only whether the measures taken were reasonable and within the legislator's margin of appreciation.[612]

445. *Charalambous* was problematic because the majority judgment had effectively held that the restriction of the rights was not in accordance with a specific legitimate aim as restrictively enumerated in Article 23 § 2 of the Constitution, but nevertheless held that there was no violation because the interference was proportional. However, this is an incorrect methodology: if the Court determines that there is no constitutionally prescribed legitimate aim justifying the interference, it may not further consider the question of proportionality and there is a violation of the constitutional right in question. The same methodology was inexplicably adopted by the majority of the Supreme Court in the subsequent *Avgousti* judgment, which related to restrictions on both salaries and pensions of employees in the public sector.[613]

446. The decision to impose a haircut on deposits of the country's largest bank and a resolution of the country's second-largest bank, as requisites for receiving financial assistance for the recapitalization of the Cypriot banking sector,[614] was challenged before the Supreme Court. In *Christodoulou*, the majority of the Full Bench of the Supreme Court held that the relevant Decrees imposing the haircut affected the legitimate interests of affected depositors only indirectly and as such the depositors did not have legitimate interest and accordingly legal standing to file recourse under Article 146 of the Constitution for judicial review of the said Decrees. It was further held that the only persons directly affected by the Decrees were the banks themselves which did not seek to have the decrees reviewed and the depositors could file civil suits against the banks in order to safeguard their legal interests as their status was that of creditors to the bank.[615] The aforementioned decision did not examine the issue of constitutionality of the Decrees but rather decided that the relevant Decrees could not become the subject of judicial review directly but only indirectly when, and if, civil suits were to be adjudicated.

612. *Charalambous and others v. Republic* [2014] 3 CLR 175 (in Greek).

613. *Republic v. Avgousti and others*, Adm. Apps 177/2018 a.o, Judgment of 10 Apr. 2020 (in Greek). *See also* A. Emilianides, 'Right to Property and Cuts of Salaries and Pensions of Public Servants', dikaiosyni, 12 Apr. 2020 (in Greek), available in, https://dikaiosyni.com/katigories/arthra/dikaioma-stin-idioktisia-kai-perikopes-misthwn-kai-syntaxewn-dimosiwn-ypallilwn/, S. Yiallourou, *The Review of Constitutionality of the Cuts of the Salaries of Public Servants due to the Financial Crisis* 2 Efimerida Dioikitikou Dikaiou 133–161 (2019) (in Greek).

614. C. Ioannou & A. Emilianides, *The Haircut of Cypriot Deposits and the Protection of Fundamental Rights*, 2 Cyprus Human Rights L. Rev. 141–166 (2013); C. Ioannou & A. Emilianides, *Cyprus and EU Following the Haircut of Deposits*, in *Cyprus in a New Era: Geostrategy, Economy, Foreign Policy* 124–153 (C. Ioannou, D. Sotiropoulos & A. Emilianides eds, Foreign Affairs: Hellenic Edition and Hippasus 2014, in Greek).

615. *Christodoulou and Others v. Central Bank of Cyprus and Others* [2013] 3 CLR 427 (in Greek).

447. It is submitted that the Supreme Court's decision in *Christodoulou* failed to produce an appropriate legal outcome. Paragraph 2 of Article 146 of the Constitution provides that a recourse may be made by a person whose existing legitimate interest, which he/she has either as a person or by virtue of being a member of a Community, is adversely and directly affected by an act or omission.[616] The affected depositors in this case, however, had a legitimate interest given that the Decrees of the Central Bank imposing the haircut of deposits had damaged or negatively influenced their own pecuniary interests. It is submitted that the Decrees in question were administrative acts of a regulatory nature which directly affected the depositors and which accordingly could, and should, have become the subject of judicial review by virtue of Article 146 of the Constitution.[617] It is undisputed that the imposition of a haircut of deposits affected the deposits of each depositor in an individual manner and did not affect the interests of the bank in a general manner, as would have been the case if the haircut was imposed on the bank (in which case the creditors would have suffered the damage in an analogous manner). It was the individual deposits and not the bank's capital *in abstracto* that was affected. As correctly noted by Judge Papadopoulou in her dissenting opinion:

> I consider that the Decrees are a classic case of application of an individual administrative act/administrative act of general application. Whereas, the relationship between the banks and the applicant is one of contract law, the Decrees introduced an administrative procedure which affects, not only the banks (which did not themselves choose to sell their operations or to bail-in), but also the applicants who have a contract law relationship with them and draw legitimate interest in disputing the Decrees.[618]

448. The Supreme Court decision effectively suggests that the only type of recourse it would entertain jurisdiction over by virtue of Article 146 of the Constitution would be one lodged by the affected banks themselves. However, these banks were, at the time, in accordance with the Decrees, controlled by the Central Bank of Cyprus – the same authority that issued the Decrees in the first place. Since the Central Bank of Cyprus could not be reasonably expected to file recourse against its own Decrees, the decision of the Supreme Court effectively implies that their legality could not be directly disputed in an administrative recourse. This is hardly a satisfactory solution.

449. Both the CJEU and the General Court of the EU held that the decision to impose a haircut on deposits of the country's largest bank and a resolution of the country's second-largest bank, as requisites for receiving financial assistance for the recapitalization of the Cypriot banking sector, did not constitute a disproportional

616. A. Emilianides, *Legitimate Interest in the Administrative Trial: A Review of the Case-Law*, 10 Cyprus and European L. Rev. 631–699 (2009, in Greek).
617. *See also Cyprus Ports Authority v. Sewerage Board of Larnaca* [2000] 3 CLR 311 (in Greek).
618. *Christodoulou and Others v. Central Bank of Cyprus and Others* [2013] 3 CLR 427 dissenting judgment of Papadopoulou J (in Greek).

interference with the right to property. The objective of the measures was to safeguard the stability of the Cypriot financial system and the measures were proportional to the aim pursued and applied in a transparent and non-discriminatory manner. It was further held that the difference in treatment between the Cypriot branches of the two banks and the respective Greek branches was not discriminatory since it was justified by an objective and reasonable aim, i.e., the need to prevent any effect from contagion from the Cypriot banking system to the Greek financial system.[619]

VIII. The Right to a Healthy Environment

450. The Nineteenth Constitutional Amendment 171(I)/2024 is the first to introduce a new individual right since the Constitution was originally enacted. It introduced the right to a safe, clean, healthy and sustainable environment with a new Article 7A of the Constitution. It covers three separate but essentially interlinked objectives, namely: (1) the establishment of an individual right to a safe, clean, healthy and sustainable environment; (2) the right to specific procedural mechanisms that allow for – or aim to better facilitate – the justiciability of the right to a safe environment including via the right to information, access to justice, and effective remedies for violation of the right; and (3) the formulation of a positive obligation of the State to take all necessary precautionary, preventive, or restorative measures in line with the principle of sustainability. These rights are subject to the typical legally prescribed limitations, i.e., public security, public order, public health or the protection of other individual rights and liberties. The language reflects the emerging standard of constitutional and legislative protection of environmental rights, as also seen in international conventions. The preamble of the amendment goes further by acknowledging the individual and collective duty to prevent environmental destruction and combat the climate crisis, emphasizing the principle of intergenerational equity and affirming the responsibility for environmental protection not only by the state but also by private entities – especially multinational corporations.[620]

619. Joined Cases C-8–10/15, *Ledra Advertising and others v. European Commission and others* EU:C:2016:701, Case T-680/13, *Dr. K. Chrysostomides & Co LLC and others v. Council of the EU and others* EU:T:2018:486. *See also* A. Emilianides & C. Ioannou, *A Financial Crisis as Limitation to a Fundamental Right to Protection of Deposits under European Union Law*, in *Staat – Religion – Recht. Festschrift für Gerhard Robbers* 937–954 (K. von der Decken and A. Günzel eds, Baden-Baden: Nomos, 2020).

620. T. Kouspi & A. Emilianides, 'From Process Misstep to Environmental Milestone: Cyprus's New Constitutional Right' April *constitutionnet*, available at https://constitutionnet.org/news/voices/process-misstep-environmental-milestone-cypruss-new-constitutional-right.

Chapter 3. Constitutional Problems of Minorities (Protection of Minorities and Group Rights)

§1. Defining Minorities in the Constitutional Sense

451. While numerically a minority, the Turks of Cyprus were elevated to Community status by virtue of Article 2 of the Constitution. Accordingly, the largest numerical minority of the island is not considered legally as a minority in view of its privileged constitutional status. There are, however, three constitutionally recognized minorities in Cyprus and such are defined as 'religious groups'.[621] The constitutionally recognized religious groups are the Armenians,[622] Maronites[623] and Roman Catholics (Latins).[624] While the Armenian and Maronite religious groups have considered that their characterization as *religious groups* does not represent their position as ethnic or even national minorities, it is submitted that the recognition of the Armenians and the Maronites as religious groups does not necessarily entail a non-recognition of their ethnic characteristics. Indeed, the Republic of Cyprus has considered that both the Maronites and the Armenians constitute *National Minorities* within the context of the FCPNM.[625]

452. In particular, the statement of the Government of the Republic of Cyprus declared that it considers that the FCPNM should apply to all three 'religious groups' of the Republic, namely the Armenians, Maronites and Roman Catholics, as well as, and without prejudice to their constitutional position, to the Turkish Cypriots living in the non-occupied areas,[626] despite the fact that the Roman Catholics are a religious and not a national minority, and the fact that the Armenians and Maronites could probably be considered ethnic minorities, rather than national minorities.[627] The Republic of Cyprus has further declared that it understands the term 'national minorities' as designating only those national minority groups who had a traditional presence on the island at the time of the establishment of the Republic of Cyprus in 1960 and who have Cypriot citizenship. In view of the above,

---

621. A. Emilianides, *The Negotiation of the Constitutional Rights of the Religious Minorities of the Republic of Cyprus* 1 Nomokanonika 11–34 (2022).
622. *See* in general A. Emilianides, *The Status of the Armenian Church of Cyprus* (Cyprus Inst. Church & State Rel. 2006, in Greek); C. Tornaritis, *The Legal Position of the Armenian Religious Group*, in *Ibid., Constitutional and Legal Problems of the Republic of Cyprus* 85–90 (2d ed., 1972); A. Hadjilyra, *The Armenians of Cyprus* (2009).
623. A. Hadjilyra, *The Maronite Community in Cyprus*, in *History of the Republic of Cyprus 1990–1999* vol. IV, 199–207 (P. Papapolyviou ed., Phileleftheros 2011, in Greek).
624. *See* A. Emilianides, *The Legal Status of the Latin Community of Cyprus*, in A. Varnava, N. Coureas & M. Elia, *Minorities of Cyprus* 229–240 (Cambridge Scholars Publg. 2009).
625. Report Submitted by Cyprus pursuant to Art. 25, para. 1 of the Framework Convention for the Protection of National Minorities, 1 Mar. 1999, Part II, Art. 3.
626. Report Submitted by Cyprus, 1 Mar. 1999, Part II, Art. 3.
627. *See also* for a wider discussion G. Kentas & A. Emilianides, *The Emergence and Regulation of Minority Religious Groups in Europe*, in *How Groups Matter: Challenges of Toleration in Pluralist Societies* 260–285 (M. Bessone, G. Galder & F. Zuolo eds, Routledge 2013); A. Emilianides, *Recognized, but Not Fully Appreciated: The Legal Status of Religious Minorities in Cyprus*, in *The Legal Status of Old and New Religious Minorities in the European Union* 97–106 (M. Ventura ed., Comares, 2021).

the FCPNM currently applies in Cyprus predominantly as an instrument for the protection of the major minorities of the island. The Maronites, the Armenians and the Roman Catholics enjoy, in addition to the international protection of a national minority, the constitutional protection as a religious minority.

453. A 'religious group' in the constitutional sense is, according to Article 2 section 3 of the Constitution, a group of persons, ordinarily resident in Cyprus, professing the same religion and either belonging to the same rite or being subject to the same jurisdiction thereof. The number of such a group on the date of the coming into operation of the Constitution must have exceeded one thousand persons out of whom at least five hundred became on that date citizens of the Republic. Such difference in the number of persons ordinarily residing in Cyprus and the number of persons, who became citizens of the Republic, was due to the fact that a great number of Roman Catholics and Armenians had retained their British citizenship, even following 16 August 1960, when the Constitution came into force. There is no possibility to constitutionally recognize in the future a new religious group, even if such a group fulfils the numerical criteria provided for in Article 2 section 3 of the Constitution, nor is it possible to remove the constitutional status of a religious group from any of the three aforementioned religious groups, even if the number of their members who reside in Cyprus, or who are citizens of the Republic is diminished, so that the numerical criteria provided for, in Article 2 section 3 of the Constitution may no longer be fulfilled.

454. According to Article 2 section 3 of the Constitution, religious groups would opt as groups whether they would belong to the Greek or the Turkish Community, within three months of the coming into operation of the Constitution. All three religious groups opted to belong to the Greek Community and now reside in the non-occupied territories, with the exception of about 100 Maronites residing in Kormakitis. In a referendum held on 13 November 1960, 1,077 Armenians, 1,046 Maronites and 322 Roman Catholics voted in favour of adhering to the Greek Community, while only five Armenians and one Roman Catholic voted in favour of adhering to the Turkish Community; thus, all members of the three religious groups became members of the Greek Community. The Constitution further provides that any individual member of a religious group may choose not to abide by the option of such group and, by a written and signed declaration, opt to belong to a Community other than that to which such group shall be deemed to belong. However, all individual members of the three religious groups abided by the option of their respective group.

455. The Representative of the Latins in the House of Representatives has expressed the view that the term *Latins* does not properly reflect the essential element of their identity, namely the Roman Catholic rites they share in common. The Advisory Committee on the FCPNM observed in its Opinion on Cyprus adopted on 6 April 2001 that the Republic could address this matter without undue difficulties and modify the name of the Roman Catholic religious group to 'Roman Catholics

– Latins' since such modification does not require a change to the Constitution.[628] On 2 September 2004, the then Attorney-General of the Republic also advised the Ministry of Interior that the intended modification in the name of the Latin religious group would not amount to an amendment of the Constitution of Cyprus and that the change could be implemented with an amendment of laws where reference is made to the constitutionally recognized religious groups. Thus, in December 2004, a proposal to that effect was submitted to the Council of Ministers for approval.

456. However, the Council of Ministers, at its meeting of 20 January 2005, decided to postpone its decision because, as it stated, the above matter 'had been associated by the Representative of the Latins with other issues that presented constitutional difficulties'.[629] Such issues included primarily the issue of who are to be considered members of the Roman Catholic religious group according to the Constitution of Cyprus. It is submitted that it is not correct that the issue of modifying the name of the Latin religious group to the Roman Catholic religious group should be associated with any other issue presenting constitutional difficulties. Thus, the Government of the Republic of Cyprus should promptly proceed to the proposed change since it does not present any constitutional difficulties.[630]

457. Article 2 section 3 of the Constitution does not provide who may be considered to be a member of each specific religious group. There is therefore no provision which stipulates who the state should consider to be a member of the Roman Catholic religious group. This is due to the fact that according to a universally recognized legal principle, being a member of a church should depend upon the law of such a church and not upon a state's law. This was the position of the Supreme Court of Cyprus prior to Independence in the case of *Tsivitanides*, where it was held that: *whether a church admits a person to its membership no doubt depends on the ecclesiastical law of that church.*[631] Thus, whether a person is a member of a specific religious group depends primarily upon the law of such group and not upon any state legal provisions.[632]

458. The only criteria which the state law may apply, apart from ecclesiastical law, in order to specify whether a person should be considered a member of a specific religious group are: whether such person is a citizen of the Republic and whether he/she resides ordinarily in Cyprus.[633] Such criteria are contained in the definition of religious groups provided for in Article 2 section 3 of the Constitution. Accordingly, it was held that a person may not belong to a religious group, defined

628. Advisory Committee on the Framework Convention for the Protection of National Minorities, *Opinion on Cyprus*, 6 Apr. 2001, para. 20.
629. Second Report submitted by Cyprus pursuant to Art. 25, para. 1 of the Framework Convention for the Protection of National Minorities, 27 Oct. 2006, Part III, Art. 3.
630. *See* A. Emilianides, *Who May Be Considered to Be Members of Religious Groups According to the Constitution of Cyprus?*, Lysias 26–31 (2006) (in Greek).
631. *Tsivitanides v. Tsivitanides* [1956] 21 CLR 111.
632. *See* G. Serghides, *Internal and External Conflict of Laws in Regard to Family Relations in Cyprus* 147 (1988).
633. *See* A. Emilianides, *The Cypriot Law of Marriage and Divorce* 173ff (Sakkoulas 2006, in Greek).

as *a group of persons ordinarily resident in Cyprus*, if such person is not ordinarily resident in Cyprus.[634] Furthermore, a person may not be considered to belong to the Greek Community, unless such person is a citizen of the Republic, since members of the Greek or the Turkish Community are by definition citizens of the Republic of Cyprus.

459. According to one view, initially supported by the Government, members of the three religious groups were fixed in 1960 and following such date, no new members may be added. The above view exempts only descendants of persons who were members of the three religious groups in 1960. The above view is not only misguided, but it is also not based upon any legal provisions. The drafters of the Constitution were perfectly aware that a great number of members of the three religious groups had not acquired citizenship of the Republic by the time of the coming into force of the Constitution. Such persons, ordinarily resident in Cyprus, could, of course, acquire citizenship of the Republic of Cyprus at any later stage and would thus become members of their respective religious groups.

460. Nevertheless, any person has the right, at any given time, to opt to become a member of a religious community. Such a right is safeguarded by Article 18 of the Constitution, as well as by Article 9 of the ECHR. If a person considers that he/she belongs to one of the three religious groups of the Republic and further the respective religious group considers that such person is indeed a member of such religious group, it would be unconstitutional and in violation of fundamental human rights, should the state refuse to recognize such person as a member of the relevant religious group, simply due to the fact that such person became a member of the religious group at a later stage.

461. Consequently, if a person who belongs to the Orthodox Church or the Protestant Church, or indeed any other church, opts to change his/her religious beliefs, then the state must accept the change. Otherwise, the right to religious freedom would be fettered.[635] Similarly, if Roman Catholics or Maronites or Armenians acquire Cypriot citizenship and ordinarily reside in Cyprus at any given time, they should properly be considered members of the respective religious group; otherwise, not only would the constitutional provisions be inaccurately applied, but also there would be a violation of the right of non-discrimination, which is safeguarded by Article 28 of the Constitution and Article 14, as well as Protocol 12, of the ECHR.

§2. The Constitutional Status of Minorities

462. The documents presented to the British Parliament in July 1960 contained a statement by the British Government concerning the rights of the three smaller

634. *Achcar v. Saad* [1979] 1 CLR 627.
635. *Tsivitanides v. Tsivitanides* [1956] 21 CLR 111.

religious groups in Cyprus.[636] It was stated that the aim of the relevant constitutional provisions with respect to religious groups had been to secure for the minor religious groups in Cyprus the continued enjoyment of the liberties and status which such groups had under British rule, as well as to maintain the enjoyment of no less extensive rights in respect of religious matters than they had enjoyed in law before the Constitution came into force. It was further stated that the member of a religious group would enjoy the same benefits as the other members of the Community to which they had opted to belong.

463. According to Article 110 section 3 of the Constitution, the three religious groups of the Republic shall continue to have every right with respect to religious matters that they had before the coming into force of the Constitution. Furthermore, prior to the First Amendment of the Constitution of 1989, Article 111 of the Constitution had provided that family law matters would be governed by the law of the respective religious group and would be cognizable by the ecclesiastical courts of such religious group. Following the First Amendment of the Constitution, family law matters of members of the three religious groups came under the jurisdiction of the Family Courts of Religious Groups; only issues relating to betrothal or ecclesiastical marriage, or nullity of ecclesiastical marriage have continued to be governed by the canon law of the religious groups even after 1989.[637] Article 111 of the Constitution was further amended by the Eighteenth Amendment of the Constitution, Law 3(I)/2023, which abolished the Family Courts of Religious Groups. Jurisdiction for all family law disputes of members of religious groups now falls under the jurisdiction of Family Courts.

464. The provisions of Articles 110 section 3 and 111 of the Constitution with respect to religious groups corresponded to the relevant provisions of Articles 110 section 1 and 111 of the Constitution with regard to the Orthodox Church. While Article 110 section 1 of the Constitution is more detailed compared to Article 110 section 3, this is only due to the fact that the Orthodox Christian religion is the religion of the great majority of the population, and thus, it was considered necessary that the extent of its competences be defined with greater clarity; however, this should not signify any difference in treatment between the Orthodox Church on the one hand and the three religious groups on the other.[638] Article 110 section 3 of the Constitution provides for the maintenance of the rights that the religious groups had enjoyed prior to independence. Such rights correspond to those of the Orthodox Church and relate to the religious groups' internal affairs and the administration of their property. While Article 110 section 3 of the Constitution does not provide, contrary to Article 110 section 1 of the Constitution, that the Greek Communal Chamber shall not interfere with the rights of the three religious groups, it is suggested

636. *Cyprus: Presented to Parliament by the Secretary of State for the Colonies, the Secretary of State for Foreign Affairs and the Minister of Defence*, Cmnd. 1093, July 1960, App. E.
637. *See* A. Emilianides, *The Cypriot Law of Marriage and Divorce* (Sakkoulas 2006, in Greek).
638. A. Emilianides, *The Constitutional Framework of the Relations Between Church and State in the Republic of Cyprus*, 1 Nomokanonika 46–47 (2006) (in Greek).

that this is heavily implied.[639] Thus, the Greek Communal Chamber, and following its self-dissolution, the House of Representatives may not interfere with issues relating to the internal affairs of the religious groups or the administration of their property.

465. According to Article 109 of the Constitution, each religious group had the right to elect member(s) of such group in the communal chamber of the Community to which such group has opted to belong as provided by a relevant communal law. Such was the Greek Communal Chamber Law 8/1960 regarding the Composition of the Greek Communal Chamber, which provided that the religious groups of the Armenians and the Roman Catholics would elect one member each in Nicosia, while the religious group of the Maronites would elect one member in Kyrenia. This specific right of the three religious groups was in addition to the right of electing and being elected in the House of Representatives. A Maronite, Joseph Yiamakis, was elected as a member of the House of Representatives on behalf of the Greek Community in the first parliamentary elections of 1960.[640]

466. Following the self-dissolution of the Greek Communal Chamber, Article 10 of Law 12/1965 provided that the elected members of the three religious groups would continue to represent their groups and would have the right to present their views before the House of Representatives; the House of Representatives would have to request for such views of the elected members of the religious groups before legislating upon specific matters concerning the relevant religious group. Law 12/1965 was held to be constitutional on the basis of the doctrine of necessity and in view of the abnormal situation prevailing in Cyprus.[641] The relevant provisions of Law 12/1965 were repeated in the Religious Groups (Representation) Law 58/1970. The Religious Groups (Representation) Law 38/1976, which is currently in force, provides that the members of the three religious groups of the Republic, in addition to the right of electing and being elected in parliamentary elections, elect, under their capacity as members of their respective religious groups one representative of each religious group, who represents their group in the House of Representatives. These representatives have the right to speak in the House of Representatives with regard to all matters which concern the relevant religious group but do not have the right to vote; their status concerning remuneration and other benefits is equivalent to that of a regular member of the House of Representatives.

639. *See also* C. Tornaritis, *The Legal Position of the Armenian Religious Group*, in *Ibid., Constitutional and Legal Problems in the Republic of Cyprus* 90 (2d ed., 1972).

640. Another Maronite Avraam Antoniou was elected as member of the House of Representatives in both the 1991 and 1996 elections, while an Armenian Marios Karoyian was elected as a member of the House of Representatives in 2006 and as the President of the House of Representatives in 2008.

641. *Cypiom Ltd v. The Police* [2003] 2 CLR 459 (in Greek).

467. It has been suggested that the presence of representatives from the three religious groups in the House of Representatives is unconstitutional and unjustified.[642] According to the above view, such participation of the members of the three religious groups in the House of Representatives violates the principle of equality which is safeguarded by Article 28 of the Constitution; this is due to the fact that all the remaining members of the Greek Communal Chamber were forced to quit their positions in 1965 when the Greek Communal Chamber was self-dissolved. It has been further argued that Article 79 of the Constitution provides that only members of the Council of Ministers may participate in the House of Representatives with regard to matters falling within their competences. It is submitted that the above view is not correct.[643] The presence of representatives of the three religious groups in the House of Representatives was the direct result of the self-dissolution of the Greek Communal Chamber with Law 12/65 and the transfer of its legislative competences to the House of Representatives. The Constitution provided for the participation of representatives of the three religious groups in the Greek Communal Chamber in order to safeguard their rights. Thus, the participation of the representatives of the three religious groups in the House of Representatives, far from being discriminatory, is consistent with the need to protect the rights of the minority groups of the Republic in a proportional manner, pursuant to the obligations of the Republic according to the FCPNM.

468. It is further observed that Article 79 of the Constitution does not impede the participation of officials, other than members of the Council of Ministers, in the House of Representatives with regard to matters falling within their competences. There could be no specific provision in the Constitution with respect to the representatives of the religious groups, similar to that of Article 79, since the constitutional legislator could not be expected to predict that the Greek Communal Chamber would have been self-dissolved. It is thus submitted that the participation of the representatives of the three religious groups in the House of Representatives is entirely justified. If anything, the participation of the three representatives to the House of Representatives, without the right to vote, even with regard to matters which concern the relevant religious group, provides less minority protection compared to that afforded by the Constitution, since the representatives of the three religious groups would have had the right to vote for such matters in the Greek Communal Chamber, should such Communal Chamber not have been self-dissolved. In view of the above, methods should be explored in order to further improve the effective participation of the representatives of the religious groups by providing for a right to vote, or initiate legislation, in matters within their competence.[644]

---

642. *See* L. Papaphilippou, *Constitutional Problems from the Participation of the Armenian, Maronite and Latin Religious Groups in the House of Representatives*, 4 Cyprus L. Tribune 626–638 (1991) (in Greek).

643. A. Emilianides, *The Constitutional Framework of the Relations Between Church and State in the Republic of Cyprus*, 1 Nomokanonika 70–71 (2006) (in Greek).

644. *See also* Advisory Committee on the Framework Convention for the Protection of National Minorities, *Opinion on Cyprus*, 7 Jun. 2007, para. 143.

Chapter 4. Judicial Control of Administrative Action

§1. Preventive Legal Protection

469. There is no possibility for preventive judicial control of administrative action.

§2. Curative Legal Protection

I. Acts of the Administration Subject to Judicial Review

470. Article 146 of the Constitution introduced for the first time the judicial review of administrative action,[645] a jurisdiction which was unknown to English and Cypriot law at the time of Cyprus' Independence. As a result, common law did not have any influence on the development of Cypriot administrative law. The structure of judicial control of administrative action in Cyprus is founded on the principles of continental administrative law. For the brief period of time before 1963, when the Supreme Constitutional Court was functioning under the Chairmanship of the German Ernst Forsthoff, the development of administrative law was primarily founded on German law and secondarily on Greek and French administrative law; however, due to linguistic barriers (since very few Cypriots are German speaking), Greek and French case-law and textbooks proved to have more lasting influence in the development of Cypriot administrative law since 1963.

471. Accordingly, the development of Cypriot administrative law is mainly based on the case-law of the Greek *Symvoulion tis Epikrateias* and the French *Conseil d' Etat.*[646] In *Morsis*, the Supreme Court held that:

> As it appears that, under Article 146, the process of judicial review of administrative acts, existing in Continental countries such as Greece, France or Germany, has been introduced in Cyprus, it is reasonable to hold that principles of administrative law, evolved in the said countries and applied there and elsewhere with such degree of consistency and universal applicability as to render them part of the science of administrative law, can in a proper case, be adopted and applied by this Court, not as foreign law applied in Cyprus, but as Cyprus law laid down by the Courts of Cyprus.[647]

645. *See* in general N. Charalambous, *Cypriot Administrative Law Textbook* (3d ed., 2016, in Greek), A. Angelides, & S. Angelides, *Administrative Procedural Law* (2d ed., Cyprus Bar Assn. 2020, in Greek), C. Paraskeva, *Cypriot Administrative Law* (Nomiki Vivliothiki 2017, in Greek), *Ibid., Cypriot Administrative Procedure Law* (Nomiki Vivliothiki 2020, in Greek), C. Melides, *Administrative Law*, in *Introduction to Cyprus Law* 87–117 (Andreas Neocleous & Co LLC ed., 3d ed., Limassol 2010); Z. Nedjati, *Cyprus Administrative Law* (1970).

646. L. Clerides, *The Influence of Greek Administrative Law in the Development of Administrative Law Applicable in Cyprus*, 1 Cyprus L. Tribune 7–27 (1974) (in Greek).

647. *Morsis v. The Republic* [1965] 3 CLR 1.

472. In accordance with Article 146 of the Constitution, recourse may be filed before the Administrative Court against a decision, an act or omission of the administration which falls within the public domain. The Supreme Constitutional Court has defined organs or authority of the Republic as those: 'specific juridical creations bearing the features of individual and concrete organic institutions of government and functioning for and on behalf of a primary legal entity, such as the Republic of Cyprus, of which they are organs or authorities in the ordinary meaning of such terms'.[648] In view of the above, the term organ or authority of the Republic includes not only organs or authorities of the central administration of the State which exercise executive or administrative power, such as the various ministries or departments but also semi-governmental organizations and legal persons of public nature, such as the CYTA, the EAC, the CYBC, the municipal councils, the improvement boards, public universities.[649] On the contrary, the Orthodox Church of Cyprus[650] or the Cyprus Bar Association[651] do not constitute organs or authorities of the Republic for the purpose of Article 146 of the Constitution.

473. In the case of *Christofides*, the Supreme Court held that the Union of Cyprus Municipalities which was registered as an association, namely as a legal person of private law, could not be considered an organ or authority of the Republic exercising administrative authority. It was consequently held that the Supreme Court had no jurisdiction to review a decision by the Union of Cyprus Municipalities to award a contract as a contracting authority, since it is only the municipalities and not their Union which may be properly considered as organs exercising administrative authority.[652] The general principle emanating from *Christofides* was that only legal persons of public law might be properly considered contracting authorities for the purposes of Article 146 of the Constitution. In the case of *Intergaz*, the Supreme Court held that the Cypriot Oil Refinery Ltd should not be considered an organ or authority of the Republic in accordance with Article 146 of the Constitution; while it had been founded on the basis of a governmental agreement which had been ratified by law, its legal status was still that of a private company.[653]

474. There are various criteria that can be considered in order to decide whether a legal person is an organ or authority of the Republic in accordance with Article 146 of the Constitution; these include considerations of whether the legal person has been founded for the public interest, the power to exercise public authority, for example, by imposing taxes or levies, or collecting public revenues, or ordering

648. *Celaleddin and Others v. The Council of Ministers* 5 RSCC 102.
649. *See Athliticos Pnevmaticos Omilos Defteras v. KOA* [1984] 3 CLR 831, *Solomou v. The Republic* 1 RSCC 96, *Stamatiou v. EAC* [1962] RSCC 44, *Miliotis v. Republic* [1968] 3 CLR 477, *Ioannou v. The Water Board of Limassol* [1984] 3 CLR 728.
650. *Autocephalous and Apostolic Orthodox Church of Cyprus v. House of Representatives* (1990) 3 CLR 338 (in Greek). *See also* A. Emilianides, *The Cypriot Law of Marriage and Divorce* 108ff (Sakkoulas 2006, in Greek).
651. *Papacharalambous v. The Bar Council* [1983] 3 CLR 342.
652. *J.N.Christofides Trading Ltd v.* Municipality of Nicosia [1989] 3 CLR 1015 (in Greek).
653. *Intergaz Ltd v. Minister of Commerce and Industry* [1989] 3 CLR 453 (in Greek).

compulsory acquisition of land, whether the status of the employees should be considered analogous to that of public servants, whether the supervision of the State over the legal person is extraordinary, or whether the State participates in the management of the legal person.[654] It is not sufficient that the act, decision or omission has been taken by an organ, authority or person of the administration; the act should also emanate from the exercise of powers in the public domain, namely the exercise of executive or administrative authority.

475. Cypriot administrative law thus applies a twofold criterion in order to determine whether an act is administrative for the purposes of Article 146 of the Constitution, by considering both the nature of the authority from which the act or decision emanates, and the nature of the act or decision in question.[655] An organ or authority of the administrative may sometimes act within the framework of private law, such as when it concludes agreements for the management of its property, such as the leasing of State property; the latter acts shall not be considered administrative and do not fall within the ambit of Article 146 of the Constitution. Similarly, a decision of the Director of the Lands and Surveys Department to locate the boundaries of immovable property does not add to or detract from the private law rights of a person but merely ascertains them by reference to their title deeds; accordingly, such decision falls under private law and does not fall within the ambit of Article 146 of the Constitution.[656]

476. The Supreme Court has held that the unilateral expression of the will of the administration is the crucial factor in determining whether the act or decision is an administrative one; the State should exercise its *imperium* by conferring rights or imposing obligations upon persons. The test to determine whether the act or decision falls within the ambit of Article 146 of the Constitution is whether the act or decision intends to promote a public purpose so as to interest the public at large or a substantial part of such public. A public purpose has been defined as 'one in which the public at large or a noticeable section of it has an interest in the sense that its proper promotion has repercussions extending beyond those immediately affecting the parties directly affected thereby'.[657]

477. Public procurement is a good example of the distinction between public and private law.[658] The Supreme Court has held that the decision of a public authority to award a contract for works, goods or services falls under the ambit of Article 146 of the Constitution, since it is an act falling within the public domain.[659] On the

654. *See also* A. Emilianides, *The Community Framework for the Application of Public Procurement Rules to Contracting Authorities*, in *Law Across Nations* 910–919 (S. Kierkergaard ed., IAITL 2011).
655. *The Greek Registrar of the Co-Operative Societies v. Nicos Nicolaides* [1965] 3 CLR 164.
656. *Antoniou v. Republic* [1984] 3 CLR 623.
657. *Ibid.*, *Midland Bank Project Finance Limited v. Republic* [1989] 3 CLR 2099 (in Greek), *Hellenic Bank Limited v. The Republic* [1986] 3 CLR 481.
658. *See* A. Emilianides, *The Cypriot Law of Public Procurement* (Dikaionomia 2007, in Greek).
659. *Medcon Construction v. The Republic* [1968] 3 CLR 535, *George D. Kounnas and Sons Ltd v. The Republic* [1972] 3 CLR 542, *Matsoukas v. The Republic* [1984] 3 CLR 1443.

contrary, a contract which is subsequently concluded by the public authority and the successful tenderer and the relationship between the two parties is governed by private law and does not fall within the ambit of Article 146 of the Constitution.[660] Consequently, the Administrative Court has jurisdiction to annul the decision of the contracting authority to award the contract but has no jurisdiction to annul the contract which has been concluded pursuant to such award. Another interesting illustration of the distinction is *Pantelidou* where the Supreme Court held, by majority, that a decision of the Water Board of Nicosia to rescind the rights of persons who had title deeds to the supply of water was one deriving from a contractual obligation and which affected private law rights. Accordingly, it did not fall within the ambit of Article 146 of the Constitution.[661]

478. Acts which are related to the exercise of legislative power do not fall within the ambit of Article 146 of the Constitution, even if they have been enacted by an organ of the executive; thus, regulations and by-laws issued by an authority or organ of the Republic in the exercise of delegate legislative power are not subject to recourse before the Administrative Court.[662] Similarly, it has been held that the omission of the Council of Ministers to introduce a bill to the House of Representatives is not subject to judicial review pursuant to Article 146 of the Constitution.[663] Acts which are closely interwoven with the exercise of judicial power are also not subject to judicial review pursuant to Article 146. This applies not only with respect to judicial decisions[664] but also with respect to acts such as the exercise of the power of the Attorney-General to initiate a prosecution or discontinue criminal proceedings[665] or the conduct of the police during the hearing of a criminal case.[666] Decisions of the Supreme Court of Judicature involving the appointment, transfer, promotion or discipline of judges were also not subject to judicial review, since they are interwoven with the exercise of judicial power.[667] Pursuant, however, to the Seventeenth Amendment of the Constitution, Law 103(I)/2022, there can be judicial review by way of an objection, but this still does not fall within the ambit of Article 146.

479. It has further been held that acts which are classified as acts of government (*actes de gouvernement*) do not fall within the ambit of Article 146 of the Constitution; acts such as the appointment by the President of Ministers, or members of

---

660. *George Zachariades Ltd v. The Republic* [1987] 3 CLR 68, *J & A Philippou v. The Republic* [1989] 3 CLR 829.
661. *Pantelidou v. Water Board of Nicosia* [1990] 3 CLR 3397 (in Greek).
662. *Theodoridou v. The Republic* [1965] 3 CLR 41, *Police v. Hondrou* 3 RSCC 82.
663. *Papaphilippou v. The Republic* RSCC 62, *Demetrios Philippou v. The Republic* [1970] 3 CLR 123.
664. *Pitsillos v. Aristodemou* [1969] 3 CLR 226.
665. *Archigos Kommatos Dikeosinis v. The Republic* [1986] 3 CLR 187, *Xenophontos v. The Republic* RSCC 89.
666. *Moran v. The Republic* RSCC 10, *Pitsillos v. The Republic* [1985] 3 CLR 2819, *Kyriakides v. The Republic* [1961] RSCC 66.
667. *Kourris v. The Supreme Council of Judicature* [1972] 3 CLR 390.

the Public Service Commission,[668] or judges to the Supreme Court,[669] or the exercise by the President of the prerogative of mercy,[670] or the termination or appointment of an honorary consul,[671] have been characterized as acts of government. In addition, an administrative act or decision may only be judicially reviewed if it has an executory character. An act is considered executory if it is determinative in itself of the rights and obligations of a person under the authority of the administration. Acts of a preliminary character, such as the opinion of an organ which has an advisory role and not a decisive one, do not fall within the ambit of Article 146 of the Constitution. Similarly, acts of a confirmatory nature which reiterate previous acts of the administration without any new elements having been examined, acts which simply inform the applicant of his/her rights or of a legal situation without creating new rights or obligations, or acts of an internal character, or purely material acts,[672] are not executory and as such may not be the subject of judicial review by virtue of Article 146 of the Constitution. The Administrative Court shall examine *ex proprio motu* whether an act is executory.

II. The Administrative Powers

480. Article 146 section 4 of the Constitution provides that upon a recourse, the Supreme Court may, by its decision: (a) confirm, either in whole or in part, the impugned decision or act or omission; (b) declare, either in whole or in part, such decision or act to be null and void and of no effect whatsoever, or declare that such omission, either in whole or in part ought to have been made and that whatever has been omitted should have been performed. The Administrative Court, when exercising its jurisdiction by virtue of Article 146 of the Constitution, is essentially a court of review and not a court of substance. Whereas it has the power to confirm or annul the decision, act or omission under review, it has no power to amend it, or to substitute it with another decision or act, or to decide what the administration ought to have done. Accordingly, the Administrative Court shall not substitute the discretion of the administrative organ with its own discretion[673] and shall not interfere with the decision of the administration so long as such could have been reasonably taken in accordance with the law and the general principles of administrative law.[674] It should be noted, however, that the Administrative Court has the power to amend the administrative act, or to substitute it with its own decision, to the extent that it refers to taxation or to a procedure of international protection pursuant to the law of the EU.

668. *Republic v. Louca* [1984] 3 CLR 241.
669. *Level Tachexaves Ltd* [1995] 1 CLR 1075 (in Greek).
670. *Demetriou v. Republic* 3 RSCC 121.
671. *Hadjiandreou v. Republic* [2001] 3 CLR 352 (in Greek).
672. *Paschali v. Republic* [1966] 3 CLR 593, *Markou v. Republic* [1968] 3 CLR 267.
673. *White Horse Distillers Ltd v. El Greco Distillers Ltd* [1987] 3 CLR 531, *Plough Inc v. The Republic* [1988] 3 CLR 145, *Andreou v. The Republic* [1967] 3 CLR 329.
674. *Kalisperas v. The Republic* [1986] 3 CLR 771, *Uludag v. The Republic* (1962) RSCC 131, *Papapetrou v. The Republic* (1961) RSCC 61.

481. Moreover, the Administrative Court shall not review the substance of matters of a technical nature (such as expert opinion, the findings of a medical board, or the report of a technical committee) so long as the administrative organ has properly exercised its discretion in accordance with the general principles of administrative law.[675] Following the annulment of an administrative act, the administration is called upon to reach a new administrative decision on the basis of the findings of the Administrative Court. Paragraph 5 of Article 146 provides that the decision of the Court is binding on all courts and all organs or authorities in the Republic and shall be given effect to and acted upon by the organ or authority or person concerned. However, it is only the operative findings of the decision which are binding on the administrative.

482. Accordingly, the fact that the applicant has been successful in annulling the promotion of another person does not imply that the applicant should automatically be promoted himself/herself instead of the other person; it might be that the administrative organ decides again that the same person as before ought to be promoted, after a thorough investigation of the factual circumstances, or taking into account material facts which it had failed to take into account, or giving due reasoning for its decision, depending on the operative findings of the Supreme Court in the case at hand.[676] New Article 146 § 5A of the Constitution provides that a law may provide that the Administrative Court may determine whether there has been compliance with its judgment and impose penalties in case of non-compliance. However, no such law has yet been enacted.[677]

483. The Administrative Court has no jurisdiction to award monetary compensation by virtue of Article 146.[678] Article 146 section 6 of the Constitution stipulates that any person aggrieved by any decision or act declared by the Administrative Court to be void or by any omission declared thereunder that it ought not to have been made shall be entitled, if his/her claim is not met to his/her satisfaction by the organ, authority or person concerned, to institute legal proceedings in a court for the recovery of damages or for being granted other remedy and to recover just and equitable damages to be assessed by the court or to be granted such other just and equitable remedy as such court is empowered to grant. The competent court to entertain an action for compensation is the District Court since such an action shall be a civil one and not an administrative one; an administrative decision of the Administrative Court annulling the impugned act or decision is a prerequisite for an action for compensation to be filed in accordance with Article 146 section 6 of the Constitution.[679]

---

675. *Vryonides v. The Educational Service Commission* [1984] 3 CLR 1567.
676. *Georghiou v. The Republic* [1976] 3 CLR 74.
677. For an analysis of the power of the Administrative Court to punish for contempt of court *see* Ch. 5, §2, IV of this monograph.
678. *Ramandan v. EAC* (1960–1961) RSCC 49, *Gavris v. The Republic* (1960–1961) RSCC 88.
679. *Hapeshis v. The Republic* [1979] 3 CLR 550, *Nicolas v. Republic* [2001] 1 CLR 983 (in Greek), *Vnukovo Airlines v. Attorney-General* [2001] 1 CLR 969 (in Greek).

III. Legitimate Interest

484. Paragraph 2 of Article 146 of the Constitution provides that a recourse may be made by a person whose existing legitimate interest, which he/she has either as a person or by virtue of being a member of a Community, is adversely and directly affected by such decision or act or omission.[680] It has been repeatedly held that an administrative resource is not an *actio popularis*, entitling every citizen who is interested in preserving law to make a resource.[681] The applicant should prove *legitimatio ad causum*, namely that the decision or act under review has damaged or negatively influenced his/her own interests. The applicant's relationship to the act, from which relationship his/her interest flows, has to exist already when the act has been challenged, and his/her injury must have already taken place or appear reasonably unavoidable. Thus, the legitimate interest must be existing at all stages of the trial.[682] The existence of a legitimate interest shall be examined by the Administrative Court *ex proprio motu*.

485. It has been held that for legitimate interest to exist, such interest should be in accordance with the law; otherwise, it could not be legitimate.[683] It has accordingly been held that an applicant who is not a displaced person lacks the necessary legitimate interest to file recourse against validity of a requisition order which explicitly limits the range of persons affected to the displaced person.[684] Furthermore, the legitimate interest has to be personal and direct. In *Ierodiakonos*, the applicant, a member of 'The Church of the True Orthodox Christians of Cyprus', applied on behalf of Bishop Epiphanios of Kitium for the issue of a passport. When such application was rejected, he filed recourse before the Supreme Constitutional Court, as it then was. It was held that the right to a recourse is personal to the person whose legitimate interest had been adversely and directly affected by the refusal to issue the passport in question and not to the applicant.[685] Similarly, a director of a company may not file recourse against a decision which concerns the company itself.[686]

486. In view of the fact that the notion of legitimate interest is contained in a constitutional provision, the House of Representatives may not define it by law. The Supreme Court has therefore stricken out as unconstitutional the attempt by the House of Representatives to introduce the notion of moral legitimate interest in the General Principles of Administrative Law Act 158(I)/1999. It was unanimously held

---

680. A. Emilianides, *Legitimate Interest in the Administrative Trial: A Review of the Case-Law*, 10 Cyprus & European L. Rev 631–699 (2009) (in Greek).
681. *Chrysostomides v. The Greek Communal Chamber* [1964] CLR 397.
682. *Maratheftis v. Municipality of Limassol* [2003] 3 CLR 228 (in Greek), *Chrysostomides v. The Greek Communal Chamber* [1964] CLR 397, *Republic v. Pericleous* [1972] 3 CLR 63.
683. *Constantinou v. Municipality of Paphos* [1998] 3 CLR 707 (in Greek).
684. *Kritiotis v. The Municipality of Paphos* [1986] 3 CLR 322, *Papaioannou v. The Republic* [1985] 3 CLR 1549.
685. *Ierodiakonos v. The Republic* (1962) RSCC 55. *See* further *Kirzis Stephanou Container Terminal & Bonded Warehousing v. Republic* [2007] 3 CLR 575 (in Greek).
686. *Lapertas Fisheries Ltd v. Republic* [2004] 3 CLR 554 (in Greek).

that the impugned legislation essentially amounted to an amendment of Article 146 of the Constitution by ordinary legislation which was accordingly contrary to the Constitution.[687] However, the Administrative Court may, in the proper case, hold that an applicant has sufficient moral legitimate interest so as to satisfy the requirement of Article 146 section 2 of the Constitution, despite the fact that he/she has no pecuniary or material interest.[688]

IV. The Seventy-Five-Day Limitation Period

487. Article 146 section 3 stipulates that a recourse has to be made within seventy-five days of the date when the decision or act was published or, if not published and in the case of an omission, when it came to the notice of the person making the recourse. The seventy-five-day period stipulated in the Constitution is of a mandatory nature and accordingly no recourse may be made after such period has elapsed;[689] this requirement may be examined by the Court *ex proprio motu*. The period may not be extended by the fact that the applicant is a minor[690] or ill; however, it might be extended in cases of force majeure, such as the coup d'etat or the Turkish invasion.[691] The onus of proof that an applicant had notice of the act or omission impeached, if such an act has not been published, rests on the party who alleges that the recourse is out of time. In case of doubt, the Court has to lean in favour of the applicant.[692] The Fifteenth Amendment of the Constitution, Law 135(I)/2020, however, has provided that a period different than the seventy-five-day period may be provided specifically by legislation. This was intended to cover resources before the International Protection Administrative Court. Law 73(I)/2018 has shortened the period for cases regarding asylum and international refugees which fall under the jurisdiction of the International Protection Administrative Court to thirty days, and, in some cases, to fifteen days.

488. Notice is complete if it allows the person interested to ascertain with certainty and precision the material and moral damage that he/she suffers from the published or communicated act. The communication must be complete because if the interested person does not become aware of the whole of the contents of the act, he/she cannot judge and decide about the exercise or not of his/her right to file the recourse. Communication, therefore, of only the operative part without the reasoning for the act is not complete and the time does not run. Complete knowledge may

687. *President of the Republic v. House of Representatives* [2009] 3 CLR 23 (in Greek). *See* further C. Kombos, *Actio Popularis and the Delimitation of Legitimate Interest: An Introduction to the Approach of the European Court and the Supreme Court of Cyprus* 3–4 Lysias 5–19 (2010) (in Greek).

688. *Olympios v. The Republic* [1974] 3 CLR 17, *Miliotis v. The Republic* [1986] 3 CLR 1341.

689. *Marcoullides v. The Greek Communal Chamber* (1962–1963) RSCC 7, *Moran v. The Republic* (1961) RSCC 10.

690. *Panayides v. The Republic* [1988] 3 CLR 2435.

691. *Potamitis v. The Water Board of Limassol* [1985] 3 CLR 260, *Yialousa Savings Bank Ltd v. The Republic* [1977] 3 CLR 25.

692. *Neophytou v. The Republic* [1964] CLR 280, *Plousiou v. The Central Bank of Cyprus* [1982] 3 CLR 230, *Tsiaou v. The Republic* [1983] 3 CLR 1068.

be inferred from a statement or action of the interested person, especially from the submission of an application for remedy containing the defects of the impeached act or omission.[693]

§3. Miscellaneous

I. General Principles of Administrative Law

489. The jurisprudence of the Supreme Court has developed several general principles for the proper application of administrative law. It has been repeatedly held that no decision or act of the administration may be inconsistent with the general principles of administrative law. Eventually, such general principles were codified in a single legislative act, the General Principles of Administrative Law Act 158(I)/99.[694] The main principles shall be briefly summarized in the subsequent paragraphs.

II. Principle of Legality

490. The principle of legality of administrative action derives from the principle of the rule of law. Section 8 of Law 158(I)/99 stipulates that the acts of the administration must be consistent with the law in force. An administrative act or decision which has been taken without a law empowering the organ or authority of the administration to take such decision or by an organ which is not competent to take such act shall be void. Section 17 § 3 of Law 158(I)/99 expressly states that the illegality of an act issued by an incompetent administrative organ may not be remedied even if the competent organ subsequently approves of such an act. Administrative action outside or beyond the powers conferred upon the administration by law would amount to an act or decision taken in excess or abuse of power. Excess or abuse of power also constitute separate grounds for the annulment of administrative acts. When the administrative organ issues an administrative act, on the basis of an application by the subject, it must be based on the status of the law at the time the administrative act is issued, irrespective of whether it was different at the time of application; if, however, the administration had failed to examine the application within reasonable time, then the status of the law at the time of application may be taken into account instead (section 9 of Law 158(I)/99).

491. Section 10 of Law 158(I)/99 expressly states that administrative organs should exercise their competences and issue their decisions within a reasonable time and without undue delay. However, the time limits fixed for the issue of an administrative act are, in principle, only indicative of the administration. An act may be declared invalid only if excessive time has passed from the expiry of the time limit,

693. *Demetriou v. The Municipal Committee of Nicosia* [1987] 3 CLR 1996.

694. *See* A. Angelides, *The General Principles of Administrative Law Act and the Subsequent Case-Law of the Supreme Court of Cyprus* (House of Representatives 2008, in Greek).

so as to have substantially affected the factual and legal circumstances of the case.[695] On the contrary, the time limits fixed for the submission of applications by the persons subject to the administration are peremptory (section 11 of Law 158(I)/99). It should be noted that administrative acts may not have retrospective effect, by virtue of section 6 of Law 158(I)/99, unless the requirements of section 7 of Law 158(I)/99, namely: (a) the law conferring the competences to the administrative organ expressly authorizes such retrospective effect; (b) the administrative act is issued in order to comply with a court judgment of the and retrospective effect is required in order to fully restore legality; (c) the administrative organ reissues an act which had been annulled for formal grounds, so long as the new decision has the same content as the first one and is issued within a reasonable time from the first and on the basis of the same legal and factual considerations; (d) the administrative act revokes an illegal act of the administration; (e) the sole content of the act is to ascertain a factual situation without prejudicing existing situations; (f) retroactivity is required in order to rectify an injustice occurred towards a person due to the omission of the administration.

III. Principles of Proper Administration

492. Administrative authorities should exercise their discretionary powers properly, within the limits provided by law and without abusing their rights. The Administrative Court shall examine whether the administrative organs have exercised their discretion within the proper limits of such discretion, and if not, the administrative decision is subject to invalidation. Whereas the administrative organ should not decide a priori and in a general way the manner in which it shall exercise its discretionary powers in future cases, it may nevertheless exercise its powers on the basis of a general policy or criteria it has pre-determined for similar cases, so long as such policy or criteria are consistent with the legislation and so far as it also examines whether the particular facts of a given case might justify a different approach. The administrative organ may further be guided by circulars or administrative guidelines of a general character which were issued by a hierarchically superior administrative organ, in so far as those circulars or guidelines are not inconsistent with the legislation.

493. The principles of proper administration impose on the administrative organs, by virtue of section 50 of Law 158(I)/99, to exercise their discretion in accordance with a concept of fairness and equity, so as to avoid unfair and unjust solutions. The administrative organs may not pursue aims which are inconsistent with the aims of the legislation[696] or act in bad faith. The obligation of the administration to act in good faith is of cardinal importance for the trust of the citizens; accordingly, the administrative organs should not alter the manner in which they exercise their discretion, thus prejudicing the interested person, unless there is a good reason. The methods used by the administration should be proportionate to the

695. *Tingiridou v. Republic* [1987] 3 CLR 1811.
696. *Michaelides v. The Attorney-General* [1984] 3 CLR 1596.

aims pursued and any interference with the rights of the citizen shall be excused only where such is necessary or justified for the public interest. The administration is not permitted to act in a manner which is inconsistent or contradictory or to invoke its own shortcomings in order to ignore a situation which is favourable for the citizen.

494. The administration has an obligation to carry out an investigation into all relevant circumstances and to reach its decision only after having conducted the enquiry reasonably necessary for the purpose of ascertaining fully all the relevant facts. Reasonable and due enquiry is an essential step in the administrative process whose lack would lead to the annulment of an administrative decision (section 45 of Law 158(I)/99).[697] There is, however, a presumption that the administrative organ has considered all the material facts which were before it, including recommendations of lower organs and the material submitted by the applicant or other persons;[698] this is in accordance with the general presumption of regularity of administrative organs.[699] Thus, the mere fact that a collective organ adopted the opinion or recommendation of another organ does not imply that there was no due enquiry.[700] The applicant thus has the burden of disproving the presumption of legality of the administrative act[701] and of convincing the Court that such was taken because the administrative organ failed to conduct a reasonable enquiry or take into account material facts.[702]

495. Misconception of the administration as to the legal principles (or their proper interpretation) governing the administrative decision,[703] or misconception of facts materially affecting the decision,[704] shall result in the invalidation of the decision in question, by virtue of section 46 of Law 158(I)/99. Whereas the assessment of the facts lies with the administrative organs and the Court shall not interfere with such evaluation so long as it was reasonably open to the administration,[705] the Court shall declare the decision to be void when there is even a possibility of material misconception.[706] Such material misconception may arise if the administrative organ has taken into account non-existing material or has failed to take into account existing material and would also imply that there is lack of a reasonable enquiry. It is further provided that the administrative organs should abide by the formalities which the law requires for the issue of an administrative act; however, section 13 of Law 158(I)/99 distinguishes between those formalities which are material for the

697. *Nicolaides v. The Greek Registrar of the Co-Operative Societies* [1965] 3 CLR 585.
698. *Ierides v. The Republic* [1980] 3 CLR 165.
699. *Georghios Zachariades Ltd v. Ports Authority of Cyprus* [1996] 3 CLR 269 (in Greek), *Gavriel v. Attorney-General* [1989] 3 CLR 3067 (in Greek).
700. *Phylaktou v. The Republic* [1973] 3 CLR 444, *Morphis v. The Republic* [1975] 3 CLR 255.
701. *Vasiotis Constructions Ltd v. Municipality of Limassol* [1989] 3 CLR 3193 (in Greek).
702. *Hadjiyiorki v. The Republic* [1977] 3 CLR 144, *Demetriou v. The Municipal Committee of Larnaca* [1986] 3 CLR 2171, *Violari v. Republic* [1988] 3 CLR 2170.
703. *Demades & Sons Ltd v. The Republic* [1964] CLR 167.
704. *Pavlides v. The Republic* [1967] 3 CLR 223.
705. *Hji Michael v. The Republic* [1972] 3 CLR 246.
706. *Kontos v. The Republic* [1974] 3 CLR 112, *Daphnides v. The Republic* [1964] CLR 180, *Municipality of Strovolos v. Pitta* [2001] 3 CLR 55 (in Greek).

decision taken and those which are immaterial and did not have any effect to the outcome of the decision. The former render the administrative act invalid, whereas the latter do not.

IV. Due Reasoning of Administrative Decision

496. It is a paramount principle of administrative law that administrative decisions must be duly reasoned. The object of the rule requiring reasons to be given for administrative decisions is to enable the persons concerned and the Court on review to ascertain, in each case, whether the decision is well founded in fact and in law. Accordingly, the reasons must be stated clearly and unambiguously; they must be read in the sense that reasonable persons affected thereby would understand them, and they should be supported by reasons which fulfil the object of the relevant legislation. Mere repetition of the text of the enactment concerned, either in a negative form or otherwise, is not sufficient (section 28 of Law 158(I)/99).[707] The extent of reasoning which is required in each particular case depends upon the nature of the decision in question. Reasoning is not based on length; a lengthy decision might lack justification, whereas a brief decision might be duly reasoned.[708] Full reasoning shall be given if the Administration sufficiently explains how it applied the law or its discretion on the basis of the facts of the case in order to reach its decision;[709] the reasons for reaching a specific conclusion have to be sufficiently explained.

497. The Administration may not rely on the public interest in order to justify its decision; the grounds why the Administration considered that a specific decision was for the public interest have to be explained.[710] It is not lawful for the Administration to rely on 'public policy grounds' without explaining sufficiently what these grounds are.[711] Nor is it lawful for the Administration to simply announce that a petition is rejected, without offering any justification.[712] The decision should contain all the material facts on which the decision is based, as well as all the relevant legal provisions that the administrative organ considered in order to reach its decision.[713] However, the Administration may opt not to refer to every single detail of the case, if this has not been crucial for its decision.[714] If, however, the reasoning may be found in documents which were before the administrative organ when it

707. *Christou v. The Republic* [1972] 3 CLR 32, *Bagdades v. The Central Bank of Cyprus* [1973] 3 CLR 417, *Rallis v. The Greek Communal Chamber* [1963] RSCC 11, *Zavros v. The Council for Registration of Architects and Civil Engineers* [1969] 3 CLR 310.

708. *Marangos v. The Republic* [1983] 3 CLR 682.

709. *Georghiou v. Republic* [1989] 3 CLR 589 (in Greek), *Nicolas v. Republic* [1989] 3 CLR 228 (in Greek).

710. *Kazamias v. The Republic* [1982] 3 CLR 239, *Adamides v. The Republic* [1982] 3 CLR 343.

711. *Carayiannis v. The Republic* [1969] 3 CLR 341, *Dekathlon Shipping Co Ltd v. The Republic* [1980] 3 CLR 630.

712. *Andreou v. The Republic* [1978] 3 CLR 85.

713. *Papazachariou v. The Republic* [1972] 3 CLR 486, *Hadjiconstantinou v. The Republic* [1973] 3 CLR 65.

714. *Savva v. The Republic* [1985] 3 CLR 694, *Orictaco Co Ltd v. The Republic* [1985] 3 CLR 1327.

reached its decision, such as opinions of hierarchically lower organs which the superior organ adopted, it is not necessary to repeat such reasoning in the decision itself.[715] The reasoning of an administration decision may not, under any circumstances, be supplemented by material which was not before the administrative organ at the time when the decision was taken,[716] or by the arguments submitted by advocates on behalf of the Administration.[717]

498. Collective organs are under a duty to keep proper minutes in accordance with section 24 of Law 158(I)/99. The inadequacy of recording a decision deprives the Court of the ability to examine how and why it was reasonably open to the administrative organ to decide in such a manner. If no minutes have been recorded, the administrative act shall unavoidably be annulled.[718] Similarly, if the administrative file does not contain material documents on which the administrative organ supposedly based its decision, the decision shall be annulled.[719] If the decision of a collective organ was reached by majority rather than unanimously, the requirement to provide sufficient reasoning is even more obvious.[720] There is, however, no requirement to keep minutes of all deliberations of the members of the administrative organ, so long as the actual decision has been properly kept.[721]

499. The reasoning provided by the administrative organ should, in any event, be in accordance with the law. The Administration may not rely on extra-legal criteria which are inconsistent with the relevant legal provisions governing the case.[722] It should be noted, however, that if part of the reasoning is lawful and it is sufficient to justify the decision, the mere fact that part of the reasoning is incorrect shall not automatically lead to the annulment of the administrative decision (section 31 of Law 158(I)/99).[723] The above principles may only apply if the fact that part of the reasoning is faulty does not also lead to lack of proper enquiry or material factual misapprehension. In any event, the reasoning should be consistent with the material facts of the case.[724]

715. *Georghiou v. Republic* [1989] 3 CLR 589, *Louca v. Republic* [1986] 3 CLR 1640, *Republic v. Myrtiotis* [1975] 3 CLR 484, *Peratica Trading Ltd v. Republic* [2002] 3 CLR 445 (in Greek).
716. *Tsikkinis v. Republic* [1984] 3 CLR 1577.
717. *Metalock (Near East) Limited v. The Republic* [1969] 3 CLR 351, *Frangou v. Republic* [1998] 3 CLR 270 (in Greek).
718. *Medcon Construction v. Republic* [1968] 3 CLR 535, *Stylson Engineering Co Ltd v. Republic* [1995] 3 CLR 491 (in Greek).
719. *Michael v. The Republic* [1981] 3 CLR 147, *Georghiades v. The Republic* [1980] 3 CLR 487, *Eracleous v. The Republic* [1985] 3 CLR 740.
720. *Georghiades v. The Republic* [1967] 3 CLR 653, *Papageorghiou v. The Republic* [1984] 3 CLR 1348.
721. *Georghiou v. Republic* [1989] 3 CLR 589.
722. *Emilios Ellinas & Co Ltd v. Ministry of Finance* [1990] 3 CLR 181 (in Greek).
723. *Pikis v. The Republic* [1967] 3 CLR 562, *Ioannou v. The Ministry of Interior* [1987] 3 CLR 1549.
724. *Jacovides v. The Republic* [1966] 3 CLR 212.

V. Principles of Natural Justice

500. The principles of natural justice should always govern the actions of the administration. An administrative organ which participates in the making of an administrative act should warrant both integrity and impartiality. By virtue of section 42 of Law 158(I)/99, any person who has a special relationship or is related, either by blood or affinity within the fourth degree or has intense hostility towards the person who is affected by the administrative act, or any person who has an interest (monetary or of another kind) in the outcome of the administrative act, should not participate in its making. The question of whether objectivity exists should be considered in an objective manner, and thus, the decisive criterion in not whether bias actually existed but whether an outsider might reasonably conclude that there was partiality.[725] It is therefore immaterial whether the person acted in good faith.[726] The principle of impartiality is consistent with the Latin maxim *nemo judex in causa sua*; the only case where a person should participate in the making of an administrative act despite the fact that he/she has an interest or special relationship in the making of the act is when the said act may not be lawfully issued by any other organ, or where the competent collective organ could not otherwise convene because of lack of a quorum.

501. The second principle of natural justice consists of the right to be heard by the administrative organ. By virtue of section 43 of Law 158(I)/99, any person who is affected by the issue of an administrative act or by the taking of an administrative measure which is of a disciplinary or an adverse nature has the right to be heard prior to the act being issued.[727] If an administrative organ intends to support its decision on allegations which have been submitted against a person, it should give that person the right to present his/her views regarding such allegations. However, the right to be heard is not necessarily an oral one; the person may, in principle, submit his/her views in writing. The extent of the right to be heard should always be considered on the basis of the actual circumstances of the case, the nature of the investigation that the administration needs to carry out and the object of the enquiry.[728] In cases of decisions of a purely administrative nature, however, which are not of a disciplinary or an adverse nature and which do not have the character of a sanction, such as compulsory acquisition, or public procurement or registration of vehicles, the right to be heard is normally not required, unless provided by law, or unless the circumstances of the case would so require.[729]

VI. Equality and Non-discrimination

502. The constitutional prohibition of discrimination extends also to the action of the administration. Article 28 of the Constitution and section 38 of Law 158(I)/

725. *Republic v. Solomou* [1998] 3 CLR 769 (in Greek).
726. *Kallouris v. The Republic* [1964] CLR 313.
727. *Louca v. The Republic* [1986] 3 CLR 1640.
728. *Kyprianou v. The Public Service Commission* [1973] 3 CLR 206.
729. *Savvides v. Republic* [1989] 3 CLR 2595, *Hjiloucas v. The Republic* [1971] 3 CLR 96.

99, which safeguard the principle of equality of citizens, entail that the administration must treat in an equal and uniform manner all citizens who are under the same or similar circumstances.[730] It has repeatedly been held that the principle of equality safeguarded by Article 28 of the Constitution does not convey the notion of exact arithmetical equality, but it safeguards only against arbitrary differentiations and does not exclude reasonable distinctions which have to be made in view of the intrinsic nature of things.[731] The Court has to assess the material facts and particular circumstances of each case in order to conclude whether there has been unequal treatment and bearing in mind that if it was reasonably open to the Administration to treat the cases differently, the Court should not interfere by substituting its own views.[732]

503. There are several cases where the principle of equality has been successfully invoked by applicants. In the case of *Christoforou*, it was held that once the applicants were admitted to the third year of the Academy in Cyprus on the strength of their previous two years record in another Academy, it could not be reasonably considered that there was room for differentiation between the applicants and graduates who completed all three years in the Academy.[733] Similarly, a decision for admitting at the Pedagogical Academy of Cyprus fifty new students, of whom twenty-five would necessarily be male and twenty-five would necessarily be female, was held by the Full Bench to be unconstitutional, since it resulted in not admitting female candidates who had superior results when compared to their male counterparts; the distinction on the grounds of the sex of the candidates could not be reasonably justified and was held to be unconstitutional.[734]

504. However, Article 28 is violated only when the differentiation is not based on an objective and reasonable justification. The existence of such justification must be assessed in relation to the aim and effects of the measure under consideration with regard to the principles which normally prevail in democratic societies. Article 28 is likewise violated when it is clearly established that there is no reasonable relationship on proportionality between the means employed and the aim sought to be realized. Bare equality of treatment, regardless of the inequality of realities, is neither justice nor homage to the constitutional principle. Where objects, persons or transactions essentially dissimilar are treated uniformly, discrimination may result.[735]

505. It has accordingly been held that a difference in treatment between an advocate and a person who is not an advocate, with respect to the registration of trademarks of a client before the Registrar of Trademarks, is an objective and reasonable

730. *Jacovides v. The Republic* [1966] 3 CLR 212.
731. *Kantara Shipping Ltd v. The Republic* [1969] 3 CLR 95, *Georghiades v. The Republic* [1979] 3 CLR 146.
732. *Kyriacou v. The Greek Communal Chamber* [1968] 3 CLR 280.
733. *Christoforou v. The Educational Service Committee* [1981] 3 CLR 255.
734. *The Republic v. Christophorou* [1986] 3 CLR 1523.
735. *The Republic v. Christoudia* [1988] 3 CLR 2622.

differentiation since such aims at the protection of the legal profession.[736] Similarly, differences in treatment of public servants with respect to salary, which are based on years of service, are not inconsistent with the principle of non-discrimination.[737] In matters of taxation, the discretion of the Administration to distinguish between different classes of taxable persons is wider than usual.[738] Consequently, there is no violation of the principle of equality simply because persons are classified differently for tax purposes, so long as the classification is based on objective and reasonable social criteria.[739]

506. Whenever the Administration decides to handle a case in a different manner than it had dealt with other similar cases in the past, such decision should be part of a wider justified new policy decision on the manner in which the Administration exercises its discretion; otherwise, the difference in treatment might be considered as arbitrary.[740] It should be noted, however, that there is no right of equal treatment with respect to illegal action of the Administration (section 39 of Law 158(I)/99). The mere fact that the Administration had acted contrary to the law in previous cases does not entail a right of the Applicant to request that the Administration also act illegally in his/her case.[741] Accordingly, the refusal by the Administration to act illegally does not entail discrimination under any circumstances.[742]

507. Starting with *Dias*,[743] the Supreme Court has repeatedly adhered to a rather limited approach to its jurisdiction to examine the constitutionality of laws allegedly violating the right to equality, which seriously undermines the constitutional guarantees against discrimination. The case of *Tsiakka* offers a sufficient illustration of this approach.[744] The Appellant's mother was a displaced person and submitted a resource against the decision to reject her application to be recognized as a displaced person. However, the Archive of Population Law 141/2002 provided that only persons whose father was a displaced person would be recognized as displaced persons. The Appellant argued that this was a clear case of violation of her right to equality, which was solely grounded on the sex of her parent, who was a displaced person. The Supreme Court rejected the appeal, holding that it had no jurisdiction to declare that the said provision was unconstitutional, since such a declaration would not automatically lead to the satisfaction of her petition to be recognized as

---

736. *Saba Kypris & Co v. The Republic* [1980] 3 CLR 149.
737. *Tsinontas v. Cyprus Land Development Corporation* [1987] 3 CLR 1766.
738. *Papas v. Improvement Board of Kakopetria* [1989] 3 CLR 322 (in Greek), *Hara Hotels Ltd v. The Republic* [1987] 3 CLR 618.
739. *Colocassides v. The Republic* [1977] 3 CLR 364, *Skyfrost Co Ltd v. The Republic* [1979] 3 CLR 1, *Commercial Company Arkozy v. The Republic* [1975] 3 CLR 415.
740. *Drousiotis v. CYBC* [1984] 3 CLR 546.
741. *Voyiazanos v. The Republic* [1967] 3 CLR 239, *Ioannides v. The Republic* [1973] 3 CLR 117, *Shamassian v. The Republic* [1973] 3 CLR 341.
742. *Lanitis v. The Republic* [1988] 3 CLR 87, *Proestou v. The Republic* [1981] 3 CLR 314, *Ioannou v. The Republic* [1982] 3 CLR 1002, *Christodoulides v. The Republic* [1985] 3 CLR 357, *Koniotis v. The Republic* [1967] 3 CLR 376, *Karayianni v. The Educational Service Committee* [1979] 3 CLR 371.
743. *Dias United Publishing Co Ltd v. Republic* [1996] 3 CLR 550 (in Greek).
744. *Tsiakka v. Republic* [2010] 3 CLR 510 (in Greek).

a displaced person; the House of Representatives would necessarily have to enact new legislation extending such right to persons whose mother is a displaced person. There is little doubt that the case-law of the Supreme Court unnecessarily refuses to judicially control the constitutionality of laws which are manifestly incompatible with Article 28 of the Constitution. The ECtHR recently held that this approach amounted to a violation of the right to an effective remedy under Article 13 of the ECHR.[745]

745. *Vrountou v.* Cyprus, App. 33631/06, Judgment of 13 Oct. 2015.

Chapter 5. Legal Position of Aliens

508. Cyprus had historically been a country of emigration, especially towards the UK, but also towards Australia, the USA and South Africa. Following the Turkish invasion of 1974, however, and the occupation of the northern part of the island, the Republic began issuing individual visas to migrant workers for employment which were for short term and restricted to specific sectors. Demand for labour in Cyprus in specific sectors, such as the tourism industry, led to the granting of visas and work permits on the condition that the worker would be attached to a particular employer without the freedom to change employer, unless the original employer consented to such a change; in any event, the duration of the stay of the worker in Cyprus ought to be of a temporary and limited nature. Employing migrants who do not have a work permit or who do not reside lawfully in the Republic of Cyprus is a criminal offence, with the penalty of imprisonment normally being imposed on wrongdoers.

509. The principal legislative instrument concerning immigration law is the Aliens and Immigration Law Cap. 105 as amended. The Aliens and Immigration Law regulates the issue of refusal of entry within the Republic of Cyprus to illegal immigrants and provides an extensive list of such persons. According to section 6 of Cap. 105, persons who are considered illegal immigrants include, *inter alia*, poor persons, persons who are mentally disturbed or who suffer from a contagious disease, persons who have been convicted to imprisonment as a result of committing murder or any other serious offence, prostitutes, or persons who are expected to behave in a manner contrary to public order or morals, or who are members of illegal organizations, or persons whose entry to the Republic is not allowed, or who have been deported.

510. In addition to the above, the immigration authorities of the Republic may refuse entry to any person who is not a citizen of the Republic. Therefore, aliens do not have an absolute right of entry to the Republic and may be refused entry unless they hold a permanent residence permit or a valid immigration authorization or unless they are temporary residents and hold a valid entry permit or disembarkation permit. According to section 9 of Cap. 105 and subject to the discretionary powers of the Chief Immigration Officer, no person shall enter into the Republic of Cyprus without a passport. Failure to do so will lead the immigration authorities to consider such a person as an illegal immigrant. Section 7A of Cap. 105 further provides that if the immigration authorities find out that a fictitious marriage has been performed, then they may prohibit aliens from remaining within the territory of the Republic, or they may cancel or refuse to renew the residence permit granted to the alien. The powers of the immigration authorities to prohibit entry into, or to order the expulsion of an alien from the Republic, although subject to judicial control, are extremely wide.[746]

---

746. *Georghiou v. Republic* [1968] 3 CLR 401, *Moyo v. Republic* [1998] 3 CLR 1203 (in Greek), *Eddine v. Republic* [2008] 3 CLR 95 (in Greek).

511. Normally, an alien will need a visa to enter the Republic, namely an authorization granted by the consular authorities of the Republic. Aliens may be prohibited from entering the Republic unless their passport has a Cypriot visa; if no such visa is demonstrated, then the alien may be considered to be an illegal immigrant. Nevertheless, the Council of Ministers may, from time to time, issue orders prescribing that passports or Cypriot visas are not required for the citizens of a certain country or for any class of persons. It should be noted that while the general rule is that a person should apply for a visa to be issued by the consular authorities of the Republic, such person may, in special cases, apply for visa at the borders for the purpose of entering or transiting from the Republic; such person ought, in any event, comply with the requirements of Cap.105 for entering into the Republic, should not have been in a position to apply for a visa beforehand from the consular authorities of the Republic, should file all necessary documents proving the unforeseen and urgent reasons for entering into the Republic and should prove that the return to the country of origin is secured.

512. The Aliens and Immigration Law has been amended on a number of occasions for the purpose of harmonizing the Law with the *acquis communautaire*.[747] The Law Concerning the Freedom of Movement and Residence of Citizens of Member States of the EU and of Members of their Family 7(I)/2007 has been adopted for the purposes of harmonization with Directive 2004/38/EC and provides that citizens of the Union and their family members have, in principle and subject to minor exceptions, a right to move and reside freely within the territory of the Republic of Cyprus.[748] Furthermore, Article 3 section 1 of the Refugee Law 6(I)/2000, as amended, provides that a person may acquire the status of a refugee, so long as s/he is outside his/her country due to well-founded fear of persecution and cannot, or is not willing due to such well-founded fear of persecution, be protected by his/her country; persecution may relate to racial, political, or religious grounds, or to the fact that the refugee is part of a specific social group. A refugee may be persecuted by the State, groups or organizations controlling the State or a substantial part of the State, or even non-state actors, so long as the state actors – including international organizations – may not, or are not willing, to provide protection from persecution or harm.

747. Sometimes very controversially, as evidenced by *Motilla v. Republic* [2008] 1 CLR 29 (in Greek).
748. *See*, however, *Bekefi and others v. Republic* [2016] 3 CLR 258 (in Greek).

Part V. Specific Problems

Chapter 1. War, Treaty and Foreign Affairs Powers

513. The Council of Ministers has the power to declare war or conclude peace treaties, or conclude any other international treaties or agreements in accordance with Articles 50 and 54 of the Constitution. As already noted, by virtue of Article 169 section 1 of the Constitution, international agreements with a foreign State or any International Organization relating to commercial matters, economic cooperation (including payments and credit) and modus vivendi are concluded under a decision of the Council of Ministers, whereas any other treaty, convention or international agreement shall be negotiated and signed under a decision of the Council of Ministers, but shall be operative and binding only when approved by a law made by the House of Representatives. All the above powers of the Council of Ministers are, however, subject to the veto right of the President of the Republic, since the decision relates to foreign affairs, defence or security.

514. The Treaty of Guarantee is arguably the most controversial part of the Zurich Agreements. The Treaty of Guarantee was signed by the newly established Republic of Cyprus on the one part and Greece, Turkey and the UK on the other part and is annexed to the Constitution as Annex II and has constitutional force. Article I of the Treaty of Guarantee provides that the Republic of Cyprus undertakes to ensure the maintenance of its independence, territorial integrity and security, as well as respect for its Constitution and undertakes not to participate, in whole or in part, in any political or economic union with any State whatsoever. It accordingly declares prohibited any activity likely to promote, directly or indirectly, either union with any other State or partition of the Island. Furthermore, Article 170 of the Constitution provides that the Republic shall, by agreement on appropriate terms, accord the most favoured nation treatment to Greece, Turkey and the UK for all agreements, whatever their nature shall be.

515. It has been considered whether the aforementioned Articles should be construed as prohibiting the accession of the Republic of Cyprus to the EU. In a joint Legal Opinion, Professors James Crawford, Gerhard Hafner and Alain Pellet correctly concluded that the Treaty of Guarantee does not prohibit Cyprus from becoming a member of a regional organization such as the EU, since membership of the EU would not constitute participation 'in any political or economic union with any State whatsoever' within the meaning of Article I of the Treaty of Guarantee. It was further considered that Article 170 of the Constitution does not prohibit Cyprus from entering into agreements which confer benefits in third states or from acceding to any agreement whatever. Furthermore, membership in the EU should not be regarded as triggering general most favoured nation obligations, a position which Turkey had recognized in the past. Accordingly, Article 170 of the Constitution would not require Cyprus to extend any additional benefits of EU membership to Turkey.[749]

516. In the *British Council of Turkish Cypriot Associations,* the applicants argued that the Republic of Cyprus did not have the capacity to start negotiations for accession to the EU, without the participation of the Turkish Cypriot Community. They further argued that the British Government ought to have taken into account the constitutional anomaly prevailing in Cyprus and voted against opening such negotiations. The British Court dismissed the application, noting that the Republic of Cyprus is an internationally recognized and independent sovereign state and British courts do not have any jurisdiction to examine the alleged constitutionality of the decisions of a foreign sovereign state.[750] The position that there is no constitutional impediment to the Republic of Cyprus acceding in the EU has been accepted by the international community and, as already stated, the Republic of Cyprus officially became a member of the EU on 1 May 2004.

517. Article II of the Treaty of Guarantee further provides that Greece, Turkey and the UK, taking note of the undertakings of the Republic of Cyprus set out in Article I of the Treaty, recognize and guarantee the independence, territorial integrity and security of the Republic of Cyprus and also the state of affairs established by the Basic Articles of the Constitution. Moreover, Greece, Turkey and the UK undertake to prohibit so far as concerns them any activity aimed at promoting, directly or indirectly, either union of Cyprus with any other State or partition of the island. There is little doubt that Article II of the Treaty of Guarantee has not been respected, especially since one of the Guarantor Powers, Turkey, continued in 1974 to occupy part of the territory of the Republic of Cyprus, de facto partitioning the island. Article III of the Treaty of Guarantee which provides that the Republic of Cyprus, Greece and Turkey undertake to respect the integrity of the areas retained under UK sovereignty at the time of the establishment of the Republic of Cyprus and guarantee the use and enjoyment by the UK of the rights to be secured to it by the Republic of Cyprus in accordance with the Treaty of Establishment.

518. The most controversial provisions of the Treaty of Guarantee are contained in Article IV of the Treaty which provides that in the event of a breach of the provisions of the Treaty of Guarantee, Greece, Turkey and the UK undertake to consult

749. *See* in particular *Cyprus and European Union Membership: Important Legal Documents* (A. Markides ed., 2002); L. Loucaides, *The Application for Accession in the EEC and the Treaty of Guarantee* 26 Cyprus L. Rev. 411–415 (1989) (in Greek); A. Syrigos, *Cyprus and the EU: Sovereign State, Negotiations and Objections from an International Law Point of View*, in *Cyprus and the European Union*, 91–106 (A. Theophanous, N. Peristianis & A. Ioannou eds, Intercollege Press 1999).

750. *R v. Secretary of State for Foreign and Commonwealth Affairs ex p. British Council of Turkish Cypriot Associations* [1998] COD 336 QBD.

together with respect to the representations of measures necessary to ensure observance of those provisions. In so far as common or concerted action may not prove possible, it is provided that each of the three guaranteeing powers 'reserves the right to take action with the sole aim of re-establishing the state of affairs created by the present Treaty'. In an opinion prepared by Hans Kelsen in his advice to the UN on the admission of the Republic of Cyprus, it was stated that the expression 'reserves' presupposes the existence of such right on the basis of the general principles of international and does not imply grant of a new right.

519. It was further stated that the said Article cannot validly be interpreted as granting the guarantors an unqualified right to intervene by use of armed force in the event of a breach of the provisions of the Treaty, since such use is justifiable only on grounds of self-defence, or under the authority of the UN; in any event the right of unilateral action would be limited by the need for recourse to the means of pacific settlement available to the States concerned in accordance with the UN Charter. It is reiterated that in the event of a conflict between the obligations of a Member State of the UN under the Charter and their obligations under any other international agreement, their obligations under the Charter shall prevail. Similarly, Frank Soskice, in his opinion dated 1 November 1963, opined that the words 'take action' could not be interpreted as referring to unilateral military intervention without the authority of the Security Council.[751]

520. Irrespective of the validity of such Article under international law, it has generally been accepted that the Turkish invasion of Cyprus and the continuing occupation of northern Cyprus could not be justified on the basis of such article as Turkey had alleged. Even if it was unreasonably considered that the Treaty of Guarantee could supersede peremptory norms of international law, it is doubtful whether the 1974 coup d'etat could be considered a breach of the provisions of the Treaty. Furthermore, no common consultation for 'common concrete action' had taken place despite invitations to such consultation. It is further clear that the aim of such armed intervention has not been the 'restoration of the state of affairs created by the Treaty', as such restoration has already taken place since 23 July 1974 and yet the Turkish military continues to occupy the northern part of the island.[752]

---

751. *See* further G. Zotiades, *Intervention by Treaty Right: Its Legality in Present Day International Law* (1965); D. Constantopoulos, *Intervention by Treaty Right and the Cyprus Problem*, 8 Armenopoulos 3–7 (1974) (in Greek); *Ibid.*, *The Right of Intervention*, 6 Intl. Rel. 41–47 (1964); C. Tornaritis, *Whether any Resort to Force or Armed Intervention in Cyprus Could be Justified Either under the Constitution or under Customary Law*, 2 Cyprus Today (1964); G. Tenekides, *La Republique de Chypre et le Droit International Il Politica* 69–88 (1962); E. Ypsarides, *The Treaty of Guarantee and the Alleged Right of Intervention*, 2 Cyprus Today (1964); T. Zoupanos, *The Invalidity and the Inapplicability of the Treaty of Guarantee* (1964, in Greek); A. Jacovides, *Treaties Conflicting with Peremptory Norms of International Law and the Zurich – London Agreements* (1966); T. Erlich, *Cyprus: 1958–1967. International Crises and the Role of Law* 69 (Oxford U. Press 1974); T. Tsatsos, *Observations on the Constitution of Cyprus* 18–20 (A. Sakkoulas 1965, in Greek).
752. *See* among others K. Chrysostomides, *The Republic of Cyprus: A Study in International Law* 117ff (Martinus Nijhoff Publishers 2000); R. McDonald, *International Law and the Conflict in Cyprus*, 19 Canadian Y.B. Intl. L. 3ff (1981); D. Constantopoulos, *The Turkish Invasion of Cyprus from the*

Chapter 2. Taxing and Spending Powers

§1. The Constitutional Framework of Taxation

521. Article 24 of the Constitution introduces the obligation of every person to contribute towards the public burden according to his/her financial means.[753] The obligation to contribute in accordance with one's financial means implies that the law might differentiate between classes of individuals so as to achieve fairness in the fiscal policy and that such differentiation, so long as it is reasonable, shall not be considered to violate the principle of equality as safeguarded by Article 28 of the Constitution. This is due to the fact that Article 28 safeguards only against arbitrary differentiation and does not exclude reasonable distinctions which have to be made in view of the intrinsic nature of things; the legislative accordingly enjoys wider latitude than usual in making classifications for tax purposes and the Court shall not in principle strike down legislation as unconstitutional so long as the differentiation is not arbitrary.[754] It has therefore been held that a Law is not inconsistent with Article 24 of the Constitution by the fact that taxation in respect of one of the public burdens was not based on the totality of one's means but only on the basis of personal income.[755]

522. However, tax legislation which is clearly inconsistent with the constitutional provisions shall be stricken out. In *Panayides*, the Applicant, who was a bachelor, has been assessed to pay a personal tax of 20% in excess of what would have been paid by him had he not been a bachelor. The Supreme Court held that such distinction between married and unmarried persons was not reasonable and contravened Articles 24 and 28 of the Constitution. In *Ioannides*, the applicants challenged the decision of the Commissioner of Income Tax, who decided that the income of their wives, not derived from their own labour but from other sources, should be aggregated, for taxation purposes, on their income. The Supreme Court reversed its previous case-law and held that the provision of the Income Tax Law which imposed upon a married man the obligation to pay tax on the combined total of his income and the income of his wife, was unconstitutional, since it imposed to a married man the liability to contribute, in addition to his own means, for the means of someone else. It was further held that the addition of the income of the wife from other sources than from her own labour to the income of her husband resulted in

---

Aspect of International Law (1978); I. Brownlie, *The Prohibition of the Use of Armed Force for the Solution of International Differences, with Particular Reference to the Affairs of the Republic of Cyprus*, in *International Law Conference on Cyprus* 198–213 (Cyprus Bar Council 1979); J. Wolfe, *The Treaty of Guarantee: Intervention and Intercession in Cyprus*, in *International Law Conference on Cyprus* 33–49 (Cyprus Bar Council 1979); C. Tornaritis, *The Turkish Invasion of Cyprus and Legal Problems Arising Therefrom* (1975).

753. *See* M. Miltiadous, *Tax Principles in Article 24 of the Constitution*, 49–50 Cyprus L. Rev. 7191–7204 (1995) (in Greek).

754. *Matsis v. Republic* [1969] 3 CLR 245, *Anastassiou v. Republic* [1977] 3 CLR 91.

755. *Hadjikyriacos and Sons Ltd* [1963] 5 RSCC 107.

unequal treatment between married men depending on whether their wives derive income from their own labour or from their own property.[756]

523. Article 24 section 2 of the Constitution stipulates that no contribution by way of tax, duty or rate of any kind whatsoever shall be imposed save by or under the authority of a law. Furthermore, as an exception to the prerogative of the House of Representatives to enact legislation with retrospective effect, Article 24 section 3 of the Constitution stipulates that no tax, duty or rate of any kind whatsoever shall be imposed with retrospective effect. Provided that any import duty may be imposed from the date of the introduction of the relevant Bill. Finally, no tax, duty or rate of any kind whatsoever other than customs duties shall be of a destructive or prohibitive nature. In a disputed case, the onus is on the taxing authority to satisfy the Court as to liability to pay tax, but where the tax-payer claims any exemption or deduction from tax, the onus is on him/her to support such claim for exemption or deduction.[757] The Court should examine whether the tax-payer is clearly within the words of the provision by which he/she is charged with tax; in case of doubt, this should be interpreted in favour of the tax-payer.

§2. Financial Provisions

524. Article 165 of the Constitution provides that all revenues and moneys, howsoever raised or received by the Republic, shall, subject to the provisions of the Constitution and of the law, be paid into and form one fund to be known as the Consolidated Fund of the Republic. In addition to any grant, remuneration or other monies charged to the Consolidated Fund, all pensions and gratuities for which the Republic is liable, the emoluments of the President of the Republic and the salaries of the judges of the Supreme Court, of the Attorney-General and of the Deputy Attorney-General, of the Auditor-General and of the Deputy Auditor-General, of the Governor of the Central Bank of the Republic and of members of the Public Service Commission, all debt charges to which the Republic is liable[758] and any moneys required to satisfy any judgment, decision or award against the Republic by any court shall be charged on the Consolidated Fund by virtue of Article 166 of the Constitution. The power to prepare a comprehensive Budget of the Republic in respect of every financial year is vested to the Minister of Finance upon receiving the estimates of each Ministry and of each Independent Office of the Republic. Such Budget shall be laid before the House of Representatives, following approval by the Council of Ministers.

525. Article 167 of the Constitution provides that the estimates of expenditure in the Budget shall show separately the total sums required to meet expenditure

756. *Ioannides v. Republic* [1979] 3 CLR 295. *See also Demetriades v. Republic* [1977] 3 CLR 213.
757. *Georgallides* [1958] 23 CLR 249, *Hadjiyiannis v. Republic* [1966] 3 CLR 338.
758. Including interest, sinking fund charges, the repayment of amortization of debt and all expenditure in connexion with the raising of loans on the security of the Consolidated Fund and the service and redemption of debt created thereby.

charged on the Consolidated Fund and the sums respectively required to meet other expenditures. The Budget shall also show, so far as practicable, the assets and liabilities of the Republic at the end of the last completed financial year, the manner in which those assets are invested or held and particulars in respect of outstanding liabilities. The expenditure to be met from the Consolidated Fund but not charged thereon shall be submitted to the House of Representatives for adoption and, if adopted, shall be included in the Budget in respect of that financial year. If, in respect of any financial year, it is found that the amount adopted by the House of Representatives for any purpose is insufficient or that a need has arisen for expenditure for a purpose for which no amount has been adopted, a supplementary budget showing the sums required shall be laid before the House of Representatives for adoption and if adopted by the House of Representatives shall be included in the Budget in respect of that financial year. The House of Representatives may approve or refuse its approval of any expenditure contained in a supplementary Budget but may not vote for an increased amount or an alteration in its destination.[759] Pursuant to the Eleventh Amendment of the Constitution, Law 100(I)/2019 and in respect of its autonomy, the House of Representatives introduces, enacts and executes its own budget, in so far as it respects the maximum limits determined by the Executive.

526. Article 168 of the Constitution explicitly provides that no expenditure shall be met from the Consolidated Fund or other Public Funds except upon the authority of a warrant under the hand of the Minister of Finance, provided that the Minister of Finance shall not refuse to sign any such warrant for an expenditure provided for in the Budget. No such warrant shall be issued unless such expenditure has been adopted in the Budget for the financial year to which the warrant relates in the Budget. If the Budget has not been adopted by the House of Representatives by the first day of the financial year to which it relates, the House of Representatives may, subject to the provisions of this Constitution, by a resolution, authorize the meeting of any expenditure required, for a period not exceeding one month at any one time but in any event not exceeding two months in the aggregate, from the Consolidated Fund or other Public Funds as they may consider essential for the continuance of the public services shown in the Budget until the expiration of such period. This is so, provided that the expenditure so authorized for any service shall not exceed the proportion with respect to such period of the amount voted for that service in the Budget for the preceding financial year.[760]

759. *President of the Republic v. House of Representatives*, App. 2/2024, Judgment of 5 Feb. 2025 (in Greek).

760. *See* further C. Clerides, *The Power to Amend the Budget in Accordance with the Provisions of the Constitution of the Republic of Cyprus*, 12 Cyprus L. Rev. 1942–1950 (1985) (in Greek); C. Tornaritis, *Legal Problems Relating to the Budget*, 1 Cyprus L. Tribune 9–10 (1988) (in Greek).

Chapter 3. Emergency Laws

§1. Proclamation of Emergency

527. Despite its turbulent constitutional history, the Republic of Cyprus has never issued a Proclamation of Emergency in accordance with Article 183 of the Constitution, suspending the effect of constitutional freedoms. As noted in *Ibrahim*, 'the fact that in spite of what has been going on in Cyprus since December, 1963, no Proclamation of Emergency has been issued under Article 183, rather than indicating, contrary to glaring fact, that no such emergency exists, strongly indicates that the present emergency is one which could not be met within the express provisions of the Constitution'.[761] Article 183 of the Constitution stipulates that in case of war or other public danger threatening the life of the Republic or any part thereof, the Council of Ministers shall have power, by a decision taken in this respect, to issue a Proclamation of Emergency. The President (or Vice-President) of the Republic shall have a right of veto against any such decision which they shall exercise within forty-eight hours of the date when the decision has been transmitted to their respective offices. The President of the Republic shall, unless he/she has exercised his/her right of veto, promulgate such Proclamation by publication in the official Gazette of the Republic. The Proclamation shall, following promulgation, be laid before the House of Representatives. If the House of Representatives is not sitting, it must be convened as soon as possible for this purpose. The House of Representatives shall have the right to reject or confirm such Proclamation of Emergency. In the case of rejection, the Proclamation of Emergency shall have no legal effect. In the case of confirmation, the President of the Republic shall promulgate such decision of the House of Representatives by publication in the official Gazette of the Republic.

528. Any Proclamation of Emergency should specify the Articles of the Constitution which shall be suspended for the duration of such Emergency. It is, however, provided that only specific Articles of the Constitution may be suspended by the Proclamation of Emergency, namely Article 7 which safeguards the right to life in so far as it relates to death inflicted by a permissible act of war; Article 10 sections 2 and 3 of the Constitution which provides that no person shall be required to perform forced or compulsory labour, Article 11 which safeguards liberty and security of a person, Article 13 which safeguards free movement and residence, Article 16 which safeguards the right to home, Article 17 which safeguards the right to correspondence and communication, Article 19 which safeguards freedom of expression, Article 21 which safeguards the right to a peaceful assembly, Article 23 which safeguards the right to property, but only in so far as the prompt payment in cash of just and equitable compensation for the requisition of property by the Republic is concerned, Article 25 which safeguards the right to carry any profession or business

761. *Attorney-General v. Ibrahim* [1964] CLR 195, at 225.

and Article 27 which safeguards the right to strike. Accordingly, the Proclamation of Emergency is not all-embracing but may suspend the application of only specific Articles of the Constitution.

529. The Proclamation of Emergency shall cease to operate at the expiration of two months from the date of confirmation by the House of Representatives unless the House, at the request of the Council of Ministers, decides to prolong the duration of the state of emergency, whereupon the President of the Republic shall again have a right of veto against such decision of prolongation. While a Proclamation is in operation, the Council of Ministers, if satisfied that immediate action is required, may, subject to the right of veto of the President, make any ordinance strictly connected with the state of emergency having the force of law. If no right of veto is exercised, the President of the Republic shall promulgate by publication in the official Gazette of the Republic such ordinance. Such ordinance, if not sooner revoked, shall cease to be in force at the expiration of the emergency.

530. Article 184 of the Constitution further provides that where any ordinance provides for preventive detention, the authority on whose order any person is detained under that ordinance shall, as soon as may be, inform him/her of the grounds for his/her detention and the allegations of fact on which the order is based, and shall give him/her the opportunity of making representations against the order as soon as may be. Such obligation is, however, restricted by the proviso that no authority is required to disclose facts of which disclosure would, in its opinion, be against the national interest. In any case, no citizen shall be detained under that ordinance for a period exceeding one month unless the advisory board has considered any representations made by him/her and has reported, before the expiration of that period, that there is, in its opinion, sufficient cause for the detention. The advisory board constituted for the purposes of such ordinances issued in a state of emergency shall consist of a Chairman, who shall be appointed by the President of the Republic from among persons who are or have been judges of the Supreme Court or are qualified to be judges of such Court, and two other members, who shall be appointed by the President of the Republic after consultation with the President of the Supreme Court.

§2. The Legal Status of the 1974 Coup

531. On 15 July 1974, there took place a coup d'etat, organized by the Greek junta then in power in Greece and led by Greek officers, who were in Cyprus for service in the National Guard. The then-President of the Republic, Archbishop Makarios, was temporarily overthrown but survived and went abroad. On 23 July 1974, namely eight days later and following the Turkish invasion of 20 July 1974, Nicolaos Sampson who had undertaken the presidency of the Republic which was entrusted to him by the armed forces which executed the coup d'etat, resigned as President, the President of the House of Representatives Glafkos Clerides assumed duties. Following his return to Cyprus on 7 December 1974, Makarios resumed his duties as President of the Republic. The Supreme Court held that during its short life, the government that came into being as a result of the coup d'etat had not managed to be legalized as having the support of the people or as having been accepted by the people even tacitly but it remained foreign to the people until the very end.[762] Therefore, the coup d'etat failed to be legalized on the basis of the substantial test, that is, its sanction by the public conscience. In addition, there was enacted by the House of Representatives the Coup d'etat (Special Provisions) Law 57/1975 whereby it is provided that the coup d'etat and the 'Coup d' etat Government' had no legal basis whatsoever.[763]

762. *Liasis v. Attorney-General* [1975] 3 CLR 558.

763. *See* L. Loucaides, *The Legal Effect of the Coup of 15 July 1974* (2d ed., 1976, in Greek); A. Loizou, *The Coup, the Usurpers and the Rule of Law*, in *Cyprus: History, Problems and Struggle of Its People* 503–533 (G. Tenekides & N. Kranidiotis eds, Hestia 1981, in Greek); A. Emilianides, *The Legal Aspects of the 1974 Coup* in *History of the Republic of Cyprus*, vol. II, 146–149 (P. Papapolyviou ed., Phileleftheros 2011, in Greek).

Chapter 4. The Power of the Military

532. The Treaty of Alliance is annexed to the Constitution as Annex I and has constitutional force. It provides that Cyprus, Greece and Turkey, in their common desire to uphold peace and to preserve the security of each of them and considering that their efforts for the preservation of peace and security are in conformity with the purposes and principles of the UN Chapter, have agreed to cooperate for their common defence and to consult together on the problems raised by that defence. It was provided in the Treaty that the Parties undertake to resist any attack or aggression, direct or indirect, directed against the independence or the territorial integrity of the Republic of Cyprus. In order to achieve this objective, a Tripartite Headquarters would be established on the territory of the island with the participation of military contingents of 950 Greek officers, non-commissioned officers and men and 650 Turkish officers, non-commissioned officers and men.[764] The said contingents should provide for the training of the army of the Republic of Cyprus and its command would be assumed in rotation, for a period of one year each, by a Cypriot, Greek and Turkish General Officer, who would be appointed respectively by the President and Vice-President of the Republic of Cyprus and by the Governments of Greece and Turkey.

533. In addition, Additional Protocol II to the Treaty of Alliance provided that a Committee would be set up consisting of the Foreign Ministers of Cyprus, Greece and Turkey and it would constitute the supreme political body of the Tripartite Alliance which might take cognizance of any question concerning the Alliance with the Governments of Cyprus, Greece and Turkey would agree to submit to it. Such Committee of Ministers should meet in ordinary session by its Chairman at the request of the members of the Alliance; its decisions should be unanimous. The Committee would be presided over in rotation and for a period of one year by each of the three Foreign Ministers, holding its ordinary session, unless otherwise decided, in the capital of the Chairman's country. The Tripartite Headquarters would be responsible to the Committee of Ministers in the performance of its functions and would submit to the Committee's ordinary session an annual report comprising a detailed account of the Headquarters' activities.

534. Article 129 of the Constitution stipulated that the Republic would have an army of two thousand men, of whom 60% shall be Greek, and 40% shall be Turkish. However, the Constitution did not provide the manner in which the percentage analogy of the officers would be distributed. The Greek Cypriots were of the opinion that there should be a unified army, whereas the Turkish Cypriots considered that there should be a mixed army only as far as the superior officers are concerned; on the lower spectrum of the military, there should be a pure Greek unit and a pure Turkish unit. When the Council of Ministers decided by majority that the army should be comprised of Greek and Turkish Cypriots in all units, the Turkish Cypriot

764. Provided that the President and the Vice-President of the Republic of Cyprus, acting in agreement, may request the Greek and Turkish Governments to increase or reduce the Greek and Turkish contingents.

Vice-President of the Republic vetoed such decision.[765] The constitutional crisis of 1964 effectively did not allow for the creation of the constitutionally mandated army of the Republic. Furthermore, the Republic of Cyprus considered that the Treaty of Alliance was violated by Turkey which committed acts of aggression against the territorial integrity of the island.[766] Accordingly, the constitutional provisions regarding the Army of the Republic and the Treaty of Alliance do not apply in practice.

535. In 1964, the National Guard of the Republic was established with the National Guard Law 20/1964. Law 20/64 was repealed and substituted by the National Guard Law 19(I)/2011 which is currently in force. The National Guard comprises of Greek Cypriot men who serve compulsory military service and has proved essential in preserving the territorial integrity of the Republic after 1964. However, units of the National Guard were used in the 1974 coup against then-President of the Republic Archbishop Makarios. Since the Turkish invasion of 1974, the National Guard has remained in a constant state of preparation for war against the Turkish military. Permanent officers of the Republic are members of the Army of the Republic in accordance with the Army of the Republic Law 36(I)/2016.[767] The military is used for defensive purposes only and remains subject to the civil government.

765. *See* Kyriakides, *Cyprus: Constitutionalism and Crisis Government* 93 (University of Pennsylvania Press 1968).

766. C. Tornaritis, *The Treaty of Alliance and the Agreement for Its Application*, in *Ibid.*, *Constitutional and Legal Problems of the Republic of Cyprus* 33–39 (2d ed., 1972).

767. This is not the constitutionally mandated Army of the Republic as it is comprised by Greek Cypriots only.

Chapter 5. The Constitutional Relationship Between Church and State

536. According to Article 110 section 1 of the Constitution, the Autocephalous Greek Orthodox Church of Cyprus shall continue to have the exclusive right of regulating and administering its own internal affairs and property in accordance with the Holy Canons and its Charter in force for the time being. It is further provided that the Greek Communal Chamber shall not act inconsistently with such right of the Orthodox Church. Following the self-dissolution of the Greek Communal Chamber, it is implied that none of the state organs to which the competences of the Greek Communal Chamber were transferred according to Law 12/1965 (namely the House of Representatives, the Council of Ministers, or the Ministry of Education and Culture), may act inconsistently with the exclusive right of the Orthodox Church to regulate and administer its internal affairs and property. Article 110 therefore confirms that the State may not interfere with the internal affairs of the Orthodox Church, similarly to the existing legal position prior to independence.[768]

537. Moreover, Article 111 of the Constitution used to provide for certain privileges of the Orthodox Church with respect to the adjudication of issues relevant to marriage and divorce of members of the Greek Orthodox Church. Prior to the First Amendment of the Constitution of 1989, Article 111 of the Constitution provided that family law matters would continue to be governed by the law of the Orthodox Church and to be cognizable by the ecclesiastical courts of such Church.[769] Following the First Amendment of 1989, however, all family law matters of members of the Orthodox Church came under the jurisdiction of the Family Courts; further, only issues relating to betrothal or ecclesiastical marriage, or nullity of ecclesiastical marriage have continued to be governed by the canon law of the Orthodox Church even after 1989.[770]

538. It has been suggested that the constitutional protection of the Orthodox Church is wider than the respective constitutional protection of the three religious groups; it has further been suggested that the state and church relations between the Orthodox Church and the State in Cyprus are governed by the *State-law rule*, similarly to Greece, *even if the control of the Church on behalf of the State is limited.*[771] The above views are hardly convincing and have to be rejected. Despite the different terminology used, the aim of the Constitution is to treat the five major religions (Orthodox, Islamic, Armenian, Maronite and Roman Catholic) in an equal manner and not to differentiate among them. The Orthodox Church, the three religious groups and the Islamic religion, all enjoy exclusive competence with respect to their

---

768. *See* A. Emilianides, *The Constitutional Position of the Charter of the Church of Cyprus*, 2 Nomokanonika 41–54 (2005) (in Greek); *Ibid.*, *Religion and Law in Cyprus* (4th ed., Kluwer 2024).
769. *See* G. Serghides, *Internal and External Conflict of Laws in Regard to Family Relations in Cyprus* (1988).
770. *See* A. Emilianides, *The Cypriot Law of Marriage and Divorce* (Sakkoulas 2006, in Greek).
771. C. Tornaritis, *The Constitutional Position of the Autocephalous Greek Orthodox Church in the Republic of Cyprus*, 4 Cyprus L. Tribune 485–495 (1990) (in Greek); *Ibid.*, *The Relations Between Church and State According to Cypriot Law*, 1 Rev. Public & Private L. 14–15 (1967) (in Greek).

internal affairs, as well as the administration of their property. Such autonomy derives from the pre-existing legal regime, prior to independence, since the Constitution has not created a new internal legal regime for the various religions in Cyprus but has essentially maintained in effect the provisions of the Ottoman law, especially Hatt-i-Humayun, albeit without affording a dominant position to the Islamic religion.

539. It has already been noted that the Orthodox Christian and the Islamic religion constitute one of the criteria of the bi-communal character of the Republic of Cyprus, since Article 2 of the Constitution provides that the Greek Community comprises, *inter alia*, all citizens of the Republic who are members of the Greek Orthodox Church, while the Turkish Community comprises, *inter alia*, all citizens of the Republic who are Muslims. This peculiarity does not, however, signify the recognition of a special status in favour of the Orthodox Church or the Muslim religion at the expense of the other religions;[772] such was simply a method of distinguishing between members of the Greek and the Turkish Community, without any further implications with respect to the status of either religion.[773] From the aforementioned constitutional provisions, it emerges that no single religion or creed is established as the official religion. As a result, there is no prevailing, established, or state religion in Cyprus. All the religions and creeds in Cyprus deal restrictively with their own affairs without in any way interfering in the affairs of the State.

540. The five main religions of the Republic, however, enjoy a special constitutional status. The state has recognized broad discretionary powers in their favour and does not have the right to intervene in their internal affairs, or in the administration of their property. Whenever matters of common interest arise, such as religious education, the State and the religious corporations debate in order to reach a common solution;[774] if, however, this is not possible, the State may reach any decision, so long as it does not interfere with the internal affairs or the administration of the property of the constitutionally protected religions.[775] It is further observed that the State is not confessional. Thus, when assuming their duties, state officials are not sworn in, but affirm their faith to, and respect for the Constitution and the laws made thereunder, the preservation of the independence and the territorial integrity of the Republic of Cyprus, pursuant to Articles 42 section 1, 59 section 4, 69 and 100 of the Constitution (with respect to the President of the Republic, the Ministers, the Representatives, and the members of the Communal Chambers, respectively). Accordingly, state officials do not have to believe in any particular religion, or even

772. As suggested by C. Tornaritis. *The Relations Between Church and State According to Cypriot Law*, 1 Rev. Public & Private L. 15 (1967) (in Greek).

773. *See* C. Papastathis, *On the Administrative Organisation of the Church of Cyprus* 36–37 (1981, in Greek).

774. *See* A. Emilianides, *The Mutual Role of Religion and the State in Cyprus*, in *The Mutual Role of Religion and the State in Europe* 25–31 (B. Schanda ed., European Consortium for State and Church Research 2014).

775. *See* A. Emilianides, *State and Church in Cyprus*, in *State and Church in the European Union*, 281–296 (G. Robbers ed., 3d ed., Nomos Verlagsgesellschaft 2019); *Ibid.*, *Law and Religion in Cyprus*, 20 Kanon 7–21(2008).

that a God exists, in order to be elected or appointed. Their only allegiance is towards the Constitution and the laws made thereunder, and not towards any religious beliefs.

541. In view of the above, the Constitution has introduced a system of coordination between the Republic of Cyprus and the major religions and Christian creeds.[776] Such a system differs substantially from the *State-law rule* system prevailing in Greece, since it is based upon the autonomy of religious organizations, which are distinct from the State and deal restrictively with their own affairs. It further differs from the separation system, since the State has recognized broad discretionary powers with regard to the main religions' internal affairs, administration of their property, family matters, and in general matters of communal character. The model prevailing in Cyprus is essentially a pluralistic model, which recognizes and embraces the public dimension of religion, while at the same time attempting cooperation with all religions. The significance of faith in people's lives is considered worthy of protection by the state, and where the function of the state overlaps with religious concerns, the state seeks to accommodate religious views, in so far as they are not inconsistent with the state's interests.

542. In consequence, pluralism is achieved through the recognition that the state and the various religions occupy, in principle, different societal structures; religious neutrality is not, however, achieved simply because there is religious autonomy but also through positive measures on behalf of the state, which aim at the protection of religions.[777] Other religions and rites, such as the Jews, the Jehovah's Witnesses, the Buddhists, or the Protestants, or the Orthodox Christians who follow the Old Calendar, enjoy religious freedom according to Article 18 of the Constitution, and are equal before the law, so that no legislative, executive or administrative act should discriminate against them. However, such religions are not considered religious groups in the constitutional sense and, therefore, do not enjoy the special constitutional status of the five main religions of the island; difference in treatment between the five constitutionally recognized religions and other religions of the island principally occur with respect to religious education, direct financing and family law matters.

776. A. Emilianides, *The Constitutional Framework of the Relations Between Church and State in the Republic of Cyprus*, 1 Nomokanonika 7ff (2006) (in Greek); C. Papastathis, *On the Administrative Organisation of the Church of Cyprus* 34 (1981, in Greek); A. Gavrielides, *Nomocanonical and Political Study on the Unfrocking of Bishops in Cyprus in Conjunction to the Exercise of their Ethnarchical Rights* (2d ed., 1973, in Greek).

777. A. Emilianides, *Secularism, Law and Religion Within the Cypriot Legal Order*, in *Religion, Rights and Secular Society. European Perspectives* 169–188 (P. Cumper & T. Lewis eds, Edward Elgar Publishing 2012); *Ibid.*, *Religious Jurisdiction and Pluralism of Legal Adjudication in Cyprus*, in *Religious Adjudication and the State* 39–48 (R. Potz & W. Wieschaider eds, Comares 2015).

Selected Bibliography

Books

In Greek

Angelides, A. *The General Principles of Administrative Law Act and Subsequent Case-Law of the Supreme Court of Cyprus*. Nicosia: House of Representatives, 2008.

Angelides, A., Angelides, S. *Administrative Procedural Law*. 2nd edn, Nicosia: Cyprus Bar Association, 2020.

Charalambous, N. *Cypriot Administrative Law Textbook*. 3rd edn. Nicosia, 2016.

Emilianides, A. *Beyond the Constitution of Cyprus*. Athens-Thessaloniki: Sakkoulas, 2006.

Emilianides, A., Papastylianos C., Stratilatis, C. *The Republic of Cyprus and the Doctrine of Necessity*. Athens-Thessaloniki: Sakkoulas 2016.

Emilianides, A. *The Secret Negotiations. The Establishment of the Republic of Cyprus (1959–1960)*. Athens: Papazisi/CECL 2022.

Emilianides, A. et al (eds), *The Institution of the House of Representatives*. Nicosia: House of Representatives/UNIC School of Law, 2022.

Kombos, C. Constantinides, A. *Kriton Tornaritis. A Selection of Opinions in Constitutional Law*. Athens: Nomiki Vivliothiki, 2019.

Kombos, C. *Cypriot Constitutional Law*. Athens: Nomiki Vivliothiki, 2021.

Konstantinidis, P. *The Drittwirkung of Fundamental Rights in Cyprus*. Nicosia: Hippasus, 2016.

Loizides, S. *After the Agreements, the New Cypriot Reality: The Constitutional Structure and International Position of Cyprus*. Athens, 1959.

Loizou, A. *Constitution of the Republic of Cyprus*. Nicosia, 2001.

Loizou, A. *Cyprus and the European Convention on Human Rights*. Athens: A. Sakkoulas, 2003.

Loucaides, L. *Topics of Cypriot Law*. vol. I, Nicosia, 1982, vol. II, Nicosia, 1988.

Melissas, D. *The Organisation of Political Power in the Cypriot State: The Electoral Body, the House of Representatives*. Athens: A. Sakkoulas, 1996.

Melissas, D. *Political Parties in the Republic of Cyprus: The Development towards Institutionalisation*. Athens: A. Sakkoulas, 1996.

Nicolaou, E. *The Constitutional Review of Laws and of the Distribution of Competences of State Organs in Cyprus*. Athens: A. Sakkoulas, 2000.

Selected Bibliography

Nicolaou, E., Michaelides, P. *Cypriot Administrative Law. Fundamental Principles. Judicial Control*. Athens: Nomiki Vivliothiki, 2019.

Nicolaou, E., Tsaousis, G. *Textbook of Administrative Procedure*. Athens: Nomiki Vivliothiki, 2021.

Papademetriou, G. The Constitutional Problem of the Republic of Cyprus. Athens: A. Sakkoulas, 1997.

Papaphilippou, L. *The Doctrine of Necessity and the Constitutional Order in Cyprus*. Nicosia, 1995.

Paraskeva, C. *Cypriot Constitutional Law: Fundamental Rights and Freedoms*. Athens: Nomiki Vivliothiki, 2015.

Paraskeva, C. *Cypriot Administrative Law*. Athens: Nomiki Vivliothiki, 2017.

Paraskeva, C. *Cypriot Administrative Procedure Law*. Athens: Nomiki Vivliothiki, 2020.

Paraskeva, C. *The Compliance of the Administration to Judicial Decisions in Cyprus*. Athens: Nomiki Vivliothiki, 2021.

Tornaritis, C. *The Genesis of the Cypriot State and its Form*. Nicosia, 1974.

Tornaritis, C. *The Doctrine of Necessity and the Cypriot Legal System*. Nicosia, 1978.

Tornaritis, C. *Peculiarities of the Cypriot Constitution and Effect on the Normal Function of the State*. Nicosia, 1980.

Tornaritis, C. *The State Law of the Republic of Cyprus*. Nicosia: Cyprus Research Centre, 1982.

Tsatsos, T. *Observations on the Constitution of Cyprus*. Athens: A. Sakkoulas, 1965.

Venizelos, E. *The Cyprus Problem, The Cypriot Constitutional Order and the Prospect of Accession to the European Union*. Athens: A. Sakkoulas, 2000.

Other than Greek

Evangelides, P. *The Republic of Cyprus and Its Constitution with Special Regard to the Constitutional Rights*. Bamburg: Difo-Druck GmbH, 1996.

Kombos, C. *The Impact of EU Law on Cypriot Public Law*. Athens-Thessaloniki: Sakkoulas, 2015.

Kombos, C. *The Doctrine of Necessity in Constitutional Law*. Athens-Thessaloniki: Sakkoulas, 2015,

Kyriakides, S. *Cyprus Constitutionalism and Cyprus Government*. Philadelphia: University of Pennsylvania Press, 1968.

Nedjati, Z. *Cyprus Administrative Law*. Nicosia, 1970.

Papasavvas, S. *La Justice Constitutionelle à Chypre*. Paris: Economica/Presses Universitaires d' Aix – Marseilles, 1998.

Pikis, G. *Constitutionalism, Human Rights, Separation of Powers: The Cyprus Precedent*. Leiden: Martinus Nijhoff, 2006.

Polyviou, P. *The Problem of Cyprus: Constitutional and Political Aspects*. Nicosia, 1974.

Polyviou, P. *The Case of Ibrahim, the Doctrine of Necessity and the Republic of Cyprus*. Nicosia: Chryssafinis & Polyviou, 2015.

Polyviou, P. *The Cyprus Experience. Constitutionalism, Fundamental Law and the Doctrine of Necessity*. Athens: Nomiki Vivliothiki, 2021.

Tornaritis, C. *The Human Rights as Recognised and Protected by Law with Special Reference to the Law of Cyprus*. Nicosia, 1967.
Tornaritis, C. *Cyprus and its Constitutional and Other Legal Problems*. 2nd edn. Nicosia, 1980.
Tornaritis, C. *Constitutional Review of Laws in the Republic of Cyprus*. Nicosia, 1983.

Articles

In Greek

Angelides, S. 'The Protection of Human Rights in the Republic of Cyprus' *Cyprus and European Law Review* 7 (2008): 154–193.
Apostolides, D. 'Observations on the Constitution of the Republic of Cyprus'. *Review of Public Law and Administrative Law* 4 (1960): 347–362, 5 (1961): 39–50, 122–136.
Christofides, M. 'The Power of the House to Amend'. *Cyprus Law Review* 28 (1989): 4333–4344.
Clerides, C. 'The Power to Amend the Constitution of the Republic of Cyprus'. *Cyprus Law Review* 26 (1989): 1951–1956.
Clerides, L. 'The Cypriot Election System and the Various Systems Abroad'. *Cyprus Law Tribune* 1 (1977): 8–16.
Eftychiou, A. 'The Doctrine of Necessity and its Application in the Cypriot Legal System'. *Cyprus Law Review* 12 (1985): 1951–1956.
Emilianides, A. 'The Constitution of Cyprus post-Accession'. In *Policy Proposals*. Edited by A. Emilianides. Nicosia: Power Publishing, 2005, 81–101.
Emilianides, A. 'Reviewing the Constitutional Review. Comments on Three Recent Judgments of the Supreme Court' *Yearbook of Cyprus and European Law* (2013): 45–88.
Emilianides A., 'The Separation between Political Power and Public Administration in Cypriot Law'. *Efimerida Dioikitikou Dikaiou* 1 (2019): 2–9.
Emilianides, A. 'Public Servants and Separation of Powers in the Cypriot Legal Order'. In *Public Administration after the* Crisis. Edited by X. Kontiades, A. Emilianides, C. Anthopoulos, Athens-Thessaloniki: Sakkoulas, 2019, 139–154.
Loizou, A. 'The Judicial Review of the Constitutionality of Laws and the Legality of Administrative Action'. *Cyprus Law Review* 27 (1989): 4161–4173.
Loucaides, L. 'Constitutional Problems of the Presidential Elections'. *Cyprus Law Review* 21 (1988): 3393–3340.
Mamopoulos, P. 'The Constitution of the Republic of Cyprus'. *Law Tribune* 9 (1961): 689–695.
Manesis, A. & Papademetriou, G. 'The Doctrine of Necessity and the Amendment of the Constitution of the Republic of Cyprus'. *Review of Public Law and Administrative Law* 34 (1990): 7–13.
Markides, A. 'Bi-Communality in the Constitution of the Republic of Cyprus'. In *The Republic of Cyprus. 50 Years of Painful Journey*. Edited by C. Pericleous, Athens: Papazisi, 2010, 187–208.
Mprinomlas, M. 'The Republic of Cyprus from an International and Constitutional Law Aspect'. *Armenopoulos* 13 (1959): 619–622.

Nicolaou, E. 'The Accession to the European Union and the Constitutional Order of Cyprus'. *Hellenic Review of European Law* 19 (1999): 23–33.

Papasavvas, S. 'Supreme Court, Constitutional Amendment and the Prospect of Accession to the European Union'. *Hellenic Review of European Law* 19 (1999): 43–50.

Papasavvas, S. 'Constitutional Aspects of the Accession of the Republic of Cyprus to the European Union'. *Hellenic Review of European Law* 22 (2002): 81–91.

Pikis, G. 'The Most Important Judgments of Constitutional Law in Cyprus. 1960–2010'. In *History of the Republic of Cyprus*, Edited by P. Papapolyviou. Nicosia: Phileleftheros, 2011, v. III, 212–217.

Soulioti, S. 'The Amendment of the Constitution and the Application of the Doctrine of Necessity'. *Cyprus Law Review* 13 (1986): 2063–2078.

Talarides, K. 'The Current Constitutional Structure of Public Authorities in Cyprus'. *Review of Public and Private Law* 3 (1967): 125–128.

Yiallourou, S. 'The Review of Constitutionality of the Cuts of the Salaries of Public Servants due to the Financial Crisis' *Efimerida Dioikitikou Dikaiou* 2 (2019): 133–161.

Venizelos, E. 'The Constitutional Review of Laws in Greece and Cyprus: A Parallel Sketch'. *Cyprus Law Review* 39–40 (1992): 51–70.

Other than Greek

Antonopoulos, N. 'Les Tendances Constitutionelles des États Avant Accédé Récement à l' Independance: La Constitution de la République de Chypre'. *Revue Hellénique de Droit International* 15 (1962): 307–326.

De Smith, S.A. 'Cyprus: Sui Generis'. In *The New Commonwealth and its Constitutions*. Authored by De Smith. London: Stevens & Sons, 1964, 282–296.

De Zayas, A. *The Annan Plan and the Implantation of Turkish Settlers in Northern Cyprus. Cyprus Yearbook of International Relations* (2006): 163–178.

Emilianides, A. 'The Zurich and London Agreements and the Cyprus Republic'. In Mélanges *Seferiadou*, Athens, 1961, v. II, 629–639.

Emilianides, A. 'The Constitution of Cyprus'. In *Encyclopedia of World Constitutions*. Edited by Robbers, G. Facts on File, New York, 2006, v. I: 240–243.

Emilianides, A. 'Accession of the Republic of Cyprus in the EU, the Constitution and the Cypriot Doctrine of Necessity' *Cyprus Yearbook of International Relations* (2007), 65–82.

Emilianides, A. 'Remarks on the Idea of a Constitutional Convention for Cyprus'. In *Constitutional Convention for Cyprus*. Edited by A. Auer & V. Triga, A. Berlin: Wissenschaftlicher Verlag Berlin, 2009, 123–130.

Emilianides, A., Ioannou, C. 'The Haircut of Cypriot Deposits and the Protection of Fundamental Rights' *Cyprus Human Rights Law Review* 2 (2014): 141–166.

Emilianides, A., Papastylianos, C. 'Citizenship and Nationality. Cyprus'. In *Constitutionalism in Context*. Edited by D. Law. Cambridge: Cambridge University Press, 2022, 330–350.

Hadjianastasiou, T. 'The European Convention on Human Rights Applicable in Cyprus' *Cyprus Law Tribune* 3 (1976): 97 – 113.

Kombos, C., Laulhé-Shaelou, S. 'The Cypriot Constitution under the Impact of EU law: An Asymmetrical Formation'. In *The Role of National Constitutions in*

European and Global Governance. Edited by A. Albi, S. Bardutzky, Berlin: TMC Asser Press/Springer Open, 2019, 1373–1432.

Kombos, C. 'Social Rights in the Republic of Cyprus'. In *Social and Economic Rights as Fundamental Rights*. Edited by K. Wojtyczek, Den Haag: Eleven, 2016, 57–86.

Kombos, C., Herodotou, A. '(Un-) Constitutional Amendments: The Cypriot Paradigm' *European Public Law* 25 (2019): 305–324.

Kombos, C. 'Legal Pluralism and Constitutionalism in the Cypriot Example'. In *Debating Legal Pluralism and Constitutionalism*. Edited by G. Tusseau, Berlin: Springer, 2020, 137–187.

Kombos, C., Herodotou, A. 'Economic, Social and Cultural Rights During Crisis in Cyprus. The Interplay between Domestic and External Normative Systems' *Constitutional Review* 7 (2021): 92–123.

Kouspi T. Emilianides A. 'From Process Misstep to Environmental Milestone: Cyprus's New Constitutional Right' April *constitutionnet*, available at https://constitutionnet.org/news/voices/process-misstep-environmental-milestone-cypruss-new-constitutional-right.

Liakouras, P. 'Looking Back to See Forward: The 1959 Zurich and London Accords and the Constitutional Order of Cyprus'. *Etudes Helléniques* 10 (2002): 47–61.

Loizou, A. 'The Effect of the ECHR on the Legal and Political Systems of Member States: Cyprus'. In *Fundamental Rights in Europe: The European Convention on Human Rights and its Member States, 1950–2000*. Edited by R. Blackburn, J. Polakiewicz, Oxford: Oxford University Press, 2001, 217–239.

Markides, A. 'The Republic of Cyprus'. In *Constitutional Law of 10 EU Member States: The 2004 Enlargement*. Edited by C Kortmann et al, The Hague: Kluwer, 2006, I-3–I-77.

Melides, C. 'Constitutional Law'. In *Introduction to Cyprus Law*. Edited by Andreas Neocleous & Co LLC, 3rd edn, Limassol, 2010, 45–85.

Pantelides, A. 'Legal Opinion on the Question of the Constitutionality of the System for the Election of the Members of the House of Representatives in Cyprus'. *Cyprus Law Tribune* 4 (1976): 29–36.

Papastylianos, C. 'The Cypriot Doctrine of Necessity Within the Context of Emergency Discourse: How a Unique Emergency Shaped a Particular Type of Emergency Law' *The Cyprus Review* 30(1) (2018): 113–143.

Tornaritis, C. 'The Constitution of Cyprus'. *International Relations* 6 (1964): 28–40.

Tornaritis, C. 'Social and Economic Rights under the Law of the Republic of Cyprus'. In *Mélanges Bridel*, Lausanne: Imprimeries Réunies, 1968, 533–556.

Tornaritis, C. 'The Operation of the European Convention for the Protection of Human Rights in the Republic of Cyprus'. *Cyprus Law Review* 3 (1983): 455–464.

Vlachos, G. 'L' Organisation Constitutionelle de la République de Chypre'. *Revue International de Droit Comparé* 3 (1961): 526–559.

Selected Bibliography

Index

The numbers here refer to paragraph numbers.

Index

Made in the USA
Middletown, DE
04 November 2026

36552528R00157